SHOOT, ASK... AND RUN!

PHOTOGRAPHING ASIA — AND BEYOND — IN A TIME OF UPHEAVAL

Being Volume 2 of
The Diaries of a Western Nomad,
Concerning the Life of the Photographer
As a Young Man Wrestling
With the Concept of Home

1989–1992

CHRIS STOWERS

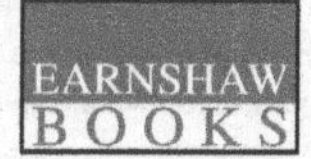

Shoot, Ask … and Run!

By Chris Stowers

Trade Paper: 978-988-8843-92-3
Digital: 978-988-8904-08-2

BIOGRAPHY & AUTOBIOGRAPHY

EB221

Cover: Troops pass a burning APC during the Russian invasion of Georgia, August 2008
        Photo © Chris Stowers/PANOS

Back Cover Inset: The author in Hong Kong, circa 1992
        Photo © Hans Kemp

About the Author page: Photo © Jennie Stowers

Published in Hong Kong by Earnshaw Books Ltd.

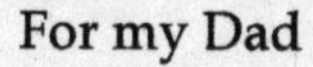

For my Dad

CONTENTS

AUTHOR'S NOTE

WHERE DOES ONE story end and another begin? This was the question I asked myself after arriving in Singapore in the autumn of 1988, at the end of an extraordinary voyage from Jampea Island aboard the Bugis spice ship *Kurnia Ilahi*—a journey that became the subject of the first volume of this three-part series, *Bugis Nights*. Barely had the sea spray dried from my sun-blistered face, hardly had I learned to navigate the stable deck of Orchard Road without staggering to the motion of invisible waves, before the nitty-gritty of daily existence poured in. The month-long voyage had consumed me, and the thrill and relief of safe arrival overwhelmed my senses. I was left hollowed out, disoriented, wondering where to go, and how to chase my next adventure fix.

Fortunately, it was then I discovered a knack for photography (maybe it discovered me?). I was able to transfer a fraction of the thrill I'd experienced on that ocean odyssey into the pages of a glossy magazine. From the vanishing vapors of one adventure, a new direction was set, and my subsequent 'career' launched.

I'd been on the road for almost two years before this first story was published and had long lost any thought of heading home. My mind was focused on exploration and echoed with the advice and entrenched wisdom of the cast and characters I'd met along the way, some of whom crop up again in the pages of this volume. Where does one story end and another begin? It doesn't, and they don't. Over time, dreams and reality merge. Eventually, they become indistinguishable, part of our ultimate journey and most epic adventure, Life.

These diaries, and this book, are a continuation of mine.

C.R.S., Taipei

1. Advice to the Young Photographer

I was a photographer long before I ever held a camera. I never wanted to do anything but travel and observe. Photography helped qualify this curiosity; it gave me permission to peek. I never dreamed I'd make a living out of it, though, and I still have difficulty calling what I do a 'career'. I guess one day I'll get found out, have to give it all up and get a proper job as an accountant or a bus driver. Until then I will carry on wandering the world, lining up my shots, and feeling I'm the luckiest man alive.

⚭

Photography is a physically demanding job. To the desk-bound outsider it can appear a glamorous profession but, in reality, it's one step up from bricklaying. It is not a life for everyone. You're always on duty, never know where you'll be one day to the next, and the pay is erratic. This hasn't stopped the academics latching on to it, though. In his book 'Camera Lucida', French philosopher Roland Barthes at least gets close with his esoteric dialectic about 'studium' and 'punctum'. But, with all due respect, he was never a shooter. Only someone who is out there every day searching for images will know the truth: that it is impossible to intellectualize instinct.

Find me a photographer who hasn't ruined their back lugging around heavy equipment, or lost their spleen by age forty getting shot at, then we can sit down, crack open a beer, and begin to discuss what it takes to make a photograph. And what photography takes out of you.

Real photographers are up before sunrise. We carry our lenses in a beat-up Domke bag. We live in an unwashed jacket of many pockets, and can tell the correct light exposure — to within half a stop—at a glance. Those who are not gifted these skills, or cannot muster the discipline, disguise themselves in beret and turtleneck, they grow pointy beards and try to pass off their poorly focused studies of the relationship between human form and function as 'Art'. These are tossers. Or pornographers. Please be clear to make the distinction.

In early January 1987, when I set off from England, clutching a one-way ticket to Karachi, I knew none of this. The world back then was a mysterious, magical and welcoming place. My brain, an innocent sponge, soaked up wise opinion, mad rant and conspiracy theory alike, according all views, and their holders, equal respect. Many of these formative facts, tips and prejudices were consumed around the communal table of the long-since demolished Khyber Hotel, in Peshawar, Pakistan.

The city was a hotbed of intrigue that distant Spring, rife with rumor: a pressure cooker brimming with refugees from neighboring Afghanistan, Mujahedeen freedom fighters (then the West's friends and allies), journalists, doctors, NGO workers, spies and other assorted adventurers—all of them fired up by fear and fury, idealism and deadlines. It was a hell of a place to arrive fresh out of high school, innocent in the ways of the world.

"We shall not cease from exploration
And the end of all our exploring
Will be to arrive where we started
And know the place for the first time."
—**T.S. Eliot** (from "Little Gidding")

PESHAWAR, PAKISTAN

February 19, 1987

THE TWIN ELEMENTS of gunfire and hashish assailed me at dawn. The first from the street below, the latter, seeping in like fog under the door. The wood-frame charpoy creaked under my weight as I sought a more comfortable position in which to carry on sleeping and ignore what I reasoned was the standard wake-up call in these parts. After all, carrying a gun in Pakistan's lawless North West Frontier Province was akin to clutching an umbrella on the streets of London. And the Japanese *had* been up all night, puffing on that huge clay bong of theirs. Tugging down on the lumpy pillow, I muffled my ears and tried to remain not unduly alarmed.

I'd arrived in Peshawar the day before, and already felt at home amid its grungy chaos. The train journey from Rawalpindi had taken six hours, as a vivid thunderstorm played itself out across the horizon, like artillery kicking off the Battle of the Somme. The Khyber Hotel was just where Stuart—the street-wise, weed-smoking Aussie traveler who'd taken me under his wing back in Lahore—had said it would be, its rooms arranged around a central skylight overlooking the hotel's first-floor courtyard. The yellow-painted walls and gray doors emitted a rather rustic French touch, out of place, and yet, like the rest of the dollar-a-night establishment, instantly homely. Centerpiece of the second-floor open area was an elongated metal trestle table, and it was there I'd spotted a young man with cropped gingery hair—and a beard of similar length—fiddling impatiently with a shortwave radio set. His thick neck emerged from an olive-green combat jacket. The smeared glasses balanced on his broad, freckled nose were aiding close-up inspection of the defective broadcasting device. This, I assumed, was Darrell.

"Here's the money Stuart owes you," I said, handing over the five, red 100 rupee notes I'd been entrusted to deliver. Despite my knowledge of electronics adding nothing to the common pool, we were able to tune in to a serviceable transmission from the BBC World Service at 7:00 p.m. and became instant friends.

Through the open doorway, I saw Tanaka emerge from the Japs' dormitory, coughing as pursued by a pungent plume of pot. The right-wing activist karate master was somewhat of a celebrity around the Khyber. The official martial arts instructor to the Mujahedeen, it was rumored he carried with him two hand grenades so, in the event of capture, he could use the first on the Russians, and, if necessary, the spare on himself.

Wide awake by now, and with no chance of getting back to sleep, I stumbled into the showers—and the Khyber Hotel's best-kept secret—hot water. I had just worked up a nice lather from the soggy bar of communal soap when a huge explosion uprooted the building. Thinking Tanaka must have accidentally triggered one of his grenades, I dashed barefoot from the showers and up to the rooftop, wrapped in a towel. The courtyard seemed peaceful enough, so I turned my gaze outward, to the horizon. A dark funnel of smoke was rising from across the railway lines, a mile or so away. That was some bomb! Sirens from emergency vehicles were already audible. The building was still swaying from the blast as I glanced down at Darrell who was pulling a military-style jacket over his pajama top. We nodded in silent agreement and, pausing only to grab my camera, rushed down to the street, taking the Khyber's staircase three steps at a time. I flagged down a passing auto-rickshaw, pointed the driver in the most conspicuous direction, and urged him to abandon all caution with the throttle.

We flew off the main road and into a maze of narrow alleys, boxed in on both sides by high brick walls topped with barbed wire and plastered with posters and political graffiti. Popping out like a champagne cork into an open area, the three-wheeler skidded to a halt in front of a mangled metal fence guarded by dozens of gray-uniformed policemen.

"A-Salaam u-Aleikom."

"Waleikom a-Salaam," I replied, using the first communication I'd picked up in Pakistan. A handshake with the most senior-looking official cemented the honesty of our intent.

"Who are you from? From which agency?" the officer demanded. I must have looked blank. *Agency*? "The BBC? Rooters?", he prompted, alluding to the homophonic British wire service.

"Yes, BBC," I agreed. *I am English after all. It's my birthright.* I tightened the grip on my cheap, plasticky Nikon EM camera, with its standard 50mm lens, bringing it into more prominent view. Darrell was already flashing his New Zealand driving license, claiming, "CIA!"

We were waved through the cordon, the first 'press' to have arrived. But bluster can only take you so far; the bloodiest event I'd witnessed up to this point in my life had been a particularly vicious rugby match. I was not prepared for the scene that confronted us. The target of the bomb was a primary school. Its former playground now a crater that severed water pipes were turning into a deep pond. An engine block—all that was left of the truck that had carried the bomb—was lodged in the stripped branches of a tree, fully twelve feet off the ground. A group of boys, too young to appreciate the gravity of the situation, were throwing around balls of mud still emitting smoke.

Darrell and I were dragged stumbling through a rubble of classrooms by a distraught teacher, his arms wind-milling as he pointed to torn and burned pages from textbooks, random items of kids' clothing, brown stains on the earthen floor. "Blood," he spat. I couldn't think where to start photographing, but obviously it was expected of me. People start to question if you don't conform to stereotype. So, I began to gather information, jotting down notes, breadcrumbs of data to help find a way back out of this vast and overwhelming jungle of insensibility.

"Name of village?" I asked the teacher. Garhi Qamardin. "And who is responsible?"

Why a school?

"It is KHAD," the teacher explained, using the acronym for the Afghan communist regime's secret police. "They stage these atrocities to turn public opinion in Pakistan against the Afghani refugees."

I knew, from reading *Newsweek* on the plane from London, that around two million Afghans had been displaced by the Russian invasion of 1979. Most of them were living now in the tribal areas, many in and around Peshawar itself. The bombing campaign was a diabolically cynical strategy, but I couldn't quite make the link: surely murdering Pakistani kids in a Pakistani school would lead to resentment against the Afghan regime and the Russians, not the refugees, who were innocent in all this?

"Chris, mate," Darrell piped up, breaking my train of thought, "some of these blokes are starting to look mighty pissed."

Indeed, so intent had I become recording details that I'd missed the growing big picture. Crowds, comprised entirely of men, were massing. Someone held up a burning tire on a stick. The police had abandoned any attempt to hold them back as they converged on the crater. I climbed atop a wall, but pointing my camera acted like positioning a Bunsen burner beneath some particularly volatile liquid. Chanting erupted wherever I focused: "Death to President Zia. Zia is a Dog!"

Some university students took it upon themselves to act as our bodyguards, and hustled us out to the relative calm of the main road.

"What the hell was that all about?" shouted Darrell, still on an adrenaline high "I don't know!" I admitted, thinking, *it's all a long way from the home I left behind forever, less than a month ago.* Rubbing my camera expectantly, as though it were a magic lamp, the tightly coiled film within a celluloid genie, I confessed, "I'm hooked, though."

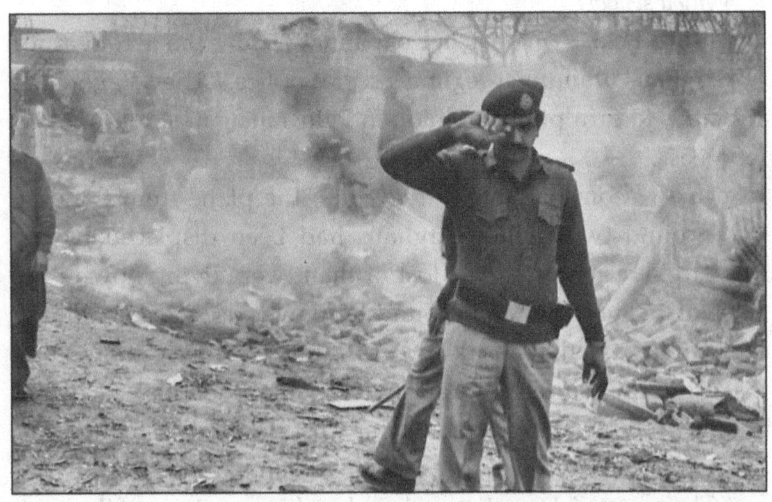

My first attempt at news photography. Bomb site in Garhi Qamardin village.
Peshawar, Pakistan — February 19, 1987.

Inwardly I shuddered with this realization; that I was attracted to things most sensible people ran to avoid.

Peshawar melted in golden twilight. Dusty beams seeped through the skylight of the Khyber Hotel, painting the communal table, and all of us sitting around it, in lurid burnt orange emulsion.

"This sort of light is best captured on 64 ASA Kodachrome, using an 81B," advised London Bus, absently, of films and filters. Tall, wiry, specks of gray streaking his black hedgehog of a beard, and of indeterminate age (he insisted he was thirty-nine, but so would I if I were in my mid-forties), the photographer from Queensland had creased eyes that indicated an over-familiarity with the sun. It was a few days after the bomb blast, and we were as hungry for news of the resultant civic mayhem as we were for tiffin.

One of the Khyber's serving boys weaved across the landing, his elbows extended, supporting a huge tray that obscured his head. Upon this unstable platform teetered a tower of freshly baked Turcoman bread, clinking plates loaded with peppered shortbread and assorted local sponge cake, several chipped and spitting enamel pots filled with ridiculously sugary, cardamom-infused tea—*chai*—two massive jars of Soviet strawberry jam, and an entire watermelon. All I saw were his spindly legs, crisscrossing beneath the groaning platter, and then the blinding explosion of teeth, on safe delivery of sacred cargo to table.

"I'll give this to the Ruskies, mate," a rare concession from The Bus, "they really know how to make jam." The bazaars of Peshawar were awash with the stuff. The Mujahedeen brought it back in crates strapped to donkeys every time they ambushed a Soviet convoy across the border. "Think of it, mate! By consuming these delicious Bolshevik preserves, we are helping finance the fight against global communism," the Bus burped with satisfaction and licked his knife clean.

Jim, a big American, made do with his fingers. The police had confiscated his Swiss Army knife after an affray with locals at the pudding shop a week earlier. The documentary soundman was here along with director Lee Shapiro to make a film about Afghanistan. They were being backed by the anti-communist Unification Church of Rev Sun Myung Moon. Lee's earlier documentary for PBS, 'Nicaragua Was My Home', had detailed the plight of the Miskito Indians, a native population resisting the Sandinista regime in Nicaragua. Their documentary about the Mujahedeen was informally titled 'Against the Empire' (both soundman and director would perish later that year when attacked by a Soviet helicopter gunship inside Afghanistan).

Left in Peshawar with nothing to do but guard the video camera while Lee returned to the States to try and secure more funding for their project, the lack of activity had started eating at him. Jim was gregarious by nature, a blond-bearded lumberjack of a man. Bit of a hippie, at heart, though a paramedic by profession. The latter was a skill the Mujahedeen were in desperate need of over the border. His partner, the director of their venture — from what I'd seen of him — was shrewd, sharp and full of ambition, and still riding high off his Nicaraguan success. We all played cards for matchsticks out on the second-floor landing, London Bus trying to engage the Yank in the game. But Jim was more distracted than usual.

"He's talking too much, to anyone who will listen," Bus confided in a concerned whisper, "telling people about his plans to cross the border into Afghanistan. I just hope Lee gets back soon."

Coverage of Thursday's school bombing continued to dominate the local papers. The official tally of victims by now running to ten dead and sixty-nine wounded. Reprisals against innocent Afghan refugees were being widely reported:

The Muslim: "Angry citizens clash with refugees."

The Frontier Post: "Violent public reaction to grisly incident."

As I was handing *The Frontier Post* to Darrell, The Mouse burst in from the staircase. The mild-mannered Aussie shooter, never seen without his bush hat or tiny Olympus cameras — his equipment being as unobtrusive as his alias hinted — had been down in Qissa Khwani bazaar.

"There's loads of police down there, firing off teargas and tearing into the crowds with *lathis*. Complete riot. Some bloke with a tray of knives is doing brisk business! Everyone's up in arms against the 'Ghans," he reported, pausing to catch both his breath and his composure over a steaming cup of chai.

London Bus, four cameras habitually slung across his torso, like bandoliers of ammunition on a Mexican bandit ("You can see him coming a mile off!" joked Mouse, referring to his giant compatriot's nom de guerre), invited him to join our game of cards. But Mouse was a loner. He'd instinctively retreated to the end of the table, out of earshot, and was already absorbed cutting off chunks of watermelon with his newly purchased flick knife.

Ted from Texas, who worked for the International Rescue Committee, an NGO dealing with Afghan refugees (bookish and, with his reading glasses and turtleneck jumper, the living embodiment of the character 'Brains' from the kids' TV show *Thunderbirds*), admired the quieter Australian's air of unflustered detachment:

"The ones who achieve *true* greatness always do so alone and in silence. Loneliness is the primal human condition. It is how a man deals with his solitude that will determine his success in life."

And, after a pause he quizzed me, "Isn't that why you are always writing so much in that journal of yours?" Then he added thoughtfully, "Keep on with the photography, it could be just the passport to adventure you're searching for."

This prompted me to bring out the envelope of photos from the bomb blast I'd had developed at Uncle Tony's, the Saddar Road photo lab. I pushed aside a dripping teapot, placing a crusty disc of Turcoman bread layered with jam out of harm's way on the up-turned lid of a biscuit tin. Wiping the table clear with my sleeve, I spread my precious black and white prints across the scuffed and dented surface.

The group discussion, as so often before, turned to photography.

"You've got what it takes to be a proper photographer," boomed Bus, "not just a snapper." Praise, indeed. "You have to remember though, mate: shoot first, *then* ask permission."

And Mouse—who respected the Bus's photos well enough but was diametrically opposed to the slash-and-burn approach he employed obtaining them—piped up:

"And when that fails, run!"

Restless by inclination, I've been running ever since ...

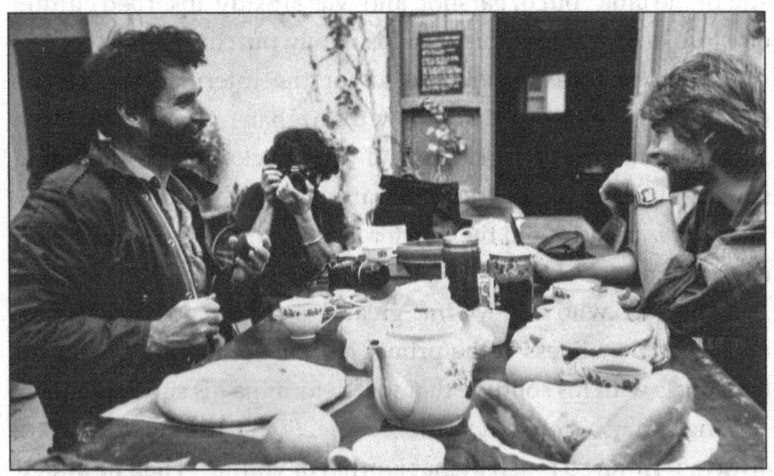

Seated around the communal table at the Khyber Hotel: (from left) Australian photographer
The London Bus, Italian photographer Alberto Buzzola, and myself.
Photo most likely taken by Australian photographer The Mouse – circa April, 1987.

PART

1

Jungle Life: February–June 1989

"Innocence is like a dumb leper who has lost his bell,
wandering the world, meaning no harm."
Graham Greene (*The Quiet American*)

Jakarta, Indonesia

February 15, 1989

If only all breakfasts were this memorable. Barely had my morning indulgence in papaya, hairy red rambutan fruits and multiple cups of coffee settled, and I'd been confirmed in a career, celebrated the freedom of a repressed nation, and received a letter from overseas. First in order of personally life-changing magnitude was the package from the publisher in Singapore containing three copies of *South East Asia Traveller* magazine. In it, my ocean odyssey of last September had been brought to life — in words and pictures — across nine pages. It opened with a double-page spread of our boat, the *Kurnia Ilahi*. That image — the first frame I ever shot on color slide film — was taken the moment I first laid eyes on the ship, unaware, at the time, of the significant role the vessel would soon play in my life. Some things were just meant to be!

You should pop in to see Mr Fong at American Express, show him this story; his office is in the Hyatt Hotel in Jakarta, and they're putting out a magazine, Anna, the *SEAT* editor, suggested in a handwritten note she'd slipped in with the magazines.

Next, the BBC World Service announced the Soviet Union was finally pulling their last troops out of Afghanistan. Did Ata

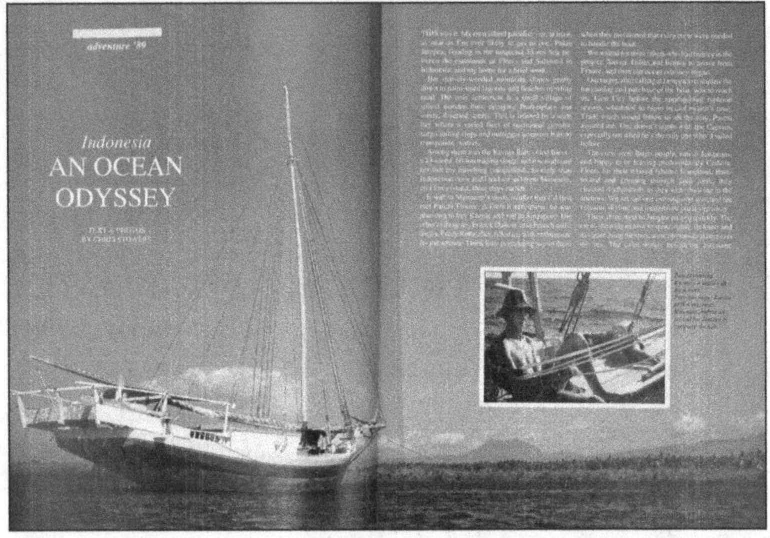

still attend the Dr Omar Khyam School in Peshawar, I wondered, instinctively tugging at the silver talisman my refugee friend had gifted me when I'd finished teaching there. It had hung on its chain around my neck ever since, and had done a pretty good job of protecting me on my travels, so far. I hoped his family would now get a chance to enjoy the peace they so richly deserved.

And then there was the postcard from Australia. It seemed my old backpacking buddy Stuart was thinking of settling down with his girlfriend, Jackie, in Perth. He'd just landed himself a job as a hearse driver and apprentice coffin maker: '... *130 people applied for the job, and the bloody fools picked me!*'

The travel bugs would soon start gnawing at his brain, I predicted.

News from far-off places has always made me restless for adventure, highlighting how I was stuck *here*, as life passed me by out *there*. The condition seemed to always kick in after I'd stopped traveling for more than three consecutive days. As a mental equation, it looked something like this:

$$S = \int_0^{n \geq 3} \left(\frac{m}{\Delta h} - \Delta f \right)$$

Where S represented my state of **sanity** at any given time; m delineated freedom of **movement**; and h was a constant, tracking whichever **hellish pit** of stagnation I found myself mired in. The current value of S was further modified by n, the coefficient of desperation to get away from h, and moderated by f, a differential used to rate the variable degree of **frustration** engendered by communicating my degree of n to the native population of h. In short, I tended to go nuts the moment I stopped moving.

My current 'h' was a day job at Peter Pan, a cram school in a forgettable suburb of west Jakarta that kept me reined in, teaching English to teenagers. Rina, the lady principal, was over the moon when I'd returned from my latest visa-run to Singapore. Her husband, less so. *He can smuggle in his own smutty videos.* Today I was scheduled to teach my first private adult student, Miranda, a close friend of Rina's. Miranda was already an hour and a half late.

"Have some more sayur asem, Chris," Rina snapped her fingers, and a serving girl refilled my bowl with the bittersweet vegetable soup, my favorite. I broke off a crumbling triangle of prawn cracker to dunk in the bowl.

"Has she forgotten, you think?"

"No, it will be her *situation* … she has to meet her new boyfriend in a car park, for safety, and the traffic, as you know, is terrible," Rina's Indonesian instincts—eager to divulge the intimate details of her friend's blighted love life—were only just overpowered, on this occasion, by her Chinese blood, which cautioned utmost secrecy and evasion in all matters personal.

She continued:

"Her husband is incredibly jealous. He is not a good man." He operated an illegal gambling den and was always having affairs with the working girls there, if Rina was to be believed. "She tells me they are getting divorced, that she really loves this new man. He's an old flame."

The embers of some particularly long-repressed emotions must have been in the process of being rekindled, for Miranda failed to show. This sudden gap in my schedule left me at the mercy of my students, who urged me to accompany them camping that night. I had just enough time to grab a spare shirt and my toothbrush, and then we were off, driving in an open-top jeep—the living embodiment of the billboards advertizing Djarum brand cigarettes that flashed by at regular intervals—out of the capital's endless sprawl of industrial slums, and up towards Bogor, the famed (and thankfully cooler) hill station. Here, unlike the more proletarian European camping experience, tents were already erected and servants on hand to carry out the most onerous tasks, like cooking and washing up. Yuppi, Andy and Oni were my star students, all ethnic-Chinese Indonesian lads. They didn't speak or read Chinese, of course, such linguistic perversion being banned in Suharto's fervently anti-communist Indonesia. And all of them had modified family names to make them sound more Javanese, further disguising their ancestral origins. We joined their friends at the scrubby site, and sat around a huge barbeque pit as instant noodles boiled in a pot.

Oni strummed his guitar, the main body of which was glued together by worn stickers honoring Eddie van Halen, the Dutch-Indonesian guitarist who was role model to half of Jakarta's disaffected youth, and unofficial figure of national pride. I joined in experimentally on the blues harmonica I was hoping to master one day. Talk turned, naturally enough, to sex. Their impressions had been set by American teen movies. It struck me I was not the best person to ask about these things as I seemed to have been conferred travel and photography as a substitute for human relations with girls.

"You must have many girlfriends, Mr Chris," Yuppi cut to the chase.

"What do you think?" I hit back with a knowing smirk. *Lying is the path of least explanation.*

"You are lucky, in your country you can sleep with any girl," Yuppi speculated, "but here we have to get married first."

Not that this seemed to diminish their fevered search for the facts of life. "We have blue videos, of course, but they are illegal." I'd never watched a porn film in my life. Odd pages torn out of *Whitehouse* or *Hustler* were all I'd ever picked out of the hedgerows on my childhood bicycle rides through the Kentish countryside.

"It is easiest just to give my driver 100,000 rupiah," Andy admitted, to general consensus, "then he brings back a prostitute, and we all watch."

The amount—equivalent to around US$50, half a driver's monthly salary—seemed to be the cost of sex education here, for the rich.

Following their natural instinct to form into councils, I left my young students singing around the campfire, getting high on bottles of sugary Sosro tea. Their youthful excitement and abundance of hormones showed no sign of burning out. Squatting patiently and ignored on the darkened fringes, beyond this privileged scholarly circle, scavenger kids waited for the party to disperse, before moving in to strip our rubbish bare.

I towered over the friend school principal Rina was introducing me to.

"Miranda, this is Chris, he's my best teacher." I hoped I wasn't blushing. This felt more like a dating service than a language session. We shook hands, her palm soft, delicate, warm. Tentative. She was not what I'd expected. What was that, exactly—something out of *The Godfather*? Miranda embodied vulnerability more than vendetta.

"Hullo Chris," she looked up, shuffling her feet like a schoolgirl, though she was ten years my senior. Normally I taught entire classes, but for this private lesson, we were left alone in an echoing classroom, squeezed into student-sized chairs, facing each other, leaning our elbows on swivel desks. Miranda had been born in Pontianak, a city in West Kalimantan that straddled the equator. And, like the place she was from, Miranda carried inside her a dual nature, being half Chinese and half indigenous Dayak.

I have to record here that I know how this is going to end. Against all reason, my wildest desires will be accommodated in this fellow human being.

"Yes, I'd like to see you again."

That was what she'd said at the termination of our initial, innocent hour. We had remained seated, opposite each other, at respectable distance and under the watchful eye of Rina's spying servants, dispatched with unnecessary frequency to refill our coffee glasses. On the surface all that passed between us were conventional pleasantries. Beneath, though, emanating from my solar plexus, I felt a surging primal energy that restricted my breathing and made my heart pound.

I had lessons with Miranda every day that week. Hers was a crash course since she was practicing for a secretarial exam, and needed as much help as she could get. Married since a teenager, she had never had a job before. Never needed one. She was in the process of moving out of her husband's home, pending divorce proceedings, and in the meantime was living with her brother and his family in the north Jakarta enclave of Pluit, where all the rich Chinese hid behind high walls in ugly marble mansions. I couldn't ask directly about the new boyfriend, it wouldn't have been appropriate, sitting there alone in our classroom, our chairs close enough together that occasionally our knees brushed.

"Sorry," I said after one such occasion, and made a show of dragging my chair back a few inches. Why this magnetic attraction? I'd locked into a pre-programmed orbit, touchdown was inevitable. I was no longer the master of my own fate.

"You need to get laid, mate," Jez advised when he and Lorne had driven over in Jez's Land Rover. Lorne was the pony-tailed musician I'd traveled down with from Singapore, when I'd first moved to Jakarta. Jez, his friend, was a young Australian photographer. The son of an expat businessman, Jez had lived most of his life in Indonesia. A series of his postcards featuring tribes from Irian Jaya's remote Baliem Valley were currently on sale at the Sarinah department store. Rina made a fuss over my celebrity visitor, overdoing the tea and cakes, and was bowled over by Jez's fluency in the national language, chiding me later about my own deficiencies in that quarter.

"Way I see it," Lorne continued, "you survived sailing from Flores to Singapore, you hitchhiked across Tibet, and Christ-knows what you got up to in Afghanistan … your account is fully paid up in the adventure department. Can't be that difficult to get your leg over. Think of it as therapy."

This was the most direct talk I'd had about sex in my life. My dad's parting advice was something garbled about 'French letters' — the euphemism favored by his generation for condoms. At secondary school, all they'd managed to do was scare the shit out of me and my classmates talking about AIDS. It left our year mentally scarred and convinced: *if I have sex, I'm going to die, horribly.*

"She's a bit of all right," Lorne appraised Miranda with the wandering eye of the bluesman. Miranda had just arrived for her daily lesson and he and Jez were on their way out, "if *you* don't, then at least leave me her number ..." I think that rude reckoning was what did it; I needed to save Miranda from all the predators out there.

But when would an opportunity for intimacy arise? I was restricted to discussing with Miranda business terminology, letter formats, and the occasions on which one uses 'yours sincerely' or 'yours faithfully' — but never 'yours truly'. All I had to go by was Rina's secondhand gossip and rumor-mongering about the chaos of her friend's crumbling marriage.

━━━━∽━━━━

Miranda fidgeted distractedly through the lesson. It transpired, after a little probing, that her husband had ripped up her English textbooks and slashed all the tires on her car. She'd had to travel over by taxi. He called up five times during our lesson, demanding to speak to her. Rina intercepted the calls, lying that Miranda was not here. But then Miranda's husband turned on Rina, too, accusing her of harboring his runaway wife. At this, Rina exploded. She could be quite scary at times. Obviously, the guy was totally deranged. Miranda was now fearing for her life and on the verge of tears. I was out of my depth. How did you go about consoling a sobbing woman, especially one for whom you felt a growing sympathy?

Finally, it was decided that Miranda should make a call to her brother. His solution was to hire eight policemen to accompany Miranda to her husband's place when she picked up her remaining jewelry that evening. Apparently, Jakarta's Finest were no strangers to supplementing their meager incomes this way.

———— ∞ ————

There followed an eventful weekend family trip to Borobudur. Mrs Rina had first posited the idea of an outing a week earlier. At the time, I tactfully evaded making any firm decision, instinctively balking at having to spend any more time than necessary being sociable in the company of my boss. But when she'd mentioned they would also be making a side trip to the recently fully renovated World Heritage temple, I saw the potential to expand my collection of photographs. Hell, I might even be able to write a story about it. Why was I not surprised to discover Rina had invited Miranda along, too? Rina and her husband, Mr Halim, their two young daughters, and Rini the nursemaid, set off in their Kijang van first, leaving Miranda and me to follow by taxi.

Candi Borobudur is located in the spiritual heartland of Java, rising amid lush, misty rice terraces and guardian volcanoes, near the royal city of Yogyakarta. The 9th Century Syailendra Dynasty temple complex—said to be the largest Buddhist temple in the world—is a repository of more than 2,500 carved stone relief panels and 500 Buddha statues, seventy-two of these being seated inside perforated bell-shaped stone stupas surrounding the central dome. The vast, nine-level monument fell into disrepair, overlain with volcanic ash and overgrown with vegetation during the gradual decline of the Hindu kingdoms in Java, after the 14th Century, to be rediscovered by Sir Stanford Raffles' Dutch engineer, H.C. Cornelius, in 1814. It was going to take all day to drive there. Miranda had brought along her shorthand textbooks, and it looked as though I'd been kidnapped for a lengthy tuition session. We made a stop for late breakfast at

Cianjur. Almost every town en route featured its own specialty dish, advertizing them gaudily across the tarpaulin drapes of countless 'warungs' — the ubiquitous street cafes. At Cianjur the specific delicacy was frog's legs — grilled, chewy, and covered in chili sauce. I made a show of enjoying them, as was obviously expected, though I'd have preferred Coco Pops. But Asia doesn't do proper breakfasts.

By late afternoon we were reduced to a crawl down Yogya's clogged main artery, Jalan Malioboro. Finally, we were able to break off, and followed a narrow alley lined with batik galleries, leather workshops and touristy shadow puppet shows. I needed some time alone, having done my 9-to-5 of etiquette for the day. So, I was only too happy to clock out now from Rina, Miranda and their girlish debate over restaurant options for the evening.

"Hey, *Belanda*! Beer Mister," the bar girls beckoned. Across Indonesia — with the notable exception of Bali, where the automatic assumption is Australia — all foreigners are taken to be from Holland, 'Belanda', until otherwise identified. I settled for a large bottle of Bali Hai at the Gecko Bar, on the fringes of the backpacking district. The beer came served in a glass of melting ice chunks. I suddenly realized how much I'd been missing my tribe and the traveling vibe. Two Dutch girls played pool in the corner, leaning over the poorly lit table, their smooth, antelope legs drawing lurid stares from the local alley cats. As the Skorpions played over the eight-track sound system, my mind drifted, wishing I were back in Hong Kong dreaming of being in Borneo. Why could I never be content with where I was? After a third beer, I felt intrigued enough to find out about the night's sleeping arrangements and wandered back to the hotel.

"Chris, there you are!" Rina had been worried. Rarely drawn out of her west Jakarta enclave, she was terrified of the unfamiliar. By contrast, as a foreigner here, I defied any such social categorization, equally at home among princes or paupers. She handed me the key to my room. My single room. Why the hell would I want to get involved with Miranda and her messed-up state of affairs, anyhow? Better, by far, to go to bed buzzing from beer and dreaming of Dutch legs leading ever so slowly up to tightly clenched Dutch ...

"Chris?" An urgent whisper and gentle rattling alerted me to someone being outside my door, "Chriiis, let me in." Miranda.

I glanced up at the clock; it was one o'clock in the morning, and Miranda was dressed as if about to take dictation. She must tread carefully. Gossip, insinuation, anonymous spite; they festered in this uneven environment where everyone was either a master or slave. Those who failed to climb the social ranking enjoyed dragging anyone above them down.

"Come in."

"I can't sleep. Can we talk?" She tugged at the hem of her short black skirt, attempting to make it more suitable, only managing to draw my attention to her bare legs.

"Sure. I'm not very sleepy, either." I was awake now, at least.

"I can't talk about things to Rina, she knows my husband. She will gossip, she can't help herself."

"Your ex-husband ..."

"We are in the middle of a divorce. My brother is very rich, luckily."

"What do you mean? He has to pay your husband ...?"

"... Rudi, my husband is called Rudi. He is complaining I use Black Magic, how else to explain why we never had any children?"

"And that is grounds for divorce?" I was getting confused; it seemed ridiculous, but sorcery was a big deal here. Indonesians — especially the Dayak branch of Miranda's family, who had hunted for heads as recently as the 1960s — were animist spirit worshippers long before Islam arrived on these shores, imposing itself as the religion of trade.

"No, my brother has to pay the *judge*, of course. Whoever pays the most will win the case. It is normal, but these things take a long time to settle."

"And your boyfriend?" Having assailed the ramparts, I felt at liberty to explore her courtyard.

"My what? Oh, I made that up. Rina asks *so* many questions, I had to tell her something."

The sanest course of action seemed to be the most direct, so I reached out and pulled her down to sit on the edge of my bed, just a few inches away from me, our legs touching, and this time no witnesses lurking, no need of false modesty.

"And what about you? You must have girlfriends?"

"No. I've been traveling too much. I never had the time to sleep with anyone." I told her, being economical with the truth.

"I don't believe you! All Western men have many girlfriends, I have seen it, in America."

"You have been," I asked, "to the States?"

"Well, of course, in the cinema."

"Then you'll have to just believe me. I really don't know what to do around women." This admission seemed to strengthen Miranda's resolve and she took my arm, starting to stroke its hair. A bead of sweat formed on her neck, swelling until it reached critical mass, then started to trickle down and disappear into the crevasse between her small breasts.

"Let me put the fan on, it is too stuffy in here." I stood up and made my way to the switch at the doorway. When I turned around, she'd unbuttoned her white, frilly blouse. Her bra, the same shade as her skin, was hardly visible beneath it.

"Why don't you kiss me, Chris?" she giggled, "for once, you will have to listen to me; I will enjoy being your teacher."

It's strange, I didn't feel at all embarrassed as she stripped me of my clothes. There can be no secrets when you are naked. And Miranda soon realized I had not been lying when I'd told her she was the first woman I'd been with. She became quite serious in her task, in fact, guiding me by hand and tongue in a variety of explorations of pleasure. I followed her lead.

"You learn quick, Chris," she moaned, her back arched and thighs muffling my ears.

"Quickly." I corrected her, on teacher autopilot.

"No, no, *slowly*, it is nicer."

Sweating, we slithered and slid over and under one another, like electric eels in a bucket, each new touch delivering increased sensation. *This* was what I'd been missing all this time. Although, having become somewhat inured to excitement of late, I have to record here I sort of expected more … more what? … transcendence? Only the truly unexpected thrills.

I awakened, tangled in bedsheets, strands of Miranda's long, black hair sticking to the pillowcase. But no sign of her. She must have snuck out just before dawn. The bill you are handed for a night of passion is a morning of pathos. We faced each other over breakfast in the hotel canteen, yawning. Studying first Miranda and then me, Rina began to make such a huge exhibition of being the eager tourist that I reckoned she *must* have known what we'd been up to in the night.

"Did you not sleep well, Chris?" she asked, full of faux concern at my untamed hair.

"Mosquitos," I replied, failing to convince her, or to deflect her inquisition.

"Was your room full of mosquitoes too, Miranda?" She turned to her friend, who was looking a bit dark around the eyes. Miranda smiled, weakly. Rina continued, all pep and vim:

"Mr Halim wants to set off soon, if we're to see the temple *and* get back to Jakarta before it is too late."

I sipped at my coffee. It was tepid, black and tasted of licorice.

"Right you are, Rina. Let me pop up and get my camera gear." Poor Miranda, I deserted her at the table, the focus of all Rina's probing.

Borobudur was more than worthy of the detour. The ancient layer-cake temple genuinely deserved its status as an unofficial Wonder of the World. I eagerly focused my lens on the bell-shaped stupas surrounding each of the structure's many ascending tiers. Visitors strained, pushing their arms through the stone lattice walls of these bells, attempting to touch the serene carved Buddhas seated within, the accomplishment of which was said to bring good luck. Getting back into photographer mode helped distract me from speculation of the possible complications that would undoubtedly lead on from last night's weakness, and very un-Buddha-like bout of lust.

Mr Halim had his own camera at the ready. He seemed always to capture me just as I reached out to steady Miranda from toppling on the uneven ramparts, or was helping her up the deep stone steps linking each level of the monument, like those of an Aztec pyramid. It was uncanny. Was he gathering evidence? Would these images return, in the future, to haunt me?

If so, I was smiling like an idiot, complicit in my own persecution.

———— ∾ ————

A couple of days later I picked up my Borobudur slides from the lab. They had turned out pretty well and, on the strength of them, I decided to pop over to the Hyatt Hotel and knock on the door of Room 526: Mr Fong of Amex. He was in, and gracious enough to see me without prior warning or knowledge of my existence.

Anna's name worked like a magic charm. I discovered he was actually employed by an outfit called Cheney Communications, based out of Hong Kong—which put out various regional lifestyle magazines—and Mr Fong was editing one of their new titles, *Expressions*, largely sponsored by American Express. He was working on the launch issue at this very moment.

"Well, if you can write me a thousand words ..." he muttered, bending over a large light box and studying my images intently through his magnifying loupe, "... I think we could use these for the cover story. Yes! Your colors really pop."

It must be the 81B warming filter London Bus had urged me to use back in Peshawar. I worried briefly that popping colors could be a bad thing, but then Fong continued, "By Monday, if that would be possible?"

He added, "This is a windfall for us," and mentioned he'd take any other stories I had, too. I mentioned the Thai island of Koh Phangan, where I'd hidden from the world over the new year, and some of my earlier shots from Timor and Flores.

"Yes, yes. Though your boat trip is not really suitable for our readers." These, I gathered, were Amex cardholders, more desirous of luxury travel advice than in tales of gritty survival. "Do you have anything on Singapore?"

Overwhelmed, I said 'yes' to all the above. I felt like adding *pinch me, I'm dreaming*, though I managed to retain a more professional veneer. The genial Chinese-Malaysian Fong introduced me to his wife Ruby, who worked in the office as his general assistant. Together they pumped me full of strong coffee and head-spinning praise. Only later, once I was again navigating the cracked and crowded pavements, having to avoid stepping on legless beggars pushing themselves along on trolleys, and being forced to dodge around the *kaki lima* carts selling saté chicken on bamboo splints; only here, with my feet planted back in the heaving, humid, diesel-choked reality of the street, did my stomach plunge. I had to now produce a story, out of thin air, over the weekend. My motivation for this was Fong's promised rate of US$0.20 per word, US$30 per picture.

I had an hour to kill before my pre-arranged meeting with Miranda in the car park behind the Sarinah department store. A foreign man walking the streets of the Indonesian capital already attracted way too much unwanted attention, but a foreign man and local woman seen together in public — alone, and stripped of the anonymity provided by being in a group — would just multiply that degree of attention to an unbearable level. So, I drew out the process, sipping my coffee at a crowded food court, swaddled in pungent kretek fumes. These ubiquitous sweet cigarettes of Indonesia are spiced with cloves, whose buds crackle when ignited by the burning tobacco, giving them their onomatopoeic name, and their tang was impossible to evade. I tethered my camera by its strap in case of grab-and-run opportunists and began to scrawl the outline for my Borobudur article on the back of a paper place mat.

Miranda arrived accompanied by her brother's chauffeur who, no doubt, was already mentally compiling the report he'd later deliver to his boss. We couldn't meet at the school any longer. Rina, initially our most enthusiastic backer, had become cold on our trysting. Perhaps she'd been talking to Rudi? Miranda suggested we direct the driver to the Horison Hotel (now the Mercure Convention Centre), a sprawling tourist complex occupying a considerable acreage of the city's polluted north shore. More immediately important than any environmental degradation, though, was the hotel's location, a world away from south Jakarta and Rudi's network of sleazy nightclub, hotel and bar owners who would soon have recognized and informed on Miranda. The room reeked of clove tobacco and the carpet was perforated with a miniature golf course of cigarette burns. An ancient air conditioner churned away, noisily struggling to push dank columns of air over the bed. Horison was, like our relationship, convenient and practical rather than romantic.

I fell inevitably, and surprisingly comfortably, into this double life. By weekday, the aspiring photojournalist and clean-shaven English teacher. In the weekends, dodging night shadows down the darkened alleyways of old Batavia. I'd be lying to say I didn't get a certain thrill out of the subterfuge: perhaps the wide range of experience was necessary? I was aware that I was probably substituting for the adventures I'd become used to, and that until recently had been provided by extreme travel. Anyhow, wasn't any experience — as long as one survived it — ultimately chalked up as 'research'? If there was one length of rope I was left clinging to, rope that would guide me back to safety after falling overboard, it was that marked 'photography'. But ropes could be used as nooses, too.

It was the week of Miranda's birthday. She couldn't slip away on the actual day, so we planned to meet on the closest Friday night to it. She'd let slip a while back that, should I be thinking of buying her a present, then a bra — to replace one I'd recently destroyed during a particularly frenzied bout of bodily unwrapping (I'd been unaware of the concept of the front-loader, until then) — would be appreciated. This simplified matters, as I had no idea what else she would like or what her interests were. But why did it have to be a bra? I would never ask her to purchase me a pair of boxer shorts. I assumed it was some sort of test women were biologically compelled to put men through, to establish their degree of devotion. In olden days, a knight would have been urged to fight a dragon. Tasked with the modern-day equivalent, I headed to Blok-M mall, a depressingly concrete consumer prison, home to pickpockets and half of Jakarta's trendy youth. I hoped I wouldn't bump into any of my students there. The sales assistant in the Pasaraya department store took pity on me. I assumed she was used to modeling on a regular basis for absent girlfriends.

"B-52" ... wait, wasn't that an American heavy bomber? A cocktail? I took a look at the slip of paper in my hand. "Er, 32-B ... which one would you buy? You look about the same size. I mean shape ... er ..."

The girl didn't blush, instead she seemed to be enjoying my evident unease and went off, soon to return carrying a wide array of likely styles and colors. I went for black. It was either that or the red. No doubt every woman who gazes into a mirror sees a supermodel looking back at her, a paragon of elegance and enchantment. Further, the appropriate and wise selection of underwear, to the female mind—I assumed, not really knowing the intimate workings of any female minds—acted not only as visual expression of her sophistication, but as a weapon to be wielded in her on-going mission to engage and entrap the man she had locked on to. What she willfully chose to ignore, though, was that men, given the choice, would opt for slutty every time, and hardly notice the upholstery. But it was the level of discomfiture—evidently on both sides—that counted.

Today was the designated Friday, so after finishing my classes I flagged down a bajaj three-wheeler and fumigated in a cloud of exhaust smoke all the way to Cikini Raya. *A Fish Called Wanda* was being screened at T.I.M. cinema there. Jakarta, little more than an exponentially overgrown village, was linked by torturously potholed, floodable, one-way streets. The speediest, though least graceful way to navigate these blighted lanes, was by orange and black painted, two-stroke bajaj rickshaws. It was best to remain mindful, as alighting, of the vicious metal door flap that would spring back and attempt to snag your trousers in its ravenous jaws. Taxies being prohibitively costly, I utilized these vehicles to get around town. They were a lot safer than my remaining option, which was to be picked up by Miranda. Her driving was awful. At least three new dents and scratches appeared on her car each week, the result of missing a turn off along the toll road, say, and reversing against the flow of traffic to get back to it.

I spotted Miranda from across the lobby. Our eyes met, hungrily. Blood starting to flow to the most awkward parts of my anatomy. Walking up to her, stiffly, I gestured that we should perhaps sit for a while, partly to disguise my growing erection, but also because it would be culturally inappropriate to display any obvious sign of physical affection, like leaping into each other's arms, in public.

"Hello, Chris. I have been longing for you," she said, staring straight ahead, getting in on the act.

"I have your bra, in my pocket," I shot back.

"Oh my God!"

"Well, you asked me to buy one ..."

"No, I mean, oh my God, over there." She jutted her chin indicating a young couple who had just entered the complex and sat down, maybe twenty feet away. Luckily, the crowds were quite dense, obscuring us from immediate exposure. "That's the brother of Rudi's sister-in-law, and his girlfriend." She shrank into the plush, red leatherette cushions.

"What of it? Why should we be scared of them? We should go up to them and say 'hi', or else they'll think it suspicious."

"No, no. Maybe they haven't seen us yet."

Rudi's relative seemed to be facing the same dilemma, painstakingly avoiding eye contact, continuing an animated chat with his girl, pointing out to her all the latest movie posters. It was she who eventually spotted Miranda and called out, "Miranda! Hello, it's me, Sissy! How are you? And this is?"

They ambled across the thinly carpeted floor.

I had to think fast. "Charly," I introduced myself, an ocker Aussie, straight off the farm, "G'day, Mate!" I don't know if this performance convinced them: one being guilty until proven innocent in the judgmental court of Indonesian public opinion. Fortunately, we made it out to the car park after the film avoiding further encounter with members of Miranda's extended family. I had enjoyed the film enormously, but was left somewhat distracted by the mental image of Miranda's husband, Rudi, transformed into the role of a demented local Otto (Jamie Lee Curtis's psychopathic suitor, played in the movie by Kevin Kline).

There was no way I was going to let Miranda return to her brother's place that night, and she had no intention of letting me off the hook with just a visit to the cinema. So, after having driven around several other low-risk options, and finding them all fully booked, we settled on the Marcopolo Hotel. Even here, though, it was necessary to follow sneaky protocol.

"You go in first and get a room. Tell me the number and I'll come up and knock on the door in half an hour," Miranda advised.

I was sure all this cloak-and-dagger skulking was doing a number on me. My paranoia, which had sunk back to workable levels after spiking in Pakistan, had returned and was giving me acid indigestion. Maybe the AIDS posters at school were right, after all? What if, inadvertently, having sex *did* kill you (or, at least, kick-start the process)?

After the initial, shaky start we'd had in Yogyakarta, I was getting better at the game; our bodies had become more synchronized now. We made love four times before the happy obliteration of sleep at around at around 3:00 a.m. Only once was our private pleasure dome infiltrated, and then just by room service — Miranda concealing herself in the bathroom during the delivery of prawn crackers and ice cream.

I feel a teeny bit traitorous to think it, what with Miranda snoring softly at my side, but is this sneaking around worth all the gray hairs?

SINGAPORE
April 1, 1989

I NEVER NEEDED much excuse to escape from Jakarta. By now, my visa was about to expire and, in truth, I was only too happy to take a breather from the place—and from Miranda. Sex was OK, but I was beginning to value my sanity above it. It was liberating to soak up again the international atmosphere of the Lion City, and to be back at Sim's guesthouse, even if the man himself was becoming crankier every time I passed through town. Sim presided over his backpacking bailiwick like a provincial magistrate of the Qing dynasty. His white vest, rolled up to the armpits, exposed a fat Buddha's belly that wobbled where it rested, like a shapeless blancmange, on the surface of his Formica desk. Dismissed to the outer perimeter of this shiny table were a clunky telephone and his cash box. Behind him the inevitable TV screen flickered away, night and day. He greeted me:

"Hey, *yan dao*. See you again, lah! Why you come back, still make no money?" Sim, like many Singaporeans, was of Hokkien Chinese ancestry and used the Fujianese expression for 'handsome guy'—his embedded sarcasm requiring no translation.

"Precisely the opposite, Sim, Old Boy," I hammed it up, in retaliation, "I am here to photograph your beautiful City State for the American Express Company." He didn't believe me, of course, but something in me must have changed; he was less cantankerous than usual, and issued me a nice lower bunk, by a window, without my having to ask for it.

"Hola!" There was a girl somewhere behind all the long hair, I was convinced of it. "I'm Felicia. We sleep together on our first night, I see!" she joked, leaning down from the bunk above me. The floodgates had opened: all these years of blissful abstinence, and now? Did they *smell* the difference?

Felicia came from Huelva, about as far south as you can go down in Spain, before hitting British rock. She was a very feminine sort of girl, if you know what I mean—one to laugh and cry and capture you with their honesty. Twenty-nine years old, though I took her for twenty-four. Wordlessly, we were drawn to each other. Holed below the water line, I was defenseless: let one woman in and, like the ocean, the rest swiftly followed. *I'm drowning in sentiment.*

〰

It was a Sunday, nothing much was going on at the hostel, so I invited Felicia to join me on my pilgrimage to Changi Sailing Club. I'd started making one, each time I came back to Singapore for a new Indonesian visa. It was here we had ended our voyage on the *Kurnia Ilahi* the previous year, and it helped the 45-minute journey on the No. 2 bus pass faster, being able to recount to my captive Spanish audience the story of our ocean adventure from distant Jampea Island.

"Are you a member, *Sir*?" a club official questioned me, his doubtful eyes—clamped on Felicia's flowing Thai silk trousers and flip-flops—signaling obvious disapproval. You could get away with murder in Singapore as long as your costume was a business suit.

"My boat is moored here," I confirmed breezily, the power of truth on my side, and strode past him. He made no further inquiry or attempt to stop us. Felicia was smiling though.

"You liar!"

"No, I'm not," I replied, pretending to be stung by her lack of faith, and eager to deliver the punchline to my story. I led her through the clubhouse, across the flower-hung patio and down to the jetty. "There, see?" In the shadows beneath the pier, submerged and tethered to a leg of the jetty, floated a native sampan—our ship's laughable 'lifeboat'—the only surviving proof of our madcap sailing adventure the previous year.

"My boat!" I announced.

We arrived back in the city at 2:00 p.m. The light at this hour, this near to the equator, was harsh but I needed to shoot some photos of recognizable Singaporean landmarks for Mr Fong's magazine. And the Merlion statue, spewing water in front of the General Post Office (now the magnificent Fullerton Hotel) seemed to be as good a place to start as any. Nearby, a hawker sat shaded by a huge, multicolored umbrella, selling his specialty snack to the lunchtime crowds: condensed milk sandwiches, sprinkled with sugar.

"Ugh," Felicia winced, "I think I'll go for the coconut ice cream." This melting confection dripped on the entrance steps between her legs as she sat watching me disappear into the ancient gloom of the GPO. There was a small chance someone would have remembered me and posted a communication via Poste Restante. I was in luck! An airmail letter from Adelaide awaited. It had been sent by The Mouse:

London Bus has gone back to YKW. Seems the end game is playing out there now. I'm still stuck here driving the taxi, though the Pacific Defense Review took a bunch of my shots … he'd penned, using our old, coded initials Afghanistan, 'YKW' … You Know Where. And then came his reply to my last letter, in which I'd opened up a bit about the Miranda situation:

… Always remember that women are the downfall of the solitary male. It's been that way since the Garden of Eden.

Biblical Adam had to learn the hard way. I was more fortunate: being cast out from Paradise never bothered a nomad; it only served to strengthen him, to make him more nomadic.

There was a thunderstorm in the night and the electricity had been cut off. Without ceiling fans to stir it, the air became immediately stuffy. It was impossible to even think of getting any sleep. Since she was up, too, Felicia suggested giving me a massage. She seemed like a practical girl, her hands were strong but not rough, and no monkey business was implied by her offer. After some laborious deconstruction of the taut coils of muscles I'd developed carrying a camera bag around all the time, she mentioned the pain I was experiencing in my spleen was from worrying too much, and that I needed to cut down on sugar. She had obviously never visited Jakarta.

"Here are my cats, Chris." It was breakfast time at Sim's. White sliced bread that tasted of polystyrene, plasticky margarine that never melted, jam of unspecified chemical provenance, and ludicrously sweetened tea made using evaporated milk, poured from a big teapot kept continuously on the boil. Felicia shoved a kitten in my face. It was part of a large litter left behind by a stray that had adopted the guesthouse. I could have crushed it in one hand. Instead, I stroked its oversized head, felt the rapid beat of its tiny heart. Mr Sim didn't like them, said they scratched his furniture. He really was in a foul mood. The days of his guesthouse were numbered. The Singapore government wanted to price us backpackers off their island.

I needed to get some serious shots in Chinatown today for Mr Fong. This could only be done alone. Non-photographers always became bored with all the hanging around.

"I'll come with you, Chris, I'll just stay in the background," Felicia pleaded. But the suggestion was as unrealistic as if I'd asked to follow her to her office, and just sit in a chair beside her desk all day. I needed to concentrate, to block out all distraction. Photography was a totally selfish occupation. She accepted my decision, though I could see I had lost some of my coolness capital in the process. I didn't make it back to Sim's until 5:00 p.m. Felicia was in a state.

"Chris, he says it's my fault—all the cats. He is going to kill them; he is mad!" She meant Mr Sim. Her mascara cascading in grotesque rivulets down both cheeks.

"Let's get out of here, let's just split. Don't let him make you cry," I consoled her, feeling pity creep in. I had a soft spot for pity.

"But what, what about the cats?"

"They'll be OK. Jerry will look after them, won't you, Jerry?" Jerry was a Tamil and a long-term Sim's resident. He worked in the oil industry, and would occasionally make real money, before gambling it all away and ending up back here waiting for his next gig. Presently he was driving a cement truck. I must have lent him S$30 already. I knew I'd never get it back. The trick with lending money, as with gambling, was to only offer up that which you could afford to lose. *Karma* had many forms of payback, and very few of them were financial in nature.

"Yeah, man, no problem. I'll look after the cats."

"You promise, Jerry?" Felicia stopped sobbing and looked hopefully at the Indian. "If you don't, I will *kill* you." I believed her.

Thus began a rather late-in-the-day search for alternative accommodation. This was prolonged by a tour of the NTUC supermarket in Sim Lim Towers to stock up on cans of Special Brew. We ended up in a much enhanced and giggling mood, checking into the Tai Loke Hotel, an old colonial house with creaking floorboards and a little garden, up on Middle Road (and long-since bulldozed to make way for the Sunshine Plaza shopping center). We dropped our bags and wandered down Selegie Road to the Cathay Cinema to see *Who Framed Roger Rabbit?* This was brilliant, even more-so when embellished by our smuggled-in beers.

It was almost midnight when we arrived back at the hotel, though I don't remember anything of the walk from the cinema. I half-heartedly offered to sleep on the floor of our room, there being but the one, obvious bed, right in the middle of it. But Felicia insisted I join her on the big mattress and that we talk about anything and everything. This I found myself very willing to do, she being a special kind of girl, living for 'now'. *Like I can only dream of doing.* Open, frank, always laughing. She made fun of my straight English ways, and coaxed me out of them; and I wondered if all Spanish women were like her?

"I'm going to kiss you now," I warned her, the earlier intake of alcohol providing me a level of bravery totally lacking in my non-inebriated self.

"Goodness, Senor, let me prepare," she swigged down the remnants of a can of Special Brew and I dove in through the jungle of her long, thick hair. She peeled off my t-shirt, and I helped remove hers. It was stretched taut across generous, smooth breasts that were underlined by just the faintest w-shape of perspiration. After much entanglement, we made love once in the night, enjoying the warmth and companionship of skin touching skin, snuggling into each other's curves. With Miranda sex *was* our means of communication. Felicia was different; with her there was no sense of urgency. There was something beyond sex: the elixir of conversation. I needed two different types of lover at the same time: one to fulfill my carnal desires, the other my mental ones.

I don't wish to seem greedy, but wouldn't it be great if the Universe could present both these qualities in the body of one, single (attractive, sexy, long-legged, smoky-voiced, traditional, independent and yet low maintenance) woman?

Sulawesi, Indonesia
April 19, 1989

I SPENT THE ten days following our night at the Tai Loke continuously on the move. Felicia had left for Thailand and, without her, I'd lost my desire, or any reason, to remain in Singapore. Then, a rather unexpected but certainly timely advance payment for my Borobudur story tipped the scales. I decided to invest all my 'winnings' in a one-way air ticket to Kota Kinabalu, and to purchase forty rolls of color slide film. I also bought a Tupperware sandwich box that could accommodate, perfectly, thirty-three rolls of 35mm film (once they'd been removed from their plastic canisters), and set about loading it with its precious celluloid stash.

From Kinabalu, provincial capital of the Malay state of Sabah, on the northeastern tip of the jungle island of Borneo, I engaged in a series of bus journeys to Tawau, before, finally, enduring a frigidly air-conditioned high-speed ferry to Indonesia's Tarakan Island.

"I see you have been to communist China," said the Indonesian immigration official there who examined my passport.

"I have also spent time in capitalist Hong Kong," I defended myself, leafing over a few pages in the document. He chopped me back on to Indonesian soil with a wry smile.

I had to lay over in Tarakan for the next two days, one of many souls waiting for the next passenger ship, a vessel of the government-run PELNI line that intermittently serviced the sprawling archipelago. Tarakan I found to be a seedy, stifling joint, the sole attraction of which—besides a porous coastline beloved of cigarette smugglers—was the entertainment of certain pious gentlemen from neighboring lands who came to partake of alcohol on such occasions their love of pleasure exceeded their fear of God. And where the only reason to go out of a night was to find a hooker.

A night voyage from Tarakan to Toli-Toli—the next link in a numerous chain of settlements joining me obliquely from here to Jakarta—was the South Seas equivalent of ascension from Hell to Heaven. In Toli-Toli. I found a berth on a local coaster that plied the turquoise waters of the North Sulawesi coastline dropping off supplies and picking up passengers from tiny, palm-fringed settlements, for whom the sea was their sole point of contact with the greater world. Rising from the horizon, on the second day of this idyllic voyage, Old Manado—*Manadotua*—appeared long before new Manado. The still-active volcanic peak constituted an entire island, a fiery exclamation point that guarded the northernmost tip of Indonesia. Next stop, the Philippines. Ethnic Chinese-Indonesians had long dominated trade in Manado, and were mainly Catholic. There were sometimes as many as two churches to a street.

I recuperated here for a few days, unwilling to contemplate the onward journey, but knowing that I must set off or lose momentum entirely. There was only one road out of the place, and that headed south, to Gorontalo. Choosing my next destination was not challenging. It was on average an easy stage, by Northern Sulawesi standards, just the nine hours by cramped minivan. The blood had stopped flowing to my legs before we'd even left the Manado suburbs. I jumped around on arrival in Gorontalo, trying to revive circulation, and started the search for a place to stay, rather late in the day.

Fritz had lived through seventy-seven years, and had owned Gorontalo's Melati Hotel for a good portion of them. "In the war I fought for the Dutch against the Japanese," he told me. We sat inside his small store, next door to the hotel, out of which he sold bottled water, single-use sachets of shampoo and laundry powder, and the inevitable Gudang Garam clove cigarettes. "They took me prisoner near the end, and I was freed by the Allies. I am lucky, a few more months and I would have starved to death, like all my friends did."

"Have you ever been to Holland?" It seemed a fair question to ask of someone born of one Dutch parent and who had fought in the name of that far-away notion.

"Not yet!" replied the old optimist, his eyes lighting up at the possibility.

I left him some postage stamps I'd collected off my various mail. In return, he presented me with a year-old copy of *Time* magazine representing probably the most recent news from the outside world to have invaded this sleepy outpost. When he heard I was heading south, he advised me, "The Muslims in Poso are fanatic, but not extreme." The difference between these two similar states would seem to be of the fine and nuanced variety favored by Indonesians.

Manga horse drawn carts clip-clopped up and down narrow streets beyond the Melati's lawn, outnumbering their motorized competition, and Widya insisted I eat not only an entire papaya but chew its bitter seeds, too. These were the best medicine against a sudden return of my diarrhea, she explained to me, patiently. Widya was Fritz's fifteen-year-old room maid, a young Bugis girl.

"Why don't you marry me?" she teased as we sat together on the veranda, she helping me practice my Indonesian.

"I'll come back in ten years," I told her, thinking seriously, if nothing else had come up by then, returning aged 32 to settle with a cute 25-year-old Bugis wouldn't be such a bad option.

She pouted, "By then I'll have five children!"

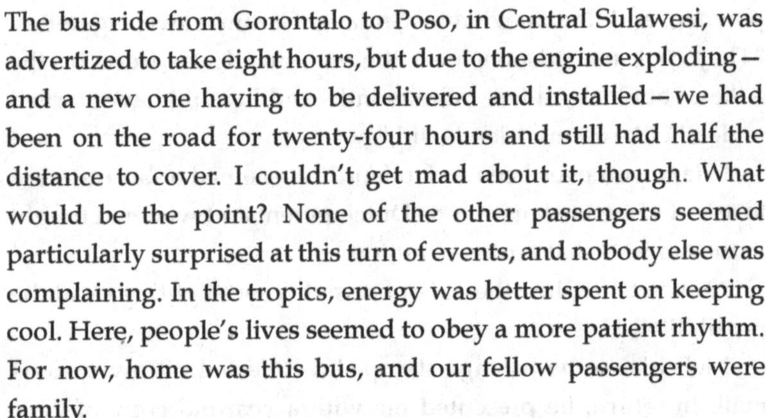

The bus ride from Gorontalo to Poso, in Central Sulawesi, was advertized to take eight hours, but due to the engine exploding — and a new one having to be delivered and installed — we had been on the road for twenty-four hours and still had half the distance to cover. I couldn't get mad about it, though. What would be the point? None of the other passengers seemed particularly surprised at this turn of events, and nobody else was complaining. In the tropics, energy was better spent on keeping cool. Here, people's lives seemed to obey a more patient rhythm. For now, home was this bus, and our fellow passengers were family.

After the passing of several stationary hours, the driver began tooting his horn, anxious to get moving now the new motor had miraculously rumbled into life. The women dashed off to gather their children from downstream, where they'd been playing in a small creek; we menfolk sauntered back from upstream, where we'd been taking a piss. The heavily laden vehicle began to move, a dusty breeze soon traveling the length of the aisle, drying off some of the equatorial sweat. My gaze escaped outwards, between the flickering coconut trees, and across the silver and blue glint of the Gulf of Tomimi, continuing on until it was lost beyond the invisible horizon.

Each new vista had moved someone sufficiently to praise it with the construction of a church, or mosque. We halted a few hours later for prayers. Here, some locals were proudly surrounding a fifteen-foot-long python they'd captured, killed, and tied to a wooden fence. The snake had been unable to slither away, being weighed down, as it was, by the recent consumption of an entire kid goat. It could have swallowed a small child with less discomfort.

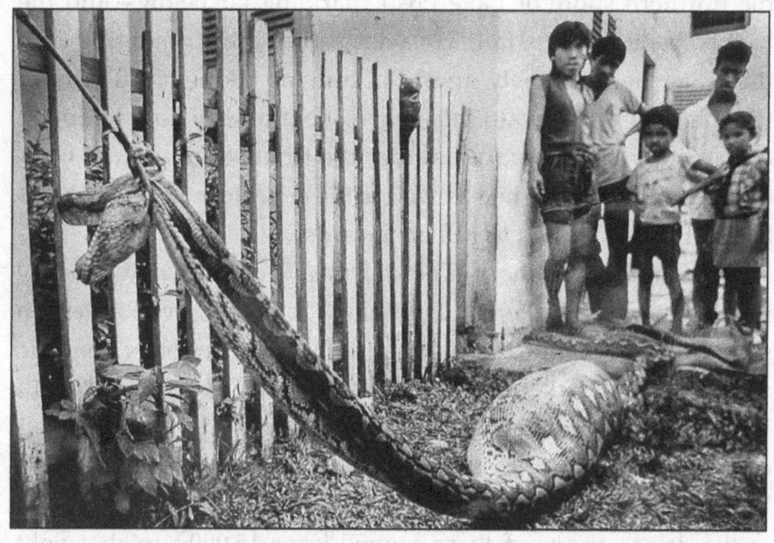

Hindu temples, resembling those in the Bali tourist brochures, began to replace the churches. By noon we were in steep descent from the hills, heading into Poso, the town's corrugated red tin rooftops looking like neatly ploughed plots of land amid the spreading green palm leaves. Here, after a brief coffee stop, I changed vehicles to continue along the grandly titled 'Trans-Sulawesi Highway' to Tentena. The van had seen better days. Its retreaded tires were bald, and nuts were missing off its wheels. The driver's mate had to secure the door by means of a custom-made wire latch, stuffing sections of old inner tube to seal and dust-proof any remaining gaps. The driver hotwired the ignition and stepped on the accelerator pedal; he tore along the single-track lane, slaloming around lazy water buffalos and dodging potholes with breathtaking dexterity and complete disregard for the structural integrity of both his van and the human bodies transported within it. A few hours later we found ourselves descending through hills of long grasses, down into Tentena — the northern shore of Lake Poso sparkling far below — and the brakes beginning to fail. We were saved from plunging into the water by the timely arrival of an embankment. The driver rammed his vehicle into this heaven-sent obstruction, whipped out a couple of bricks from under the front seat and, in a well-practiced routine, rushed to wedge these behind the rear wheels before the van started to roll backwards.

The road ended here. The only way forward now was by ferry, across the lake, to Pendolo. Rainwater evaporated in steamy vapors from the baking surface of Pendolo's concrete wharf. A small ticket office at the end of the jetty stood backlit by the headlights from a row of Toyota Land Cruisers, their engines revving in anticipation of the next leg of a journey I was beginning to convince myself was never going to end. I handed to the driver of one of these rugged jeeps 15,000 rupiah — eight dollars — it seemed an excessive amount for a mere sixty-mile journey.

The reason for the inflated fare, and necessity of transport by muscular 4WD vehicles, soon became apparent: mud. A mountain of the stuff that took all night to traverse. The Toyota was tossed like a boat in a storm, water flooding in through cracks in the floorboards and through the door gaps. Windscreen wipers were pathetic against such a deluge of sludge and muck, so a young boy was roped to the hood of each vehicle, clearing a space with his arm for the driver to peer through.

——∞——

Toraja Land — *Tanah Toraja* — this was a different world; claustrophobic, animistic, ancient, and dripping with coffee plantations. The Bugis of the south — who can't fathom why anyone would choose to live away from the sea — called its inhabitants the 'People of the Uplands', and feared it as a place steeped in death. Wooden *Tau-Tau* effigies were placed standing in cliff-top alcoves, staring out over the land, while the physical corpses they represented were suspended below in hanging wooden caskets, until the ropes holding them up rotted.

I'd arrived, by chance, during a three-day funeral celebration. As dictated by the Torajan's polytheistic *aluk* belief, animals were required to be sacrificed before the spirit of the deceased could continue on its journey to *puya*, the Land of the Souls. Particularly prized were gentle, timid 'kerbau' — water buffaloes; and today twenty-three of these, and dozens of pigs, were going to be offered in an orgy of mud and blood-letting.

Utilizing my credentials from *Matra* — a magazine in Jakarta that had recently re-run my *Kurnia Ilahi* story — I made it through to the front of an expectant crowd, just as the first surprised and resentful kerbau was disturbed from munching a tuft of grass, its neck and both hind legs being lassoed by expert ranchmen. The groaning ruminant was brought down, its rear legs being pulled from under it, and its neck twisted at an acute angle, exposing the jugular. An official dressed in funereal black, his head wrapped in a blue bandana, stepped up; he stroked the flinching beast's neck with the flat of his machete, and then began to hack, the buffalo's eyes widening in pain and terror, its flabby carcass shuddering. I hid behind my camera while shooting the hot, maroon fountains that gushed from the stricken animal's throat. Guilty, bloody-red droplets stained my clothes.

From high above, where the coffin lay draped in red cloth on a teetering wooden dais, the dead man's three widows began a mourning wail. The killing would go on all day, but when they began slaughtering pigs, I'd seen enough.

"One buffalo is equal to four pigs," informed Abdul Madjid, the personal photographer of the governor of South Sulawesi. He was a small, energetic man, his spectacles held together by masking tape. A battered old Ricoh SLR slapped against his chest. He offered me a kretek. I accepted, for once, in need of sweet clove to burn away the acrid taste and overpowering stench of sacrificial blood. "I can see you are a photographer, not a tourist," he went on, "they would never get so close." We sat smoking silently, enjoying the shared camaraderie of our absurd profession for a while.

On the way back into town there was a torrential downpour such as is only ever experienced in the tropics: rain so heavy that the earth jumps up to meet it halfway in muddy explosions. Children scampered off into the undergrowth, emerging soon afterwards carrying huge banana fronds they'd chopped off and fashioned for use as umbrellas. Back at the guesthouse, I soaked my already-soaked trousers in a bucket of petrol, hoping to wash out the bloody stains. And later, mindful of unfinished business in Jakarta, I took the night bus to Makassar, from where a PELNI ship was scheduled to depart for Surabaya. Even diluted by a few thorough rinses, my trousers continued to emit powerful gasoline fumes. At least these kept the mosquitos at bay.

***

My official berth for the two-day voyage on the *K.M. Kelimutu*, one of PELNI's distinctive, cream and rust-hued East German-built fleet, was down among the hard beds and communal interrogation of 'ekonomi' class. The atmosphere there was composed in equal measure of stuffiness, smoke and sauna, and defeated me. I moved my backpack to sleep in the open air and sea breezes up on the top deck. Wrapping myself in my Pakistani blanket, I lay at the base of the ship's bright orange funnel staring up into the sparkling sky, and tried to make out which of the stars was the one for Surabaya. Ever since picking up the rudiments of celestial navigation on the *Kurnia Ilahi* when sailing to Singapore, eight months earlier, I'd retained the habit of trying to guess which heavenly body would lead me to my destination, even when not at sea.

That every mile now traveled was bringing me a mile closer to Jakarta somewhat overshadowed my last few days of freedom, just as Sunday afternoons as a kid were always ruined thinking about the prison of school the next morning. As with all capital cities, Jakarta had for years acted as a magnet for transient populations from across the country; these came in search of jobs and social improvement. All too frequently, the same economic migrants would be left living in the makeshift slums that tended to surround the base of most of the capital's skyscrapers, the same gleaming towers the luckiest among them had found temporary and dangerous employment helping to construct. I was confused at the latent sense of duty that seemed to be compelling me to leave behind the tranquility of the provinces and return, instead, to the urban jungle, and the unpredictable beasts that preyed within. Did separation make the heart grow fonder? Or just encourage lust to grow stronger? Was the answer: either, both, or none of the above? I had missed Miranda slightly more than Jakarta on those rare occasions my thoughts had turned to either. Maybe *she* was my unfinished business? After all, as St Augustine put it, 'I was not yet in love, yet I loved to love ...'

Later in the day I found plenty of time to ponder such age-old conundrums, jolting on the train back across the productive paddy fields and coconut groves of bustling Java, the most heavily populated of all of Indonesia's many islands, and where hardly an acre of fertile, volcano-fed loam is left unclaimed by agriculture, or untouched by residential development. What makes Man want to push out Nature so? From where comes this compulsion to impose order and control? In contrast, the tangled trees and vines, and all the insects and animals of the jungle lived in perfect harmony, never wasting a thought about Man.

Midnight and Jakarta: an unpleasant conspiracy of time and place. Waiting to whisk me from Gambir Station to Pluit, though, was Miranda, semi-clad in the back seat of her brother's chauffeur-driven Mercedes. I revised my earlier bleak assessment up a notch.

JAKARTA
May 4, 1989

SOME IDIOT MOTORIST deliberately attempted to run me down today. This I was sure of. The conveyance of a motor vehicle in the Indonesian capital was not—as would appear to some freshly disembarked first world observer—conducted entirely at random. Operating deep inside the pulsing gray, nicotine-caffeine-infused, organic sub-strata of the native Jakartan brain, was buried a pretty effective algorithm capable of computing and predicting myriad swerves, sudden detours, and the appearance of objects that, by rights, should not exist within a hundred yards of any functioning expressway. To the confused foreign onlooker, his mind dulled into conformity by restrictions of logic, legalistic codes, structured monetary penalties and all the cumbersome practical regulation of the progressive society, traffic in Jakarta resembled little more than a fairground dodgem ride. Of this I was well aware. However, when *everyone* drove in the same instinctively haphazard way, then an overarching pattern of natural chaos formed, and equilibrium—albeit of a rather reactionary sort—over time, and through much instructive denting of side panels, could not help but be established.

Then you had chaos by design. Targeted chaos. And I am sure, this morning, I had been a victim of this, latter, operating system. The incident occurred as I was walking back from the post office. I had just started across the narrow road bridge over the stinking canal that bisected Jalan Puri Indah. As usual, it was safer to walk in the road than on the pavement; that unpassable minefield of missing bricks, smashed glass, skeletal umbrellas, and general dumping ground for piles of rank, oily sludge dredged from the poisoned waterways below.

I sensed rather than saw the sudden flash, a moving blur, and leapt instinctively to one side, reaching out to grab the bridge's low parapet as I dove. My survival instincts at this moment zoomed in on the rusted and buckled rail, the only barrier saving me from a plunge into the bubbling broth. Was the driver of the car Miranda's husband Rudi? I was too shocked to think to record the model type or number. It had been white, though, that much I remembered.

———— ∞ ————

The following morning, still in travel-mode after Sulawesi, I headed out to take photos before my classes began. I walked all the way to Slipi interchange to document the street kids there who sold newspapers, kreteks and salted peanuts to motorists stuck in the eternal 'macet' — traffic jam. I got some nice shots, and was left largely un-harassed. The kids were, I think, surprised more than anything to see a foreigner showing up at this hour; happy that someone cared enough to record their work. Soon, though, my eyes were stinging and reddened by leaded petrol fumes. I made the mistake of rubbing them, only adding sweat to the volatile mix trying to blind me. It was time to head back to the school anyway, so, with a level of functioning vision now returning, I wandered back to Peter Pan. There, in the bathroom attached to my spartan quarters, I washed off the morning's dirt with a short, sharp 'mandi'—the local word for an inevitably cold shower. After toweling off, and dressing in crisply ironed shirt and trousers—the housemaid insisted on putting creases in the legs of my jeans—I heard Rina's voice, from the living room, raised in alarm.

A maid screamed, the door to the courtyard was flung open, and a man appeared, blinking in the immediate sunlight. In his raised right hand he brandished a machete with a flashing foot-long blade. Instincts are funny things, ignored at our peril. I took in the intruder's puffed face, his hair—slicked-back and blackened with dye—the expensive silk batik shirt: Rudi. My instincts shouted, 'RUN'! But the only way out was through the house, and Miranda's enraged gangster-ex blocked that route.

Like most Englishmen, I am instilled with a deep-seated abhorrence of violence and cheap theatrics. The further I found myself from it, the prouder ambassador I had become of my faraway country, and its culture derived of a blessedly mild and pragmatic climate. No problem, surely, was so serious that it couldn't be solved rationally, and civilly, with a quiet chat over a nice cup of tea? Here in the tropics, by contrast, heat and spice dominated. People were primed by the elements of fire to run amok. As Rudi advanced, knife in hand, I didn't feel scared as much as very abruptly homesick.

Before he had time to lunge, I grasped an armful of washing off the line, and charged at my assailant. His blade slashed down ineffectively on the bundle of cloth, and I pushed Rudi off balance, gaining enough time to make it into the main house. There, Rina was mouthing something, her arms pointing towards the front door and the street. There was no time to look back. Buying a few seconds, I toppled a desk in my wake, hoping Rudi would stumble over it, and rushed into the front yard. Flinging open the iron door that led to the street, I slammed right into the white Toyota sedan that had been parked strategically to block this exit. The only way out now was over its roof, my foot gaining just enough purchase on the rear door handle to launch me sliding over and across the boot, and rolling right into the busy and confused flow of traffic pouring along Jalan Puri Indah.

Should you ever find yourself in a similar situation, it is best to not waste crucial moments expecting any help from the middle classes. Their doors remain sealed to disturbance. The very poor and the very wealthy alone have, or fear, nothing to lose by coming to your aid. Miranda's family fortress being on the far side of the city, I opted for sanctuary with Agus, an impoverished photographer, who lived in his wooden booth, down by the canal. Friends through our mutual interest in cameras, I often directed the bajaj to stop a block short to visit him when returning from Jakarta.

"Gus, Gus! Ini saya, Chris," I banged my fist on his door. It creaked open, letting out a carcinogenic perfume of cigarette smoke and photo developing chemicals.

"Ah, brother Chris. Welcome!" Agus seemed to have been expecting my flustered arrival. He swiftly closed the door on us. Agus—'Gus' to friends—was a younger version of Ho Chi Minh; he had the beard, the professorial air. A pair of smudged reading glasses hung as always around his neck, attached to a chain made of elastic bands. His main clientele were the local houseboys, maids and drivers who came to him for their identity card portraits. His booth—as well as being his home—acted as his darkroom; the enlarger for this being a hole drilled through one of the wall panels. In front of this free and abundant light source, Gus would clip the negative he intended to make a print from, projecting it via the lens of a magnifying glass held in a vice, onto an awaiting scrap of photographic paper. Moving the celluloid strip backwards or forwards, minutely, until the image came into focus, he would open a flap and count off in steady seconds the appropriate exposure, having already factored in the sun's intensity, and for any shifting cloud cover. He worked alone, and I viewed him as one of those naïve masters whose primitive output would one day be stumbled upon by the metropolitan artistic elite.

On this day though, right now, I needed Gus's 'enlarger' for a more immediate purpose: to spy through its pinhole aperture. I lifted the flap and peaked out, taking in a fair sweep of Jalan Puri Indah. The coast appeared clear. What would I have done if Rudi had caught up with me, anyway? I was not the naturally aggressive type. Relieved of the immediate responsibility of self-defense, I cast my mind back to the only time I'd reacted in rage before, as a teenager, when I'd slammed the bathroom door on my father after some hormonally charged argument. His finger had been caught between the door and its wooden frame, bringing the first tear I'd ever seen to my father's eye. But that was accidental.

"Here, I just made coffee," Gus handed me a chipped mug filled with brown liquid, "Pak Rudi is a crazy man, you must be careful. These people are not level-headed; they are not like us photographers. They have no patience." Of course, I should have guessed Gus would be clued up on all the goings-on inside Rina's household. Her own servants were frequent customers of his, habituated to view the exchange of juicy gossip as polite and correct behavior. I told Gus of my earlier fireside experiences at the campsite, before Miranda and sex; two long months ago, when life was innocent, and I'd thought I had everything worked out.

"Mas Chris," Gus sighed, using the familiar term of respect, "travel and photography are not a replacement for human relationships; they are there to keep you out of the mess of other people's lives. To save you from yourself." I decided to save myself.

I snuck back to the school a few hours later, making sure no white vehicles were parked or passing anywhere nearby. Rina was obviously disappointed, and in a bit of a state.

"What will I tell the parents of my students?" She had been charging a premium for their kids to be taught by a native speaker. But she agreed, "You can't stay here, it is too dangerous." She meant for her. She paid what she owed me for the week with a US$100 note, which was going to be a bitch to exchange into more tradeable, smaller denomination local currency.

I grabbed my backpack and headed off in the midday heat, a vague sense of sadness at having to leave in such circumstances and not being able to say goodbye to my students. But it was better this way. A couple of bajaj drivers lounged in the shade of the tree opposite. They looked around, expectantly, and called out to me for custom. I ignored them: it was safer always to hail the moving vehicle. I walked to the end of the lane and caught a three-wheeler on the busier thoroughfare it joined there. Getting in, I informed the driver, "Menteng". Paranoia was bubbling irrationally inside me now. I imagined Rudi having half of Jakarta under surveillance. Taking the precaution of alighting a few hundred yards from the Marcopolo Hotel, I continued on foot. The bajaj driver would be unable to reveal my final destination, even under threat of torture.

That evening my hand hovered over the telephone in the room. I really should talk to Miranda, to at least let her know I was OK and that I was leaving. But she'd want to meet, and very likely succeed to talk me out of that decision. So, instead I busied myself rearranging the furniture, pushing a large sideboard up against the door, wedging it into position with two chairs and a hat-stand. Let's see Rudi and his mob break through *that* in a hurry.

My spirits in need of fortification, I lined up all my lucky charms on a wobbly bedside table, the only substantial piece of furniture not otherwise engaged in anti-intrusion operations. First, I took off my necklace and polished the antique silver Afghan talisman hanging from it. This was inscribed with verses of the Koran, a gift from Ata, my former student in Peshawar. Next, the small bronze Buddha statue that traveled everywhere in one of the pockets of my camera vest. This was a reminder of my month-long trek over the Tibetan Himalayas the previous year, and had been presented by Jack, a Chinese rare herb smuggler — on leave from his job at the Pepsico Joint Venture in Guangzhou — at the conclusion of a particularly grueling section of that journey. These totemic companions had seen me safely through many perilous situations, and it didn't feel at all odd to be talking to them as I worked to bring a gleam back to their tarnished surfaces. I was not talking to myself; I was not going mad. Besides, other than these mementos, I had only my diary to confide in: only my camera to offer a way out.

2. In Defense of Restlessness

I first attempted escape through a hole in the garden fence, aged six.

"I'm running away from home!" Granny was next door in her kitchen at the time and took the news matter-of-factly.

"I'll make you some sandwiches, then." Having herself jumped ship to Cape Town as a young girl back in 1926, she knew what I was going through. Restlessness: the ancestral curse. From a tender age I felt compelled to get away (to where exactly was of little concern); a lifetime of adventure was the only possible future worth aiming for.

I wished I'd been born in Africa like my Dad, and his before him. Having once left Rhodesia, though, neither of them were granted the opportunity, nor felt the urge, to return. Granddad, carrying his infant son off the ship at Gravesend in 1938, planted his feet for the very first time in the tidal mud of an alien Motherland, just in time for The War. And I'd always wondered if, at this point, as the chill wind swept unchallenged across the treeless marshes, fleeing towards the contemptuous English Channel, he realized that he'd never return, never again feel the burning African heat through the thin cotton of his tropical shirt? His golden Sun God, replaced now by a pale milky disc, had lost its power to blind. And he was dispirited.

I never met Grandpa Stowers—he died three weeks before I was born. But he was with me as I grew up, leafing through the imaginary topography of the family's 'Reader's Digest Atlas of the World', and peeling back the pages of albums of fading photos: primed and ready to swap in a heartbeat the gray-stained skies of southeast England for the sepia-bleached photographic promise of lion hunts, and picnics on the Veldt.

The restless gene can never be extinguished, though perhaps it does skip the odd generation or two.

KALIMANTAN, INDONESIA
May 7, 1989

ALL IT TOOK was a one-way ticket to Banjarmasin and things started to look up. I was one of fifteen souls aboard the twin turbo-prop Bouraq Airways flight, five of whom were the crew. The journey to the provincial capital, seated at the southernmost tip of Kalimantan (as Indonesia calls the main bulk of the island of Borneo under their control) took two-and-a-half hours, skimming 10,000 feet above the Java Sea — low enough to make out individual boats and waves with the naked eye. It was not the most regulated of aircraft: my legs rested on a couple of wooden crates that half-blocked the emergency exit, and the two air hostesses came to occupy the seats either side of mine and chat away merrily whenever not engaged with the more onerous demands of their job. Trying to come up with a witty acronym for the airline proved tougher than usual. The short ones were always easiest: Pakistan's PIA — 'Praise In Allah', for instance, or the Philippines' national carrier PAL — 'Plane Always Late.' Indonesia's own international airline, Garuda, was known among the expat community as a euphemism for the country as a whole: 'Good And Reliable Under Dutch Administration.'

I was getting somewhere with the end letters of Bouraq '... Rudimentary Aircraft Quality', when the pilot executed an impetuous banking maneuver, and threw us in a death-dive towards the jungle. I searched frantically for the separate ends of the seatbelt that had been alluded to, but not actively insisted upon, during take-off, and risked a glance through the oil-smeared windowpane. Below, approaching rapidly now, ran the ugly brown knife slash of the Barito River. Slightly east of this lay the gray mess I assumed was our final destination. The turgid Martapura River also made its way into the sea here. The entire region, from the vantage point of our plunging eagle, was nothing more than a vast, sandy delta, a collection point for all the mud and flushed refuse of the jungle, and repository of diamonds, rubies and gold. The British East India Company once knew it as 'Tamborneo' until the Dutch took over and named Banjarmasin their capital of all Borneo.

Before leaving Jakarta, I'd telephoned the Said household. I'd taken it as a good omen that the number I'd been given a year ago still worked, and was soon connected to a squealing Melda. "You are really coming? When?? Tomorrow???" Ever since we'd met a year before in Australia, she and her sisters had been urging me to pay a visit to their south Kalimantan hometown. Indeed, the option of pulling in to see them — and, simultaneously, carrying out repairs on our rapidly deteriorating ship — had almost led to mutiny during my earlier voyage on the *Kurnia Ilahi*. Now seemed the perfect moment to take the Said girls up on their offer. Still, I hadn't expected the welcoming committee. Or the banner:

"Well Come Mr. Kris (Fotografer)"

The bearer of this was Budi Setiawan, a bright-eyed, bushy-tailed member of the South Kalimantan Tourism Bureau. Indeed, I had the impression he was the *only* member of the South Kalimantan Tourism Bureau: given his personal enthusiasm, employment of a second representative would have been superfluous. He ushered me outside to his waiting jeep, chattering nonstop, a walking one-man advertisement for the wonders of his sorely overlooked province.

"Welcome to the Venice of Asia!" he spouted, grinding the Suzuki into gear and sending us careening out of the airport compound. Soon we were speeding above a maze of sampan-clogged canals on narrow, clattering, road bridges constructed of indestructible *ulin*. This dark-stained 'iron wood' (*Eusideroxylon zwageri*), Budi explained—dismissively ploughing through a sea of becak pedicabs, scattering them like marbles—is used in construction in low-lying and coastal regions across Kalimantan, Brunei and Malaysia, where it is highly valued for its durability and tendency to strengthen with prolonged exposure to water.

"I am horning, I am horning!" he shouted at the enraged cyclists through his open window.

"Where are we going?" *Help, I've been hijacked by a genial madman!*

"I will take you to your hotel. The Governor has arranged everything. Don't worry!" he beamed, worryingly. The mirrored-glass façade of the Batung Batulis Hotel approached flashily, signaling discord with my limited budget.

"Budi, I can't afford this. Can't you take me to a cheap losmen?"

"Don't worry," the beaming guide repeated, "The Governor is paying; you are his guest!" Now I *was* worried. Who was this mysterious "Governor" ... the local mafia kingpin? Had Miranda's ex called ahead?

"Stop the car, Budi!"

"Wait, Mr. Chris. We are here."

And then I recognized the faces of the three petite girls standing on the entrance steps, in descending order of age: Lela, Melda and Dewi Said. It was like being back in Brisbane again, where my job had been to chaperone them, and a bunch of other exchange students, around World Expo '88, for a local language college.

"MacGyver!" shrilled Dewi, who had christened me thus after the star of her favorite TV show.

"It's so good to see you!" I said, in genuine relief. "But how did you know I'd be at this hotel?"

"Why, our Papa, of course," explained Melda, as though to a dim but dear child. It turned out he *was* the Governor, after all — of the entire province of South Kalimantan.

———∿∿∿———

Gubernatorial immunity had its advantages. Being left in peace, however, was not among them. It soon became apparent that Budi and his jeep had been turned over to me for the duration of my stay in Banjarmasin. At all times one, two or the complete hat-trick of First Family daughters — and their various school friends, all native Banjarese — accompanied me, clearing a path through the usual minefield of hassles and rip-offs that faced the lone and vulnerable foreign visitor. My diary entries slipped during these few hectic days.

Just after dawn was the perfect time for a photographer to visit the floating market in Muara Kuin, a few miles out of central Banjarmasin. I ripped through several rolls of valuable film — replacement rolls of professional-grade color slides being hard enough to locate in Jakarta, let alone at this forested outpost — unable to stop myself from shooting, yet sufficiently aware of light, angle and fleeting opportunity to kick myself for having missed a million more 'National Geographic Moments'. Here, women hidden beneath lampshade hats, formed a watery traffic jam between bobbing rows of houses, shops and toilets, all constructed and floating on log rafts. Their hand-paddled canoes were laden to the gunwales with exotic fruits: huge bananas, spiky rambutans and fibrous, lizard-skinned salaks. Spices, firewood, coconuts, paraffin, rice and cassava were all hawked here from their bobbing decks; medicines, farming tools and kitchen utensils, too. In one instance I spotted a pyramidal stack of endangered turtle eggs.

Dark afternoon clouds sagged over oppressive acres of riverside mangroves, and we piled into a small 'Klotok' pump boat. These ubiquitous craft were named after the distinctive chug of their 5HP engines — *klotokklotokklotok* — and passengers were forced to lie forward on their benches as the pilot navigated beneath some of the lower bridges. Then suddenly we broke free from the clogged canal and began bumping and jarring across the deep, rapid channels of the Barito, heading to Monkey Island.

I've never trusted simian intentions, theirs being too close to human ones. The bravest denizens of 'Pulau Monyet' had even mastered their innate hydrophobia, leaping from overhanging branches and swimming out to our launch before we'd even landed. Damp, furry hands deftly pickpocketed our bags of peanuts, and I was left with only a bunch of bananas to appease the expectant welcoming committee of apes massed at the pier.

The sky continued to brood. We were halfway back across the Barito when lightning cracked the air's humid mask, and raindrops began to machinegun their approach across the watery surface. Dewi, startled, grabbed my right hand, a move not missed by her elder sister, who grabbed my left one. Together we sat, linked in mutual reassurance against the raging elements, until the boat nudged us back to reality, colliding heavily with a wooden quayside ladder. Deafening thunder greeted our first steps ashore, and the streets and windowpanes shook with Nature's fury.

In the evening, my ears still ringing from the thunder, I paid a courtesy call on Governor Said at his palatial official residence. A short, rotund, jovial fellow, he was convincingly, if abruptly, apologetic: *I've been so busy, so sorry, unable to meet you at an earlier juncture.* Pleasantries paid, and souvenir photographs duly taken, I was next whisked into a separate and lengthier audience with the girls and their mother: for sweet tea, gooey coconut cakes, and for them to squeeze out of me any juicy gossip I could supply about my brief encounters with the Jakarta TV stars staying at my hotel. The whole of the city was eager to hear how positively Banjarmasin was going to be portrayed in the epic soap drama currently being filmed here.

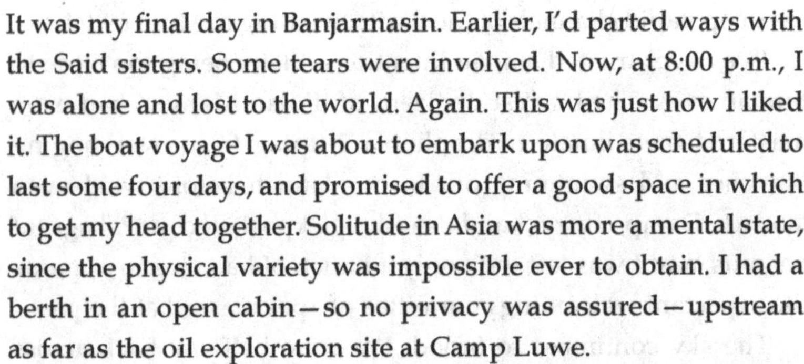

It was my final day in Banjarmasin. Earlier, I'd parted ways with the Said sisters. Some tears were involved. Now, at 8:00 p.m., I was alone and lost to the world. Again. This was just how I liked it. The boat voyage I was about to embark upon was scheduled to last some four days, and promised to offer a good space in which to get my head together. Solitude in Asia was more a mental state, since the physical variety was impossible ever to obtain. I had a berth in an open cabin—so no privacy was assured—upstream as far as the oil exploration site at Camp Luwe.

"There's an American who works at Luwe, for the UNOCAL oil company. He'll be able to set you en route for Kal-Tim," Budi assured me, referring to East Kalimantan Province, though he couldn't remember the Yank's name. It all sounded a bit hit and miss. On my map the Barito River to Muara Teweh resembled 400 miles of highly agitated tapeworm trapped in an unappetizing aspic of jungle and swamp. But ever since my *Kurnia Ilahi* story had been reprinted in Jakarta's *Matra* magazine, my readership had demanded adventure. I was going to have to give it to them.

Later, aboard the riverboat, the air was thick enough to slice with a machete. The diesel engine burbled comfortingly, and I was cooled by occasional splashes of river water, coming in through the low, open window. Miranda's gangster ex, Rudi, would have to be spectacularly bent on revenge to pursue me into this particular heart of darkness.

"Hey, Mister, Kodak!" It was the local way of asking for a photo. People saw my camera and assumed a pose. It would have been undiplomatic of me not to snap them. But I was mindful to ration my shots; I had only eight rolls left. My bunkmates on the ferry were Muji and his girlfriend Hatty. Muji said he'd represented Indonesia in the javelin at the Olympics in Seoul last year, throwing seventy-four meters. And Hatty used a handheld CB radio to chat with family further up the river in Buntok.

"There are still tribes out there using blowpipes and poison darts to kill wild pigs, Chris. You cannot talk to them in Bahasa, they know only a dialect of Banjarese."

A Hong Kong kungfu video played on board, *The Challenges of the Lady Ninja*. A 1987 veteran of the low-budget Hong Kong movie scene myself, I kept a sharp eye out for Edowan (Dutchman Edowan Bersma, star of more than 200 low-budget movies by HK director Godfrey Ho. The most famous of which were *Thunder of the Gigantic Serpent* (1988) and 1989 classic *Zombie vs Ninja*), or any other backpacker friends who may have had a role in this one. Outside, entire islands of logs—lashed together in V-formation, like the fletching of an arrow—were being towed downstream. One tug up front seemed to be sufficient to control

1,500 logs at a time, stretching a quarter of a mile. Crews of workers lived in small wooden huts erected on top of the logs, replete with clothes drying on washing lines and wooden toilet outhouses.

Life for these river dwellers seemed not so unremoved from those of the Bugis pirates of the Java Sea: the continued existence of both depended on water. Only the fish tasted different. A young mother tended to her baby in a small hammock, the child being swayed to sleep with the roll of the boat. She seemed totally contented with her lot. Scrap Gorontalo, I should come back *here* in ten years or so, find a beautiful maiden, marry, build a few bamboo huts and a jetty leading down to my speedboat. I could charge tourists to guide them through the forest. Assuming any trees would be left by then, of course.

Muji and Hatty alighted at Buntok. Alarmed screaming erupted as the boat set off. Too many heavy crates had been loaded at the fore, causing water to surge over the deck and flood the cabin. A general panic set in—passengers grabbing their belongings, crashing for the exits. But boats, as I had recently learned, were fundamentally buoyant objects; they usually righted themselves. I helped the deckhands drag boxes aft, and the vessel stabilized. Still, I made sure to wrap my camera in a dustbin liner, and eyed possible escape routes out the window. If we sank, I'd grab this bag, along with my hat, and swim for it.

Afternoon fell like lead: we would soon be crushed by dusk. Two young boys, with the light skin tone and almost Chinese looks typical to some Dayak tribes, paddled up to my window, balanced intrepidly on a log. They urge me to photograph a bird of prey they had found, spreading out its wings over a span of three feet. It was a type of kestrel, I think, with a markedly hooked beak and disconcertingly large, bright yellow eyes.

"*Ini burung setan*, Mister. Kodak!" A devil bird.

May 14, 1:30 a.m.

Muara Montallat. It won't be marked on any map. If you ever find yourself here, don't stop.

I'd sensed something was wrong, even in my sleep, and sat up, as if slapped by some invisible demon. The ferry was moored midstream. All about was deadly calm. For safety, I'd been resting my head on my valuables, but that pillow now felt less bulky. Fear, that lamentable laxative, wrapped itself around my gut and tugged down, hard. I took a hesitant peek inside the purse, noting that the zip was open. All my local currency — US$50 worth of it, reward for many hours of teaching at Peter Pan School — money I'd carefully changed into lower denomination notes at the bank in Banjarmasin, had been swiped. Thankfully, my traveler's checks and US dollars (being of no immediate use) had been left intact. A local trying to exchange foreign cash would be lynched on suspicion of theft alone. At least this local sense of jungle justice resulted in 'honest' thieves, marginally preferable to the dishonest variety.

I flicked through my dictionary until coming across the expression for 'thief' — a useful addition to my growing Bahasa lexicon — 'orang pencuri'. And then went to practice its use on the captain of the ferry. He reluctantly delegated a couple of his crewmen to carry out a ship-wide search, taking me aside to warn me about the presence of 'taranculars'.

"Taranculars?" I repeated. "You mean, like spiders?"

"No, no. *Taranculars*." The captain began a hopping mime across the wheelhouse, arms raised in front of him, eyes closed as if in a trance, and his upper lip drawn back to expose vampire-like fangs.

"Ah, Dracula!" I clicked. Yes. Apparently, evil spirits lurked along these dense and shady shores; my bunk neighbors all nodded in enthusiastic agreement: this was better than a TV show. One of the bloodsucking undead must have reached in and snatched my cash through the open window. Such evil spirits were known to be able to walk on water, after all. What possible alternative explanation could there be?

The captain and I paddled in one of the moored ferry's sampans, upstream at 4:00 a.m., when there was just enough light to distinguish between sky and water. Arriving, we scrambled up the muddy indented steps of a steep embankment, made our way to the tiny police post nearby, and shook awake Jimmy, its resident slumbering sergeant. I knew I'd never get my stolen money back, but I wanted an official report, as proof of its passing.

It took about an hour, once the various balls had been set in motion, for typewriter, paper and the least-desiccated ink ribbon to be located, transported to, and assembled in one spot. Jimmy's boss, a local captain, having been roused from his home, accepted a pack of kreteks for his efforts and began to dictate the official version of events as stated by me, and seconded by the captain of the ferry. Dutifully and diligently, Jimmy (not the world's most natural stenographer, it must be admitted, but the best that could be found before dawn in the middle of the central Kalimantan morass) typed the words dictated by his superior using the Columbus Method—first discover a key, then land on it—favored by the Indonesian police force.

A further forty-five minutes was consumed as the single-page report was tapped out, the heroic Jimmy being saved from further clerical exertion by the morning call to prayer.

———— ∞ ————

Most of my fellow passengers were bound for Muara Teweh. The settlement conformed to Nature's contours like a dirty blanket thrown over the bank of the river. Standing on the roof of the ferry I counted around a hundred houses in it. The largest and most institutional of these were of concrete, and resided higher up the riverbank; the majority were constructed lower down, of wooden planks with balconies extending over the water itself. From these rickety platforms, children dived into the swirling Barito, and women squatted, pummeling clothes on frothy washboards. The ferry, lightened now of half its human cargo, shrugged off this last vestige of civilization and burbled on up to Camp Luwe, carrying supplies for the thriving Pertamina/ UNOCAL joint oil venture there. The turgid, brown river narrowed, the mangroves closed in, and heavy branches loomed over us on the sharpest meanders. As the afternoon grew late, we landed at a jetty in a clearing. The village headman—the 'Kepala Desa'—met me off the boat. He thrust his visitors' book under my nose. From its pages I learned I was the third foreigner to have trodden this way all year (the other two being the British tourists Budi had accompanied, back in January).

Pak Misran, was a wiry old Muslim who wore a sparse, gray beard, balancing these whiskers with a neat black *peci* hat, atop. He was officially obliged to accommodate me in his house for the duration of my stay. I couldn't imagine the mayor of my Kentish hometown being so generous as to receive into his hearth and home a lost and lone Dayak tribesman. I also doubted the existence of any municipal book for visitors to sign. And they called *us* civilized? It was as if we, in the West, were done with caring.

Camp Luwe was, in fact, two distinct settlements. Luwe Hulu, a peaceful, grassy acre atop an eighty-foot-high embankment surrounded by pastel-painted wooden stilt houses, coconut trees and bushes bursting with colorful tropical blooms and wild chili peppers. And then there was the UNOCAL compound down by the riverfront, contained by a fence, operating around the clock, and floodlit at night. They were kept from each other by a wide, red-mud trail, indented with Caterpillar tracks. Gratefully, I dumped my backpack in Misran's shaded parlor and asked my official host where I could find 'the American'. He pointed across the muddy divide to where a lanky Westerner, in his mid-forties, sat sipping coffee from a scratched glass in the shade of a small warung.

Budi had informed me in advance of a daily jeep the oil company ran along logging tracks, forty miles inland, to Hara Gandang; that small village would make a good kicking-off point for my planned trek to the east. Wondering how I was going to broach the subject of a free lift, I squelched across the rutted track, hovered at the far end of the plank he was sitting on, and ordered a coffee.

"Hello," seemed as good a place to start as any.

"Why don't ya get down here," he nodded towards the splintered bench, as an afterthought adding, "Hell, you're not an Aussie, are you?" his baseball cap turned in my direction, its long peak keeping his eyes hidden in shade.

"No, no. English. Chris."

"That's better," though by his tone I could tell by not much, "Ahm Travis." He swigged back his glass, draining it, and I ordered him another, so as to prolong the encounter.

"Bless your heart."

"You're the American, right?"

"News travels fast."

"Much to do out here?"

"Well, it ain't the busiest parish, that's fo' sure, but I like it well enough, flying the whirly bird." Travis was from Louisiana (he pronounced it, 'Loozana'), and had worked as a helicopter pilot for various oil exploration companies for almost ten years, all of them spent in harsh and remote backwaters. Luwe, I gathered, was something of a holiday camp by comparison.

"Ain't so much diff'rent here than back in the Bayou." Before that he'd flown a combat Huey in Vietnam. He was a man who seemed to appreciate time spent alone and in contemplation, not given to wasteful speech. Mind you, for the US$8,000 a month paycheck he was pulling in—and nothing in the immediate, what, thousand miles in any direction worth spending it on—I'd have been happy to risk solitary confinement here, too.

"I understand there's a jeep to Hara Gandang in the morning?"

"Rain's turned the logging tracks to a quagmire. Once the trees are down there's nuthin' to bind the soil together."

"Oh. Get many visitors up here?" I feared my questioning would prove too much for a man habituated to the company of one. Instead, I'd opened a spigot.

"From tahm t'tahm. It's all right as long as they're travelin' alone. One at a tahm I can tolerate the most noxious soul," he blew across the steaming rim of his glass, "No, you'd have to be pretty despicable for me not to give you the tahm-a-day. I'm a magnet for the crazy ones, though—they always seem t'find me. Not that you're one of 'em, of course," he added, quickly, "but you can't keep anyone out, can you? We're all entitled to a point of view, and who's to say yours is any less valid than mahn? No, only when dealin' with the masses do I lose mah patience. I will always favor the flawed over the follower."

"You've read Mark Twain, perhaps? *Whenever you find yourself on the side of the majority, it's time to pause and reconsider ...*"

"You're right there. Probably not right in the head, mahnd; hell, who of us ain't a li'l batshit, coming to a place like this out of choice, eh? Ah mean, it ain't normal folks' behavior. But at least you're cutting your own path through the undergrowth."

"Probably be nicer to fly over it ..." I decided to nudge the subject along a little.

"Yeah, look, don't worry, I thought to mahself the moment you turned up, 'Travis', I says, 'you gonna have to pop this'un over in the chopper.'"

Sensing I was on solid enough ground to explore a bit, I went on, "So, why do you do it, live out here, I mean?"

"It beats workin'!"

He went back to studying the chipped rim of his coffee glass, and I suspected that was all he had in him for the day. But isolation is a dam that thoughts build behind. Overflow was inevitable, given time and opportunity.

"Nah, I'm done with all that; the periodic payments, the repetitive relationships, not to mention the periodic payments for those repetitive relationships. The whole steady drip feed, tryin' to poison me that *without thangs, how will anyone know how successful Ah am.* Got it all raht here. And all they got are their debts and nagging ex-wives and soon-to-be-ex-wife-new-girlfriends. Well, here's to that!" And he swigged the rest of his glass back and spat out the grinds.

Borneo was perfect country for the nomad. Only a generation or two removed from hunter-gatherers, the populace was, on the whole, understanding of a man's urge to wander, and generously accommodating of those who did. And language wasn't such a barrier now I'd memorized around five hundred words of Bahasa. I could communicate most basic needs, intentions, and immediate directions.

Flying in to Hara Gandang the next day caused quite a stir, though I didn't have much time to appreciate my first flight in a helicopter, being too occupied at the time, simultaneously trying to capture aerial shots out the cabin door, and retain my molecular presence within. Vibrations inside the aircraft were so vigorous I had to crank my shutter speed to 1,000th/sec., the highest it would go, to ensure a stable image. The Barito, glinting mercurially in the midday sun, fell behind to the west. Travis had another mission and couldn't hang around.

"Watch out for the bad juju!" he shouted against the roar of the rotors. I was more immediately concerned with keeping possession of my hat than his warnings about jungle voodoo.

I hired a couple of village lads, Doryanto and Suderson, who were willing to guide me as far as Damai, for 10,000 rupiah a day, each. They would only travel together as a pair, each being unwilling to make the return trip alone. It would be a four-day trek, across the border from where we were now, in Central Kalimantan, to Damai, in East Kalimantan Province. From Damai, passenger ferries ran down a tributary into the mighty Mahakam River and on to Samarinda on the coast.

Rivers were the expressways of the interior. The visitor book of Pak Hadrat, the Kepala Desa here, informed me I was continuing in the footsteps of Budi Setiawan and his two British tourists, Paul Bainbridge and Robert Ferguson. Before them, a lone German biologist had been the last representative of the European race to pass this way, fully twelve months ago.

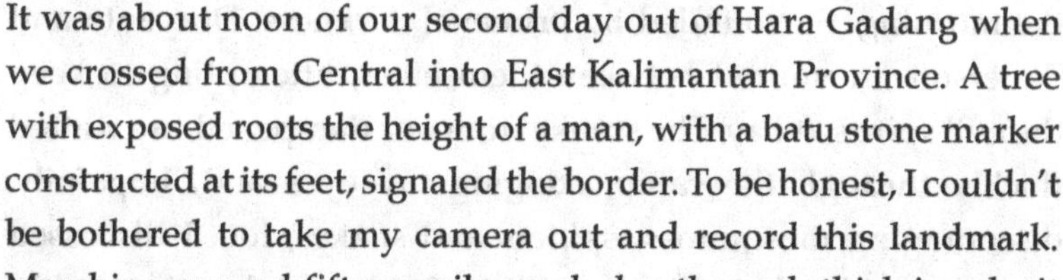

It was about noon of our second day out of Hara Gadang when we crossed from Central into East Kalimantan Province. A tree with exposed roots the height of a man, with a batu stone marker constructed at its feet, signaled the border. To be honest, I couldn't be bothered to take my camera out and record this landmark. Marching around fifteen miles each day through thick jungle, it was as much as I could do to keep breathing. I had seen nothing but trees all the way. We may have been traversing the equator, but it was dark under all the layers of leaves, and surprisingly chilly at night. Cicadas, monkeys and birds combined to produce a deafening, multi-layered forest symphony that sounded for all the world like farmyard animals, chainsaws, ringing telephones and the squealing brakes of a slowing train. This type of wilderness was claustrophobic.

At night we made camp beside a swift-flowing brook that forced a rare rupture in the tree canopy. My gaze turned upwards to be met by a deep sea of stars. Silhouetted palm fronds swayed at the perimeter of my vision. I wondered if Adam and Eve had had a similarly restricted view. It was as though God, gifting them a verdant Eden, had made sure any gaps in it compelled them to lift their eyes in His direction, alone.

Previous travelers had left behind raised wooden platforms, called 'pondoks', erected at convenient stages along the trail. To my eye they were often the only such indicators of Mans' footprint at all. We sheltered in one of these crude cabins, its roof matted together of dried leaves. My clothes were heavy with sweat and swamp water. The first night I had made the mistake of falling asleep still wearing this familiar uniform, being too exhausted to change, and woke at dawn shivering. Tonight, I followed the example of my guides and placed my trekking clothes on top of a pole, keeping them away from any ground dwelling jungle critters, and allowing them to dry out before reuse in the morning. Surrounded by primeval darkness, Doryanto and Suderson murmured between themselves, attempting to keep the evil spirits at bay. The smoke from our dampened fire wafted thickly through the camp, stinging my eyes and, hopefully, discouraging mosquitoes, spiders and snakes, too. I discussed with my guides their favorite subject, food. And then, inevitably, we arrived at girls and marriage. I told them I fully intended to have six different wives, one on each continent. This, they agreed, made perfect sense, since mine was obviously destined to be a life of travel, and it wouldn't do to find myself lonely in any corner of the world. They themselves would stick at just the four, being pious and observant Muslims.

I began to understand why it was called the 'rainforest'. Water permeated the air, hissing softly on the leaves above; it fed miraculous brooks that spouted from rock and crevasse. Dawn mist evaporated from giant ferns that nodded like green giraffes, their long necks weighted with condensation. When it wasn't actually raining, steam filled the air, making it hard to breathe. My clothes remained damp, despite all my efforts to dry them. Worse, leeches scented our approach, thrusting themselves from leaves and grass stems to latch onto our clothing or ankles as we passed. They worked their way towards any moist spot, seeking warm blood at waist, armpit, in between toes, and at the groin. The soil we trod was a thick clay, which clogged the tread of my boots. I managed only to slip and slide, and struggled to keep up with Doryanto and Suderson in their flip-flops.

And then I lost sight of both my guides. We had been wading through a deep, swampy depression. Water, thick with mud from some impatient broken riverbank, flowed fast and high, up around my chest. They had gone ahead, I assumed, to seek dry ground on which to deposit our packs. I struggled on, holding my camera bag above my head, inching cautiously across a series of submerged, invisible logs. It was like playing tropical Twister, having to grab at any thin sapling or overhanging creeper to correct my balance. I couldn't help but laugh; my situation was so ridiculous, so vulnerable. I was as insignificant as any other insect in the vastness of this uncaring wilderness, my existence no more important than that of a millipede, or lantern bug.

That I'd brought myself to this point voluntarily just added to the absurdity. But then, charging from the mental undergrowth, came a condition far more deadly than physical attack by some better-adapted feral beast: doubt.

What if they'd planned to abandon me here all along, a helpless fly stuck amid this vast web of trails and creepers? How could I have been so trusting, so dumb?

Fear poured in, filling the vacuum left by my departing Faith. It was on the verge of branching off to form its own religion called Hysteria, when I caught the faint, desperate call of Suderson, rising above that of the rippling mire, somewhere to the east, giving direction and renewing my hope.

By midday even my guides needed to make a halt—whether to assess our correct location or because, beneath the tough guy act, they were as exhausted as I, will never be known. Doryanto quickly gathered some tinder and twigs and started a small blaze, drying out a few larger logs on its perimeter. A while later, he built up a pyramid of these branches over the twigs and soon a fire was raging, and a pot of coffee on the boil. The sudden and unexpected domesticity of kettle and hearth obliterated any earlier concerns I'd had about abandonment and treachery. Suderson asked for a fishhook from my survival kit, and eight feet of nylon cord.

I asked, "What's your bait?"

And he showed me three live yellow crickets he'd collected in his hat, having pulled their legs off so they couldn't escape. I was skeptical. But ten minutes later, the hunter returned, bearing three nine-inch-long fish. These we baked over the open flame, which had worn down now to a nice, even glow. They had an earthy taste.

Our next obstacle was the Sungai Ngahan, a river wide enough to warrant a name. It was also, thanks to all the recent rain, too deep to ford, even if we carried our packs on our heads. Suderson swam across to retrieve a half-finished raft from the opposite bank. This we bound with newly cut bamboo poles. The contraption floated surprisingly well. It was buoyant enough to bear our packs and my camera bag. That left the transport of us three humans. We were too heavy to sit on the platform, so we clung to its sides and kicked it along, angling our crossing against a strong current. I tried hard to cancel out images of anacondas during the five minutes it took to reach the far bank.

From the Ngahan River we trudged on eastwards. Eventually the forest gave way to a clearing as night surrenders to dawn: imperceptibly, and inch-by-inch. The fringes of cultivation appeared at first subconsciously — the economic cluster of mango trees, a regulated row of pepperbushes, the ploughed furrow — the hand of Man revealing itself in the uniform and purposeful arrangement of Nature. And then settlement was sensed: drifting wood smoke infused with the fat of grilled pork and smoldering tobacco leaf; a track worn down by the routine footsteps of daily activity; the barking of dogs and laughter of children tumbling carelessly in the benign shadow of their ancestors raised in caskets. And, around the last corner, a startling glimpse of guardian spirits carved on the village totem pole.

This was Intu Linggau.

Suderson's parents lived on the outskirts of the village, in a stilt hut raised fully ten feet off the ground, and under a rusted corrugated iron roof. Lopsided wooden steps led up to its front (and only) door. Here, the elders sat cross-legged, surrounded by piles of half-completed rattan mats — the construction and sale of which generated the majority of their income — as we weary travelers took refuge out of a sudden afternoon deluge. They didn't appear surprised at the unannounced emergence of their sole male heir from the undergrowth. Ever the dutiful son,

Suderson presented his red-gummed old Dad with a fresh bag of chewing tobacco.

I examined my condition. By this stage, the fifth day of our trek from Hara Gadang, my feet had become white and blistered by constant immersion in water, and covered in weeping sores. There was a healthy new growth of mold starting to colonize the interior of my camera lens, too. *That* wasn't there a week ago.

Dumping our bags, I hobbled along with my faithful guides to the main hub of the settlement, a half-mile further along the increasingly peopled track. The center of the settlement proper was delineated by a crooked longhouse, in which more than twenty families lived in communal contentment. With the exception of Suderson's parents, who were kept on the outskirts due to their devotion to the Muslim faith, the population of Intu Linggau was 80 percent animist and 20 percent Protestant Christian.

News of our arrival had traveled fast. The village primary school teacher, energetic and thinning of hair, was himself one of the twenty percent. Our Protestant kinship, and elitist communion in the English language, was sufficient to establish him as my tireless local guide, and he took it upon himself to induct me in the ways of Intu Linggauian society, when all I really wanted to do was fall asleep under a dry roof for a week.

"We should go and see the dead man," the school master urged. Apparently, an old man had passed away earlier that day, at about the same time Suderson, Doryanto and I had emerged from out of the jungle.

"He. It. The dead man ... won't mind, I suppose?" I queried.

"No, no, come." And we trod a maze of grassy paths, chickens clucking in confusion at our feet, a tethered bull chomping on the green, and a cat, I noticed, with a long tail—unusual in Indonesia where the short-tailed gene is dominant.

The corpse was laid out in the corner of a large, airy room, wrapped tightly from head to foot in white sheets. His head was propped up by two Bibles, and a rattan mat had been rolled out to cover his hollow chest. His elderly widow squatted nearby, rocking sorrowfully on her haunches. She didn't object to my request to photograph the scene, or really recognize our presence at all. It was gloomy inside the hut, and I had no flash to help light the scene. So, in a darkened corner, I rolled off a half-shot 100 ASA film, leaving its tail sticking out of the canister. I marked the frame number on this tail using a Sharpie pen, for future re-use, and slotted in a fresh 400 ASA, the fastest film I had (erroneously, I had thought the jungle would be a bright place). Next, I motioned the teacher to redirect sunlight in through a high window using the shiny base of a biscuit tin. I imagined this would create quite an atmospheric image.

As we were leaving, a presence half-man, half-eagle, emerged from the shadows of the cassava field. In his hand, he shook a spear ringed with feathers, and bells jangled around his ankles. His headdress flowed with the colorful plumage of exotic birds of prey, and a painted mask concealed his face. His head floated, as if detached, upon an ivory necklace of wild boar tusks. There was no doubt about it: this was the shaman. He entered the hut we'd just left, and I started to return, to catch the show. But the schoolteacher tugged at my shirt, the element of fear in his eyes genuine, and made me reconsider any such course of action.

Back in the village center, I bought a pack of biscuits at a wooden shack that offered an inventory of cigarettes, snacks and sweet tea. I popped back to the home of headman and offered them to my host. He was using a CB radio powered by car batteries to report my safe arrival to his peer, Pak Hadrat, back in Hara Gandang. The headman's aged parents, one of his uncles and his wife, his own wife, a random assortment of their combined six young children, two cats and a pet monkey completed the household's hectic inventory. I sat mesmerized by his young wife, who couldn't have been far removed from her teens, as she suckled a newborn at perky breasts. Catching my gaze, she smiled back, proudly, the picture of contented innocence.

〰

All night I tossed and turned in sweaty torpor, in and out of vivid dreams in which I was smashing my head against a brick wall, trying to break through, to escape the rising floodwaters that were reaching up to my neck, to my nostrils, sinking, drowning …

When I was ten years old, I had had a fever. It burned at 105°F. Given my body temperature is naturally one degree lower than normal, I should have died. It was six months before I fully recovered. Primary school was a Victorian institution, a prison I knew one day I'd get away from. Chilly hallways, and high windows that limited distraction by the comings and goings of the outside world. There were only forty-five of us students, spread so thinly we'd sit through the same lessons two or three years in a row before moving up a class. No homework, nothing to tax the brain; fertile ground for daydreams of escape. Before the illness, I was an extroverted child, a big fish in a small pond; I won all the running races and sang sweetest in choir. After the illness, I withdrew, became insular, introspective. And then I moved to secondary school in a larger village and became just another brick in the wall … deranged, distorted teachers, canes poised to inflict pain, Rudi and his slashing machete … get out, RUN AWAY! The delirium continues. I'm lying flat, passing through a cloudy white tunnel of sky, flickering green and silver. Paddles dip, in and out of sight. Gurgling, roiling, foaming, flowing. Water slaps against logs, motors chug, there are shouts and haggling, half-glimpsed smiles and frowns; language half-understood, tones buoyant, reassuring. Moisture: all is wet. I must get up … yet some extraordinary force keeps me pinned to the bed. It is a bed, no longer moving, no longer rocking. I am wrapped in cotton, damp now with sweat, piss and blood. Have I passed into the spirit world, too? When will the shaman pay his visit? Felicia dabs at my brow with a cool sponge ... 'Don't worry so much and cut down on the sugar', I hear her laugh. Out in the brilliant diffusion beyond the shuttered windows, vibrant voices full of life. A fan stirs phantoms of air, a rooster crows. The door whips open, fuzzy faces lean over, friendly outlines. Then it is night again. Blurry vision ...

"Welcome back, Mr Chris!" beamed Doryanto.

"Dory ... where are we? S-Suderson?" The interior of the hut was bright, painted in cool pastel shades, shocked by reflected ripples of light from the river that gurgled and lapped just below the window. My last clear memory had been of falling asleep, wrapped in an oppressive funeral shroud of impenetrable foliage, bathed in the humid vibration of a chorus of insects and predators ... but my eyes opened now to light.

"I am here," came a lower-pitched voice from the corner. "Don't worry, you are safe. This is the house of my sisters. We are in Damai." *How did I get here?* Fifty miles of forest trail and rivers, erased from memory. It was now Friday. I had been out of it for the last two days. "We have to leave you now, for prayers. Then we must begin our journey back to Hara Gandang." A flicker of concern must have crossed my face. "Don't worry, stay as long as you like. My sisters will look after you. Don't forget to write about us, in your story, yah?" I promised him, solemnly, that I would.

"You are lucky; the fever has burned away. It must have been a powerful curse from the witchdoctor." So ran the diagnosis of Emmy, one of Suderson's bevy of sweet sisters. Or a dose of Travis's jungle juju, I thought to myself. My rational-self denounced black magic as so much superstitious mumbo-jumbo, yet given my present fragile state of physical recovery, the jungle and its mysterious spirits and powerful sorcery — just a suggestive stroll away — I decided the wisest approach would be to keep an open mind on the subject.

It was fully two days after regaining consciousness before I could even contemplate diving back into the chaotic world of travel. I remained in Limbo here in Damai — up the jungle, not yet at the sea — but travel on I must, at some point. I was on first-name terms with most of the shopkeepers and warung owners along the embankment of this bustling, frontier settlement, and sought to memorialize my time here setting up portrait shots of the plentiful, willing subjects. But on rewinding the roll of 400 ASA film that I'd first inserted back in Intu Linggau, the strip jammed, exactly as had happened once before in Tibet. I was fully aware that the rational explanation for this, in both cases, was atmospheric: excessive humidity loosening the glue on the blackout bar the film fed through into its metal canister. I knew that humidity was my Devil, something scientific and explainable. But rational thought didn't help. I had lost all my shots of the dead man in Intu Linggau, as surely as if the shaman himself had placed a direct curse on that roll of celluloid. I changed films and decided to catch the next boat to Samarinda and the coast. I vowed never once to look back at this place.

It was easy to relapse into river life. The voyage took around forty hours, though time by wristwatch was becoming an increasingly irrelevant detail. Years and decades: these were the units that mattered more, that were still worth planning for. Eventually, they, too, would be deemed insignificant when measured against the only period of true importance, a lifetime.

Tugboats nudged at barges flattened to the waterline by mountains of coal. Logs collected in meanders like so many discarded giant toothpicks. Riverbanks, raw and exposed, tumbled red into the ravenous flow of the Mahakam River. As the jungle receded in the face of industry, so the sky expanded in its place. Plywood sawmills massed like teeth on both sides of the mouth of the mighty waterway, while rubber factories belched sweet, stinging smoke from chimneys taller than trees. If the forest was God's Eden, then Hell was entirely a creation of Man.

I was surprised to find a fellow European aboard. Milano was thirty-two years old, and — despite the Italian-sounding name — a Frenchman. A self-taught witchdoctor, healer and herbalist, and professor at a university in Senegal, he had spent the last twenty-two years living in Africa. He was returning from Melale, upstream, where he'd viewed a rare 'black orchid' — although, in reality, the flower was just a 'very dark shade of green'.

"Plants have a vibration, an individual wavelength, if you like. I can look at a plant, touch it, and it tells me which disease or organ it is designed to cure." His eyes bulged unnaturally, like those of Marty Feldman, as though amazed by his own discoveries and powers. At any moment, I expected them to start spinning around, attempting hypnosis. Despite extensive travels across Africa, and several years studying the ways of tribes in Senegal, Tanzania and Madagascar, this was the first trip he'd made to Asia.

"To tell you the truth, I'm disappointed," he let on. He'd been wandering through Malaysian Borneo for a couple of months now, visiting some extremely isolated Dayak settlements before reaching this point. "In Africa, people dance to communicate, and sometimes I go into a trance with them for a whole weekend, just listening to the drums, telling me how to move. Here they are listless, they are losing the knowledge of their own plants and traditional medicines."

I informed him the spirits of Intu Linggau appeared to have retained at least a degree of their original potency, and he jotted down the settlements' name and location in his battered spiral notebook, saying he would seek out the village and its shadowy shaman.

"I have written two books on the subject already," he continued, "all about medicines, cult spirits and tribal customs, but it is almost impossible to get the publishers in Paris interested."

The thing that really struck Milano, though, was something that I'd just been taking for granted:

"In Africa," he said, "one thing is absolutely taboo. People will *never* go to the toilet in the river. It is just not done!" I imagined he'd been having a hard time adjusting: in Asia, rivers were seen as convenient waste disposal units. He told me he was heading south, to Balikpapan, in the morning to secure a berth on the Indonesian government-operated PELNI ship, leaving from there to Tarakan. Milano hoped to make it to the coastal oil city on time and I told him I'd join him. I was too exhausted after my illness to countenance traveling alone.

Despite it being almost midnight by the time we'd moored in Banjarmasin and found a hotel room, I spent half the following hour submitting to the luxury of a tepid shower. Mud washed down my body in rivulets, and I shaved off the straggly beginnings of a beard that had grown quite full in the three weeks since running away from Jakarta. I hardly recognized the gaunt face that stared back at me from the cracked mirror.

TARAKAN, INDONESIA
June 3, 1989

THE VOYAGE ON the PELNI ship MV *Tidar* was luxurious. The upgrade to a cabin for the 24-hour cruise—inclusive of three meals a day—spectacular. There were even tablecloths! But Tarakan … Oh, Tarakan! Some places just existed to rub me the wrong way.

It started and ended with a huge fuss at the immigration office where, it transpired, I could only depart the country with an official visa, not a mere tourist stamp. My argument against this was logical, unassailable: since I'd been stamped in *at this very same port of call* with a tourist stamp, a mere seven weeks earlier, it was not my fault to have failed to anticipate any problem in being allowed to leave by the same route, now. But Asian logic, like taste in music, appeared to not be universal.

"Ah, but they should not have issued you a tourist stamp in the first place!" the high-ranking officer responded.

"By 'they', you mean your *own* officers, who obviously are unaware of their own rules?" I knew I was breaking the cardinal rule in dealing with Indonesian officials—just as surely as if I had been taking a massive crap in the Zambesi River, upstream of a group of washerwomen from the Veekuhane tribe—that rule being never argue. And don't even *think* about losing your temper.

"You will have to return to Balikpapan and fly to Malaysia from there. There is nothing more I can do," the officer dismissed me, airily. As well as being a time-wasting diversion, I simply could not afford the additional cost such a flight would incur. But on Tarakan He was The Law, and The Law *could not* be wrong. Even when, in my opinion, he was.

At this low point, my feelings about bureaucracy, in fact *all* the emotions I'd been bottling up over the last few months, boiled over. They manifested themselves in my spitting on the tourist stamp in my open passport. I regretted the action instantly, of course, but there was nothing that could be done: a great glob of phlegm was now dribbling slowly across the imprinted head of the Pancasila eagle, Indonesia's sacred symbol of national unity and justice. That did it:

"Get out of my office!" roared the red-faced official. And I was about to storm out, I really was. But the buck stopped here. Wiping my visa page clean, smudging the purple ink a little in the process, I adopted the posture of the penitent, and started the consumption of a massive slice of humble pie.

"But, Sir, you don't understand. All my money was stolen in Muara Montallat," — police reports can be useful — "I was forced to trek through the jungle and almost died from fever. I am sorry I spat on your stamp, but I am at the end of my tether. Please help me."

It was a command performance. I think there was even a tear in my eye by the end of it. And it was totally believable because, like the best piles of steaming horseshit, it contained the nutritious fiber of truth. We struck a deal. The immigration officer would give me an exit stamp if I just got the hell off his island. There were no more flights that day, so I agreed to take the first flight to Malaysia in the morning, settling on the 8:00 a.m. Bouraq service to Tawau, in Sabah. It was a one-way ticket, naturally.

Sabah, Malaysia
June 4, 1989

TARAKAN AIRFIELD WAS just that, a field. Emaciated chickens scraped for worms at the base of the control tower. There was no x-ray machine or baggage check, even though my flight was an international one. I chewed a strip of gum offered by a nice Indonesian businesswoman who was waiting for a later flight, and grew bored squashing lazy flies and over-fed cockroaches with my flip-flops. The immigration chief turned up, in person, to make sure I honored my word. He carried in his pocket a little inkpad and rubber stamp, especially for the occasion. The aircraft for Tawau was a tiny, twin-prop—all luggage was weighed and then stowed in its nose cone—and it had seating for just ten passengers. The backwash of the turboprops as we prepared to take off bent the papaya trees on the perimeter in prayer, and we began to jolt across the uneven grassy strip, bumpily gaining speed. The pilot pulled up in an unexpectedly steep climb and we brushed first the treetops and then the bay, at barely 3,000 feet.

From the air, Sabah—one of the states of Borneo belonging to Malaysia—appeared more orderly than its Indonesian neighbor;

at once exotic yet familiar. It was part of the same island, yes, but less fantastical than Kalimantan, as if the very streets, trees and rice fields were sensitive to the faintest adumbrations of *Pax Britannica*.

It was a Sunday, so the banks were closed. I had just enough cash for a bus ride on to Sandakan. The notion of staying a moment longer than necessary in Tawau didn't occur to me. Where does it come from, this compulsion toward perpetual motion? I traveled to stay sane, felt more alive when vulnerable, and rested most peacefully numbed by exhaustion.

It took until the evening to arrive at the sweltering port city. I eked out my few remaining ringgits at a cheap restaurant, happy to rediscover the edible ecstasy of *roti canai* — the ubiquitous and delicious, flaky, fried pancake offered at Indian restaurants throughout Malaysia, Brunei and Singapore — with all its attendant curry sauces. I washed down this poor man's feast with glasses of syrupy *kopi-C* — strong coffee mixed with sugar and evaporated milk. Just before closing time I asked the Indian waiter where he stayed, since locating budget accommodation had suddenly become a concern. He directed me to a doss-house-cum-brothel with thin plywood walls and filthy toilets a few floors above the restaurant. This cost five ringgits — about a pound — a night, and was the cheapest place in town.

The next morning, I awoke feeling none-too refreshed following a night of bedbugs and close-by erotic moaning. I began to hitchhike out of Sandakan towards Sabah's capital, Kota Kinabalu. After an hour, a beige-painted, mud-splattered Toyota Hilux overtook me, slowed, and reversed at speed. Jerry, its driver, was an ethnic Chinese plantation manager heading into KK for supplies. A new road layout confused him, momentarily, and he pulled the truck over (enveloped shortly afterwards by our trailing plume of dust and grit) to ask directions from a road repair crew. This group comprised a couple of ethnic Indian laborers and their Malaysian foreman. "What language, lah?" asked Jerry, and they soon elected as the *lingua franca* neither the country's official language Malay, Jerry's native Cantonese, nor Tamil—no, not even the Esperanto my Grandmother had so ardently studied in her late years—but English. Home is as much semantics as it is settlement.

The lowland plantations bowed down in worship of Mount Kinabalu, the giant rock that dominates northeast Borneo and rises to 4,000 meters at its peak. Some antediluvian colossus must have placed his foot on Banjarmasin way back, when the plates were forming, and pivoted the entire landmass on the spindle of the equator, sinking the south into swamp and launching this northern tip closer to the stars.

"Pretty good, lah?" Jerry followed my elevated gaze, and then shifted focus to look down at my feet, "Say, why you not wear shoes? Dangerous all the sharp objects and snakes, you know," he mentioned in genuine concern.

I told him of my travails in Kalimantan, how I would have to sell a few photos or find work teaching English before I could afford to replace my ruined boots. Now, the nicest Chinese you will ever meet live in Sabah and its neighboring Malay state, Sarawak. Perhaps this phenomenon arose because they found themselves a distinct minority, and had to take care going around being especially kind to everyone? They believed in fate, too. At the end of the drive, Jerry insisted on going out of his way to drop me off at the ferry terminal, and that I accepted, "as a gift, to pass on to the next person in need," seventy ringgits, in cash. This was a lifesaver, I had to admit, and almost exactly the same amount I had lent earlier to Jerry (same name, no coincidence) at

Sim's guesthouse, in Singapore.

The Universal Bank of Karma. I'd trust it over Barclays, any day.

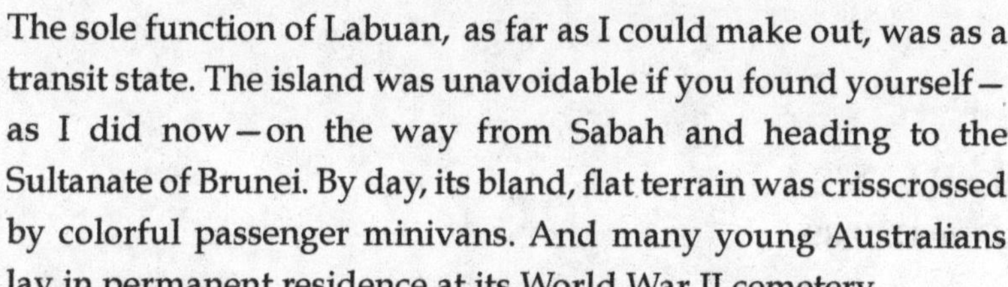

The sole function of Labuan, as far as I could make out, was as a transit state. The island was unavoidable if you found yourself — as I did now — on the way from Sabah and heading to the Sultanate of Brunei. By day, its bland, flat terrain was crisscrossed by colorful passenger minivans. And many young Australians lay in permanent residence at its World War II cemetery.

At the end of a long day, refreshing zephyrs swept down off the South China Sea, and sunset unleashed Labuan's dark secret: bars, pubs, music shops, karaoke parlors, hair, massage and whatever-else-you-want salons; restaurants, cinemas and fronts for gambling and prostitution ... all fueled by customers from Brunei, who dripped with petrodollar prosperity, and were hungry to release the natural urges they'd had to repress at home, just two hours away by high-speed hydrofoil.

Brunei

June 17, 1989

BRUNEI WAS THE natural place to conclude a story that so far existed only in my head — and on thirty rolls of undeveloped slide film: "From Banjarmasin to Brunei: A Trans-Borneo Adventure".

But it was an expensive spot to stage a finale. My flip-flops had finally given up the ghost. And walking barefoot along the trimmed grass verges and well-swept sidewalks of Bandar Seri Begawan, while therapeutic, was drawing looks of disapproval from the toffee-nosed prisoners of passing air-conditioned 4WD vehicles. The light blue weather-boarded exterior of St Andrew's Anglican Church beckoned to me, as did the lady wielding a pair of pruning shears in the shrubbery: Grace, the Vicar's wife.

"You can sleep in the Sunday School shed for free, if you like," she offered.

Considering my wild and bedraggled appearance this was a rather brave and Christian leap of faith. I accepted her offer, of course. At night, I made up a bed on the raised platform beneath a blackboard, using pew cushions as a pillow.

The problem with coming to the end of an adventure abruptly like this, of course, was *what to do next?* I'd been so consumed with surviving the journey that I'd put no thought into what would happen after its conclusion. Start another? To where? With what funds? What if I'd stayed in Hong Kong, back in 1987, or had never left England in the first place? Would I even *be* a photographer now? So many alternative futures were discarded so casually, burning through life in our curious, wasteful rush. Sanity was best preserved by ignoring all the possible paths we could have followed and, instead, relishing the present.

The Churchill Memorial Museum was situated nearby. Its air conditioning and lack of entrance fee beckoned me inside. I sought solace with my fellow countryman as recordings of his heroic wartime speeches played quietly, like prayer, in the background. From out of nowhere, tears poured from my eyes, and fiery resistance stirred in my soul. I was the only visitor. For an hour I attempted to channel inspiration from the Great Man. I thought back to my own home, located close to Chartwell, Churchill's beloved residence, and of the hop fields, oast houses, gently rolling woodlands and chalky uplands of the perfect Kentish countryside. A lump in my throat joined the salt streaming from my eyes: one day I would return. One vaguely specified day. But right now, it was Winston's youthful reports from the North West Frontier Province — of what in his time was British India — that dragged me into a completely different memorial landscape: of Peshawar and *The Frontier Post* — whose 'official poet' I had once briefly been — and I felt a stab of guilt at having let my more whimsical and tender side wither on the vine. *Travel forces open the heart, only to toughen it against emotion.*

Later the same evening, I went to watch an American film: *Naked Gun*, at the Regal. This resulted in a bout of stomachache from laughing so much. Afterwards, I sipped a thick, sweet coffee at a roadside stall, lit harshly by long fluorescent strips. A British expat left behind his copy of the previous week's *Time* magazine: 'MASSACRE IN BEIJING', shouted the cover type. A new name had been added to the glossary of infamous tyranny while I was lost in the swamps and forests: Tiananmen Square.

I devoured the article. How could I have missed this? History was like a landslide: it built up imperceptibly, fissure by overloaded fissure, and buried you under a pile of rocks when you least expected it. This was the story of the bloody decade! It neatly solved the problem of what I had to do next, though. The spirit of Churchill had spoken.

I needed to get out of the jungle and back to Hong Kong.

PART 2

Sensitive to Light: January 1990–July 1992

"Where you come from is gone, where you thought you were going to never was there, and where you are is no good unless you can get away from it."
Flannery O'Connor (*Wise Blood*)

3. Travel in the Age of Instant Gratification

I am a dinosaur. I belong to that odd minority who prefers travel to be slow, incremental. Uncomfortable even. You should feel travel, be jolted by it and in that discomfort be reminded you live.

The methods I favor are the ship and the train. Traveling this way, feeling every rail joint and ocean swell, is not at all swanky. It is far from what the holiday brochures preach (what you're buying into there is the glossy photography and, let me tell you, a photo can be a misleading thing. It's what I choose to make it). The less frantic the mode of transport, the less emphasis placed on arrival, the greater the suspension from time and place. Destinations are just the alibis we tell people so they'll let us go.

Nowadays, practically every corner of the world has been conquered and explored, settled, exploited, measured and mapped; built over, fought over, flown over; ploughed up, cleared up, blown up, upgraded, updated and uploaded. Geographical curiosity, in the age of the internet and Google Earth, seems an irrelevant passion. Aimless wandering is fast becoming an indefensible occupation, its proponents viewed with suspicion. With every destination in the world merely a screen click away, each minute must be accounted for, every route researched in advance, hotel room pre-booked, eating place peer-reviewed and experience boasted about on Instagram.

Emptying your mind so as to soak up random experience and enjoy freedom of thought now borders on heresy.

HONG KONG
January 1, 1990

YOU AREN'T GIFTED many decades in a lifetime. A New Year's Resolution List was in order to mark the beginning of the '90s:

- Learn a foreign language (Cantonese? Indonesian, easier).
- Learn to play musical instrument (Jazz piano, ideally, though not particularly transportable. Harmonica?).
- Get a steady girlfriend. NOT married. Preferably from HK (practical), or Scandinavia/Holland (closer in height).
- Quit teaching. Concentrate 100% on photography.
- Drink less alcohol (remember: quality not quantity).

Health: OK, I guess. Worrying bouts of dysentery persist. Gray hairs at last count: *fifteen*.

Wealth: HK$2,874.88 (about US$370) in Hang Seng Bank & US$150, in traveler's checks.

Equipment: Nikon FM body (one), 24mm f/2 + 85mm f/2 lenses, tripod, filters (81B, tobacco split gradient, & yellow, for shooting black and white)

"The beers are cheaper in Silvermine Bay," John persuaded me. My fellow English bunkmate at Lucky Guesthouse was wise on both booze and bargains and, being only too eager to shake off the dusty English teaching uniform of the day, I'd followed him along the pulsating pavements of Tsim Sha Tsui. Dodging fake Rolex salesmen and through icy blasts of air-conditioned electronics stores along Nathan Road, we dived down narrow alleyways where greasy ducks hung dripping next to stalls laden with erotically carved pieces of ivory and counterfeit cassette tapes.

Changing pace and mode of transport, we hopped on the Star Ferry and crossed to Hong Kong Island, Victoria Harbour slowly giving way to an advancing tsunami of neon-lit skyscrapers. Hot, oily fumes emerged from the vessel's subterranean engine room, along with a mechanical orchestra of grinding gears and throbbing cylinders. An old seaman, dressed in dark blue sailor suit, steadied himself on the gunwale before launching a heavy rope to his counterpart on the pier, both vessel and pier juddering upon impact. A bell clanged and water churned as the propeller went into reverse. The gangplank slammed down and crowds rushed off into an alien world of business, order and colonial landmarks. John and I turned right and caught the ferry to Lantau Island, aiming to test my fifth resolution, at The Flagstaff.

"...vermin...B...Hot..." the neon red signage of Silvermine Bay Hotel blinked appetizingly as we docked in choppy waves at the swaying jetty. I remembered this Lantau, wind-blown and salty-aired, from the last time I'd lived in Hong Kong, a few years back. At the pub, a largely expat crowd was slumped over and around the bar already. John bought the first round. Friends of his, Mo and Colin, then bought a round each. Peer pressure obliged me to purchase the next round. Each round meant one less roll of film I could afford to feed my camera, but allowances had to be made for the dawning of a new decade. The sequence was repeated, this time in reverse. We'd missed the message it was a 'Turban Party'. Someone was kind enough to lend me their woolen scarf, which I wrapped around my head. Computer programmer Simon had his skull encased in a bandage, painted with red nail polish 'blood'.

"I'm Captain Danger," said he, already two sheets to the wind, "the Lantau Island Superhero." It was a nickname he'd picked up following a particularly spectacular bicycle crash in Tai Tei Tong.

"That's the thing about being an expat, you don't have any choice in your friends, we're all expected to stick together, like a football team," lamented Mo, a bubbling peroxide crewcut New Ager, dressed florescent and artsy. "So, what are you, then?"

"I'm a photographer," I replied, hiding behind that lofty aspiration, rather than admitting that my bills were still largely paid teaching English.

"Ooh. You seem a bit young," said Mo. A lot of people reacted this way: there was such a pre-conceived notion about photographers. Generally, cameramen were imagined as mature womanizing loners: part James Bond, part Marlboro Man. A rugged sophisticate—one who could stare down an enraged lion in the Serengeti while charming the pants off a blond with worldly-wise banter and an adept adjustment of cufflinks. I peered into my pint in search of a witty comeback or cracking escapade to relate. But only bubbles rose through the amber.

Mo's partner, Colin, was a left-wing architect and intellectual, an Elvis Costello fan wrapped in a tweed suit. He struggled through mounting decibels to tell the story of the time he'd been thrown out of Czechoslovakia, but no one was sober enough to pay him much attention. Seems he was the spitting image of a political activist whose face had been plastered on wanted posters across the Eastern Bloc. He'd been arrested, transported through East Germany, and unceremoniously dumped off in West Berlin after his true identity had been confirmed. The experience hadn't diluted his delusions about Socialist Paradise at all. At midnight we all hugged each other and 'lah-lahed' our way through the nonsense words of *Auld Lang Syne*.

And then I met Jasmine Jones. Half-Welsh, half-Indian. Looking good after eight pints of Lowenbrau. She was twenty-five.

"I was married to a squaddie for two and a half years. Did my time. Thought, 'Fuck this', and took up with a biker gang ..." That was her short version, anyway. She could strip a semi-automatic rifle *and* balance a carburetor. *The interesting ones always get their hooks in.*

——— ∾∾∾ ———

"Are you sure about this?" I ventured. It was 4:00 a.m. and we were outside The Flagstaff. Jasmine, seemingly sober yet unable to walk, had managed to squeeze herself into a shopping trolley from the nearby supermarket.

"No bloody buses this time of night," she said, "you'll have to push."

Two hill ranges and two hours later — the downhills were trickiest, no brakes — we reached her flat in Pui-O. She mentioned she was looking for a tenant, and appeared to think I'd make a suitable candidate. We talked for an hour or so, until sunrise. It was chilly inside her living room, like being in a tomb, but with cushions. Asian builders don't waste money on extravagances such as double-glazing, central heating or insulation. I snuggled inside one of her oversized woolen sweaters, and crashed out on the shag pile carpet.

The morning was heavily clouded and humid, and I awoke

late in it with a splitting headache. I reached her kitchen sink in a state of conflicted alarm: should I throw up in it directly, or wash the dishes first? Last night, Jasmine had mentioned something about being an 'artist'. If by 'artist' she meant living in a dump, then she was a real Picasso.

"You should come out here next week. I could use you to photograph some of the scenery I've been commissioned to paint, Christopher." Christopher? She referred to me like my mother when I was a child and had done something wrong. I got a kick out of it, but didn't let Jasmine know of her victory. Half of bloody Lantau Island was probably gossiping falsely by now about how we'd slept together last night.

I returned to the police sirens and pneumatic drills of Kowloon. This was home now, an urban stew of noise and crowds; the exotic, chaotic canvas for my photographs. Lantau, by contrast, offered clear views and dirty living, and was a distraction from my mission. I went to the Cherikoff Café on Nathan Road for a restorative chicken curry with rice before the evening screening of *The Gods Must Be Crazy*, at Harbour City Cinema. Jasmine joined me in the flickering darkness, merging my worlds. She'd been over in Admiralty, checking if her parent's pub, The Prince of Wales, had survived the worst of the previous night's blowout.

After the film, we strolled along the nearby waterfront:

"I think the audience rather missed the point; they were all laughing at the black actor and showed him no sympathy at all," I said to her.

"The experiences of a Kalahari bushman and a Coke bottle are probably a bit beyond their usual sphere of social interaction. The Chinese aren't particularly racist, not as long as they have a chance of making money off you," Jasmine advised. "Their pragmatism will always keep any wilder instincts in check. Why ruin a profitable situation? Besides, we should all think ourselves superior: the issue of racism only arises when a society starts doubting itself. No, it's the opposite condition that nurtures hatred, insecurity," said Jasmine, who wouldn't for a moment admit to personal weaknesses, but had obviously spent some time brooding upon the weaknesses of others. She continued, with feeling, "If only people were more confident in who they were and where they were from…all this self-doubt just leads to intolerance."

"While men are decent to me, I try to be decent to them, regardless of race, color, politics, creed or anything else," I recited from distant memory.

"Who's that…Martin Luther King?"

"No, Biggles," I replied (referring, of course, to 1946's *Biggles Delivers the Goods*. My primary school had been well-stocked with the literary output of Captain W.E. Johns, and the daring escapades of his fictional flying ace, James Bigglesworth), "but you are comprised of two tribes and cultures, and are living in a third. How do you reconcile them all?" I wondered, "Doesn't one of them dominate?"

"Who said anything about reconciliation, dear Christopher? I just have double the confidence."

Double trouble, more like it. Jasmine would knock the stuffing right out of my ballpark, if I let her get close enough. But there was truth in what she claimed; the Universe seems to embrace the self-assured—I shuddered, involuntarily, remembering Pascal, captain of our boat, the *Kurnia Ilahi*, backlit by lightning and urging us on into a storm—and blesses them with a certain degree of impunity.

A few days later and a familiar laugh and booming voice — one loud enough to overpower the ever-present din of jackhammers and car alarms from the street below — echoed around the reception room of the guesthouse.

"Absolutely ludicrous…" Marc Johnson was one of the old Lucky Guesthouse crowd. The last time I'd bumped into him, two years ago, I'd taken some photos for his modeling portfolio. "Chris? Mate! Hey, that modeling card worked a treat. I got a gig for Yamaha and did some catwalk in Tokyo."

He'd had Monica, the Lucky Guesthouse landlady, translate all the most vital phrases into Chinese and Japanese characters:

Marc Johnson
Height: 185cm / Eyes: Blue-Gray
Hair: Light Brown / Penis: 79cm

"Couldn't understand why the receptionist girls were always giggling, but then someone explained the character for 'waist' Monica had used was north Japanese slang for 'dick'. Absolutely ludicrous…!"

January 13, 1990

ANOTHER BIRTHDAY. GENERALLY, I let them slip by undetected, but I must have told someone when I was drunk on Lantau. Jasmine called, and was most persistent in inviting me to a get-together at The Prince of Wales later. I did not view this as a movement toward relationship. Miss Jones and I had got off to a too-familiar start in the hothouse of inebriation, whereas romance, like a primrose, grows best in the walled and shaded garden of the imagination. No, it was her uninhibited, far-ranging conversation, and general demeanor of wildness, that drew me to Jasmine. Besides, I could never introduce a girl with tattoos to my parents.

My reverie was broken by conversation from the lower bunk. The little French guy, who looked like a ballet dancer and worked as a masseur, was quizzing Marc about opportunities for work in the Japanese film industry:

"And what about porn? I 'ave for eight years done zis in my country." He persisted, quite unabashed, "Vairee good money. You perhaps 'ave some experience?"

It took a lot to knock Marc off his wicket: "Not really, no, I was just an extra, you know. In some *normal* films. I wouldn't know about ..."

"You mean you did eet only with women? But I do eet with men, too. A hole is a hole, after all. What does it matter, man or woman? And they pay more for eet that way."

I grabbed my camera and deserted Marc in his discomfort. Becky from the Group Photo picture agency had called yesterday, asking if I had any pictures of businessmen using handheld phones. They were the latest trend. Bulky things. What was the point of them, when Hong Kong bristled with public phone boxes on every corner, and calls within the territory cost just HK$1, no matter their length? Surely the more communication gadgets you had, the more desperate you made yourself appear?

I began shooting at lunchtime, trying to distill order from the chaos of Central District's crowded streets, noting how the elements of photographs swirl continuously around us, like countless stars in an infinite galaxy of light, color and form. The photographer's skill lay in predicting when all this infuriating movement was, for an instant, going to align — and to be in the best position, with the right lens, using the most suitable film and combination of shutter speed and aperture to capture it — before the magical moment passed.

The party at The Prince of Wales ended up being a Reggae night. Here I unearthed a talent for dancing to Bob Marley that should, in a fair world, have remained buried. My spasmodic movements were unleashed upon the unsuspecting regulars of the bar, the product of over-indulgence in a particularly vibrant cocktail, the 'Tequila Slammer'. These toxic concoctions I blame for making this entry a day late. I remember only roaring through the wormhole of Aberdeen Tunnel, heading to Stanley Village in Jasmine's red, soft-top MG sports car. It was rather a cramped ride since, accompanying her in the tiny convertible, was the huge Zambian DJ, Fwananga and, squeezed in the passenger space euphemistically referred to as 'the back', Max and I. Max was an American artist, one of Jasmine's inner-circle. "A Berkeley man," he said, as though that title alone explained his vivid green woolen beret and Sherlock Holmes pipe. Somehow, Max had managed to strap a wildly flapping canvas to the roof by means of a single bungee cord. This, his latest 6' x 6' masterpiece, was part of his upcoming installation that consisted of intimate renditions of the splayed labia of all the girls he'd slept with in the past year. Snatch preview, all you lucky passengers still awake on the top deck of the No.70 bus.

The next morning, nursing several degrees of hangover, Jasmine suggested we head to The Boat Club for breakfast. This sounded suitably civilized and sobering, but turned out to be the Army's sailing club. Here, four amiable squaddies — Speed (who had just been court-martialed for hitting an officer), Taffy, Bernie and Richie, practically indistinguishable in their uniform crewcuts and moustaches — were frying up eggs to go with their white bread and baked beans, and were listening to *The Archers* on British Forces Radio. "Aw righ', Jazz," they welcomed us to join them. I thought of my best friend, Mark, currently based in that other (Port) Stanley, down in the Falkland Islands, and wondered if he was enjoying a similarly epicurean repast? The soldiers ignored Max's suggestion to paint their Land Rover the colors of the rainbow, and continued on dabbing with the conventional khaki and black in their tins and on their brushes. Max, pretending to be offended by the poverty of their esthetic judgment, staggered off down the beach and attempted to store his latest rendition inside his twenty-eight-foot-long wooden yacht.

━━━∾∾━━━

Today marked three years, to the day, since I'd escaped from England. I believe 'escape' is not too dramatic a description: certainly, any suggestion of return left me shuddering from mental images of window bars, balls and chains — all the assorted paraphernalia of imprisonment. Connections were made quickly in Hong Kong; they had to be. People were continuously arriving or leaving, and employment opportunities were correspondingly dynamic. Backpacker hostels like Lucky's, being the channel through which many of us initially funneled, became the eclectic repository of discarded books of those who had gone before. I started to leaf through some of the volumes lying around. These included William Golding's *The Color of Light* (I started to read this, thinking it must be about photography. It was not.). Why do so many writers create characters who themselves are writers? I guess it's inevitable, what with scribblers being stuck at their desks all day long, staring at a typewriter or blank sheet of paper. They can't all be out there having adventures, like us photographers. George Orwell's *The Road to Wigan Pier*, which came across as more of an economic survey…I have to say I preferred *Homage to Catalonia*; and *the* book of the moment, Milan Kundera's *The Unbearable Lightness of Being*…This I read all the way through. I was left confused as to whether the work was pretentiously brilliant, or merely brilliantly pretentious. I am sure it made a lot more sense in the original Czech.

Note: must discuss this with Colin. He may have read a copy since his incarceration at the Czechoslovak border.

A new student started English lessons that evening. Wendy Wong. She was a year older than me, and an actress — in local repertory theater, not the movies. She was a serious and attractive girl with whom I felt an instant rapport. She explained how she could have many more roles, but didn't want to suck up to the play directors or casting agents.

"I'd rather stop acting and be a secretary," she said, with some feeling. But then she admitted it'd be hard to give up acting. "It's something I am good at, it comes naturally. I imagine like photography is to you?" She was astute, too.

John, my bunkmate, had been handing out free tickets for the grand opening of Soho, a new disco in Lan Kwai Fong (he'd got them off of Jean Paul, who'd given up smuggling gold, ever since they'd installed a metal detector at Kathmandu airport, and was now working as a carpenter. He'd been doing Soho's interior decor). On a whim I asked Wendy if she'd like to come along, and to my great surprise, she said, 'Yes'.

Huge crowds blocked the street in front of the disco. A fellow Lucky Guesthouse resident was on duty as a bouncer and, recognizing me, nodded us through. The interior of the club was a mix between a cave and the cockpit of a spaceship.

"You made it, then?" shouted Marc over the ear-splitting music, "absolutely *ludicrous!*" He was dancing with a stately Mexican girl who'd been at the guesthouse a week, Layla. I was not sure what Wendy would make of my cosmopolitan friends; nightclubs were not really my scene, but *she* didn't know that. Deciding alcohol would help, I pushed through to the bar and ordered some Kirin beers. Wendy's mouth opened and closed as thunderous music pounded, and I pretended to listen to what she was saying; it was a good excuse to lean in closer to those luscious lips of hers. She seemed happy enough, but pulled me outside at 11:30 p.m. If anything, the crowds were denser now.

"I have to catch the bus home, or my mother will worry," she said, my head still ringing with Chaka Khan. "I had a nice time, thanks." A quick peck on the cheek and she was gone. I turned and re-entered the club.

"I bet Marc you'd not come back," admitted Layla.

"Oh yes? What'd you lose?"

"A kiss, apparently," Marc pretended to be inconsolable.

We partied on and I recollect dancing very close to Layla, her abundant brunette tresses flying in my face, lights flashing, music pounding, the old tribal ritual. The chance of catching a ferry back over to Kowloon was willfully ignored.

"I guess we should take a taxi?" I posited at around four in the morning. But the boats would start running again in just a few hours, and it seemed a waste of cash and a free sunrise.

"Or you could collect your winnings..." Layla tempted. We wandered down to Blake's Pier, where a number of other couples seemed to have been caught similarly short. Overcome by a sense of chivalry, I wrapped Layla in my jacket, and we snuggled together as fingers of pink cloud began to rip through the black bin liner of the night sky. I wanted to film this woman, to freeze-frame her every movement and gesture. Her head rested naturally on my shoulder. I lowered my chin to catch a glimpse of her becalmed profile and was engulfed by the upward waft of her perfume; a humid steam of wine and promise.

Back at Lucky's and my days were beginning to all start the same; with my feet hanging out the end of a comically short, lower bunk bed. My every movement brought forth a cacophony of creaks and metallic explosions from worn-out springs and stressed joints. I pulled aside the curtain made of hanging towels and drying clothes that provided my only privacy and territorial claim, and looked out at the familiar view of un-scrubbed, high-rise window cages and dripping air-conditioning units, directly across the narrow expanse of Hankow Road. This was the view of Kowloon the budget traveler either soon became accustomed to, or went mad from. To check what the weather was doing necessitated cricking your neck ninety degrees and gazing directly upwards. In one vital sense, though, this day was not going to be like all the rest of my days here, since today I was starting a new part-time job in Causeway Bay. I'd answered the ad for a proofreader at an academic printing house, and today would begin wielding the power of God, or at least His blue pencil, over the learned professors whose various papers and theses—due to reasons of outsource and thrift—were placed before me for commanding edit. I had even gone to the expense of purchasing a nice paisley tie from Temple Street night market, so as to best blend in with my fellow commuters.

Seasonal Occurrence of Potential Ice-Nucleating Bacteria on Douglas Fir Foliage and Seed Cones occupied my initial morning, and taught me some surprising things about agar, along the way. And then there was the paper, for a Canadian university, about acorns. What an utterly indulgent sector academia is! Two years' grant money to reach the same conclusion any good farmer, or his grandmother, would know by instinct or from folklore. In one case, an exhaustive test on the moisture content of acorns had been performed, the results of this research throwing illumination on how their fertility was affected if they were dried:

- naturally,
- by freezing, or
- kept moist

Cue drum roll and the earth-shattering discovery that, to retain maximum fertility, you had best keep your nuts moist... something I was finding impossible to *avoid* here in the tropics.

———⌇———

I went via Color Six, the photo lab in Stanley Street, after morning classes were over. I'd had some 10" x 8" Cibachrome prints made up there of Wendy I'd taken in Victoria Park, to help her when she was auditioning for roles. I planned to give them to her during our lesson in the evening. I was determined not to mention anything about it being Valentine's Day; she might think I had an ulterior motive. Obviously, I *did* have an ulterior motive. But, if she was the girl for me, she'd appreciate the more subtle approach.

Before then, though, Layla tracked me down just as I was changing my shirt in the front dorm of Lucky's, and said something flattering about my chest muscles. She had tickets to the matinee screening of *When Harry Met Sally*, down in Harbour City. It was an offer I couldn't refuse. The audience was sparse at this early hour, and largely engaged in snogging. I sank deep into my chair when Layla screamed out loud with uncontrollable laughter at the scene in which Meg Ryan faked an orgasm.

———— ∞ ————

I popped in to see Bill Cranfield, the editor at Cheney Communication's HK office. He had received no news about the payment for my Toraja story, so I felt I could guilt him into a coffee, free use of his fax machine and a chance to photocopy my latest texts and caption sheets on his Xerox. When you take into consideration the cost of camera equipment, slide films and processing, having duplicates made of the best slides (at HK$15 a pop) to leave with Group Photo, not to mention air tickets and accommodation…and all of this up front—'on spec' to use industry speak—I felt as though I was embarking on an expensive apprenticeship. But there was no other way to gain experience and stockpile material for the CV. What was it I was stockpiling, anyway? In what way was I improving the state of the world by delivering lifestyle stories for the mild titillation of a credit card-owning elite? I needed to sink my teeth into something more serious. I think this stab of conscience was all Layla's doing. Photography, she seemed to suggest, was a tool to help me prove my worthiness.

The night before, for example, we had been discussing politics:

"I can't be in Mexico right now. I was involved in some political activism. My father is Palestinian, you see?" she confided. I'd nodded, my expression serious, not wishing to seem shallow or ill-informed. "Don't look so worried, I didn't kill anyone," she smiled.

The PLO had been big news when I was growing up in the '70s, of course, something to do with Munich. I'd not paid much attention, though, being only five years old at the time. Maybe I lacked the radical gene? Blessed with insufficient curiosity, I had never been diverted by a cause.

"I don't trust movements," I said, absently stroking Layla's hair, "I couldn't even make it in the Boy Scouts. It's a good thing, on the whole. It's all such a colossal waste of energy getting worked up about anything."

"But that means you have no passion! What is life without passion?"

"Surely you can be passionate without having to blow things up?" I was surprised by the intensity of feeling bubbling inside me. Layla was smiling, coyly: *you see, you have emotions, after all!* her expression seemed to say.

"And what about those heroes of yours, those revolutionaries? Hypocrites, the lot of 'em!"

"Hey, what? Chris, I come from the Third World, remember? People don't lead nice, cozy, Radio Four-at-teatime lives there. It's brutal. Tough measures are sometimes called for."

"Perhaps, yes, I'm sure you're right. I'm sorry…" I conceded, but then thought *what the hell, bridges are for burning,* "but only the rich can afford to be revolutionaries; the rest of us need to earn a living. You know what they call a penniless revolutionary? A criminal! The jails are full of 'em!"

My blood boiled whenever I was assumed posh, just because I was shy and politely spoken. My dad was a welder, and I went to a state school. My mother was forever darning our socks and, as kids, she made our clothes; my jeans were always more patches than trouser. Our house didn't have a telephone, the TV was black and white, and the family car always a hand-me-down from Granddad after he'd bought a new one.

"I don't come from some privileged middle-class background like your comrade Che, or your beloved Karl Marx! They never worked an honest day in their lives. I mean, Marx *was* a journalist for a while, if you can call that 'work', but he was married to a baroness from the Prussian ruling class who bankrolled him. So, he was a hypocrite, too! You know why communism won't work? It's not rocket science. People want *stuff*. They like to show off and to improve their position in life. You'll never change that. People are only ever equal on their deathbed."

"Wow. You've been holding that in for a while." Layla, instead of being repulsed at my slamming everything she stood for, moved in closer.

"Oh, I'm inquisitive about places, and I adore geography," I allowed, "I'm just indifferent to people and their motives. You're right. It must be different in Mexico. In England, causes are things you drop odd change into charity tins for; they leave you basking in the warmth of self-satisfied benevolence. Like prayer."

"We pray in Mexico too, you know. A lot. And I don't believe you are as faithless as you pretend." She stared out across the park, brooding. A gray squirrel paused, hesitant to continue its approach to our bench. After a while she continued, "I envy you, you know? I always end up getting so involved. But you, you're so self-assured."

"It's nothing to do with confidence; just a willful avoidance of doubt. It's all a matter of perspective: nothing is important, in the long run. I haven't met a problem yet that won't sort itself out after two months in the jungle." I gave her the benefit of the wisdom I'd gained recently in Borneo.

"So, photography is ideal for you, then," a hint of exasperation creeping into her voice, "you can spend your entire life on the move *pretending* to care about things. I don't know, maybe you even do care, in your way, but you're never going to stick around long enough to get tied down by any one of them. There's always another subject beckoning. You're the perfect observer."

Was she criticizing my politics, or my attitude toward

relationships? "In fact," she continued, "you are the most dangerous type of revolutionary there is: one without an ideology. And stubborn, to boot!"

"I'm a photographer, dammit." Aren't we supposed to be firebrands for social justice? My job is to expose the corrupt in a blaze of truth, not to get bogged down in the details. Layla had managed to stick her needle in, though; there was nothing for it. I was going to have to clear out my bank account and make a trip to shoot something impoverished and worthy. But what and, more urgently, where?

I woke to the slow, rhythmic swaying of the bunk bed as the Spanish couple above me squirmed, furtively, making love. Out in the hallway someone was trying to hawk a golf ball up from their lungs. The day at Lucky Guesthouse had begun. It was at this low point I discovered Layla had gone to China. She had alluded to the intention the night before, when we were down on the Kowloon waterfront. I had been trying to describe in words, and failing, how I felt about her. I should have written it down: a list of Layla-ish attributes she could have taken with her to read for amusement. To start with there was her name. You don't meet girls called 'Layla' in my insular Kentish hometown. In addition, I liked her nose; it was prominent, and suggestive of character and spirit. And her kiss. Honestly, I could spend hours lost tongue-tied with her. We did. It had been as innocent as that between us, so far. And I felt proud just to walk beside her; she had such presence. I wondered at times what she saw in a kid like me (she was 28, after all). So, it was not a total surprise to find she'd bugged out, but it was a disappointment. She was heading to China, ostensibly to improve her ink painting technique but the real reason, I imagined, was to lie low with her communist fellow travelers. I found her note addressed to me propped up on the dormitory table:

Please be happy. Each of these are kisses I didn't get to give you.

— Layla

And, in a bowl, she'd left five oranges and two mangoes.

———— ∽∽ ————

I passed Ocean Terminal on my way to the Star Ferry the next morning. I couldn't help but notice the pride of the Russian Sovcomflot fleet, the cruise ship *Maksim Gorkiy*, moored nose-to-nose with the ultimate symbol of American capitalism, the *Trump Princess* super-yacht. The US businessman owner of the latter was hoping to sell his vessel for upwards of US$100 million (unsuccessful in finding a buyer in Hong Kong, the vessel was finally sold to Saudi Prince Al-Waleed bin Talal, the following year, for US$20 million). The huge vessel looked quite ungainly. But then money has never been an automatic guarantor of taste.

It was a dry morning at Victory, my job that day being to proofread a bunch of economic texts. The apex of my day being reached with a linguistics paper:

"… as Burke & Klotz (1958) maintained & Schrinkwurtle et al. (1969) endorsed, being derived from Kantist theory, without the cognitive semantics of the Cartesian influence, the cat did actually sit <u>on</u> the mat."

Deciding it was very much the author's argument to stress 'on' in his concluding sentence, I resisted my urge to underline 'did' and send academia into a tailspin.

Now, the best—and, I would contend only positive—thing about such mundane office work is the mental freedom it allows to plan for future travel. Such interludes of static employment are, therefore, as necessary as oases are to the Bedouin, for refueling and recovery before once more venturing forth into the arid unknown. This morning, for instance, as I churned through a spectacularly dull treatise titled *The Buddha as an Owner of Property and Permanent Resident in Medieval Indian Monasteries*, I'd decided the destination for my next trip would have to be the Philippines. Not only was the country the closest equivalent Asia had to a South American banana republic, but I really needed to start racking up new countries, if my target to visit ninety of them before dying was ever to be achieved. Since Cory Aquino had become president, there had been continuous coup attempts against her government by former Marcos supporters and disgruntled army officers. The most recent was just a few weeks back, when renegade Cagayan provincial Governor Rodolfo Aguinaldo led a 200-man force to seize the downtown Hotel Delfino in Tuguegarao, in a failed uprising that left at least twenty people dead. So, the potential for interesting incidents was looking up, and English was widely spoken in the Republic of the Philippines, making it easier to work independently on stories.

Oh, and to travel there was cheap—always a 'plus' to the cash-strapped freelancer.

The mere act of taking this mental decision seemed to have telegraphed itself through the ether to Derek Maitland, editor in chief of *Pacific Traveller* magazine. I'd been in his good books since he had used my Borneo adventure feature a few issues back. So now I thought it polite to check if he needed anything from the Philippines. To my great and pleasant surprise, he wanted *four* stories. A series! One was to be about festivals, one to feature holiday resorts (he said he'd give me some useful contacts before my departure), another about 'culture', and a fourth we left open for the time being, maybe some unexplored new paradise destination? There was talk of an isolated island called Palawan becoming the next Cebu.

"To put that in an Indonesian context for you, it's like Lombok becoming the next Bali. It could be huge, and it's impossible to find any pictures of the place," Derek said, tempting me further.

Waiting in my post office box this morning was a hand-painted postcard from Layla from Guilin. The image she'd painted resembled a fossil:

> *Dear Chris,*
>
> *I hope you are in very good health, 'cause I'm not. Being treated with Chinese traditional medicines and hope to be better very soon. This little town is very nice. I think of you often and hope to see you in HK later.*
>
> *This shrimp is from my first class of Chinese water colors. Very romantic, no?*
>
> *— From my heart, Layla*

April 5, 1990

CHING MING FESTIVAL: Tomb Sweeping Day. There was to be a Pro-Democracy rally from Statue Square to Victoria Park. I rushed over as fast as the Star Ferry could take me to join the estimated 5,000 protesters. Their number swelled to easily double that after police, press and passersby were factored in. People had started gathering much earlier, selling rebel t-shirts and distributing yellow cotton bandanas: I tied one to my belt and another to my camera strap.

The event truly kicked off when a young, grief-stricken protester, dragged himself up the steps to the Cenotaph, on his knees. There, he kissed a bunch of flowers before laying them down reverentially, and running away from the glare of the press, tears filling his eyes. The monument itself — a replica of Lutyens' war memorial in Whitehall, London — looked on dispassionately and, I have to say, some of my fellow photographers seemed as unmoved by the unfolding human drama as the masonry. One hard-bitten veteran, who resembled the Hollywood actor Sean Penn, and was carrying two camera bodies and a tripod-mounted 400mm lens over his shoulder, muttered, "There won't be any trouble. Nothing violent ever happens in Hong Kong. Everyone has to go to work the next day." He sounded disappointed.

I chatted with one of the organizers, Sam Ho, who introduced me to a Mr Siao. He was from Mainland China, and spoke only Mandarin. Siao was a former Wuhan University student. I'd sailed under his home city's famous bridge, on my way down the Yangtze River, back in 1987. Siao was twenty years old, and living illegally in Hong Kong. He had taken part in the pro-democracy demonstrations on the Wuhan campus in the spring of '89, and had had to make a run for it in July that year. He managed to sneak across the border from Shenzhen into Hong Kong through the network of sewerage drains along the border. His family members were still in Wuhan, and his elder brother, he reported, had been detained by the authorities. He was trying to gain amnesty in Taiwan and, until that process began to move, the HK authorities were tolerating his continued stay in the territory. This sounded like a great story, and I jotted down notes, along with Sam's contact, just in case any of the magazines I visit showed any inclination towards this sort of feature.

Soon the march set off amid much loud and furious shouting through megaphones, and any normal traffic on the streets and pavements was brought to a standstill. The rally ended in Victoria Park at the base of a twenty-foot-high replica of the Goddess of Democracy statue—the original had been centerpiece of the Tiananmen Square protests—a plaster of paris knock-off of the Statue of Liberty. Wreaths were ceremoniously laid at its base, and then everyone drifted away.

MANILA, THE PHILIPPINES
April 15, 1990

THE HONG KONG Tourist Association magazine had featured one of my pictures on its front cover. It was my first sale through the Group Photo agency, and copies were on display all over Hong Kong's Kai Tak airport. I gathered up half a dozen of them and then headed off to find my departure gate.

After the concrete jungle of Hong Kong, the palm tree silhouettes flashing along Manila Bay were an exotic welcome back to tropical Asia. So, too, were the endless slums between the bay and Manila Airport. To the photographer, where there's poverty there's opportunity. Shantytowns were the same wherever you found them, and in their contradictory mixture of chaos and neatness, pollution and pride, hardship and hopefulness, was discovered a misplaced familiarity, like arriving back to a home that'd been disfigured by war.

Looming out of the gathering darkness, Spanish colonial-era churches and the floodlit facades of municipal buildings hinted at earlier imperial glory. Traffic was thick and varied: battered taxis, open-window buses, motorbikes with low-slung sidecars competed with chopped World War II-era Jeeps — extended for up to twenty passengers — bearing names such as 'Jesus' and 'Gift of God'. It was a crazy, honking, exhaust-fumed parade, backlit by the neon confidence of corporate America: McDonald's, Dunkin' Donuts and KFC.

Through all this, street kids scrambled, bloodied by the red aura of taillights, their faces smudged black, and smiles beaming white in contrast. The youngest held on to your hand, trustingly, and asked for money or pens; the slightly less young offered to take you to see their 'sister'. The watershed of innocence seemed to be age eight.

Farther from the waterfront, down the backstreets and alleyways of Ermita and Malate, scenes of desire and redemption played themselves out in a variety of erotic Stations of the Cross.

"Hello Joe," a female voice croaked, bored, from the shadows, "you wanna girl?" And then, more cautiously, "a boy?"

My camera offered a degree of immunity. I hung around a lamppost, rolled off half a 100 ASA film and replaced it with a faster one — a 160 Tungsten — that I pushed two stops to 640. Grainy, full of contrast: a suitable canvas upon which to paint with minimal light. The interior of Malate Church was illuminated, the faithful kneeling for Sunday Evensong, whilst prostitutes lingered in the lane outside, waiting for their evening regulars to emerge. A few roads in, and sailors strutted, preening white peacocks in uniforms representing a dozen far-off nations. They sat at bar stools on the pavement outside strip-lit hovels. Barely-clad girls beckoned and cooed mechanically, from second-floor balconies — forlorn Juliet's serenading an endless procession of Romeos. The strained vocals of drunken karaoke, country & western, and rock & roll battled it out through swinging doors, embraced in the cool shudder of air-conditioned moisture. Inside, dead-eyed topless dancers gyrated on raised stages, bathed in pink luminescence. And out on the street, drunken transvestites pranced and catcalled, doormen snagged and tugged at sleeves, and pimps pimped:

"Hey Joe! Psst, you wanna girl, Joe?"

〜〜〜

I spent two days killing time on Mindoro Island, the closest proper beach resort to Manila. It was one of the destinations on Derek's list. I couldn't afford to stay in any of the luxury resorts he expected me to photograph, obviously, but a dollar-a-night hut on the beach suited me nicely. It also listed hourly rental options designed to encourage prostitution.

Extra Roomer ... 20 pesos.

Extra Roomer (w/bed) ... 50 pesos.

I am not a beach person. I detest the constant battle with sand and its tendency to ruin cameras. Give me the mountains, any day. The sea was as calm as a millpond during the two-hour pump boat voyage back to Batangas on the Luzon mainland. The local bus to Manila was puttering out of the depot, and I leapt onboard. As the vehicle passed through the main gate and turned onto the highway, a female security guard looked up from her post. Our gazes locked. She had the most beautiful almond-shaped eyes I'd ever seen. A sticker on her desk—they love stickers, in the Philippines—declared: *I love your eyes.* It was the perfect shot, missed. I rued this loss of God-given material for much of the journey back to the Capital. *I'm here to work,* I chided myself, *not to daydream.*

I was back in Manila by 1:00 p.m., reinstated at the Malate Pensione. This hardwood-paneled mansion—seemingly constructed from the trunks of half an endangered rainforest— retreated from the bustle of Adriatico Street to reveal a lush and shaded inner courtyard, tinkling fountain and a tall, languid Dane, slumped sweating in a wicker chair. I could tell from his camera vest and red and white-checkered Cambodian scarf he was a fellow photographer.

"Carl," he introduced himself in a feral growl, stubbing out the remains of his cigarette in order to shake my hand. His grip was strong and calloused, the result of a lifetime carrying cameras. We slipped easily into conversation.

Carl had travelled across Sudan twice in the early 80's, and been photographing hotspots in Asia for years now. I was quite envious of all his adventures. He signalled to the hovering waiter.

"This heat is something else. I can't stop sweating. And there's never a clear day; it's all the time hazy. Typical tropics. But there's loads of shit going on, if you know where, and who to ask. Why don't you come with me later? Let's wait for it to cool down a bit, first. Drink a coffee. Don't be so stressed out. Pictures only come when you are relaxed."

And that was how I came to discover Smoky Mountain.

Carl and I collapsed our tall frames into a motorcycle taxi, he on the pillion, shaded by a stretched plastic canopy, and me safeguarding our camera bags in the sidecar. We rode out to Tondo, the impoverished Manila suburb easily located by its steaming volcano of trash. On its decomposing and unstable slopes subsisted a swarming army of scavengers. We arrived in mid-afternoon; I needed to wrap my scarf around my face from half a mile away, acrid fumes irritating my eyes, nose and throat.

A boiling black river ran through this foul and forsaken land, like oily lava, nurturing islands of coagulated refuse thick enough to stand on. Rubber tires smoldered, and children and women fought over the new piles of rubbish tipped off the backs of continually arriving trucks. No item was too insignificant not to consider recycling; bottle caps, flattened battery cells, sections of cardboard, even discarded vegetables—never too rotten to be cooked up for dinner. A shantytown of lean-tos made of, and almost indistinguishable from, the surrounding detritus, dominated the lower slopes. Emboldened rats rustled and plopped through piles of plastic bags into thick puddles of toxic ooze. Carl had been here before and the kids mobbed him as he handed out sweets and cigarettes. We split up—it was best to work alone. Sunset arrived early—daylight defeated by the thick pall of hopelessness that sat atop and smothered this place.

I hope Layla appreciates the effort I've made to get these pictures ...

Back at the Pensione, I spent an hour scrubbing my clothes attempting to rid them of the stink. My mind would take longer to purify. Carl joined me in the small garden, out back, where smoking coils had been lit to ward off mosquitoes. We sipped our San Miguel beers in silence, and then headed to Rosie's Diner on Del Pilar Street to indulge in their 'famous' chili con carne, mini-burgers, and milkshakes. The juxtaposition of poverty and plenty was so marked and magnified in a place like Manila, the only way to cope was to go with the flow, to give thanks for not having been born in a slum, and to pray never to end up in one. It was no surprise that religion grew rampantly in such fertile soil.

"Wherever you are planning to head now," Carl advised, "just make sure you're back in Manila by May first. Things will get interesting around then."

⌀

Alphabetically, 'Palawan' was situated between 'pain' and 'paradise', and what would be the worth of any Eden without a little suffering endured in its attainment? Arriving in Puerto Princesa, its main port, thirty-six hours after having set sail from Manila, the towering William's Line flagship *Dona Virginia* listed slightly as she entered the palm-fringed bay, a cautious nautical Gulliver nudging through a patchwork welcoming committee of

Lilliputian outrigger canoes. Mighty the glorious ferry may have appeared to those staring up from sea level, but conditions had been cramped in my sauna-like communal cabin below decks. I felt I'd suffered enough pain, and was looking forward greatly to my heavenly reward.

I was also mindful of the fate of its competitor, Sulpicio Line's vessel *Dona Paz* that had caught on fire and sunk in these waters in December 1987, leading to the loss of over 4,300 lives—the worst peacetime disaster of the 20th Century. (I recalled with gruesome fascination watching reports on the TV at Lucky Guesthouse of survivors being snatched at night by sharks as they clung to the wreckage). Her sister ship, the *Dona Marylin*, sank during a typhoon with the loss of 389 lives, just ten months after that. I joined my fellow passengers in tossing coins from the promenade deck, blessing our safe arrival. Far below, kids dived from their sampans to reclaim our sinking silver treasure.

A single dirt-track road led from Puerto Princesa, four hours north to Roxas. I was relegated to the back seat of a bus that had no doors or glass in its windows. Each time we stopped, a trailing cloud of grit caught up and swamped us. Next, I endured two hours bouncing on the pillion of a motorcycle taxi, cutting across the top of the island east to west, to Port Barton. Here, brilliantly decorative fishing canoes lay tilting on the beach, and I found sanctuary at the Shangri-La Bungalows, owned and run by a German named Lothan, and his Filipina wife.

"I haven't met anyone called 'Lothan' before," I admitted.

"I am named after a 14th Century Germanic king who was popularly known by his subjects as 'Lothan the Stupid'. I don't think my parents knew this when they christened me. He had syphilis and spent the last thirty years of his life in torment, you see."

Apparently, the government planned to construct an airport

at nearby San Vicente, as well as a road from Port Barton to El Nido, all in the name of pulling in the tourists.

"But people in Palawan are not so keen," Lothan let on. "There are gold reserves here to rival those of South Africa, and they would rather become a separate country than be forced to share that wealth with Manila."

Sun set early behind a purple veil, and I walked barefooted up and down the beach with Lee, a cool American girl who had traveled in Africa for a year, and was now working in Japan. The sand squeaked beneath our feet, and young girls ran up offering us fresh jellyfish and stingrays. We shared a double bed at the bungalows to save money. I thought to myself how it would be quite an achievement if I could leave the Philippines without having succumbed to sex. It would be a sign of maturity.

In the evenings, we washed using a bucket, as there was insufficient water pressure to work the shower until the rainy season. Time passed naturally, free of the flickering demands of television, and I read hungrily through an article by Hunter S. Thompson in Lee's month-old copy of the *San Francisco Inquirer*. His comments and testosterone-laden writing style reminded me of the way photographer London Bus used to brusquely analyze world affairs.

Most Palawanian settlements looked outwards to the sea, the interior of the cigar-shaped island being an unforgiving treachery of limestone gorges and barren 'bundoks' – the Filipino word for mountainous and difficult-to-access rural inland tracts. The term was adopted by US military personnel during the 1899-1902 Philippine-American War as the boondocks. People here were habituated by luck and location to simply hop in their outrigger whenever they needed to visit a neighboring village. Accordingly, Lothan arranged a pump boat for our 25-mile voyage south to the island's main attraction, the St Paul Subterranean River. This entailed a choppy four-hour journey. The sea was predatory, and had been churned milky-green by a squall that had us crouching over our bags beneath a tarpaulin most of the way. We were dropped off in knee-deep waters in a deserted cove, and waded ashore, like MacArthur landing on Leyte. A blistered sign read "St Paul Subterranean National Park" (now the Puerta Princesa Subterranean River National Park and, since December 1999, a UNESCO World Heritage Site), and free permits were issued from a small hut with a tin positioned in the hope of collecting stray donations.

Locals, wearing miner's hats with lamps attached, paddled Lee and me in through the mouth of the cave aboard a narrow canoe, the sound of crashing waves reverberating until we were deep inside. Total darkness descended, and blissful coolness enveloped us. Colonies of bats screeched and flitted, their droppings pungent and agricultural. After ten minutes of relaxed oaring, there came a physical change in air pressure. Our eyes no longer able to see, sound became the dominant sense. A guide shouted out, his voice echoing from a dozen unseen walls and crevasses. We had come to the middle of a massive chamber. The guide's powerful torch picked out distant stalactites, hanging from the ceiling like suspended daggers.

Twilight awaited us as we emerged from the cavern, along with the poser of where to sleep for the night. In the interests of photography, I decided to trek back overland to Puerto Princesa. I sought, above all else, authenticity in my images. I would have to escape the conveyor belt rush of the tourist trail. Toward that purpose Lothan had scribbled me a rough map, advising that the journey overland back to Puerto Princesa should take two days. I arranged to meet up with Lee there, two days hence, on Friday. She—sane girl—opted to head back to Port Barton in the pump boat, leaving me alone to sleep for free on the floor of reception hut No.3, next to the cave mouth. The door wasn't locked. I felt again that intoxicating headiness released by total vulnerability. This was travel: a few alien place names jotted on the back of a cigarette packet, a compass suggesting direction, and my water bottle filling, drop by pure drop, from a bamboo splint jammed between two rocks. There was a rough trail leading to the beach at Sabang that locals told me took about an hour and was stunning at sunrise.

Sabang was a tiny fishing village, the only visitor accommodation there being a single, two-room bamboo hut with an oddly prescient sentence printed on its door mantle (some passing traveler, it would seem, being intent on spreading the gospel of Kurt Vonnegut):

> *'The invitation to a strange journey is like a dancing lesson with God.'*

If I'd had the luxury of time, I would have lingered a day or two there. But it was still forty miles to Puerto Princesa, and who was I to deny the Lord a last tango in Palawan? An uneven track of chalk and compacted sand led inland, ancient bullock carts creaking slowly along this from rut to runnel. Most of the way was void of human life. The privacy encouraged me to blast away on my harmonica, and soon I was able to work up a fair rendition of *God Save the Queen*. The farther we stray from home, it would appear, the greater the gravitational pull of its nostalgia.

Already I envisaged the villages en route—Cabayagan, Tagnipa and Masaduan—thriving, rustic market places populated by hearty yeomen, honest and good of cheer. Perhaps a refrigerated box would be found residing in the shade of a cashew nut tree at the center of one of these Elysian hamlets, its contents of chilled San Miguels to be served by rosy-cheeked wenches dispatched to welcome the weary traveler off his trail? I kept to a rough southeasterly compass bearing, and cursed my imagination and its dangerously deluded fantasies. For a start, Palawan was in the midst of a terrible drought. Tall grasses collapsed, tired and brown. Bundok after bundok I trudged, thankful for my wide-brimmed hat for shade. My eyes were narrowed slits, guarding against the light and heat that shimmered up in visible waves from the road's white surface. My water bottle was almost empty, and I hadn't brought along any food, as usual. By 4:00 p.m., I was staggering like a zombie, sustained by the occasional cooling gust from the distant coast. In its final lucid moments, my brain directed me to double down on my bet, cut through the undergrowth, and clamber down the cliffs to the sea. I came out on a smoothed white sand beach, upon which stood a single, driftwood hut.

"Masaduan?" I asked its initially startled inhabitant, getting my hopes up. It would seem I'd overshot the place by a mile.

"I am Sebastian Gulay," the middle-aged occupant introduced himself. Confident, compact, quite bald, "I am with the Philippines Planters Association." And, it transpired, the Jehovah's Witnesses, too: selling seeds and saving souls, door-to-door.

"I have no hair, but my wife is young," laughed Sebastian as I accompanied him on his rounds. He was heading toward Masaduan, anyway, the settlement a veritable metropolis comprising ten stilt huts, half of these teetering on spindly legs out in the estuary.

"There will be some boats going to Baheli tomorrow morning, and from there the bus to Princesa is quick. But first you must join my friends and me. We are going fishing," said Sebastian, exploding again with laughter. Entertainment options being limited, I hesitantly accepted his invitation. You never knew when a good picture would present itself. Sebastian rowed me out to a deserted fishing hut.

"You can stay here tonight. We will come in the boat at sunset to collect you." He left me some *lato*—dried seaweed—and a half-filled bottle of water. "Don't worry, it is not drugged. This is not Manila!" His laughter followed the receding tide out across the bay.

'Saving Face', 'Asian Family Values'—call it what you will—etiquette matters in the East; never a move, sigh or gesture is missed. Ever. Sebastian, for example, would consider it rude and a sign of my distrust—worse, following his specific assurance that I was safe there, a personal insult—were I to have taken my luggage with me on the fishing expedition in order to keep an eye on it. The alternative was to blindly trust my new acquaintance, go fishing with him and his pals, and leave all my possessions behind, free to be pilfered. Nobody knew where I was, after all. Not that I could tell you where 'here' was if you tied me to a pole and stuck a last cigarette in my mouth. There was vulnerable, and then there was stupid, and as I sat dangling my feet over the waves, chewing on a sheet of crisp *lato* waiting for my Fate to turn up in an outrigger canoe, I began to worry I may have strayed across the border into gullible.

Then I realized the solution to this social dilemma was actually hanging on me. I quickly transferred all the valuables from my backpack into the numerous pockets of my camera vest. Never underestimate how much stuff can be dispensed of in this way. The garment was a wearable bag. I plumped up the dirty laundry inside my backpack, leaving it in plain view on the verandah, thus saving my own face, and Sebastian's, with his friends. Later, as the boat pulled to, Sebastian grinned. I jumped aboard and the captain opened up the engine. We slapped across jagged little waves out into the gulf.

"What exactly are we fishing for, Sebastian," I shouted through cupped hands. Twin paraffin lamps in the center of the boat cast our shadows outwards, like the menacing rays of a black star. "Squid?" I'd heard they were attracted to bright lights.

"You will see soon. Is your camera ready?" Not for the first time, I wished I could afford a flash unit. Suddenly the helmsman swung us in a tight U-turn and killed the engine. Two of the fishermen reached into a box in the bilge, bringing out taped sticks of dynamite. Touching the fuses to the flame in the oil lamps, they lobbed their grenades as far as possible from the boat. A moment later synchronized explosions erupted, one on either side of the vessel, forcing the sea upward in great fountains. Silvery fish rained down on the narrow deck and floated belly-up on the surface of the water. Sebastian burst out laughing at my startled—and somewhat dampened—appearance, and insisted on a repeat performance so I could get my exposure right this time. Our gunwale forced to the waterline with the weight of the catch, we made it back to my hut, grilled fish speared on twigs over an open fire on the verandah, and passed around a bottle of Tanduay Rum.

"You see, Sir Chris? This is not like Manila, at all!"

Manila

May 1, 1990

I AWOKE SCRATCHING at an angry welt of red sores around my torso. Prickly heat? Mosquitoes? Bed bugs?

"There you are," Carl, dressed and ready for action in his photographer's uniform, accosted me before I'd had time for coffee. "I told you something would be happening today. Go get your camera and come with me!"

I got it, and on the way found out where we were going and getting to, and why. Rizal Park: Labor Day rally; fun and games.

May 1. May Day. Two Filipinos meeting is a reunion; three makes it a festival. Thousands had gathered in Rizal Park, ice cream and balloon vendors pushing their carts around the outskirts of a huge congregation of union workers and their families. I chatted to some of these, who were eager to tell me of their campaign for an increased minimum wage (they wanted a 17-peso raise from the current 89 pesos per day).

On the fringes, gathering in mobs—no more than a petrol bomb's throw from the heavily guarded US Embassy—gangs of younger, more militant activists squatted, holding banners demanding "US BASES OUT!"

"See? Those are the guys to watch," Carl advised, and he introduced me to Edwin Tuyay, one of the most prolific of *Asiaweek's* photographers. I remembered having seen his spread on last December's coup attempt here. They dashed off to greet some other photographers, over from Hong Kong: every violent demonstration for them was a family gathering. They stuck together, shooting as a pack, too. Safety in numbers, for sure, but all their pictures would end up looking the same (though that was mainly my resentment speaking, not having a cushy full-time position like theirs). That was the advantage of working for a news outlet. You were guaranteed to make a sale, no matter what you shot; more importantly, you could keep an eye on the competition. I scanned the crowds. The local Filipino newspaper photographers didn't seem interested in the demands of the working-class masses: no, they were all up on stage, waiting to shoot each new speaker as they stepped up to the microphone. I, alone, was lost in the freelance mire. I couldn't compete with Carl and the others, who'd be wiring their shots from their news agency offices by midnight for tomorrow's papers, or couriering their films out to Hong Kong (the colony being a hub for such publications as *Time* and *Newsweek*, both with fully functioning bureaus there — and regional newsweeklies, like *Asiaweek*, the *Far Eastern Economic Review*, and many others) this evening.

The crowds cheered and waved their flags wherever I pointed my camera, and deafening roars exploded at the conclusion of each stirring speech. Mingling with notebook and pencil, I asked questions, since I'd no particular deadline to meet or quota to fill. It seemed the polite thing to do. After all, it wasn't *that* long ago I had been riding through English winter storms for Mercury Couriers making decidedly less than minimum wage as a motorcycle messenger. But I was careful not to take sides. I did the same with the police, too. They were from the Western

District division, and were leaning casually on their riot shields. Many were happy to joke, chat and pose for a shot. By 4:30 p.m., just as the temperature became bearable and the light was getting soft, the masses began to trickle away. Typical. I realized the mission of news photography was to capture the moment, but I wanted to go one step further and immortalize that moment in interesting light. As a freelancer, and to satisfy my own personal sense of esthetics, it was imperative to strive for that golden marriage between action and art.

And then things started to boil. Riot police edged in from Roxas Boulevard and the US Embassy. The militant crowd, far from packing up their banners and going home, started pulling sticks and bricks out of their backpacks, and setting fire to rough cardboard effigies of Uncle Sam and President Cory Aquino of the Philippines. The irony—that many of these virulently anti-American militants were dressed in NY Yankees baseball caps and Levi's jeans—was lost as the scrum of newspaper photographers, suddenly energized, dashed down from the stage, every man for himself. There was a lot of pushing and shoving going on, and I noticed Carl working with two camera bodies, a 24mm lens on one, and 85mm on the other. Up this close, though, only the wide angle was really useful, and he swapped lenses fluently when the first camera body ran out of film, like a soldier exchanging magazines when out of ammo.

Note to self: I really have to get a second camera body.

The local police, who had told me they weren't allowed to carry guns in their holsters 'in case of mistakes during public disturbances' had quietly been reinforced by hundreds of elite balaclava-wearing special forces, who had no such reservations. Clad in black riot gear, with bulletproof vests and gas masks, they wielded four-foot-long batons, were loaded with CS gas canisters, packed .45 automatics, and were backed up by rows of

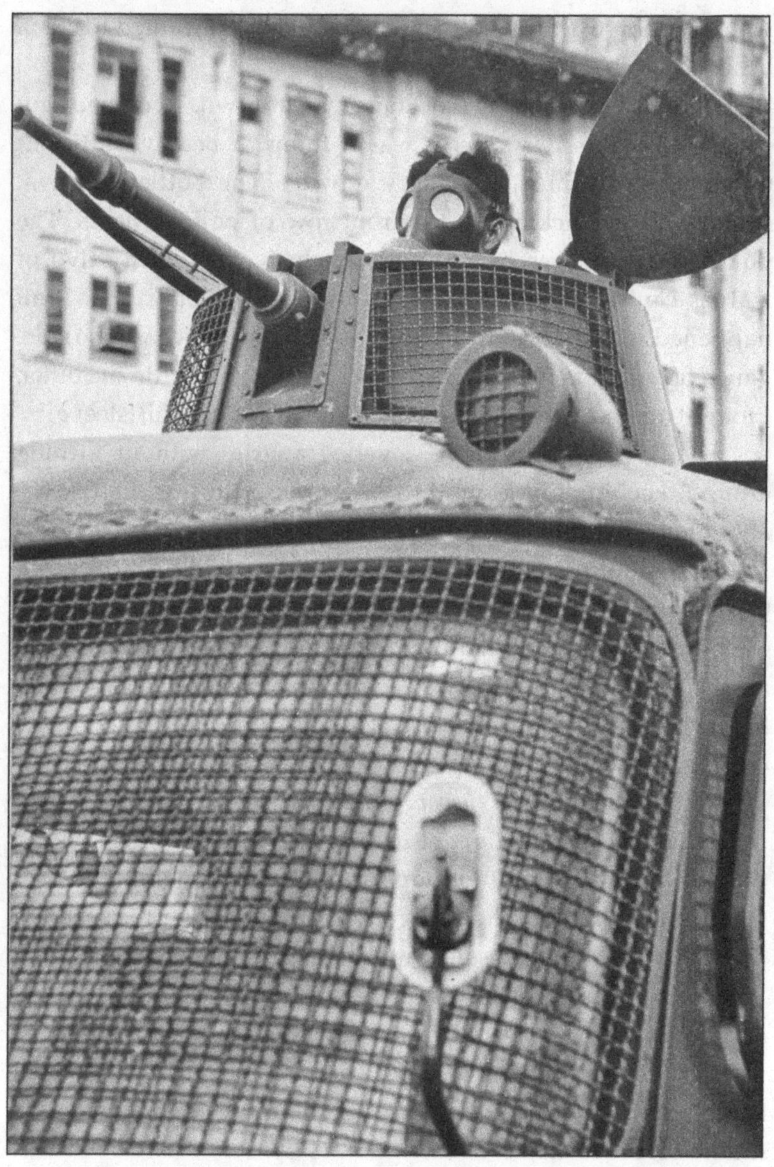

Riot police in water cannon vehicle during violent protest. Manila, Philippines — May 1, 1990.
Photo: Chris Stowers/PANOS

water cannon trucks. And they looked like they wanted to crack heads.

Suddenly a Molotov cocktail was thrown. I craned my neck to trace its fiery arc; it was a thing of beauty, sufficient to momentarily hush the angry crowds. The bottle smashed, sending flames licking up the front row of police shields. The police response was instant and conclusive: a return salvo of teargas canisters, fired back over my head in retaliation. It all happened so fast. I was in a great position: the police on one side, gangs of agitators with scarves covering their faces, on the other. I fought against someone tugging violently at my shirtsleeve.

"Fuck off, I'm working!" I yelled angrily without turning around, keeping my ground, trying to wrench free. Battle was about to commence.

"Get out of there, you idiot. You'll be crushed!" I recognized Carls' smoky baritone, edged with irritation.

"Jesus," he yanked hard and I fell back in his direction, just as the opposing front ranks closed and clashed; sticks upon helmets, bricks onto heads, teargas shots dropping right into the crowds, water jets erupting.

See?" yelled Carl, "*never* get in between the police and protesters like that again, got it? Not if you want to live." With that, he climbed swiftly on top of a bus shelter, joining two or three other photographers already there, shooting the ensuing melee from the relative safety of a vantage point.

I made it back to the Malate Pensione by 9:00 p.m., dazed and dejected. Along Del Pilar Street, it was all sex and supper as usual, no indication that a major battle was being fought just a few blocks away. The guesthouse restaurant was closed already; *still* no bloody coffee.

I had no chance to see Carl before leaving the Malate Pensione the following morning. Instead, I slipped a note under his door, apologizing for having sworn at him during the riot. I felt sure he'd understand. I spent the four days after that in Cebu, a big island, and as such, just another landmass. Things became more memorable after I boarded a ferry to tiny Bohol, the island famed for its 'Chocolate Hills' — dome-shaped limestone hillocks covered in scorched grass like the burial mounds of some ancient race of Goliaths — and for the opportunity to explore pristine coral. Only on small islands can you still pretend to be a castaway.

Food continued to be a disappointment in the Philippines. This was odd, considering its fertile volcanic soil — where you could drop a 10 peso note in reasonable expectation of a money tree sprouting on the spot — and considering the abundance of seafood, just waiting to be plucked (or dynamited) from the surrounding oceans, and where all manner of exotic fruits and vegetables abounded. Instead, the choice at Fred's Fud Hauz was always the same: fried chicken and rice, fried pork and rice, or *tapsilog* for breakfast: fried beef, with egg and rice.

On my final morning away from the capital, I rose, as usual, at 5:30 a.m. with the sun. Pulling my camera jacket over my naked torso, I waded along the placid shoreline in search of breakfast. It was not a long beach, perhaps half a mile: Bohol Dive Club was situated at one end, and Alonaville Dive Center at the other. A couple of bloated old Germans were up and about already, accompanied by their tiny Filipina girlfriends. The couples were opposites in every way, except perhaps in sharing a desire to escape the mundane reality of their existences.

Having arrived back to the Malate Pensione late the night before from Cebu, I was slightly perturbed by the knock on my door, waking me early and, before caffeine, befuddled.

"Phone call, Sir."

A call? For me? I didn't know anyone there. I reasoned it must be for Carl. After all, we did look similar: tall, camera vest, three day's stubble. I stumbled downstairs to the lobby.

"This is Chris, are you looking for Carl?" The receiver wedged between my jaw and shoulder, I leaned into the doorframe, yawning.

"This *is* Carl, man. Listen, I'm at the Convention Center for a press conference. They won't let me in wearing a t-shirt. Get here as quick as you can with a shirt, take a taxi, I'll pay." I rushed out onto Adriatico Street and flagged down a cab.

"Terrible news, Sir, last night." Why do all taxi drivers feel the need to talk?

"Huh?"

"In Angeles, Sir. Those poor GI's." It appeared the New People's Army — communist rebels — had executed two American servicemen at the entrance to Clark Air Base in the night. A planned provocation on the eve of talks about the extension of the lease on US bases in the Philippines, which was due to expire in September of the following year.

The driver screeched to a halt at the base of the long ramp leading up to the Convention Center. My fake press card got me past security. Carl beamed when he spotted me across the concourse.

"You got here fast. Good. Here, give me your shirt." He eyed my cotton drill trousers. "This is Jan." I shook hands with Carl's comrade journalist.

"Jan works for Dutch radio. Be a good fellow and give him your trousers, will you? They won't allow in anyone wearing jeans."

I began my striptease in the corner of the lobby, Carl and Jan shielding me from public scrutiny. Now, here in the tropics, I opted to go what Yankees call 'commando'. Luckily, my shirttails extended just far enough to save embarrassment and arrest for public exposure. Jan handed me his jeans in exchange for my chinos. They were a perfect fit.

Rushing off to catch the press conference, Carl shouted back over his shoulder:

"Rizal Park tonight, alright? Another demo."

I bumped into Carl at 3:30 p.m., across from the US Embassy. He was acting sour and melancholy, both at the same time, having missed the chance to photograph a clash outside the Central Bank earlier due to being preoccupied with an attractive female friend of his. They had been in a café on Del Pilar discussing the joys and pitfalls of relationships. Carl really does have a colorful background of this sort. He should write a book.

I had made sure to stuff my pockets with fresh slide films (I was down to my final four rolls now, out of thirty-six for the entire trip). I even remembered to bring along my Walkman. Choosing a sound track for a riot is almost as important as the selection of camera film. There are some situations — very few, I'll admit — that the Bee Gees don't have covered: civil disturbance being a glaring omission in their playlist (well, at least on the *Saturday Night Fever* album, the only one I had with me). I chose an alternate C90 cassette, and made sure the batteries in the player were new.

There must have been five hundred riot police out, far more than for the Labor Day rally. And they were not as keen on me taking their photos this time, either. I wandered off in the direction of Rizal Park.

"Sir Chris?" a voice hailed me from the lengthening shadows. "It is me, Doddy." I remembered the name; but his face had been obscured by a scarf when I'd interviewed him on Labor

Day. Doddy was here with his fellow workers from the nearby Bayview Prince Hotel.

"I am better prepared this time," he smiled, pulling a gas mask half way out of his backpack for me to see. His colleagues held big square signs printed with a litany of demands, covering all their bases, as it were:

	to AIDS
NO	to NUKES
	to BASES

Polite clapping was reserved for a pair of guest speakers: an Australian who droned on about campaigning for Aboriginal Rights, and an American who told, stutteringly, of his (surely unsuccessful) efforts to eject US bases from Hawaii. Things only started to come alive when local firebrand speakers came up on stage, getting the blood boiling in Tagalog.

At 5:30 p.m. — sunset — the Chief of Police announced through a megaphone, "You must disperse in ten minutes. Go home in ten minutes!"

Ten minutes came and went. Activists and police faced off, each daring the other to blink first. The Chief came on again, his megaphone screeching, "We give you four minutes to disperse!"

A combative victory cheer rose from the student protesters, who had no intention of moving, and taunted the authorities by parading a model of Uncle Sam astride a tin foil nuclear missile. I had a fresh 400 ASA film loaded, and pushed this to 800 as the light decreased. It was good enough for now; I could still shoot f/4 at 1/250th sec. shutter speed. But with each passing minute, my options diminished by a stop. Soon my lens would be at maximum aperture, and I'd need the support of a lamppost to get a steady shot. 'Hail Mary' territory: it being a miracle if anything turned out focused or correctly exposed.

Militant students in the front ranks were readying for a violent encounter. Quite a number of photographers had come prepared for the same eventuality, towels tied over their faces and readying swimming goggles. One chap had a high-tech gas mask and helmet. "He's just come back from Korea, they do really serious riots over there," mentioned Carl, enviously.

The Mayor of Manila, Mel Lopez, was called in for some last-minute mediation, attempting to prevent a televised bloodbath. The Press, as a body, I sensed were greatly looking forward to one. I hoped I'd never become so jaded. In the end, violence was avoided; Uncle Sam burned on his ICBM and the crowds dispersed noisily down UN Avenue, under close scrutiny of the police.

I was rather disappointed I didn't get the opportunity to check out my riot soundtrack: *Joy Division*. The descending crescendo of drumbeats on their track "Twenty-Four Hours" perfectly simulated a salvo of teargas canisters raining down. Carl dashed off to savor the authentic delights of Raymonds Bar, whilst I joined a bunch of other photographers heading to the Hobbit House. Established in 1973 by former Peace Corps volunteer Jim Turner, the bar employed only dwarves—commonly shunned in the Philippines as evil spirits—providing steady employment for generations of 'little people' who often came from the slum settlements of the capital. Later, we all joined up again at The Right Spot. This bar was *the* journalist's hangout, a café owned by Australian expat Richard. Business was booming, given the gathering of the Press Clan and their expense accounts. "This is nothing.... you should have been here during People Power, it was *insane!*" he said, referring to the popular revolt of February 1986—also known as the EDSA Revolution—that led to the ousting of President Marcos.

The following day, ramped up on strong coffee and spirited along by ibuprofen, I discovered I had run out of camera film. It was with reluctance I dragged myself away from Manila to fly back to Hong Kong. Some places just grow on you; the people you meet there more so. In the Philippines, I believe this had something to do with a common and shared sense of fatalistic humor and appreciation of irony. Invisible bonds, unforced, bind us closer.

HONG KONG
May 18, 1990

THE LETTER SAT **alone in my post office box:**

Dear Chris, I had hoped you would come here, but guess you can't act so impulsively — you have to work and plan things a little harder, I understand — but I really wanted to be with you around here.

I see many travelers and people but I have not met someone who feels as special as you, and most English people here seem to have no soul. You are really different.

I wish my English was better and I could write more like an adult and less like a child. Traveling is so hard emotionally — because you see and absorb so much and there is no way to let that all out.

I feel drained and lonely — I find all these Anglo people so uniform and ignorant about ethnic cultures. You are so much more sensitive and you are so beautiful, too — I remember your feet so well, I remember your smile, and your voice.

I wonder why I feel fear and sadness all over? Have a mango for me, and think of me kissing you — Layla

No one had ever admired my feet before (or, at least, admitted to it). I re-read her letter and hoped she would come back soon.

I jumped off the tram in Causeway Bay, pushed through the crowds, climbed four floors up the staircase of a regular apartment building above a mahjong parlor and a fashion store, and was soon back at Victory, into the thick of proofreading "Reliability in comparative & ethnographic observations: the example of high inference father-child interation measures". Was 'interation' even a word? This, followed by a philosophical discourse titled "Towards a post-modern Hermeneutic ontology of art: Nietzschean style and Heideggerian truth" had me considering the possibility of hanging myself with my paisley tie, but I ended up just reaching for the Nescafé and aspirin an hour earlier than usual.

Nietzsche's take on this, of course, was far more succinct— "We have art lest we perish of the truth." And, were he alive today, I'm sure he would add, "and academia to use ten words in place of one".

❧

I'd been putting off calling Derek, the *Pacific Traveller* editor. While my Philippines shots had turned out pretty well, I had failed to shoot any 'festivals'. I'd been diverted by the adrenaline rush of news events. The Palawan slides looked lovely, though, and gave me the confidence to ring up.

"Ahh, Chris. Yes. Listen, sorry to disappoint, but the sponsors haven't come through for the Philippines supplement, so we can't run any of your stories at the moment. Would you mind coming into the office later to pick up your Kalimantan slides?"

Shit. It looked like I'd be stuck teaching for a while longer. I'd exhausted my savings on the Philippines trip, too. I could probably sell a few individual stories to other magazines and slowly recoup my losses. Over time, everything balances out. Still, Derek sounded upbeat enough.

The aroma of roasting coffee wafted from the Greco-Egyptian Coffee Co. and helped pull me up the steep incline of Old Bailey Street, from Hollywood Road. The *Pacific Traveller* office sat above it, overlooking the prison attached to Central Police Station. Derek was in.

"Take a seat. I'd like to have a word with you." He assumed a confidential tone.

Uh-oh, what have I done wrong now?

"We're going to be taking on a few new titles, one of them an inflight mag. Plus PT is going monthly soon." This translated to demand. "I'll be looking for five stories for each title, every month." I made the appropriate noises, those of congratulations followed by an expression of concern at how much extra work would soon be piling up on his desk. I decided that, since he held all the cards, I'd let Derek deal the next hand.

"I was impressed by the way you put the Kalimantan story together, fleshing it out with details from your diary of the time. And you seemed to know what format I wanted, without me having to coach you." I basked warily in these compliments.

"I want to assemble a core group of about six regular contributors. Are you interested?" as if reading my mind, he continued, "It'll be good experience for you, to hone your skills." Funny how things come together; he even pointed out how my proofreading had played a part in his decision to ask me.

"Yes," I said. Of course.

SHOOT, ASK ... AND RUN!

June 3, 1990

TODAY WAS THE **first anniversary** of the Tiananmen Square massacre. Seemingly the whole of Hong Kong was out on the streets. A veritable who's who of the news-photo community assembled in camaraderie and eager anticipation of making sales, the rally being a prime contender for the front pages of newspapers around the world. Carl was easy enough to spot, his head passing above the general crowd, his Cambodian scarf tugging red and white in the breeze. He was chatting to Andy Hernandez, the *Newsweek* contract photographer. Filipino Andy, whose coverage of the Benigno Aquino assassination in 1983 and overthrow of Marcos had helped launch his career, was on a roll: he had actually been in Beijing last year. This was a particularly meaningful assignment for him.

In the midst of this turbulent sea of around 200,000 marching, chanting souls, I was not completely surprised to bump into Siao, the former Wuhan University student. I'd telephoned Sam Ho earlier, who had confirmed he and Siao would be attending, though precisely where we'd meet had been left frustratingly vague. I'd just assumed we'd bump into each other. Trusted, Fate tends to lead you to your destination: forced, it always leads you astray. Siao recognized me with a smile; he had a bandana tied around his head, and was carrying a huge banner. He raised this, and I took a shot of him in the middle of the Queensway, demonstrators filing by on either side. This time, instead of heading for Victoria Park, the procession looped up and around the racecourse in Happy Valley, before culminating outside the heavily barricaded offices of Xinhua News Agency, the official Beijing propaganda outfit in Hong Kong.

I spotted Hong Kong photographer Leong Ka-tai, owner of the Group Photo agency, and his manager Becky in the crowds. Ka-tai, low key and low of voice, visually resembled the Dalai Lama more and more each time I came across him. Like The Mouse back in Peshawar, he favored the stealth approach to photography, always carrying a tiny Leica rangefinder, as compared to the usual bulky Nikon and Canon SLRs favored by the press mob.

"It's all a bit tame, compared to the petrol bombs and teargas of Manila," I commented, having to shout to make myself heard against the ritualistic and repetitive demands being chanted by the crowd.

Becky nodded, explaining, "You know the Chinese language — important things you have to say three times."

After the march, a bunch of us headed back to Central to wind down with drinks at Club 64, in Lan Kwai Fong. Becky knew its owner Grace well, so we had good seats (the bar's name was a none-too-veiled reference to the June 4 date of Tiananmen massacre. It was popular with the media crowd and subsequently became Club 71, alluding to the July 1, 1997, Handover date).

Since I read it every day, I decided to pop in to the offices of the *South China Morning Post* in Quarry Bay, and strong-arm any likely looking editor I could find in the place. Armed with my portfolio, and sheets of Philippines slides, I lingered at reception like a malevolent spirit until eventually being shuttled to the desk of Nancy Wong, who edited the weekly *TV Times* supplement. By chance, Nancy was looking for a short destination piece to fill her travel section. She seemed to think my Palawan piece would do nicely and offered me £100 for it. I desperately needed funds to increase my range of camera equipment, so I accepted. And it was a foot in the door.

"Have you got anything on China?" she asked as I was readying to leave. All the magazine editors I'd contacted recently had made the same request. They were desperate. It looked like I would have to make a trip across the border.

Later, Sam Ho called, catching me at Lucky's. He asked me for a copy of the picture I'd taken of Siao. I owed it to Siao, he was a good kid, just trying to make his way in the world.

I handed in my notice as proofreader at Victory, effective that day. I couldn't see National Geographic's Steve McCurry moonlighting as a copy editor, and it was impossible to imagine Magnum's Henri Cartier-Bresson ever waiting tables. No, it was obvious that I'd have to sever the umbilical to my day jobs. Only that way, by taking photography seriously, would I force myself into a corner. There was nothing halfway about it. There was nothing halfway about the HK$2,680, secondhand, 35mm f1.4 Nikkor lens I bought at *Photo-Scientific* on the way home to celebrate this decision, either. It left my bank account flat-lining.

"Nice," admired Hendrick, fitting my latest acquisition onto his Nikon FE and lining up a few shots, "real shallow depth of field". Hendrick was a lanky Dutch photographer with a ponytail and a distinctive nose he used to sniff out trouble and beautiful models for his fashion shoots—often they came as a package. He had been living at Lucky's for a few weeks now. The Dutch were a race to whom God had been particularly generous, I felt, bestowing upon them not only aptitude and attitude, but *altitude*: the only Europeans that I, at six feet, two inches, was compelled to look up to.

Hendrick had been in Beijing the previous summer, too, shacked up in a hotel in risky liaison with a Mainland Chinese housewife as gunshots echoed and tanks rolled in the streets outside (luckily for him, and even more-so the girl, the authorities had been distracted by events far more immediate than their philandering, at the time).

"It will be tough, letting go of the regular income, Chris," Hendrick, five years my senior, counselled, "but only by letting go can you move ahead. Believe me, I've been there. What possible alternative do you have? To proofread the words of others? To teach English to those who will go on to leave you behind? What price can you put on your life? The way I see it, you have no option. You are a photographer. If you don't grasp the opportunity now, you'll live always in regret."

"But what if I'm no good? It's all such a matter of chance, being in the right place at the right time. It's not really a stable basis for a career, is it? What if I'm denying my inner, I don't know… my inner accountant?"

"The ability to photograph isn't really a thing that can be taught. It's something you feel by instinct; it's closer to acting or singing than bookkeeping. It's a sensitivity to light."

Answering the communal phone at the guesthouse was always a bit of a lucky draw. Back when I first lived in Hong Kong, in 1987, I'd picked up the ringing receiver and, having informed the caller that the person they were searching for was out busking on a unicycle at the Star Ferry terminal, had been cast in his place as the lead role in a Vietnam War movie, being filmed for cheap out in the New Territories. This morning the call actually was for me. It was Wendy:

"I am acting in a play tonight, can you come? I will tell them to let you in for free." Community theater was not really my thing, but Wendy definitely was, so I felt unable to refuse. Her company, the HK Repertory Theatre, was performing a local play, *72 Tenants*, out at the distant Sai Wan Ho Civic Center. I sat on the top deck of the tram for half an hour, my gaze lost down the bustling side street markets, filled with people who, having first tried at the incense-infused temples, now attempted to banish evil spirits here with a clashing combination of commerce, neon and noise.

Wendy was co-starring in the comedy-drama production. She played a widow (or a distraught mother, I couldn't quite tell; it was all in Cantonese, and she was bathed in heavy greasepaint). Hers was easily the most convincing and professional performance of the entire, extensive cast.

"Really? Do you think so?!" She glowed in my praise afterwards, and grasped my hand, warmly. Then one of her fellow thespians, Calvin, appeared in the doorway and she instantly released her grip. Damn all this Asian propriety, it's positively Victorian: all you encountered were bar girls, or virgin brides. Where were all the happily liberated in-betweens?

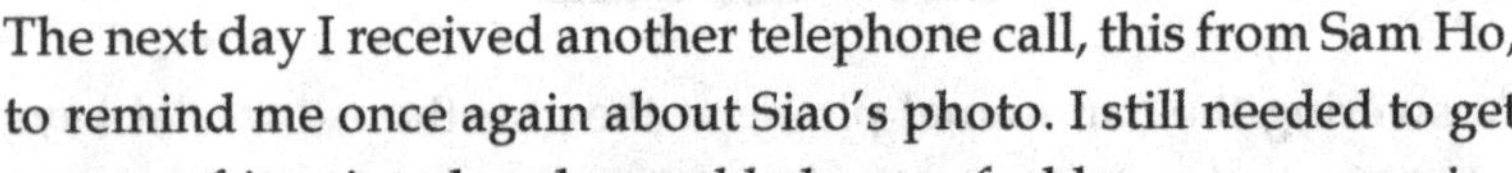

The next day I received another telephone call, this from Sam Ho, to remind me once again about Siao's photo. I still needed to get a copy of it printed and mumbled some feeble excuse, covering my natural procrastination.

"Have you heard?" Sam added, all intrigue, "the Hong Kong government are going to charge five pro-democracy leaders here for unlawful use of loudspeakers." That woke me up. I couldn't believe it. The HK Government equals Britain. We'd never lick the Chinese jackboot. Surely not?

"Siao wants to meet soon. He's scared he'll be sent back to China if he stays here much longer. The Taiwanese are taking too long to process his request. He's thinking of jumping ship to

America," revealed the pro-democracy activist.

I agreed to meet with Siao at the Cenotaph on Monday.

"I can't be there, though," said Sam. Was he washing his hands of the whole affair?

At midday, Layla walked in to the guesthouse, no advance warning. I feared she must have gone cold on me during her time on the Mainland and that any feelings she'd had for me failed to make it back across the border with her. There's an emotional peak in everyone's soul. Perhaps Layla's heart had grown fonder climbing it? Or had it descended the slopes of disillusion on the far side? I should have shown more passion and followed her to Guilin…

"Chris …" she sighed. And her sigh was a reprieve. All the old feelings came flooding back. I stepped towards her and she ran and jumped into my arms.

"I was afraid I'd never see you again," I mumbled into the thickness of her hair, choking up, about to start crying, too.

At sunset we took the ferry out to Lantau. Skyscrapers began melting into the inky-blue waters of Victoria Harbour, pushed beneath the weight of the sun's swollen red fist. We sat down on the throbbing lower deck listening to Sade sing "Smooth Operator" on my Walkman, one earpiece each; our heads together, hair entwined. A fine sea spray disturbed by the passing hydrofoils and hovercraft coated us, like evening dew.

"At moments like this I wish the world would end," she said, "wrapped in memories and sensations," and we'd cuddled up even tighter.

I recognized a couple of the Flagstaff regulars as we were alighting, and we followed them into the pub. Jasmine taxied over from Pui-O specially to meet me, excited about her book project, and still wanting me to shoot various mood scenes for it. I grabbed the bull by the horns.

"This is Layla."

"Ah, Christopher's mystery Lady," Jasmine purred, and I could tell Layla had picked up the faintest *frisson*, informing her that Miss Jones was more than a casual acquaintance: women are highly evolved in that way — like those snakes and toads that are able to sense earthquakes days before they occur. To my immense relief, she and Layla hit it off. In fact, they shared a lot in common, and their discussion soon took a sharp turn into feminism that left me nursing my Lowenbrau in exclusion. I was saved when Colin and Mo showed up, like the cavalry.

"She's very nice," smiled Mo, "was beginning to think you preferred men."

"Who was, you?" my face burned.

"No, Jasmine. She seems to approve of this one, though."

And on the late ferry back to Central, Layla snuggled up close:

"We should find a place to be together, some place private."

Afterwards, strands of Layla's hair sticking to my flank, her hot breath on my chest, she told me she was leaving for Thailand the following week.

"I don't expect you will come to find me ..." she left the invitation open.

Was I doing something wrong? I'd never yet had a relationship survive the introduction of sex. Leading such an unpredictable life, it was perhaps inevitable: relationships became just another element of adventure. They built to a climax, and then the characters moved on to populate a new story.

———— ∿ ————

I was enjoying teaching more now I knew I'd soon be quitting. During our hour-long session I asked Wendy to write down my interview questions for Siao, in Chinese. Later that afternoon I set off with my camera, notebook and Hendrick's cassette recorder — minus the trench coat and felt fedora — feeling like a proper investigative reporter.

It was 4:30 p.m. and I spied on Siao using my longest lens (the 180mm) from the shadows of the Mandarin Hotel. He cut a lonely figure, lingering at the base of the Cenotaph. I came out into the light and walked up to him, getting pretty close before he turned. This was an exposed spot. We retired across the road to Statue Square and hid anonymously amid the bustling crowds. Once settled, he read carefully through my list of questions before committing himself to tape. He answered both lengthily and fluently. I'd been worried he was going to just give a brief 'yes' or 'no' to each question, but instead he let it all out, for half an hour, filling up one side of my TDK.

We shook hands goodbye. For him, these could be the last few weeks of relative tranquility, if he really was going to follow through with his plan to stowaway to the States. And I was off to China in the morning with my new lens and thirty-six rolls of slide film, a big investment. I almost forgot: "Siao!" I shouted. His retreating figure hesitated halfway across the square, worried perhaps that the game was up, that this had all been some elaborate sting. He turned slowly.

"*Ni de zhaopian.*" I closed the gap and handed him the photograph I'd taken of him at the rally.

Since there was no safe storage place for it at Lucky's, and I was not going to take the cassette tape with me to China and risk Siao's incriminating confession falling into communist hands, I decided to seal it in a self-addressed envelope, and left it inside my post office box instead.

SOUTH CHINA
July 7, 1990

TIME IS A deception. Half an hour earlier, I'd stepped off the No. 164 Guangzhou Express in Kunming, deafened by pre-dawn stillness having spent the previous fifty-four hours from Guangzhou in the clattering train's 'hard seat' class. Thirty minutes later, all my wealth — in true Marxist fashion — had been stealthily redistributed, and I was facing the 1,500-mile-long slog back to Hong Kong.

It happened something like this. Alighting the train, hungry, I'd crossed the vacant square in front of the railway station to where old ladies wearing white caps and cotton facemasks were mass-producing worker's breakfasts of congee, fried dough sticks and warm soya milk in steaming vats. I set about photographing them before lowering myself into a seat — presumably one constructed for a small infant — to eat. My mind, relaxed for the first time in days, reveled at being back in the Chinese heartland again.

The Kunhu Hotel next door offered dormitory beds at an affordable 4 foreign exchange certificates (FECs) — less than a dollar a night. I signed in, leaving my pack resting against a pillar, just behind me. The sleepy receptionist took her own sweet time jotting down my particulars. When I turned, my backpack was gone. It wasn't so much the gaping void previously occupied by the bag that alerted me to mischief, but my hat—which I'd left on top of the bag—lying, incriminatingly, on the worn carpet. I glanced at the receptionist, she *must* have seen what was going on behind me, but received only her zombie gaze. Everything but the clothes I stood in and the passport fortunately in my hand at the time, was gone.

Items lost: my camera and all its lenses (including the beautiful new 35mm, purchased specifically for this trip); my flash unit, blanket from Peshawar, diary and address book, photos and mementos—all gone—even my Youth Hostel card (with its decade of painstakingly collected hostel stamps), and my chopsticks. What was left made a much shorter list: my passport, hat, compass, and the equivalent of RMB130 in Foreign Exchange Certificates (about £13). The train ticket back to Hong Kong, alone, cost 170 FECs. So, something was going to have to give; and it wasn't going to be me. I'd just 'given' plenty.

Roused to passion, I woke the hotel 'security' guard who tripped along, tucking his pajama top into his uniform trousers. He, in turn, raised the hotel's taxi driver and, along with two other hotel officials, we rushed off to the city's long-distance bus depot. It was the way a fevered mind focused in crisis, with pinpoint clarity, but all of those points out of order. I could only reason that if *I'd* stolen a backpack, I'd try to get as far away from the scene of the crime as possible.

It was a futile venture from the outset, expecting to locate one backpack, one guiltily sweating brow, among the hundreds of buses and thousands of dozing passengers, all heading out across Yunnan Province at this shadowy hour; and carrying with them how many tens of thousands of items of luggage? But defeat was not an option the Stowers blood would concede — not when some miserable, work-shy commie bastard was trying to make off with my single lens reflex.

I returned bagless to the Kunhu. The hotel's façade, now illuminated by optimistic morning sunlight, made me feel the opposite: deflated, and resigned to fate. Freed of the burden of possession, I was still a temporary hostage to bureaucracy. Without official Public Security Bureau confirmation of the theft, I was open to accusation of having sold my belongings for profit when exiting the country. The PSB staff were dressed in scruffy military-style uniforms, and annoyed at being disturbed from the routine counting-off of the hours of their day. This poisonous air of communal lethargy actually inspired a heady joy to surge through my body: the transformative realization that, having nothing left to lose, I was finally free — as they would never be.

Things had certainly changed since I was in China last. Maybe it was the reality of life in this post-Tiananmen era? People had become colder, mimicking the steely practicality of their government. Indifference reigned. Three years before, when I had last traveled here, theft from a foreigner would have been unthinkable. The black market was harder to find now, too, and the exchange rate, when I eventually tracked down a money changer, was a miserly 125 RMB for 100 FECs. I cashed all my remaining FECs into Renminbi, literally 'People's money'. Benefitting from the rate, I could now afford to purchase the following essentials with which to navigate my new life: paper and envelopes, a replacement diary, a knife/fork/spoon set with can opener gadget, nail clippers and enamel mug, a bar of soap and tube of toothpaste with brush, some 3-in-1 coffee sachets, 50 grams of loose tea (jasmine), a hand towel and, for transporting this bounty, a handsome brown leather satchel with one-eighth inch thick hide — 34 RMB from the No.2 Worker's

Safety Equipment Supply Store.

Back at Kunming railway station—surprising how small the formerly commanding edifice appeared now, in daylight—the train was already pointed back towards Guangzhou. Renamed the No.166 Kunming Express, the service was scheduled to depart at 1:00 p.m. Protected by a halo of self-righteous indignation, I marched right up to the ticket counter, and thrust the local Chinese fare of 73 RMB—all I had left—through the grill. In my pocket I rubbed my lucky bronze Buddha. I needed all the native luck the talisman could summon right now. It worked. Instead of insisting I pay the inflated foreigners' fee of FECs, the clerk didn't even look up as he slid my local-priced ticket beneath the grille. *There is such a thing as Karma. I'm sure of it now!*

The return journey to Guangzhou took even longer—fifty-six hours. I'd been wearing the same clothes since setting off from Hong Kong. One advantage of living in and breathing a continuous fug of cigarette smoke was that my senses were soon deadened to the sweet bouquet of body odor. The floor was thick with several days' accumulation of spit and fruit peelings, cigarette ash, sticky watermelon juice, rice and slops.

I was having fun, picking up a few words of Mandarin, playing cards and drinking tea with fellow passengers, who happily shared their slices of fruit, red-bean cakes, and endless cigarettes. I felt oddly accepted here, among these honest, working class folk. I felt as though I was some weird-looking, long-lost family member who had returned after a lifetime away, still familiar with the gestures of his clan, yet unable to recall any of the words of his childhood tongue.

With no camera to lose, I sat back, enjoying the passing scenery for what it was, rather than feeling compelled to distill and capture it on film. Perhaps it is impossible to record life and have a real experience at the same time. This state of mental relaxation brought on total recall of all the important names, addresses, postcodes and even telephone numbers from my stolen address book. I rapidly jotted these down before the mental portal slammed shut. Somewhere close to the Guangdong border new passengers boarded; their language was rapid fire and challenging, Cantonese being a dialect that achieves maximum efficiency in the shout.

A young man, his spectacles thick and with heavy, square frames, squeezed in between the wilting bodies slumped on the bench opposite me. He introduced himself as Jackson, said he was a middle school teacher, and knew some English, having spent two years at the Foreign Language Institute in Nanning. There, he'd been taught by Australians (and had obviously been influenced by them, pronouncing 'a' as 'i', in the Aussie manner). I was the first foreigner he'd encountered since leaving the institute the previous year. Since we were unlikely to be eavesdropped on by our slumbering fellow comrade peasant-workers, he let his guard down.

"You know, I support in some ways those who were protesting against the government." A cautious reference to the events of the previous June. "One thing they were asking for was to have a choice of jobs." This seemed a reasonable enough expectation. "At the moment, it all depends on what exam results you have. These dictate what university you are sent to. And what university you have been to dictates what job you are given."

"How long do you expect to teach at middle school?" I asked. He was only 22 years old.

"Maybe for all my life at this school," he replied, staring down at the floor.

Communism appeared to be a contract the State drew up with

the People when they were at a vulnerable low point. In China, it had succeeded in dragging the majority of them out of extreme poverty, but at usurious cost to their personal freedom. So many wasted lives. Jackson stared past me, bleakly, just at the start of his. Talking to Jackson at least helped add some perspective to my own present plight.

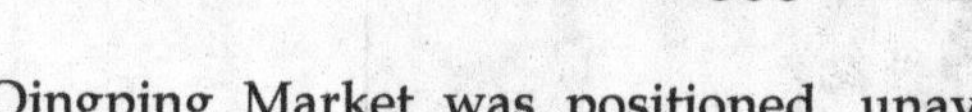

Qingping Market was positioned, unavoidably, between the youth hostel on Guangzhou's formerly elegant—and still tree-lined—foreign enclave, Shamian Island, and the minibus depot. Here chickens and ducks clucked and squabbled, tied by their ankles in feathery bundles, and tossed carelessly into bloody corner puddles. Shanks of goat and bellies of pigs hung dripping from myriad butcher's stalls. But it was the more exotic inventory that gave the place its reputation: rare animals cowering in filthy cages, like a nightmare zoo. All for the chop and the pot. Live turtles and toads, snakes pickled in alcohol, small deer, monkeys, giant dried centipedes, bats, seahorses and, worst of all, household pets, pleading with their eyes to be taken home; hopeful of reprieve, still trusting of evil humans, even at this late stage.

Out back, dogs were slowly tortured on hooks—the locals said this helped increase their production of adrenaline, keeping the meat fresh longer—and then drowned, sometimes still alive, in cauldrons of boiling water. That made it easier to peel off their pelts. I couldn't watch. My blood began to boil like the water in those bloody bowls. I felt an overpowering urge to liberate some of these poor animals. But how far would I get? The stall holders had dead, dark eyes and wielded viciously sharp chopping knives. They would misinterpret my rescue mission as the actions of a madman, one set on disrupting their

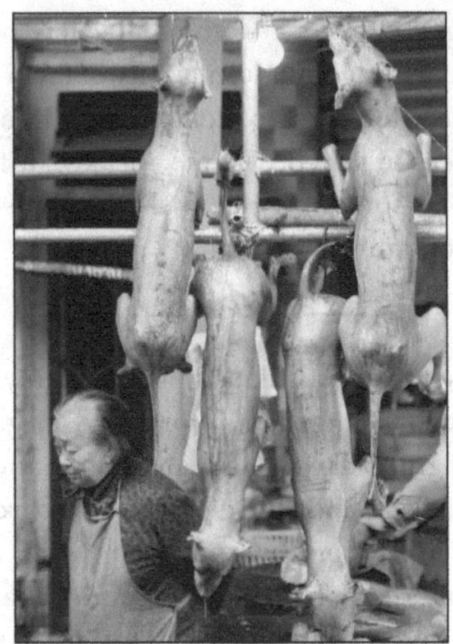

Dogs on hooks at a stall in Guangzhou's Qing Ping market,
photographed on a return trip to Guangdong province,
China — 1990. Photo: Chris Stowers/PANOS

business, impeding them — sin of sins — from making money. Our instincts were diametrically opposed: our sentiments mutually incomprehensible. I sensed the Chinese, unlike the Filipinos, did not do irony.

The only recourse left was to take photos and bear witness — and if my camera had not so recently been stolen, that's what I would have done. I resolved to return as soon as possible and put the record straight. *Two alien species inhabit this planet, and two alone: people who love dogs ... and those who eat them.*

On my last morning in China, I boarded the minibus from Guangzhou to Shenzhen. A ride by public transport tells you as much about a country as do its culinary habits — and Guangdong Province was as good as a country — the south of China being separated from the north by language, cuisine, business acumen and the Yangtse River. "Heaven is high and the Emperor is far away," as the Chinese saying goes.

The driver swerved his van viciously through oncoming traffic, accelerating and braking in erratic bursts. The peasant woman beside me, perhaps unused to motorized transport, called weakly to the driver, asking him to stop the vehicle. She scuttled out to throw up while the other passengers impatiently yelled at her:

"*Fai di-ah, fai di-aaah!*" Hurry up.

To the Cantonese, time equaled money. Business was their intrigue; profit the driving force. Beijing was, indeed, a long way off. Their reference point, instead, was freewheeling Hong Kong, just across the border. Chinese citizens required permits to enter the Special Economic Zone of Shenzhen, a dustbowl of ripped-up paddy fields, new warehouses and factories—already crumbling—where the residents of shanty villages survived by recycling plastic bottles, glass and cardboard beside rivers

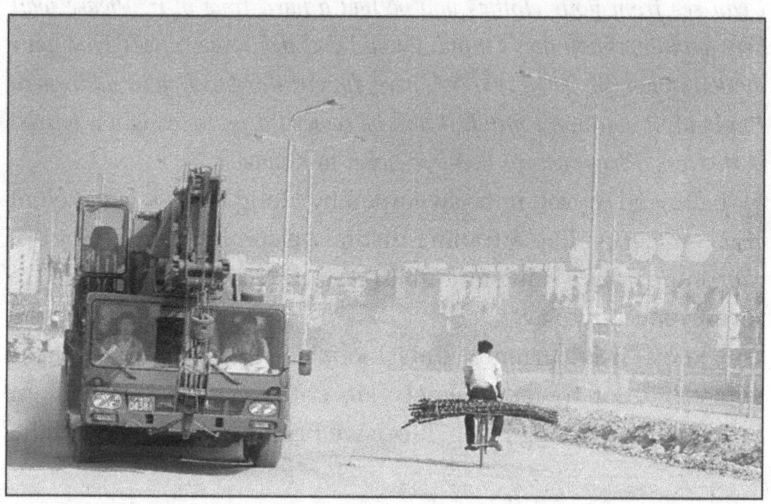

Shenzhen, China, in 1990 - shortly after my first visit – today a megacity of over 12 million inhabitants that overshadows neighboring Hong Kong. Photo: Chris Stowers/PANOS

frothing with raw chemical discharge. Was this to be the fate awaiting Hong Kong after 1997? Open the borders and let the masses flood in?

"Where is your camera?" the Chinese immigration official demanded, eyeing the customs declaration I'd made entering the country a week ago. I brought out the PSB theft report from Kunming. The official grunted. No degree of sympathy. What had I been expecting, *understanding?* Instead, he just waved me on in an arrogant, offhand manner. *Yeah, and have a nice day, too!* I walked the footbridge to freedom at Lo Wu, across a stinking canal, thinking of escaped student Siao and how he'd had to swim through *that!* And then signs began to appear, in both Chinese and English, proudly emphasizing the distinction between Us and Them:

'No smoking, no spitting'

"Hello, Sir. Welcome to Hong Kong. No money, Sir? Not a problem. I can see from your clothes you've had a hard time of it. Please wait here a while, if you don't mind. Would you like some coffee? Had your money stolen, Sir? Never mind, here, fill out this form, your address in England, if you don't mind, it will be easier for us to explain a tourist in distress. Please accept this free ticket to Kowloon."

I allowed myself to be swamped by Hong Kong's benevolent civic efficiency, like a trauma victim welcoming a huge shot of morphine. Make mine a double. We'll be handing it all over in seven years, anyway!

I know it is currently unfashionable—largely among those who have not traveled widely—to criticize the ingredients of Empire. But in Hong Kong, I feel, we British got the recipe right.

HONG KONG

July 13, 1990

I WAS BORN on a Friday the thirteenth. That superstitious date had always been lucky for me.

"Chris?" It was Derek from *Pacific Traveller* on the phone. "I would like you to photograph Hong Kong; we need pictures of everything. I'll pay for your films and processing and, of course, for all the photos we publish. Think of it as a *carte blanche*, a license to shoot."

My first ever photo assignment! Deciding, going forward, that honesty would be the most valuable policy, I accepted Derek's kind offer, and then told him I had no camera or lens with which to shoot. Derek, appreciating the irony, was full of sympathy and promised me an advance with which to replace the equipment stolen in Kunming.

Further Friday the thirteenth good fortune awaited at the post office. Two letters had arrived, both of them containing checks. One was from Cheney Communications in Singapore enclosing payment for two photo essays I'd left with them, half a year back. A picture from one of these pieces — featuring the Kuala Lumpur skyline — had made it to the front cover.

The second came along with a letter from my Mum—a check for £500! A belated tax rebate for the time I'd worked as a motorcycle dispatch rider, a lifetime ago.

The Universe strives for balance, and good luck will always follow bad. Sensing there was no time to waste, that the planets had aligned in my favor today, I took a leap of faith and called Winnie, the receptionist at the Hong Kong College of Language and Communications, and informed her of my decision to quit teaching. Photography was now my only path forward.

The next day I slid enthusiastically out of the guesthouse, down four floors of carpets that were in the process of being moved out of the fifth floor to the street, and were blocking up the entire staircase. Heading over to Central District, loaded with Derek's money, I luxuriously surveyed the many models on offer in the camera stores along Stanley Street, the island's main photography emporium, before downgrading my expectations a notch. Finally, I settled on a secondhand Nikon FM2 from Mr Poon, at *Photo-Scientific* (my first professional camera body) and, later, three used prime lenses from David Chan's, over in Champagne Court, an Aladdin's Cave of shops dealing in secondhand camera equipment just off Kimberley Road. These comprised the essential focal lengths: 24, 85 and 180mm. Oh, and a Domke bag in which to carry this bounty.

Change was in the air. Not only was John going to be moving out of the guesthouse to live on Lamma Island soon, but Hendrick was also talking of relocating to Lantau Island. Though it went against the nomadic grain, I realized I'd have to quit the guesthouse lifestyle, too, if I was serious about staying in Hong Kong for the long term.

Flicking through the *South China Morning Post* and wandering through Wanchai a few days later—I was at the junction of Johnston Road and Fenwick Street at the time, near the tramlines; a location I shall remember with the clarity some people reserve for lunar landings—my attention was caught by a headline:

Chinese Stowaway seeks new life in US
By GISELLE MILITANTE
A Chinese refugee who says he was a student
in the June 4 pro-democracy movement, stowed
away on a container ship to seek a new life
in the United States. Siao Guang Ming ...

I had in my possession a tape recording of—what could reasonably be assumed—the *only* interview carried out with Siao, just days prior to his departure. I rushed to a phone box and put a call through to the SCMP features department. My enthusiasm was dampened when the receptionist told me I'd need to call back tomorrow, after 4.00 p.m., and talk to News Editor Philip Crawley.

This twenty-four-hour reprieve turned out to be fortunate, however, as my suddenly newsworthy cassette tape needed to be translated back into English. I couldn't trust just anyone in this task. Automatically, I thought of Wendy. But her address and phone number had been among those lost in Kunming. Frantically, I scoured the Hong Kong telephone book for her number. Wong is just about the most common name in the Territory. There were dozens of Wendy Wongs and W. Wongs listed, and these I tried first. No luck. So, I resorted to calling all the plain Wongs of Ho Man Tin Estate (where I recalled she lived). I started at the top of the list and worked down. On the fifteenth call I got lucky. A gruff male voice told me *"Deng, deng"* — wait.

A few seconds later, a female voice came on the line:

"Wei? Yes? Who is this?" I recognized the voice of this particular W. Wong. It was Wendy, *my Wendy!*

"Wendy? It's Chris. Thank God! Sorry to disturb you like this. Listen, can we meet? It's slightly urgent."

We met at a *Café de Coral* off Nathan Road.

"My Mandarin isn't perfect," Wendy warned me up front. The fast-food joint was full of chattering office workers. She listened with some intensity to Siao's answers, which I played back through the headphones of my Walkman. I was transfixed by the small crease of concentration forming on her smooth forehead, like a crack in a Ming vase, as she jotted down notes on a sheet of A4 paper. When it was done, I felt like kissing her, but restrained myself, knowing the awkward social situation that would have placed her in, here, among her peers.

"I'll call you," I said, dashing off, "at least I've got your number now!"

———— ∞ ————

"Hello, News Desk ..." Crawley listened with admirable patience to my breathless and, looking back on it, roundabout explanation. "Look, we'd be interested in seeing it, for sure. But you'll have to talk to Simon Beck. He's your man. Tomorrow, though. He's not in today."

There was a full moon that night, and I was praying for better luck under it than its predecessor in China. The SCMP out of my hands until tomorrow, I borrowed Hendrick's tripod, and set out to shoot the city at night. Up on the Peak — the mountain that dominates Hong Kong Island — the air was rare, and views unparalleled. In late afternoon light, I rode the funicular Peak Tram up to its terminal station. The city shook off its gray concrete coat as the car, pulled by cables, hummed up an incline of 45 degrees. It emerged a thousand feet higher, and into a world dominated by sunlight, breezes and tropical foliage. It was the perfect place to start gathering material for my *Pacific Traveller* assignment, and I had the ideal film on which to capture the city below: some super slow Kodachrome 25 ASA Mr Poon had sold me for half price, since it was close to expiry. It was superior celluloid, and had but one flaw: Kodachrome could be developed at one of only a handful of dedicated Kodak labs around the world. The closest to Hong Kong was in Japan. After posting the exposed rolls in the yellow envelopes provided, it would take a few weeks before the processed slides were delivered back. My luck held: it was a clear evening, and I began to shoot using a combination of all my lenses, probing the city as it reacted and transformed in the changing light—an urban chameleon.

'*Hong*' and '*Kong*', separately, the two words didn't project much glamour. It was a place to live and work in, big, dirty and frustrating, a pushing, sweaty grind. Invoked as one, however, sitting on the low wall that ran around Victoria Peak and gazing down upon the neon-lit glittering metropolis, humid vapors licking at my shirt and hair—I closed my eyes and was back sailing the Java Sea on the deck of the *Kurnia Ilahi*—those exact same proletarian syllables brought instead a lump to my throat.

Due to its agreeable harbor, and a fortuitous alignment of time and geography, a magnificent city had arisen, providing safe haven, hope and fortune to millions. Seven years from now and all this would be handed over to the bureaucrats of Beijing. No wonder some people were calling it 'The Great Chinese Takeaway'.

"What's the dark area, the bit with no lights?" a woman's voice drifted across, her harsh Australian accent breaking my reverie.

"That's the sea, Darling," replied her mildly exasperated escort.

It was 2.00 a.m., slightly beyond the sensible time to make a decision about getting down from the mountaintop. A taxi would be too costly. The buses and tram had stopped operating, hours ago. So, I was stuck for the duration. I located a suitably sized drainage ditch in which to lie, and escape the worst of the wind. While my brain was still functioning, I remembered to stick my tripod up, to mark my position, like a snow pole in a blizzard. I'd be in the perfect position to photograph sunrise over the city in a few hours. Somewhere above the parapet I heard the slam of a car door, followed by the drunken stumble of approaching feet. Posh voices were singing, their words slurred in inebriation—expats. A shadowy bulk loomed above my trench, teetering on the edge, tottering back and forth, and unzipped his trousers:

"What's that?" he asked, to no one in particular, "Oh, it's a bum," he concluded, and started to pee over my shoes.

"I'm not a bum, I'm a photographer!" I exploded, rising like Dracula from his coffin, ready to prove my point by picking up the tripod and waving it around. The well-fed figure in the tuxedo staggered backwards in surprise, slaloming his spray over my legs. After gaining his composure, he apologized for the sprinkling, and left me a half-drunk magnum of champagne to accompany my night vigil.

With the champagne buzz wearing off, and the sun rising over Kowloon, I began the second stage of my shoot. It was the same city, photographed from the same position, but the light now coming from the east was well worth the wait. Easing my aching joints into motion, I jogged back to Peak station and boarded the first tram of the day down to Central. From there, I called Sam Ho. He'd not heard about Siao making it to the US yet, and I was glad to be the bearer of good tidings. I wanted desperately to change out of the clothes I'd been wearing all night, and which were now stained by expatriate piss, and to dump off the bulky tripod. But the next call I put through was to Simon Beck at the SCMP, who said we should meet immediately. So I boarded the next train to Quarry Bay, sniffing commuters giving me a distinctly wider berth than usual.

"Heading out somewhere?" Simon took in the tripod.

"Just coming back, actually." I replied.

I liked Simon; he was young, smart, and took me seriously. He was not at all affected by the arrogance and cynicism I'd begun to expect from members of the Press. He had short hair and kept tugging at his forelock. I waited in expectant silence as he read the transcript of my Siao interview.

"Well, we may have to 'newsify' it a bit," that was the word he used — *newsify* — "… and I'll have to run it past editorial." He called in Steve Shroud, the American photo editor, who took my negative of Siao raising his banner, returning it half an hour later, having made a print. I was buzzing from lack of sleep and excitement at the whole news process. It was not about the money — a picture in the SCMP paid HK$500 (US$60 then, as now. In 1990 this was enough to live on for a week, though. Today, it covers an average good meal, if you don't drink too much) — no, it was the *game* that counted: making it to print.

There was nothing else I could do for now, so I wandered back to Lucky's feeling suddenly very tired. Thinking I really must get some sleep soon, I made a drowsy call to Simon at 5:00 p.m. He had already called Sam and verified my Siao interview story.

"Look, I really want to use the piece, and soon," he said, "but the editor isn't convinced it's not all some elaborate hoax designed to raise publicity for Sam's pro-democracy Alliance group."

Welshman Giles was back at the guesthouse early. He usually worked nights, bartending at a boozy Tsim Sha Tsui joint called Memories.

"Got there and the place was shut down. The manager couldn't pay me off in cash." So, instead, he'd staggered home with three crates of beer and as many bottles of Johnny Walker and tequila as he could stuff in his backpack. An absolutely ludicrous party ensued on the fourth floor. I joined in for a while, but couldn't concentrate on drinking. My gut told me the SCMP would let me down, that they'd not run my story. So near yet so far: the story of my life.

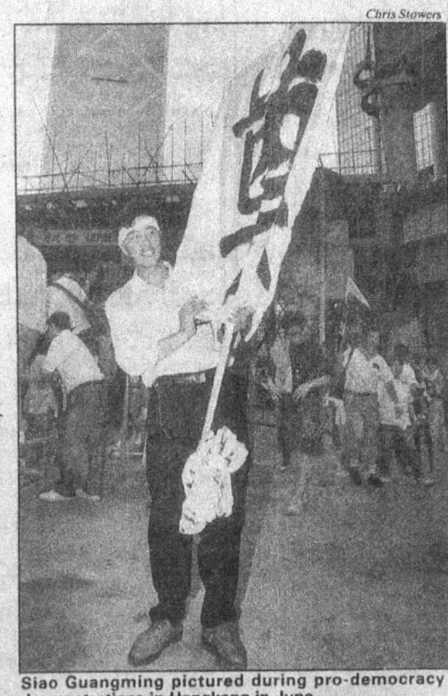

Student fled in fear of China

By CHRIS STOWERS and staff reporters

Chris Stowers

THE mainland student being held in the United States after escaping aboard a cargo ship from Hongkong, fled because he feared he would be sent back to China.

After a year of hiding in Hongkong as an illegal immigrant and working with pro-democracy activists here, Siao Guangming said that he escaped to the US because he felt he had no future in the territory.

In an interview conducted only days before he secretly boarded the Neptune Orient container ship Neptune Diamond, Siao warned: "Next week I'm going to America and will continue fighting for the people of China from there."

However, the first his colleagues in the Hongkong Alliance in Support of the Patriotic Democratic Movement in China knew of his disappearance was when it came to light in Saturday's *South China Morning Post.*

Hongkong International Terminals (HIT) said yesterday that shipping lines should tighten their onboard security to safeguard against illegal entry of per-

(Cont'd on Page 2, Col 6)

Siao Guangming pictured during pro-democracy demonstrations in Hongkong in June.

August 7, 1990

MY STORY AND the photo of Siao were splashed across the front page of the *South China Morning Post*.

Later, I met up with Wendy. She was eager to see the story she had helped make happen. I treated her to a meal, something Japanese, and she showed me an advert for a room for rent. We traveled out to far Kwai Chung to view the place. It measured barely fifty-square-feet, but that was fifty-square-feet of privacy currently unavailable to me at Lucky Guesthouse. I would still have to share the bathroom with the other residents of the flat. You know you're settled when you don't have to queue for a shower.

Buoyed by my SCMP exposure, I decided to rent the place, on instinct: sometimes luck has to be forced in order to change it. I wanted to disappear into Hong Kong, to dissolve into its noise and odd vapors, to become a part of its molecular chaos. My camera and photos could represent me, in place of anatomy. It was the photographer's dream—invisibility. Where better to start than twenty-three floors above an industrial estate in the New Territories?

〜〜〜

I never saw my new flat mates, let alone my neighbors. Like mice, when they heard me open my door they'd hide away until I'd vanished down the lift. My white t-shirts soon turned light purple, drying on the bamboo pole extending from my single window, wreathed in smoke from the dyeing factories below. God knows what this was doing to my lungs. Similar housing blocks towered around mine, and at night the rumble of traffic and air conditioners droned like the inner workings of a gigantic

175

ship's engine room. Having no TV and no one to talk to, I'd taken to spying through my long lens, with the lights out. Opposite, there was a girl who never closed her curtains. I amused myself making up some intriguing backstory and wondering how I'd react if ever I were to bump into her at the local supermarket. The best glimpse so far had been when she'd stripped to her slip, but then she turned her lights out. Who knows, maybe she spied on me through binoculars in return?

At breakfast, news on Commercial Radio warned of trouble brewing in the Gulf. Iran and Iraq were now threatening to join forces in a 'Holy War' against the US. When would my generation be called up to fight our own Vietnam? Peace, after all, is cyclical; war, inevitable.

Slogging on with the assignment to photograph Hong Kong for Derek, I took the Star Ferry over to Central in the morning. The fare had just risen to HK$1 on the lower deck, but I could always find something to shoot on each crossing. The remit of my new assignment was monstrously vague, and all my deadlines were self-imposed. The freelance photographer needs self-discipline above all else. Later, in the afternoon, I took an edited selection of a hundred shots — the distilled result of all my efforts of the week — to Derek in his office. Last week he'd been disappointed with the work I presented, which left me feeling guilty. I'd redoubled my efforts this week.

"Two hundred percent better than the last lot," he said, straightening up from the light-box, "I'll keep 'em all."

"Thanks for the kick up the backside, you know ... last week," I told him, relieved. His approval meant a lot. I'd no one else to judge my work, or to push me.

"We can always provide that!" he responded.

September 16, 1990

BLAST FROM THE past, today. Claudia was in town and today was her birthday. We met on the third floor of Chungking Mansions for a celebratory dinner at *Delhi Mess*. She was combining a freelancing assignment—for a German magazine (reporting on the situation in Hong Kong in the run-up to Handover)—with a holiday, and was on paid-leave from her government job. Visually, she had remained unchanged in the three years since we'd met in Tibet. Her shoulder pads were a bit more severe, perhaps, as befitted the costume of a career civil servant of the Federal Republic of Germany. But her new status as a Seriously Employed Adult—like her clothing—was just a disguise. Her center was still as mushy as ever.

Oddly, and despite being the tenant of a cramped but perfectly adequate—and so-far untested—love nest, any desire between us, beyond mutual company and conversation, appeared to have been left suspended in the thin air of the Himalayas, and washed up on the sands of a couple of spectacularly tropical Indonesian beaches. I was no longer her "idiot boy", prey to bouts of naïvely optimistic enthusiasm. Perhaps it was all the letters we had sent each other in the interim. Words had piled up to create a wall of respect, one that repulsed invasion by barbarian lust.

"We're re-unification crazy in Germany at the moment. Hong Kong could learn from watching how we handle it," she enthused, speculating she might have to uproot and move to Berlin soon from Bonn. "You'll have much more reason to visit me when I'm in a big city like Berlin!"

I left Claudia with forty slides in two plastic sheets to help illustrate her article. The magazine paid 80 DM for each image

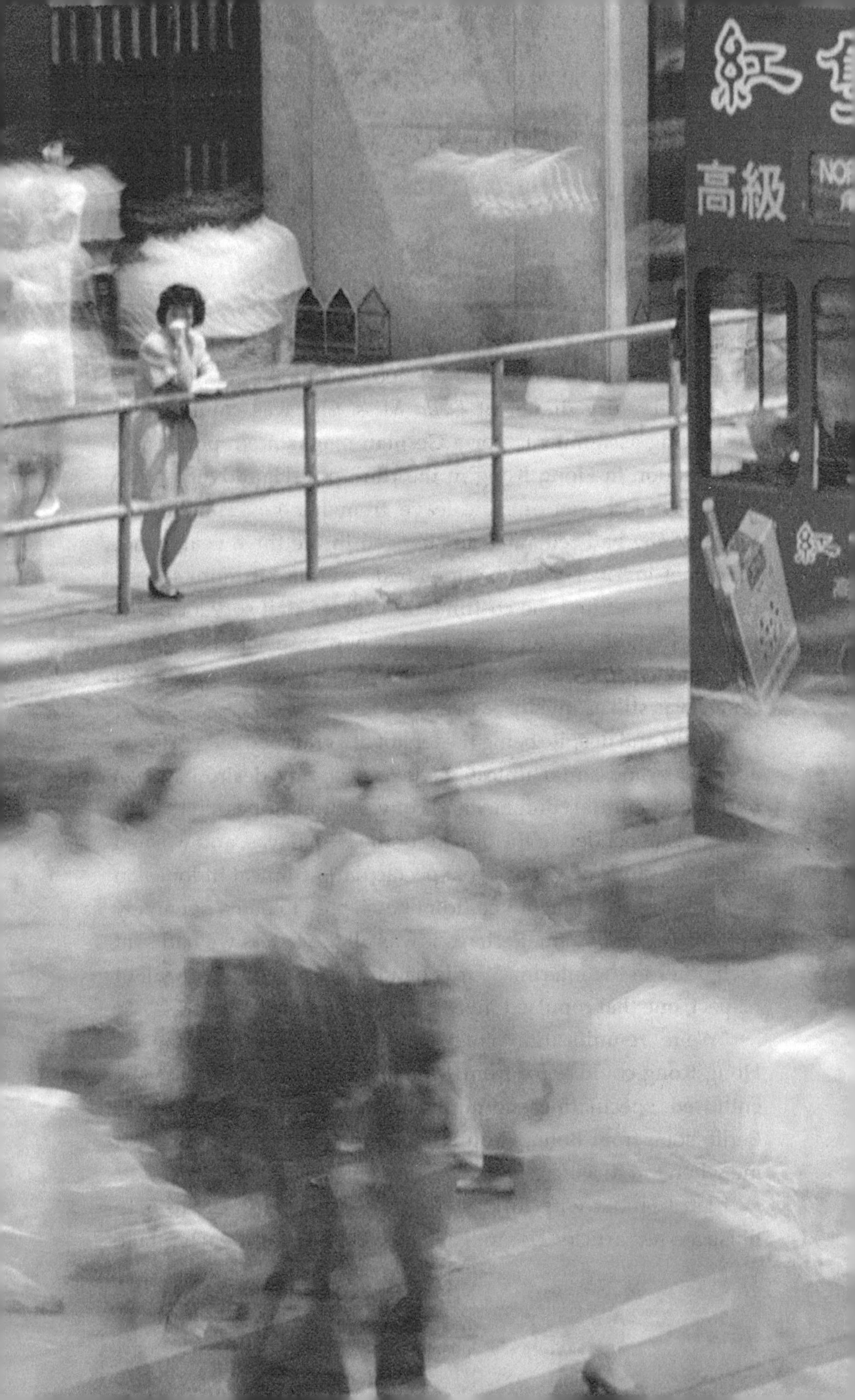

紅
高級
NO

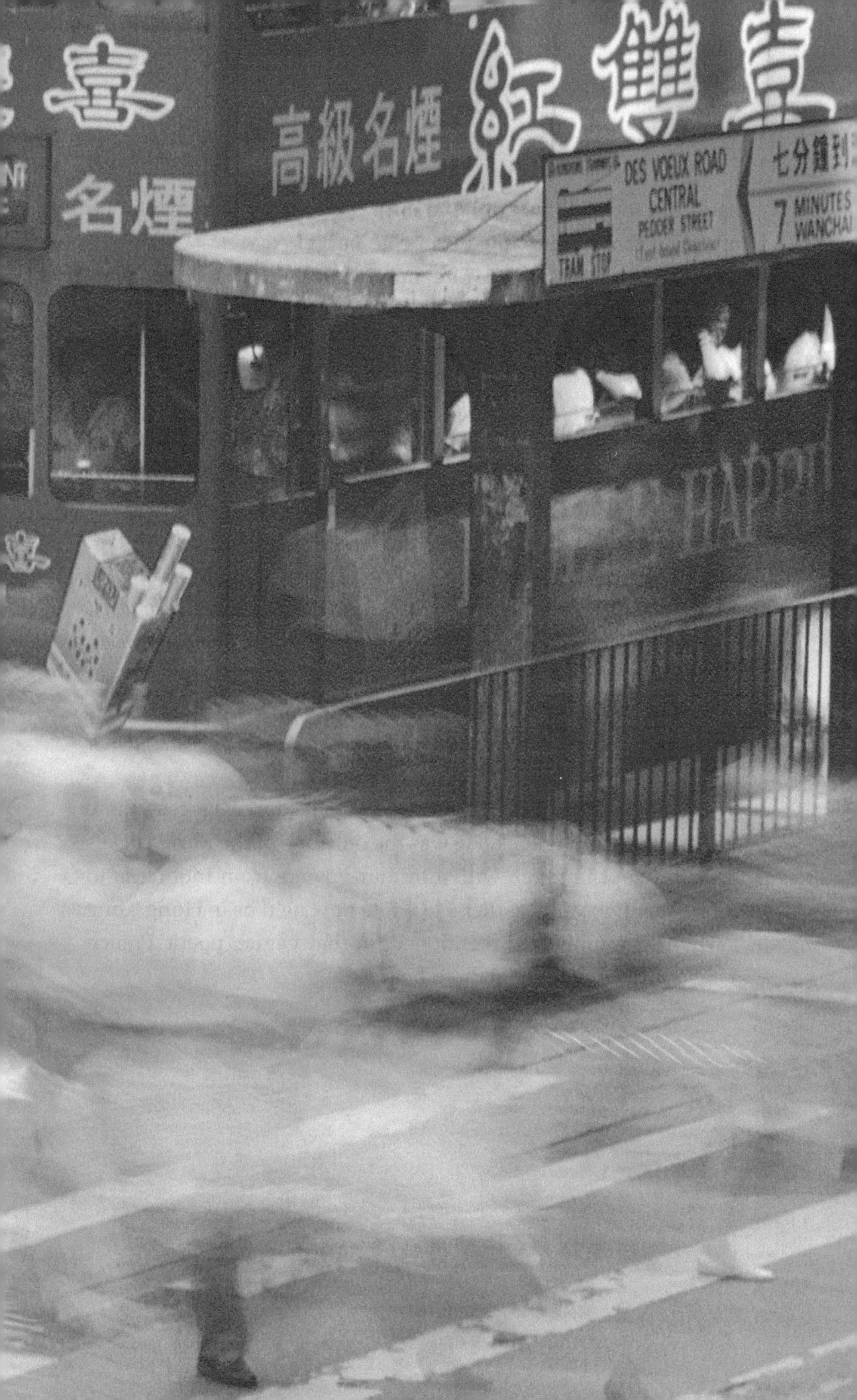
喜 紅 雙 喜
高級名煙
名煙
DES VOEUX ROAD
CENTRAL
PEDDER STREET
七分鐘到
7 MINUTES WANCHAI
TRAM STOP
HAPPY

used, not too shabby; but more important than money would be my breakthrough into the European market.

At the post office, a rare missive from London Bus had arrived, from the US. The Aussie photographer commiserated with me losing my camera gear in Kunming:

I have a solution mate, keep your slides in a safe box and your street cameras on you at all times, shithouse to shower ...

Unable to find enough work there as a shooter, he'd resorted to programming computers for the US Department of Agriculture:

... It beats taxi driving. I got fat because I hated that taxi shit. I bashed one passenger and dragged two others out of me cab. What fun. I'm writing a book on it, done 50 pages so far ... I'll be moving to Downtown DC soon, where it's cheaper and more cultural, very racist very violent (399 murders last year), lots of horny government women. I get a bone just thinking about it. Keep at the camera work, it's not easy, there's a lot of rejection, but it's self-satisfying ...

And he left me with his prediction *"There will be war between USA and Iraq no doubt, 100 percent sure of it."*

Right at the back of the box, hidden in its darkest recess, there was a letter from Franck. He was the only one of the *Kurnia Ilahi's* crew I'd kept in touch with after our voyage from Indonesia to Singapore two years earlier. He wrote how he'd be in Hong Kong early next month, and mentioned, in that vague, poetic French way of his, something about a boat.

Previous pages: Pedestrians swarm around a tram on Des Voeux Rd., Central, Hong Kong - 1990. This image was used to open the story Claudia wrote for a West German current affairs magazine, payment for which was to prove pivotal, later on in my travels. Photo: Chris Stowers/PANOS

4. On Love and Rigging

It was the summer of 1988 and I was twenty-one. I had been on the road for eighteen months and gathered many adventures under my belt. Justification for such restlessness, however, was beginning to wear thin. What I needed was purpose, travel without which was but a wasteful extravagance. I carried my cheap Nikon EM camera everywhere, and was beginning to view the world through its standard 50mm lens, focusing on everything, seeing nothing.

In the end, purpose found me.

Her name was 'Kurnia Ilahi'. It was a rather tempestuous love affair (the sort photographers are particularly prone to attract).

'Kurnia Ilahi' was a seventy-foot-long Bugis perahu, a spice-trading sloop made solely of teak; she possessed no engine, radio, survival equipment, or other unnecessary utilities. The moment I first saw her, I knew I would join the bunch of French desperados who were in the process of buying her and help them sail to distant Singapore. I had never been more certain of anything. That perilous, month-long ocean odyssey became the subject of my first-ever published story and photographs. It launched a career that is still bobbing along today, more than three decades later.

Hong Kong
October 7, 1990

"ALLO? OO EEZ zis?" It was not Franck, as expected, but a French female voice that answered my call.

"This is Chris, is Franck there?"

"Allo, Chris, zis is Fabienne, *attendez … Franck, téléphone.*"

Fabienne, it transpired, was Pascal's girlfriend. Pascal? *The* Pascal? Yes, of course, he was captain now of *Windfall. Come out to Sai Kung this evening, it will be like old times!*

Reminiscing about sailing with Pascal was like asking Fletcher Christian about all the good times aboard the HMS *Bounty*. Still, our voyage on the *Kurnia Ilahi* had been two years ago . . . Maybe the man had changed in the interval. Once again, curiosity got the better of me.

Beautiful early morning light probed the steep valleys and unexpected grasslands of the New Territories. Sai Kung sat on an eastern promontory, all white villas and blue roof tiles — an Oriental Costa del Sol. Our rendezvous was the Newcastle pub. Franck was the first to see me enter, then Pascal stood up, his face a huge, wrinkled smile. I chided myself for having remembered him so unfavorably. He was one of life's movers, without whom idle slobs like myself would never be challenged to achieve anything out of the ordinary. Extreme reactions were his territory.

I was next introduced to another Frank, from Pascal and Franck's hometown of Evreux, in Normandy, and to Fabienne, many years Pascal's junior. She seemed enchanted by the adventurer's larger-than-life spell. I guess we all were.

Across a table cluttered with empty Carlsberg pint glasses, Franck sat silently; and I knew I'd get to catch up with him, later, alone. For now, Pascal held court. He'd just visited Vietnam. The former French colony was opening up for the first time since the war, and Pascal smelled opportunity.

"Tourism. It will be bigger than Thailand!"

Red wandered over; he was a Canadian working at the Clearwater Bay Golf Club and Marina. *Windfall* was currently in dry dock there.

"Captain," he saluted Pascal, before taking a stool and helping himself to a beer. "That's some vessel you have there. Everyone is jealous."

The backstory was this: Pascal was now working as a glorified caretaker of the *Windfall*, a US$1.5 million, Swan 61' luxury racing yacht owned by eccentric HK expat financier John Watson. Part of the deal allowed Pascal to charter the vessel out of Phuket, Thailand, in return for making the occasional trip to Hong Kong, when summonsed. In this case, the boat was needed for the birthday party of the owner's daughter. Franck, who was trying to blot out the fast-approaching reality of his compulsory military service in France, was sailing back to Phuket with Pascal. And they were going via Singapore.

"Zis time we will 'ave the biggest bloody boat in Changi Sailing Club!" Pascal exclaimed, a vengeful glint in his eye, alluding to our previous visit there in a run-down wooden cargo boat.

"*Windfall* has *everything*," Franck informed me; radar, a fax machine, satellite navigation and electric winches, three refrigerators, a video and stereo sound system, a huge Volvo engine, even air conditioning. *Kurnia Ilahi's* polar opposite in the opulence stakes. "Too much things ..."

At the conclusion of our boozy lunch, we all piled into Red's Suzuki Vitara jeep and he steered us to the Club. We ate curry on its patio, and casually basked in our connection to the dark blue and white hull being re-painted down the rails; the longest, tallest, sleekest-looking boat in the entire marina. Surrounded by friends, old stories surfacing, my flat in Kwai Chung felt suddenly very far away, my time spent in Hong Kong an omission of mass stretched thin between points of *real* life and contact, like the space between planets. It was like joining the *Kurnia Ilahi* crew, back on the eastern Indonesian island of Flores, all over again.

"You know, I'm going to have to come with you ..." I blurted out, and Pascal happily agreed, making me promise to write a story about this adventure, as I had done our last. They were aiming to leave in a week, at the latest, with or without me. My grip on life in Hong Kong was tenuous; all I had to do was open my hands and drift away.

It was dark outside and too late to head back to the city, so I crashed with the others at Red's villa. Franck was unconscious already, jet-lagged after his flight, one that had been delayed an extra day, in Amman, due to developments in the Gulf after Iraq's invasion of Kuwait.

<hr>

Departure date was fast approaching. Hendrick suggested I move my worldly belongings (these filled two large rice sacks) to the spare room of his new digs on Lantau Island. Today he traveled up to Kwun Tong to help me move my bags. It took us the best part of the afternoon to reach his freestanding house, one replete with rooftop and low-walled garden, and which sat on the edge of a basketball court in Tai Tei Tong, in the Silvermine Bay hinterlands.

"Sorry, I don't know how long I'm going to be away," I warned, thinking he deserved the truth of it. To which he replied in Zen-like manner, "Take as long as it takes."

Ironically, now I was more distracted and about to decamp, Wendy started acting more warmly towards me. We met at a McDonald's on Austin Road before I left for Clearwater Bay and my new berth on the *Windfall*. I told her I was going to live on Lantau when I returned.

"I'd like to live out there too," she mused, dreamily. I didn't risk spoiling the moment by asking if she meant *with me*. It was much safer to package that image up, unshattered, to savor during the coming voyage.

Later, back at the marina, *Windfall* looked magnificent— freshly repainted and restored to her element, the sea. The surround-sound jingling and clattering of wires against masts, and of water slapping the hull, soothed me instantly to sleep.

October 14, 1990

"ATTENTION, ATTENTION!" I sat up with a start, banging my head on the cabin's low ceiling. It was 7:00 a.m. and Pascal was testing the on-board tannoy system. T'annoy us.

I accompanied Fabienne to the Sai Kung supermarket. We overindulged on supplies. I threw in a bottle of whisky and one of tequila as my contribution. We pushed our twin, overloaded shopping trolleys back along the main street to the petrol station, where we picked up ten cans of engine oil and coolant. A taxi was refueling, so we transferred all our goodies into it for the journey back to Marina Cove.

Red was deeply envious. He wanted to sail away, too, but his cushy job at the Yacht Club kept him handcuffed to Hong Kong. He followed the contours of the coast road out to Bay Head driving the club's Mini-Moke, keeping pace with us as we sailed in a more direct line, heading for open sea. He dropped his trousers and mooned us as we passed by. Perhaps this was the Canadian way of wishing us good wind for the voyage.

I was the first to be sick. Next was Franck, then Frank, and, for the first time in her life at sea, Fabienne. Pascal, of course, just sat there knocking back whisky and laughing at us. We'd entered into very rough seas. *Windfall* was equipped with an auto-helm. I dialed in our course of 210°. There was very little else to do, bar hold on tight, check sporadically for neighboring ships on the radar screen (some of the wave crests were so high they registered as blips, too), and watch the tip of the mast thread itself in an endless figure-of-eight pattern around Orion's Belt.

We set the steering rota in three-hour shifts through the night, 9:00 p.m. to 9:00 a.m., and I assigned myself the dogwatch, 3-6:00

a.m. I couldn't stay in my cot, anyway, as I was being thrown about too wildly. One of the fridge doors had already broken; we jammed it shut using a Marlboro packet and some string. So much for million-dollar technology.

The moon appeared an upturned crescent; a malicious, thin-lipped Cheshire Cat grin indicating some foreknowledge of my future it was having far too much fun keeping to itself. The speed indicator on *Windfall's* instrument dashboard glowed green and often rested, ominously, at 6.66 knots. A dark cloud passed the lower half of the lunar body leaving devilish shiny horns protruding on either side.

Voyage – Day 2

(300 miles SSW of Hong Kong)

We really were flying now. *Windfall*, a racing yacht, was averaging 10-12 knots. The sea remained turbulent; a typhoon was closing in from the east, our priority being to beat it to the Vietnam coastline. Hiccups replaced yesterday's sickness, and I rediscovered my sea legs.

"Chris, do you believe in God?" Franck launched into one of his serious conversations now that we had time to relax a little around the table at dinnertime. Storms tended to bring on an appetite. From the galley there came a crash, and swearing in French, as Fabienne struggled against the violently tilting deck to produce a whole roast chicken and potatoes. The completed bird offered itself to all sides of the table, sliding on a film of spilled gravy, a trick we found quite amusing after the consumption of a second bottle of wine.

"Well, there's something out there, for sure. Whether he, she, or it takes the form we commonly associate with our Christian 'God', I doubt. But you have to wonder: why go to all this bother, to create an entire Universe ... All this ..." I cast my eyes out over the tall waves, "... random nature? No, I imagine there's a pattern to it, at the atomic level, I mean."

"So, God is some great physicist ... it makes as much sense, I suppose, as any other religious explanation, and is just as unprovable."

"I think God is embedded in Nature. It's the perfect system. Like the waves, nature just keeps changing form, adapting, sometimes evaporating entirely, only to materialize elsewhere as rain. You can never beat something so submissive yet wholly persistent."

"It is so. Only when you abandon yourself to nature can the true adventure begin. And yet, inside this boat, we pretend Nature doesn't exist, or, at least, that we are Masters of it; we're isolated from reality, the radar acts as our eyes, the auto-helm for arms and legs. As long as the food and diesel hold out ..." mused Franck, wanting now to go on deck and smoke a cigarette.

"... and all it will take is one 'uge wave to wipe out your precious civilization!" Pascal intervened, breaking our reverie and dishing out our evening's duties.

At sea, the skipper *is* God.

Voyage–Day 3

(700 miles SSW of HK)

The barometer had plunged a dozen millibars overnight. The problem with all this labor-saving technology was the free time it left you to worry about information you hadn't previously known you needed.

We picked up our very own Vietnamese refugee: a little bird that'd been blown way off course. He sensed we were his last chance, circling *Windfall* all afternoon, trying to land. But each time he flew in close, a gust of wind would blow his weightless body out to sea; and whenever he got too near the sail, he was sucked into its slipstream. At one point he landed on a winch, way out on the prow, but hadn't sufficient grip to hold on. We all gathered to watch his valiant struggle, rooting for the little fella.

"*Ah, merde!*" Frank exclaimed, as the bird splashed into a wave.

We were sure it was the end of him … but then up he fluttered, the tough little fighter, and we all cheered. Finally, at the limit of his energy, he simply dive-bombed the deck. Pascal rushed forward, the tiny creature offering no resistance when scooped from his landing place, under the dinghy.

By 9:00 p.m., we celebrated reaching the geographical halfway mark, way ahead of schedule. The little bird was recovering well and fluttering about the main cabin.

Voyage–Day 5

(90 miles NNE of Singapore)

We had covered a thousand miles from Hong Kong in less than a week, but now there was no wind, the sails were reefed, and we were forced to rely on the 140hp Volvo Pentax, chugging along at 1,400RPM and a reliable, drudging 5 knots. Taking advantage of the temporary stability, I was winched up the mast by ropes fed through a motor to photograph from its vertiginous vantage point.

The last time I'd found myself in such a vulnerable position, dangling fifty feet above a swaying deck, was on the *Kurnia Ilahi*. That time, I'd been attached by frayed ropes to tiny sweating humans, far below, and the seas were very rough indeed. I shot off half a roll of slide film thinking how one of these images would make a nice opening spread for the story I was writing about the voyage.

Fresh water always becomes an issue after a week at sea. *Windfall* was equipped with a desalination unit, thus reducing the amount of drinking water we'd had to physically carry on-board. But this ran on diesel, and we needed to preserve all our fuel to run the engine.

There was a short but intense rain shower just before sunset. Recalling our time on *Kurnia Ilahi*, we all ran about on deck in a festive atmosphere, clad only in our underwear, with soap and shampoo. Sensing, with animal instinct, the closing presence of land, 'Gilles' — as we had named our little feathered stowaway, in honor of our *Kurnia Ilahi* shipmate who couldn't make this trip due to being detained by the same French authorities he used to work for, as a drugs officer — perked up. He circled the cockpit once, as if to take a final compass bearing, and then shot off west in the direction of the Malay Peninsula.

Singapore
October 22, 1990

Changi sailing club hadn't changed, only our means of arrival at it. And even that bore some similarity to the hallowed events of two years ago. We moored at the same floating Shell station, this time to pump in 1,000 liters of diesel — rather than cadge a tow from a tug — and replenished our depleted fuel tanks. Once again, it rained as we set off from boat to shore in the dinghy. This time we avoided sinking, though the script was ruined somewhat by a stuffy official who challenged our captain on the jetty: "Are you a member here?"

"No, but I soon will be," Pascal muttered darkly and marched off to obtain our temporary membership in the clubhouse. Upstairs at the bar, we ordered sirloin steaks and Tiger beers and sat around the same table we'd colonized after arriving on *Kurnia Ilahi*. Even the waitress was the same, Alice — and she remembered Pascal. *Everyone remembers Pascal.* It was Franck who found our sampan, the holed lifeboat from that earlier voyage. He rushed over to the table, exclaiming excitedly and pointing across the patio,

"It's over there, they've turned it into a picnic table!"

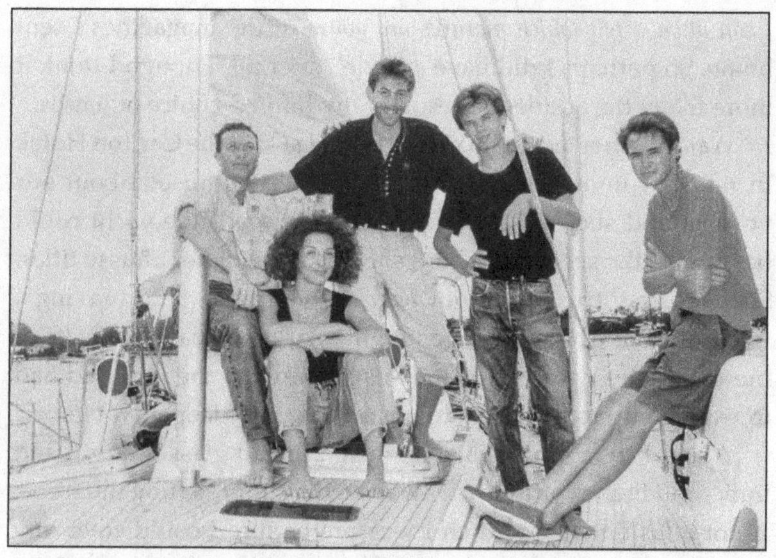

(From left) Pascal, Fabienne, me, Frank and Franck, aboard Windfall *at Changi Sailing Club in Singapore, October 22, 1990. Two years earlier Pascal, Franck and I, along with 4 other crew members, had arrived at the same club aboard the Bugis spice boat* Kurnia Ilahi, *a voyage that inspired the first volume in this series,* Bugis Nights.

When occasionally we photographers come to shore, magazine photo editors and art directors are our first port of call. One of Singapore's busiest publishing houses for lifestyle magazines was Shusse. Their art director Wai-fong was a devotee of British graphic designer Neville Brody—who had provided such bold visual direction to *The Face* magazine in the 1980s, as well as design record covers for Depeche Mode. She liked the way I framed my photos, leaving her plenty of space to add text and play with graphics, rather than filling the entire frame with subject matter, as news photographers are trained to do. Frankly, I'd not realized I was doing this, but nodded my head, pretending this stylistic arrangement had been intentional.

Long ago, The Mouse had told me to "think of every shot being a double-page spread." My mother had written saying,

I can always tell which pictures are yours in the magazines I sent home. So perhaps I did have a 'style', after all. Though I think it more likely the accidental result of my limited choice of lenses.

Wai-fong treated me to rich seafood *Laksa* at the Carlton Hotel. In return, I invited her out to *Windfall*. I'd enthused about our voyage, and she expressed an interest to see if the yacht could be used as the set for a fashion shoot for one of her Shusse titles. She was very trusting of our new acquaintance, later braving a ride out from Changi Village into the darkened bay in *Windfall's* motor dinghy. I steered us into a sandbank on the way and had to wade in up to my knees to push us off into deeper waters.

Aboard the yacht, Fabienne mixed us tall glasses of gin and tonic, and Franck strummed away on his guitar, setting the scene. If not a fashion shoot, then I was pretty sure I could cover my costs by flogging Wai-fong the story of our voyage from Hong Kong. (Duly, this appeared in *MAN* magazine, a few months later).

November 23, 1990

THE HEAD OFFICE of Cheney Communications had recently relocated from Hong Kong (where apparently there had been a big party with all the sacked employees throwing darts at an effigy of their former boss, American businessman Chris Cheney), to Singapore. Englishman Nigel Simmonds was the main editor of their surviving titles, having escaped the cull. He grumped about "being put out to grass" down here in the Lion City. He was a laugh to be around, though. Quickly assessing my penniless situation, he let me stay at the huge apartment on Robin Road he shared with his public relations girlfriend, Gilly.

News Flash: **MAGGIE THATCHER STEPS DOWN**

I'd left home vowing never to return to England until this occasion, confident in the assumption *She'd* always be there, like Queen Elizabeth, or malaria. Nigel, one of her staunchest supporters, organized a party to lament the Iron Lady's passing. I drank all his beers and vodka-oranges in subversive celebration. Another British girl joined us. Claire was a PR manager for Saatchi & Saatchi in Singapore. She admitted,

"There wasn't a hope in Hell I'd have been given this position back in the UK." And of what did her well-paid job consist? "Well, mostly I talk to people over lunch."

Nigel brought out his guitar, jamming along with Eric Clapton on the CD player. I joined in on harmonica (I *must* have been drunk since, like most Brits, I consider death preferable to embarrassment) and regaled my captive audience with slightly embellished tales of escape from Rudi and his machete.

We ended the evening sitting on submerged deckchairs in the swimming pool, only our heads above the surface, sipping white wine as rain daubed gentle ripples in the chlorinated waves.

Malaysia
December 5, 1990

THINGS WERE FALLING into place. Even Mr Fong had been moved from *Expressions* in Jakarta to their office in Kuala Lumpur. I stayed with him and Ruby at their family home in the suburbs of Petaling Jaya and he asked me to shoot an ambitious, three-part article, detailing the lives of the *Orang Asli*, the Negrito indigenous peoples of the Malay Peninsula. At last, something socially significant I could sink my teeth into. Requiring very little encouragement, I set off energized, shooting around the tea plantations of the Cameron Highlands where many of the marginalized, former forest-dwellers lived, often in abject poverty.

———∾∾∾———

Arriving back in the Malay capital a week later, Mr Fong got straight to the point, deflating me as gently as possible with the news that the *Orang Asli* 'series' had been shoe-horned into a single article. He'd need far fewer photos from me than originally anticipated. First, the Philippines, now Malaysia. I realized some people saw me as a hopelessly optimistic dreamer, and didn't take me seriously as a result—Nigel cynically joked, "All journalists start off as idealists, become realists, and end up as cynics"—but I felt in my bones that these pictures would be useful one day, if not immediately and in the glossy pages of Fong's American Express publication.

Free to travel wherever the road led once more, I set off north by bus to Penang. But a night spent tossing and turning in a cheap Love Lane guesthouse failed to improve matters. In fact, I don't think they'd changed the bed linen since its previous occupant had sweated in it. I awoke feverish, with red sores appearing all over my torso. Trying not to imagine myself into a state of panic, I waited for consultation, perched on a wooden bench outside a crowded local government clinic. An Indian lady doctor called me behind the curtain, inspected the inflamed areas, took my temperature and authoritatively pronounced:

"Chickenpox. Take these tablets, one a day. Use this lotion to reduce itching. Don't scratch or you'll be scarred for life. And avoid pregnant women and eating meat."

Not bad service for the outlay of one Malaysian ringgit.

Sumatra, Indonesia
December 13, 1990

ITCHY, ITCHY, ITCHY. Apply more lotion. Must resist the itch.

I took a morning ferry across the strait from Penang to Medan in sultry Sumatra. From that concrete metropolis, a further six-hour bus ride climbed 1,000 meters above sea level, to Lake Toba. This was the only place on the equator near and naturally cool enough to speed convalescence. Toba, the largest volcanic lake in the world, filled the caldera of a super-volcano some sixty miles in length. In the center of this stupendous natural phenomenon floated Samosir Island, home to the Christian *Batak* tribe. Here they resided among pine trees and paddy fields, eating pork and living in wooden houses whose roofs rose at both ends to resemble multiple boat prows in a clustered harbor. I sensed a story coming on, but knew it would be a few days before I could risk raising the camera close to my pox-corrupted face. With my hat on, and scarf covering the worst of these eruptions, I wandered the dirt tracks down by the pier, feeling sorry for myself, and trying to avoid as many pregnant women as possible. To be frank, there were plenty worse contenders: poor lepers and cripples, and beggars with no arms or legs.

To help pass the time, I read through a crumpled copy of *The Fountainhead*, lent by Lee-chung, one of the senior female editors at Shusse. She was a mature, assertive firebrand Wai-fong had warned had a reputation as a 'man-eater'. I'd hate to ruin my hard-won, wholesome reputation by letting on that I really wouldn't mind letting myself be consumed, from time to time.

JAKARTA
December 31, 1990

NEW YEAR'S EVE. Kids run through the maze of alleys leading off the main backpacker street, *Jalan Jaksa*, blowing horns made of glistening gold cardboard. It was going to be a 'dry' celebration, this year. Beer was prohibitively expensive in Indonesia. Instead, I became absorbed in the general flow of people, all heading to MONAS Park. At the center of this public area lay Merdeka (or freedom) Square. Thrusting through this was the 132m tall Monumen Nasional, the most recognizable landmark in Jakarta. Teenagers roared up and down the parade on their motorbikes, and other revelers rode in groups of twenty or thirty, high up in the backs of trucks waving the national flag. At 8:00 p.m., a sudden deluge sent everyone laughing and scuttling for cover; but it was impossible to dampen Indonesian spirits for long. At midnight, floodlights illuminating the needle-like tower — known tongue-in-cheek as 'Suharto's last erection' — were extinguished, and a few feeble fireworks set off. These were followed by a laser display that sent the latest Indonesian Tourism Bureau slogans flickering up the side of the phallic monument:

'Visit Indonesia Year, 1991' and:

'Let's Go Archipelago'.

And someone got *paid* to come up with these?

Although it was eighteen months since I had last been in Jakarta, I still kept a wary eye open for anyone approaching at alarming speed with a meat cleaver …

5. The Photographer and the Nomad

Nomads are drawn naturally towards photography. We're like those aliens who adopt human form so as to move around without raising alarm. Taking photos offers to us the respectable cover of profession. This makes sense: photography is selfish and essentially rootless work, most effectively practiced alone. We—and I adopt the convenience of the majestic plural in reference here to 'photographer' and 'nomad'—find society disconcerting, best kept at arms' length, used mainly as a pool in which to fish for images.

We are duplicitous: we need society to feed on, even as we long to escape its grasp; we seek anonymity, yet glow with inordinate pride to see our names printed on the communal page. We dream of being invisible, set free to follow our whim, and in solitude find space for our images to develop. Sure, corrosive doubt creeps in during the long hours of isolation, but like gold prospectors, we're lured ever on by the elusive hope of capturing one great shot, the one that will make a difference, the one that, above all, history will remember us for.

Nomads, like photographers, are not natural joiners. Neither are we particularly good at getting stuff done. The Mongol hordes of Genghis Khan, for example, raped and pillaged successfully across half the surface of the world but, unlike the monumentally organized Romans, failed to leave any trace of domination bar the fossilized hoofprints of their sturdy mounts. Nomads are inherently restless. The element we inhabit is the periphery; the place you think you see flashing by, and that evaporates the instant you turn to focus.

Nomads do not do meetings. When we attempt to—and I

suspect the last time the Bedouin gave it a serious bash was just after taking Damascus in 1918, with Colonel Lawrence in the chair—egos become quickly bruised. Trapped within four walls, even opulently decorous ones with gold-plated fixtures, we are easily suffocated and become agitated by the lack of horizon to head for.

Bloody nomads! You can't tell if they're coming or going. Their unpredictable migrations infuriate the settled inhabitants of 'normal' society (though it is really our freedom and detachment from daily concerns that breed such resentment). In contrast, a nomad hardly thinks of society at all. He doesn't pity the settled; he simply fails to understand or appreciate what it is they have settled for.

Like the nomad, a photographer never arrives; he's at home wherever he is, forever in the moment. Moving on is easy. Just click the shutter, advance the film. History is wound into darkness, a fresh frame is exposed, and along with it the promise of a new start.

～∞～

It's a lifestyle choice, people tell me, this trade-off between financial security and freedom. But, as with falling in love, I doubt we have a choice at all. Once that first step has been taken, you can never go back. Leaving home aged twenty is like walking off the edge of a cliff: the best you can hope for is to land on something soft....

HONG KONG
January 17, 1991

I'D BEEN AWAY from Hong Kong for three months, but nothing at Lucky Guesthouse had changed: the same dank towels languished over the end of each bunk bed; the tea-sticky plastic stools remained layered with abandoned playing cards and cigarette ash; residents still huddled around the TV in the common room, glued to a spectacular war movie ... only it was not a movie. The US and her Allies had launched Operation Desert Storm earlier that morning. As I had been flying back to the territory from Singapore, so aerial bombing of Baghdad had begun. I called up Hendrick. He urged me to move out to Lantau where he'd been looking after my luggage and had a spare room to rent.

"I'm trying to get to the Gulf," he said, reading my mind, "that's where the news is."

My post office box was crammed full with letters from three continents. I concentrated on the 30 percent that was not junk mail; among this, a solid 300 DM worth of traveler's checks from Claudia, along with a copy of her magazine story featuring my photos. There were a few checks from *Emphasis*, the inflight magazine people, and payments from Derek at *Pacific Traveller* for stock images used. And there was a begging letter from the Philippines where, it would appear, I'd handed out my business card a little too liberally. I became lost in correspondence on the ferry out to Lantau, sailing beneath the same type of, thin, upturned crescent moon that had so haunted my departure on *Windfall*. This one looked a whole lot friendlier.

Alighting, I followed the narrow, raised concrete pathways from Silvermine Bay ferry terminal to Tai Tei Tong village. The air was humid and echoed with comforting sounds; the clattering of Mahjong tiles, the honking geese, the scraping of metal spatulas in giant woks, and the deafening croak of bullfrogs, their mighty yet invisible army amassed in the neatly tilled vegetable plots and lotus ponds along the way. Finally, the hollow echo of basketballs and squeal of tortured sneakers on the ball court signaled arrival at Hendricks' place. *I live here now, too.*

The next fortnight zoomed by. I was let loose in the darkroom — formerly our ground floor kitchen — to learn by trial and error how to develop films and print black and white pictures. Every waking hour, when it was not absolutely essential to be elsewhere to make money or to eat, I locked myself in, under the red glow of the safety bulb, breathing in a heady mix of developing chemicals and fixer fluid, slave to the feverish joys of creation. Hendrick patiently showed me the ropes; how to blind-load films into developing tanks, operate the enlarger, make test strips and do basic dodging and burning as images formed. He drilled me in the importance of keeping the chemicals at a stable temperature of 72°F. I was hooked the instant my first image appeared, magically, out of white photographic paper.

Color was loud, distracting, undeniably sexy. From it, patterns emerged; peripheral designs, suggestions of emotion, dreams. Being seen in reflection, color was ephemeral, its tones changing according to heat and distance, and with the angle and brilliance of the sun. Shooting black and white was a very different matter: it compelled you to focus on people and, in particular, their eyes. Black and white was expression, raw sentiment; a fusion of honesty and composition. Shooting both color and black and white at the same time risked overloading the right side of the brain—that tasked with processing spatial and visual relationships.

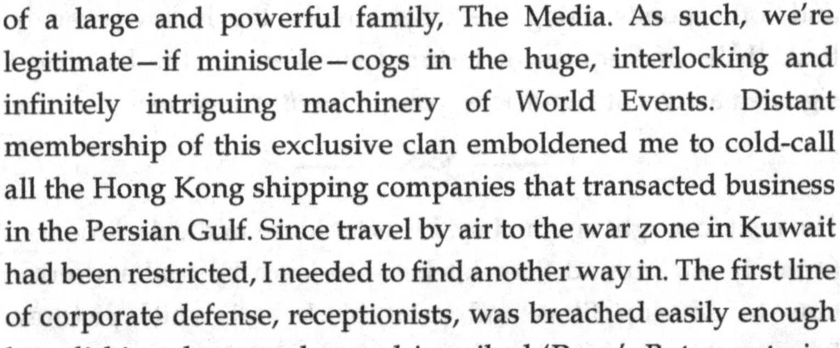

Photographers are, essentially, loners. We're the black sheep of a large and powerful family, The Media. As such, we're legitimate—if miniscule—cogs in the huge, interlocking and infinitely intriguing machinery of World Events. Distant membership of this exclusive clan emboldened me to cold-call all the Hong Kong shipping companies that transacted business in the Persian Gulf. Since travel by air to the war zone in Kuwait had been restricted, I needed to find another way in. The first line of corporate defense, receptionists, was breached easily enough brandishing the sacred sword inscribed 'Press'. But secretaries were another matter. *Please fax us your request* was their usual delaying tactic. I persisted, finally getting through to a Mr Janssen of a popular Dutch shipping line.

"You are a registered seaman, of course, Mr Stowers?" Janssen kept any trace of irony or impatience out of his voice. Somehow, I didn't think the phony, laminated *MV Darwin Hunter* crew credentials—that, in 1987, I had used to gain access to the subsidized beer at the Mariners Club in Kowloon—would pass muster this time.

"Then I am afraid I am not sure what we can do for you. It is mostly a matter of insurance, you will understand."

"Mr Janssen, I will sign any piece of paper releasing your company from responsibility of my personal safety. It really is just a matter of my temporary relocation ..."

"... from Hong Kong International Terminal to Jebel Ali, yes, you said. I understand. But this is a most unusual request. Please do one thing for me?"

"Yes, anything," I eagerly agreed.

"Fax through your request, and I will see to it that the matter is taken up with my board."

I crossed Janssen off my list and started on the Asian lines. The Japanese inability to say 'no' saw me passed up to a high-ranking member of management in a company based out of Kobe, Mr Isiki. He listened most respectfully and sympathetically to my request, agreed that the Press must be free to report independently from trouble spots around the world, and even admitted that the shipping lines were "having trouble these last weeks in finding crew who are willing to enter the most dangerous Gulf region."

On this last point I seized, offering my sweat and toil in either engine room or galley, on any of his Gulf-bound ships. But it was to no avail: in Japan, decisions were referred up the chain of command. The Emperor must have a particularly full In-Tray.

"Hendrick, I want to chuck it all in. This job is tough enough as it is, without all the barriers and obstacles placed in our way. Those guys shooting for *National Geographic* have it easy. Their fixers arrange everything in advance; helicopters laid on for aerial shoots, money and time no object. They are free to concentrate on their job, and just shoot!"

"If it were that simple," replied the calm voice of reason, "half the world would become photographers."

He'd given up on the idea of traveling to Baghdad, anyway, having been persuaded to shoot a swimsuit issue for a local sporting magazine. He went off on a tangent: "Gandhi says the things that will destroy us are politics without principle, pleasure without conscience, wealth without work, knowledge without character, business without morality, science without humanity and worship without sacrifice." I'd not asked for the lecture but, as usual, the Dutchman's sentiment was timely. "At least two of those categories apply to us photographers. It is in fact imperative we *do* struggle for our goals. If things come to us too easily, we never will appreciate them, and we will never learn."

I'd tried the open approach, now I decided to deviate. My next call was to Sam Ho at the HK Pro-Democracy Alliance.

"Hi, Sam? It's Chris. Listen, do you still have contacts at the container terminal?" I was in luck. A cargo vessel, the 10,000-ton *Prosperity*, was departing for the Gulf on February 6. Precisely *where* in the Gulf, he was none too sure. It couldn't be such a big place, surely? It was just a *gulf*. I phoned up the representative of *Prosperity* in Kowloon.

"I'm calling from the *South China Morning Post*." I embellished. "We're doing a story about the Hong Kong shipping industry and will be sending one of our photographers, a Mr Flynn, down on the fifth. Will 4:00 p.m. be a good time for you?" My cut-and-paste SCMP letterhead passed scrutiny after I'd mangled it through the fax machine. In return, I received an official invite to board *Prosperity*, for the following Tuesday. I had been carrying the fake press credentials of 'Charly Flynn' ever since I'd had them printed and laminated at a stall down Koh San Road, passing through Bangkok. It was time to bring my swashbuckling alter-ego out of retirement.

Work over for the day, Hendrick and I strolled into Mui Wo to meet Wendy off the early evening ferry and show her the new flat. Feeling blasé, I treated us all to a feast of king prawns with chips at The Flagstaff pub. I needed a distraction, something to stop me thinking about what it was I was thinking of doing. Our bravest acts are often our most foolish. They terrify us only in retrospect, when allowed sufficient time for contemplation. But direct action was the only sure way to stave off boredom, derail frustration and ensure our attractiveness to the opposite sex.

"You have wonderful hair," Hendrick complimented Wendy. It was a statement of fact: he was in fashion and knew about this sort of thing. He seemed a little more lost for words than usual, handed Wendy his business card after the meal and headed back to the house, leaving the two of us alone in the pub.

"Listen, Wendy, I will be heading off on a risky assignment in the next few days."

"Really?" She didn't seem particularly impressed.

"Yes," I played my trump card, "to the Gulf." It fell flat. She didn't follow the news.

"To play a game?"

"Not golf … Gulf … you know, the war?"

"So, you'll be going away, again …" she grabbed hold of the only part of the conversation she had any investment in. Honestly, talking with her was like playing drunken darts: I only hit the bull's-eye by accident.

The fifth arrived; neither date nor nature indicated this day would be any more or less memorable than the four days of February that had preceded it. I headed over to the Kowloon container terminal. The shipping company's fax invitation saw me past port security, a guard insisting on driving me in an electric golf cart to where *Prosperity* was berthed. Captain Yunus, a Malaysian, couldn't have been more obliging.

"Where do you want me?" he gushed, posing on the bridge, cranes twizzling around like the keys in a giant wind-up toy as containers stacked on the deck far below. Having a genuine interest in sea travel, it was easy to make up questions. And let's not get started on all those exotic sounding ports. Yunus, straight from Central Casting with his trim gray beard, had visited them all. Aden? *The chai is too sweet.* Colombo? *Too many crows.* Mombasa? *Too many Indians.* Osaka? *The girls are too pretty ...*

"Captain, where is your final Port of Call on this voyage?" I ventured.

"That would be Jebel Ali," he said, and inwardly I cheered, "Dubai." Hmm ... in the neighborhood, then ...

"And how long will that take?"

"Well, via our usual stops at Singapore and Karachi, twenty-seven days."

I hadn't expected that. The supplies hidden beneath the lighting equipment in my bag were sufficient for ten days, tops. I'd have to reveal my presence somewhere, once we were on the High Seas. I asked for a tour of the ship, and Yunus happily complied, sending me off with his First Officer, a Filipino named Alfred. Sam had already briefed me on the best hiding places aboard a ship, these being the engine room or the storage units. These days, lifeboats were sealed capsules. People only hid away in them in the movies. Sam had helped pro-Democracy activist Siao slip into an unlocked container on the wharf. Even at this late stage, I wasn't sure if I was going to go through with it. I told myself: *only if an opportunity presents itself.* Alfred was from Batangas. I praised the beaches of nearby Mindoro Island, where I had languished a few days last year. It turned out he'd been staying at the next resort along, at the same time.

"Probably, Sir, we walked past each other on the steps of Jollibee restaurant! And may I ask Sir, do you work for some other magazines?" The most prestigious publication my pictures had appeared in was *Asiaweek*. Alfred began hopping around like a child on Christmas morning.

"You are an *Asiaweek* photographer, Sir? You're famous!"

Alfred's reaction was entirely understandable, if overly generous: *Asiaweek* had been held in high regard in the Philippines ever since it editorialized in favor of the People Power Revolution, back in 1986, helping sway popular and international support for the ouster of the Marcos dictatorship.

Seven p.m. I'm concealed in the paint locker; the fumes are overpowering. The big ship's engines began to throb, the prelude to departure. Could this finally be it? The option of stowing away had never been far from my mind. I'd had a chance, back in 1986, before ever leaving England. Back then I was a motorcycle messenger, and delivering Admiralty charts to the 5,000-ton *MV Salamander*, moored off the Isle of Grain. But I'd bottled-out at the last minute. More recently, my voyage on the *Kurnia Ilahi* from Flores to Singapore had felt a lot like running away to sea, even if I was part of the crew, not a stowaway. As the perfume of one adventure wears off, so the addict searches a new fragrance to adore. Part of it is romance, but mostly it is reaction to boredom.

Earlier I'd given Alfred the slip, doubling back and down a few decks, preparing to say I'd lost my way, missed my footing, banged my head. *Where am I?* The whole Oscar-winning act. But Yunus ran a tight ship. The door to the paint locker was pulled open and I blinked adjusting to the sun's setting rays. I decided to come clean.

"I'm sorry, captain. I was trying to get to the Gulf, to take pictures of the war."

"He's an *Asiaweek* photographer, Sir." Alfred, at his captain's side confirmed.

"*Asiaweek*, or not, I can't have undocumented aliens stowing away on my ship. It's the law of the seas." He soon relented, "I admire your determination, Flynn," he harumphed. "As far as I care, you're free to leave, but you'll have to find your own way out. Good luck!"

I shook hands with Yunus, and then with Alfred, who lowered the gangplank.

❧

The Bakker family were Dutch compatriots of Hendrick, and our neighbors on Lantau. They'd returned to Holland for the month and asked me to house-sit the farm building they had painstakingly renovated into a beautiful, whitewashed home — replete with blue and white Delft tiles and a scale-model windmill in the vegetable garden. Henk, the gruff, bearded Bakker patriarch, guided people on tours of Mainland China, though his true vocation was that of missionary. He and his wife had three teenage children, all of whom grew up in Hong Kong and spoke fluent Cantonese. Their eldest, Inge, was a top-flight model. Least agreeable of my new responsibilities was to care for their opinionated and stubborn dog, 'Tuen'. I felt like the Lord of the Manor, all the space and privacy; the *cutlery*; and choice of new bedroom in which to sleep each night.

Tuen didn't want any fussing, and had taken to following me down to the ferry whenever I left the island, before going off to cause god-knows-what trouble among the local population of available bitches. This morning, though, he actually boarded the boat, and I had to pull him, snarling and resisting, back to the house. Growling at each other, I locked him inside and rushed back, disheveled and cursing, to find my boat had sailed, making me seriously late for my assignment, a portrait shoot for *Asian Business*. The magazine was a new client of mine, whose picture editor, David Sutton, I'd met at the Press Club, in Wanchai. I was anxious to make a good impression. I'd chosen a nice location; the roof of a car park down by City Hall, with Norman Foster's modernist Hong Kong Shanghai Bank HQ as the backdrop. Fortunately, my apologies for tardiness were accepted and I soon slipped into 'photographer mode'. This professional state of being brought forth an uncontrollable sweat—no matter the weather or environment—which increased in direct correlation to the degree of concentration I exerted through the lens. I was concentrating so hard now, in fact, that I went through an entire roll of film, only becoming aware of an odd lack of resistance when winding on each frame. A cold stone plummeted to the bottom of my stomach, an event of such tectonic magnitude the resultant splash must have registered on my face: "You've forgotten to put a film in, haven't you?" drawled my good-natured subject, an Australian expat, in HK to introduce new hi-tech ATM machines.

Arriving back on Lantau mid-afternoon, I reached the farmhouse and discovered Tuen's revenge. The imprisoned mutt had ripped electricity cables out of the wall, shredded the curtains, punctured the seat cover on the sofa, clawed deep marks down the piano leg, and left all his food and water scattered across the polished white flooring. The creator of this mayhem tilted his head to one side, awaiting my reaction, eager to up the stakes. It would have to be the night I'd invited Wendy over.

I rushed to clear up the most obvious mess before Wendy arrived. She brought along, as chaperone, fellow thespian, Calvin. I don't know. Maybe he was her boyfriend? I couldn't tell, and felt it impolite to ask. She loved the cottage. She was standing at the piano, admiring a photo in a frame, as I stood in the kitchen doorway, admiring her in turn.

"She's beautiful!" Wendy said.

"That's Inge, she's a model. It's one of the photos I took for her portfolio," I told her. Wendy seemed at odds tonight, distracted.

"What a cute dog!" She transferred her attention. Tuen, the manipulating mutt, allowed her to tickle his tummy, a maneuver that, if I had tried, would have resulted in the loss of my hand. *I see through you, Matey.*

"Yes, he's got personality," I admitted.

We moved the party upstairs, where we ate pizza and broke open some drinks sitting outside, on a small terrace above the kitchen, under the inspection of a solemn moon. The Style Council's *Café Bleu* drifted up the staircase, escaping into the shadowy clasp of overhanging branches. The scene was set for seduction. That *had* been my plan.

Wendy's cheeks were reddening after just her first glass of wine, and she happily accepted a second. The problem with fancying an actress was never knowing when she was being sincere or practicing the scenes of her next performance. Photographers are like that, too, I guess: superficial. How else could we coax complete strangers into adopting ridiculous poses, develop instant trust, and establish sufficient rapport to put the subject at ease? By nature, I was the opposite of all that; shy and insular, and at a loss when it came to small talk. My element was the cave; my home the confessional. But a camera, like a stage costume, helped overcome the handicap. If I kept playing the photographer long enough then, who knew, maybe one day it would all just become instinct. I left Calvin and Wendy deep in discussion, and popped downstairs to renew our drinks. When I returned, Calvin was staring up at the moon with a startled expression on his face and muttering in rapid Cantonese.

"Is this a scene from your play?" I asked, intrigued. He had captured the mood of a petrified on-looker perfectly. I twisted my head, following his gaze. Wendy was pacing unsteadily along the central spine of the steeply sloping roof, as though balancing on a tightrope in a strong gale, her arms outstretched, and a half-filled wine glass in one hand.

"How the hell did she get up there?" I shrilled, trying to find somewhere to place the drinks.

"I ... I couldn't stop her. What do we do?"

I began to climb the tiles, but they shifted under my weight and I feared the whole roof would give way. I could only join Calvin and stare, transfixed as Wendy, laughing and talking to herself, reached the eaves, paused, and then executed a wobbly pirouette, and started her erratic promenade back along the ridge.

Finally, she was able to exorcise the demon that had seized her, and slithered down to our waiting arms. She glared at poor Calvin, who made some excuse to go off and sort out his bedroom for the night, though the evening was yet young.

"I don't like men," Wendy slurred, "can't be trusted. Can you be trusted?"

"Sure, Wendy." I sat her down on the terrace wall, and placed an arm around her shoulder, concerned she'd lean back too far. It was the closest we'd been, physically, since holding her hand to get into *Soho*, the night we'd first met. "Is it Calvin?"

"Who? Calvin? No! Don't be ridicilous!" she slurred, ridiculously drunk, her face the color of a rose patch. "He doesn't love me."

"Who? Calvin? Calvin doesn't love you?"

"No, silly."

"He must be a fool not to love *you*, Wendy."

Slumped now against my side, she looked up at me. "That's nice. You're sweet, Chris. You know, *you* should ask me ..."

"Ask you what, Wendy?" I said at the moment her head slumped to her chest. She was down for the count. Calvin, who had popped up to ask for a towel, helped me carry her to her bedroom and we laid her out fully clothed to sleep it off. Although the evening had been far from perfect, a result had been achieved: I felt closer to Wendy than ever before now her mask of perfection had slipped.

Carl was browsing the overflowing shelves of equipment at *Photo-Scientific*, the Hong Kong camera mecca, looking dapper, his neck swathed by a new Cambodian scarf, and an unlit cheroot dangling from the corner of his mouth. The laconic Danish photographer invited me for lunch at the hallowed Foreign Correspondents' Club, of which he was a member. We dragged ourselves up the steep incline of Wyndham Street to 'the most famous press club in the world'. Seated at the polished wooden bar, tickertapes behind us spewing the latest news like minced meat from a grinder, Carl signaled to a member of staff, whom he addressed by name, asking for the drinks list. I was thinking of saying something asinine about how rarely we bumped into each other despite living in the same town, when he started to relate his latest adventure, last month — in Bangladesh.

That month had been April and, during it, one of the deadliest tropical cyclones in recorded history swooped out of the Bay of Bengal to lay waste to much of Chittagong District. More than 138,000 people had been killed, and Carl just happened to have been traveling there at the time. The newspapers were still printing follow-up reports of the ensuing humanitarian disaster. Carl had dashed for Dhaka Airport, boarding a flight to Paris as most of the international press were arriving. Even though the wire services had gotten initial images out by that time, he understood the unique value of his photos. So, apparently, did *Paris-Match*, who used his shot on their cover, and in a large photo spread on the inside pages, netting a huge pay-check.

Photographers are only ever one natural disaster away from having a good year.

May 22, 1991

Rajiv Gandhi Assassinated, screamed the headlines. I took Wendy to eat at the Sri Laksmi in Lan Kwai Fong, by way of national commiseration.

"He was married to an Italian, you know."

"Who, the waiter?" she asked, distractedly, glancing over my shoulder before throwing a curve ball: "A woman seems interested in you, at the table over there."

I turned to look. Penelope.

"Chris, it *is* you! And your friend?"

I made the introductions. One of my first acquaintances after arriving in Hong Kong in 1987, fresh off the boat from Shanghai, Penelope had once owned an art gallery on Hollywood Road and encouraged me to put on my first ever exhibition of photographs there. I hadn't seen her for ages.

"An *actress*, how interesting," enthused Penelope, ignoring Wendy. This was why I liked to keep my female friends separated. A photographer, by nature, is neutral. Like soda water, he blends well with anything. Women, on the other hand, were more spirited, like vodka or whisky. Perfect on their own, but a guaranteed headache when mixed.

"And this *lady*?" purred Wendy after Penelope had returned to her group, "she sells junk?"

"She used to sell art. The New Age market is more profitable for her, these days." I tried deflecting the topic, but Wendy was alert now, more attentive. This sudden discovery of my covert life, beyond that of our own immediate relations, had increased my value. We held hands and wandered down to Blake's Pier. Purposefully, I ignored the last sailing to Mui Wo, wanting to see how far the limits of Wendy's newly invigorated hospitality would extend. She let me stroke her hair. Considering the glacial pace of this romance, it was quite a breakthrough. *I must be in love, or else the frustration would kill me.*

And here we were, back to long-suffering St Augustine: was I merely 'in love with loving'? Did I love the *idea* of being in love with Wendy more than I would the reality of an actual relationship? After all, plenty of people seemed entirely content living their lives in the pursuit of perfection; few ever caught it. It would be quite a disappointment to attain that level of paradise, only to discover she snored and farted, like the rest of us.

It was by now 3.00 a.m. and, after seeing Wendy off on the all-night tunnel bus to Kowloon, I wondered what to do with myself. I'd missed the last ferry, by hours. The waterfront was deserted. Nobody actually lived in Central District; it was all skyscrapers, banks and businesses — a ghost town after the daily work exodus. But one industry looked to be thriving. Down on Des Voeux Road, beside the resting tramlines, hundreds of workers made delivery of newspapers, hot off the printing presses. Sorting the pages and folding supplements with hands encased in ink-stained cotton gloves, they stacked the shelves of myriad magazine stands in time for the morning rush hour. Hidden Hong Kong. I took out my camera and slowly began to work my way into their acceptance.

A few weeks later I received a call from Deborah (she hated being called 'Debby') the new *Asiaweek* photo editor. The weekly magazine would be printing my photo essay about the

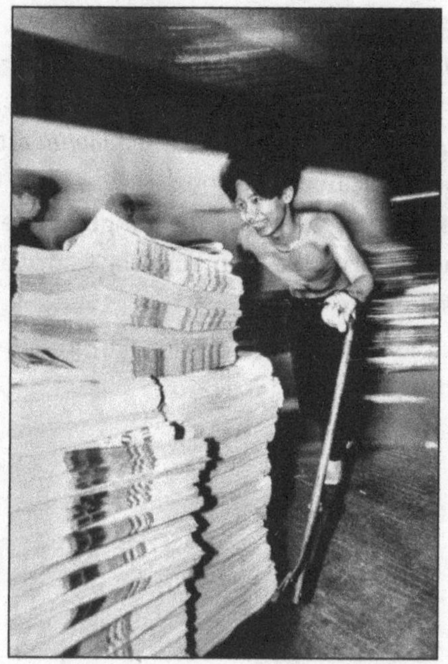

newsvendors in this week's *Eyewitness* section. Four double-page spreads, at US$200 per photo!

"Hey, well done," I basked in Hendrick's praise later. *Eyewitness* was the gold standard for half the freelance photographers in Asia. "This is what it's all about: telling a story in four, strong, double-page spreads. Let's celebrate!" Any excuse to break open the *Bols*. Genever was the Dutch national spirit, and Hendrick warned me: "This is the old stuff, clear, but like whisky. You'll like it," he said, confident in advance of my approval.

〜〜〜

The world was entering a particularly parlous state. I worried that 'society' might soon lose the benign stasis that allowed me to dip in and out of it at will. Where to start:

- Imminent collapse of an international bank, the
  BCCI (in HK, where money was worshipped, this
  was like contemplating the end of religion);
- Manila Airport closed, still, fully a *month* after
  Pinatubo's volcanic eruption;
- Massive flooding all along the Yangtze River basin;
- Practically every village in Yugoslavia declaring
  itself a sovereign state;
- Soviet Union, falling apart, goes cap-in-hand to the
  G7 meeting in UK.

July 21, 1991

BCCI, OR THE 'Bank of Crooks and Criminals' as the wits were terming it, was the money launderer of choice for such luminaries as Saddam Hussein and General Noriega. Given Hong Kong's laissez-faire financial regulatory atmosphere, BCCI had been an extraordinary success in the territory. The upstart outfit had beaten the likes of longer-established rogues, J.P. Morgan and Citicorp, in establishing a branch across the border in China's Shenzhen Special Economic Zone. Rather regretfully, the Hong Kong Office of the Commissioner of Banking had, a fortnight before, ordered BCCI to cease its operations in the colony. There was rumored to be a protest of all those depositors fearful that their savings would evaporate.

I made sure to arrive in Central early, and had just crossed Statue Square when a well-dressed Chinese woman approached and asked if she could use some of the masking tape off the roll hanging from my camera bag. "It's for the police," she explained, handing some lengths of tape to the two constables trailing her who used it to fix their walkie-talkies. It looked as though they were expecting things to get rough.

Suddenly, a mass of vocal protesters surged from behind the Bank of China Building, pushing angrily at the thin police line. I leaped over a railing and dodged the trams trundling down the center of Des Voeux Road. There was a TV camera crew bobbing about to my right, but no other photographers. I had no idea it would all kick off so early.

"Cut!"

Thought it was too good to be true. They were filming a scene for a Cantonese soap opera. Masking tape woman approached me again, megaphone in one hand, script in the other, and asked if I would like to play a photographer in this scene. Obviously, I looked the part. I declined her offer, though; by now a platform had been erected back in Statue Square, and the *real* protesters were starting to arrive. The turnout was a slight disappointment, around five hundred worried and angry souls, many of whom hailed from Hong Kong's Indian and Pakistani business communities (and found themselves united, for once, against a common enemy). Their demands were made both in Cantonese and English:

"WE WANT OUR MONEY BACK!"

I made a quick film check: twenty shots remained on the roll of Tri-X black and white loaded in my FA body, and there were seven precious frames of Ekta400 in the FM2. Still, it only took one great image …

First came two excruciating hours of speeches. As captain Yunus would no doubt have observed, it was really *too* hot to be marching at this time of day, and the BCCI's habitually office-dwelling depositors plodded off toward Victoria Park in lackluster mood, suffering in the 90 percent relative humidity. A flamboyant girl with bright orange and blue streaks in her voluminous hair passed slowly, sitting on the tailgate of a curb-crawling van. She was talking loudly into a brick-like mobile phone. Finishing her live report for *Commercial Radio*, she ordered the American photographer sitting next to her to scoot up, and motioned me to join them.

"Hi, I'm Luisa Tam," she announced. I'd heard her voice over breakfast, many times. "This is Stephan Ellis from Reuters. He's leaving Hong Kong soon. Come and join us at the Press Club later."

I was absorbed, at that time, in Mochtar Lubis's book, *Tiger! Tiger!*. The Indonesian author was a Batak, his ancestors coming from Sumatra's Lake Toba—in the cool climes of which I'd recovered from chickenpox the year before. His compelling and mystical recreation of the life and spirits of the Indonesian jungle brought the village of Intu Linggau and its witchdoctor back to mind. I saw again the girls bathing in the river in their sarongs; heard the multi-layered orchestra of tropical insects, and thought

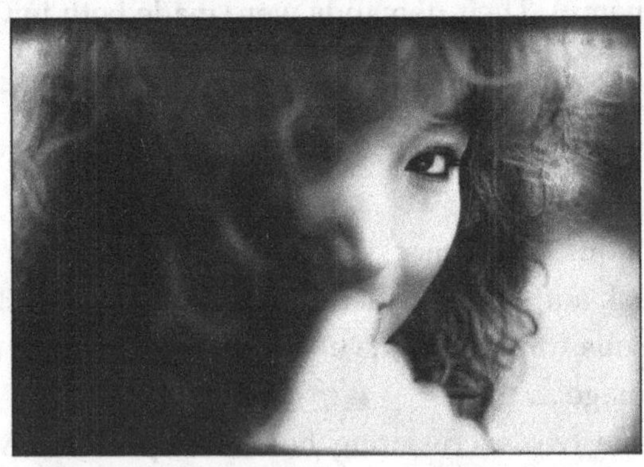

The irrepressible Luisa Tam, photographed in HK, in 1991

my time in this concrete jungle is merely transitory.

Working for weekly magazines, I mused to myself—since there was no-one else immediately available to muse with—was a relative luxury, and well-suited my pace of production. *Asiaweek* wrapped on Thursdays, for example, so any news that happened after that—apart from absolute emergencies, which could still be squeezed in on a Friday—had to wait until the following issue. It allowed a decent amount of time for productive pastimes, such as reading. I hated scrambling around competing with the newspaper and wire service types, trying to get my images out on the same day. Although I had to admit to a certain thrill, later, sipping my coffee in *Delifrance* café on Gloucester Road, listening to Luisa's report—the one that she'd phoned in beside me from the back of a moving van a few hours earlier—as it made the headline news on the 5:30 p.m. bulletin.

"Do you ask everyone you just met to marry you?" I had to shout at Luisa later, over the noise of the Sundowners, a band playing to the patrons of the crowded Press Club in Wanchai.

"It's a business proposition. Think about it. I get a British passport and you can use my flat in Hollywood Road anytime. Makes sense." Having consumed a line-up of gin tonics and B-52s, I had to admit I was warming to the practical benefits of such a strategy. With 1997 coming up, it helped to have options, immigration-wise.

"Look, there's Maria." Luisa shifted focus, probably to preempt me raising the hypothetical subject of conjugal rights. "Maria, meet Chris. We're going to get married." The stately South African reporter took this breaking news in her stride, as though I were not the first potential husband Luisa had introduced her to this week, saying dryly:

"Congratulations."

We all ended up back at Maria's flat, lying strung across her huge sofa listening to Chris Isaak's "Wicked Game" album, further mixing the drinks and mistaking all those dreams for desires.

SEOUL, SOUTH KOREA

August 29, 1991

THE ASIAN TIGER economies were rarely out of the news: Hong Kong, Singapore, Taiwan, South Korea. The latter was being touted as 'the shoe factory of Asia', but the country had obvious ambitions to move up the technology food chain into electronics. They were all chasing Japan. And photographers? We were chasing their trends. On the streets, every day, observing people, their fashion choices, all the latest consumerist whims; we were style spies. And although most of us weren't privy to the boardroom decision-making processes of Li Ka-shing or Akio Morita, we were, inevitably, among the first to spot each new wave of innovation as it swept in, unfiltered, through our lenses. Even the least faddish among us could begin to predict whose pop stars, which luxury brand, regional cuisine, iconic skyscraper, nightlife scene or property market was about to boom, and to adjust their travel plans accordingly. The trick was to have fresh pictures on hand *before* these stories ever broke and photo editors even thought of needing them: images of oil refineries in Kaohsiung, people using mobile phones in Central Seoul, banks that were about to expand (and others on the verge of implosion), Buddhist monks praying for alms outside a Starbucks in Sapporo; the remit was as vast and varied as the desires, greed and invention of the human mind. Judging my photo archive rather narrow in this department, I allotted myself two weeks, and a budget of sixty rolls of film (based on my four-roll-a-day habit) to branch out and make a sweep through South Korea. If I selected my topics wisely, I reasoned, the images should sell like spicy kimchi.

It always takes me two or three days to get used to shooting in a new country: people react differently to the camera, and to the person pointing it. I had arrived this afternoon, and was already completely out of my depth. While appreciating the softer, more melodious Korean tongue (a relief after the aural assault of Cantonese), and the coffee (Koreans were addicted to caffeine, with vending machines offering super-concentrated paper cups of the stuff on every street corner, for 200 won a shot), it was shocking to me how muscular the atmosphere was. The pavements, for example, despite being nowhere near as crowded as those in Hong Kong, were a battleground upon which I was relentlessly barged and jostled by rather aggressive Korean male commuters. I put this down to them being sore at still having to have the Americans protect them from their northern relatives.

And then there was the angular Korean *Hangul* alphabet, differing so from the florid *Hanja* Chinese characters it had been adapted from. To the uneducated foreigner, Chinese calligraphy resembled nothing more than a fortuitously aligned accident in a noodle factory, whereas the regimented format of Korean script—introduced by King Sejong in the 15th Century in the interests of mass literacy and national identity—was orderly, self-contained and logical. Written as a style guide to accompany the introduction of these new hieroglyphs in 1446, the *Hunmin jeong-eum haerye* noted of *Hangul* characters, "A wise man can acquaint himself with them before the morning is over; a stupid man can learn them in the space of ten days." Staggering beneath my overloaded backpack, it took three hours just to find a hostel agreeable to my budget; time better spent, perhaps, trying to memorize brush strokes so I could work out from which tube station I was alighting.

Further baffling, having arrived here directly from cash-obsessed Hong Kong—and indicative of a spiritually zealous trait embedded in Korean culture—was the middle-aged man, dressed in nothing but sackcloth, hobbling barefooted down the length of my train carriage dragging a huge wooden crucifix over his shoulder. The cross, which must have weighed more than he did, was at least six-feet long, and had little wheels at its base to ease movement. No one paid him the slightest bit of attention.

I do not understand these people. Thank God I do not understand these people.

BUSAN
August 31, 1991

ALL I KNEW of Korea was obtained watching *M*A*S*H*. The nation was still, technically, at war with itself, and a heavy US troop presence tangible on the streets. In late August 1950, the battle of the Busan Perimeter was raging. The North Korean Army, having advanced far down the peninsula, were facing United Nations forces—consisting mainly of Republic of Korea, American and British troops—here, on the fringes of Busan. This southeastern pocket was the only area of the ROK to remain unconquered, holding out until MacArthur's counterattack at Incheon the following month.

I like plucky port towns.

Busan was the down-to-earth, proletarian antidote to Seoul's flashy cosmopolitanism. The city had hills and views, seagulls and the thriving Jagalchi fish market, all of which surged into life in the early morning sunlight. I'd come straight down south to Busan yesterday, by bus, fleeing the overwhelming capital. Damage from a recent typhoon was evident along the way; the bent electricity pylons and abnormally swollen and boulder-strewn rivers. Outside of Seoul, Korea was a different country, its small towns populated by an ancient race who wore the traditional costume of baggy white trousers tied at the ankle, and wide straw hats, as they worked in ginseng fields.

Busan's spectacularly undulating skyline was dominated by Busan Tower, thrusting 120 meters above Yongdusan Park, and from the observation deck of which a magnificent vista stretched across to Yeongdo Island, with its active shipbuilding yards and cliff-top coastal trails.

"No photo!" screamed an official, as I was about to take a shot of the stunning view. This country was officially *paranoid* about photography. I lowered my camera, not wanting to cause an incident, but only because I'd taken a few frames before he'd spotted me.

The electronic light meter on my Nikon FA was playing up. It was something I would have to get seen to when I returned to Hong Kong. The idea, of course, was not to need a light meter at all, to sense exposure. To this end, I was continuously compensating for glare or shadow as I walked along, gauging the light, its intensity and direction. An alleyway could be viewed as a tunnel, at the end of which a character was a silhouette, or as a cave mouth, from which he emerged into blinding sunlight. Snap decisions had to be made whether to expose for darkness or highlight. Non-photographers tended to miss all this, of course: ask them how the sun hit a building and they'd mumble some unhelpful generalization about it being *bright* or *nice*. In truth, they had failed to notice. *We photographers are particularly pedantic about this sort of thing.*

There was a US consulate in Busan. It hid inside a high-walled compound, guarded by chisel-jawed, baton-wielding Korean officers. I walked past the complex on the wide pavement. I had pre-set my exposure and managed to focus and shoot off one frame—featuring a guard, with the consulate signage behind him — before he raised his arm and shouted, "Do not take camera here!"

I waved at him and walked on, only to be swiftly intercepted by two very pleasant yet persistent Korean gentlemen, smartly dressed in identical gray silk suits. *What are you doing here? Working?*

"No, walking, walking ..." I demonstrated, marching the fingers of my right hand in the air.

There's a very interesting International Market you can walk to, just down the street, one of them suggested, directing me away from the consulate.

The game was on: the more I was told I couldn't exercise my right to take photos, the more I just had to try. After a changing of the guard, I crossed back to the consulate, this time firing from the hip, triggering the camera using a cable release in my pocket. I'd only get one shot at it. But on first attempt the shutter didn't fire, the winding arm having snapped shut against my body. I retreated around the corner and jammed the winder open with a folded business card. Back again. This time I used a street map for cover, returning to the entrance and pretending to search for an address, the camera half-obscured below. I walked past three times, exhausting my range of confused tourist expressions. There was no way of telling if these shots were sharp or how they were composed, but the 24mm lens was a wide net; it usually caught some fish.

A guard rushed over, crossing his arms in repeat of the official position toward photography. I was unsatisfied with my work so far. You only truly *feel* a photo through the viewfinder, with the camera steadied between eyebrow and nose, lining up those twin semi-circles to achieve perfect focus.

I looked around. The traffic rushed by. How could I have been so stupid? The solution to my dilemma was obvious.

Tracing the bus routes back a couple of stops, I jumped aboard an old chugger I was pretty certain would pass the consulate compound. Standing near a right-side window—even though plenty of seats were available—it was with increasing tension I approached the target. If the traffic was too thin, we'd zoom past leaving precious little time to shoot, let alone make all those tweaks and adjustments necessary to transform a snapshot into a photograph. Fortunately, the bus slowed, marooned in a tailback at the traffic lights. I was able to shoot off five frames, in quick succession.

"You!" A shrill whistle was blowing, and a guard began charging through the traffic, waving his baton like a sabre. My fellow commuters kept their heads down, eyes averted. Up ahead the lights changed to green, but the traffic was slow to respond. The guard was closing in on the bus. I looked to the driver. His face, reflected in the rearview mirror, was hard to read. Suddenly he blew his horn, swung the steering wheel in a wide arc, and sent the bus lurching into thinner traffic, leaving the consular staff behind, choking on diesel fumes.

I love plucky port towns.

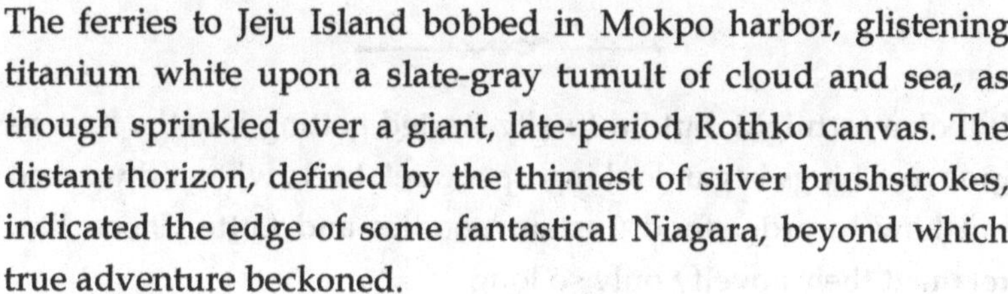

The ferries to Jeju Island bobbed in Mokpo harbor, glistening titanium white upon a slate-gray tumult of cloud and sea, as though sprinkled over a giant, late-period Rothko canvas. The distant horizon, defined by the thinnest of silver brushstrokes, indicated the edge of some fantastical Niagara, beyond which true adventure beckoned.

Jeju was the Korean answer to Hawaii: a sub-tropical honeymoon getaway. Stressed-out city folk and star-crossed lovers flocked there, leaving behind the tensions and expectations of mainland conformity, to be refreshed by the natural scenic beauty of ocean-drop waterfalls and the island's guardian volcano, Hallasan, South Korea's tallest peak. The latter had stubbornly refused me an audience for two days, preferring instead to hide behind a veil of thick cloud. I wandered half-heartedly through the streets of Jeju city. A rhythmic chanting drifted down from an open second-floor window. Curiosity dragged me up the staircase by the camera straps.

Inside, I met bearded martial arts master, Ko Kwang-Ho, owner of the *Kung Jung* dojo. Kung Jung was a form of martial arts discipline resembling Taekwondo, the better-known Korean self-defense method. Master Ko was not in the least perturbed at my unannounced visitation and intruding cameras. Instead, marshaling his young charges (around twenty boys aged 10 to14), he instructed them to perform a variety of traditional *hyung* set moves. I used my little Metz32 flash unit to help freeze-frame the action of their rapid-fire kicks, punches and leaps. Through Ko's assistant, I learned, "Kung Jung is as much about building character as it is about exercise or defense."

I'm not sure why, but I left the small academy feeling good about this set of shots, which had been economically captured on a single roll of film. They made up for, in terms of culture, what — through lousy weather — I'd missed of the landscape.

〜〜〜

It took a fortnight, but I'd finally started getting into the Korean groove. Things began looking up a week back, when I'd worked out how to order food. Instant noodles and Lotte Choco Pies retained their novelty only so long.

And then, there was Kwong.

"Can I talk?" she asked when I answered her knock on my door, dressed only in a towel. My room had no window. There was barely enough floor space to walk around the mattress. She lived in Room 10, down the hall. She said she was bored. I was, too, so I let her stay. I detected in her a sparky character, one prisoned unfairly and by circumstance under the short-haired, tarty guise. We sat on my mattress and she did, as promised — talk. And I remembered Claudia's wistful analysis, back in Tibet, *You are a listener. You are patient. You will find women are attracted to that.*

Kwong had five brothers and an equal number of sisters. They were like a pack of stray animals, she said, leaderless following the untimely death of her parents.

"It is a shame on us, they died from drugs. We are outcasts in this society. I work in a club at nights," she ran a hand through her short hair and smiled weakly before continuing, "I must have been bad in my past life, *this* one is a punishment."

Scavenging a living around the US base in Itaewon, she had lost her virginity when she was 15 to a 35-year-old, married American English teacher. She was married once herself, too, but the child from that doomed union — she didn't say if it was a boy or a girl — had died in a car crash, aged just two. She herself was only twenty-six.

We moved to the *Twilight Zone* café, for coffee. After half an hour she made her excuses.

"I have to go *arbeit* now," using the German term for work.

I headed out to arbeit, too. It was near the end of my trip and I was becoming increasingly reckless in my pursuit of shots. This evening I sidled up a bit too close to some tattooed Korean gangster types, taking pictures in their faces.

"Whaddaya want — what's your problem?" One of them challenged me in some sort of homegrown Hollywood lingo, but I was six inches taller and armed with a tripod, so I stood my ground. But then he untucked his shirt, revealing the handle of a semi-automatic pistol at his belt. Checkmate.

I'd promised Kwong I'd pop by her workplace later, Country Club Heaven, on Hooker Hill in Itaewon district, one of many dubious bars and bordellos set between discos with loudspeakers blaring out into streets full of hawker stalls. Groups of US servicemen wove by in tribal segregation: Blacks, Latinos and Whites, unified by their Flat Top haircuts, and supported by lithe ladies dressed as dungeon mistresses or schoolgirls.

"You came!" Kwong said, breathlessly. I didn't recognize her when I walked in. It wasn't just the bar's dim lighting. She was dressed for work in pointed silver shoes with five-inch heels, a body-hugging miniskirt, and silk blouse encircled by a wide, shiny black belt. Her hair was moussed up and her eyes, those of a Korean Jean Seberg, were lined in thick black kohl. She was stunning, and sat there puffing on a local *88 Lights* cigarette, enjoying the effect her looks were making.

I bought Kwong a standard bar drink, one comprised more of soda than whisky. This assured ten minutes of her time before she had to go and rejoin her cohorts at the bar, sitting on the laps of a bunch of Western businessmen. Laughing at their expat jokes and challenging them to bar games, the girls won with ruthless and practiced ease, forcing the men to buy more drinks in penalty. After a few hours of this, the leader of the ruddy-faced gang of four, a Brit known by all as "Banger", called for the bill.

"180,000 ruddy won?!" he exploded, "You crooks. Swindlers! I'm not paying this." The Americans in his party, embarrassed, would rather—judging by their anxious looks—have paid the exorbitant US$250 bill and gotten the hell out of Dodge. They urged him not to make such a fuss, but Banger's back was up and he was having none of it.

"I'll see you're blacklisted by the entire diplomatic community. This place is finished. You hear me? Finished!"

Kwong slid into my dark observatory.

"He wanted to have sex with me," she shuddered at the mention, whether involuntarily, or to spare my feelings I couldn't tell. Maybe she *was* a prostitute, the lines were so notoriously blurred, but she didn't act like one. Not around me, anyhow. In fact, she refreshed my beer for free, and we toasted the protesting Banger as he and his entourage were ejected by the club's part-time Sumo wrestler bouncers. It seemed only fair, since our drinks had been charged to his bill.

We wandered the neon-plastered city in the early hours, stopping to drink soju and fruit juice, and eat kimchi with rice from street vendors along the way. Back at the hotel Kwong brought the TV set from her room into mine and we lay back on the mattress, legs entwined, watching the *Arsenio Hall* show. Summonsing the patience of a wildlife photographer, I waited to see if this rare bird with her beautiful plumage would migrate back to her room. But by *Johnny Carson*, she'd drifted off to sleep, snoring faintly through a nose she'd told me had once been broken by a gangster's slap.

Quietly, I got up and locked the door.

September 13, 1991

THE NAME OF the nightclub was Utopia; the sort of place dreams came to die. Being Friday night, the place was pumping full of beautiful bodies, joyful skeletons fingered by strobes of ultra-violet light. Kwong stood on the dance floor, a stately six-feet tall in her highest heels. It wasn't long before I heard my name being called.

"Chris! Hi, Chris, over here!" It was Inge, the missionary's daughter. *What the heck?* And sitting beside her in the booth, a besotted young GI. "I'm here on a fashion shoot," she trailed strands of her long, blond hair over the empty soju glasses that cluttered the table, rising to kiss my cheeks three times, in the Dutch style. "What are the chances?"

"Chris ...?" A familiar, deep voice boomed from behind. I turned to find my Hong Kong flat mate doing his impersonation of an Oktoberfest waitress, two pints of beer grasped in each hand, and a look of bemusement angled across his face like an arriving wave.

"Hendrick? You didn't say you were coming to Korea."

"Got the job after you left, man. Small world, Inge's doing an ad for a new shampoo, got me in on the gig. And this is ...?"

Belatedly, I introduced them to Kwong, who had been shifting distractedly beside me.

"Miss Kwong. Kwong, meet Hendrick and Inge, my friends from Hong Kong, and ...?"

"Timmy, from Texas, Sir, Ma'am." Timmy jumped to attention. They shuffled up and we all squeezed in around the small table.

"You just thirsty, or someone else joining us?" I asked Hendrick, nodding in the direction of the four glasses of lager he'd thumped down on soggy placemats. Before he could reply, a vision in silk slid in from behind, twisting around to position herself with intimate ease across his knees, her face hidden by a shiny black waterfall of hair, one arm folding around his neck, like a swan settling into its nest.

"I'm tired, Hen'ri, so tired," this languid figure said without looking up. Something about her voice rang an alarm bell, one locked in a cell, deep in the basement of my gut. Before my brain could locate the correct bunch of keys and send down a search party to investigate, Hendrick's mystery girl raised her head, my heart jumping as the rosy cheeks rolled into view. Wendy.

"That night at the Flagstaff, I thought you knew, man!" Hendrick anticipated my pique.

"You could have warned me," I searched his face for a reaction, a glimmer of guilt, perhaps, but all I encountered were the careworn lines, the eyebrows raised in slight surprise. It was a lived-in face, one that, like its owner, had transcended long ago any pointless concerns about physical appearance.

"Hey, you know me; if it wasn't for the women, I'd be a monk," he protested, staring placidly right through me. It was as though he and I were locked alone in this swirling club. The others fought to gain entrance and understanding.

"You know Wendy?" piped up Inge, from the perimeter. "She, too, was in our advert, you see how nice her hair is." I knew how nice her hair was; my dreams had been entangled in visions of it for over a year. I should have acted faster, followed my instincts. Wait too patiently for a kettle to boil and you are left only with steam.

Wendy glared blinkingly at Kwong. My date for the night glanced back at her. The look on Kwong's face was one of detached bemusement. This wasn't just a play with which she was familiar, it was a repeat performance: the story of her life.

"Chris," Wendy attempted to sit straight, her dignity somewhat lost when she slid off of Hendrick's lap and he had to haul her up from the floor, "that night at the farmhouse. You should have kissed me. But you weren't interested in me …"

It was Timmy from Texas who, unwittingly, defused the situation, pointing out, "Hey y'all, this bar is closing down, we need to find another place."

Inge, normally so aloof in her fragile beauty, hung on every word and gesture of her young soldier, as though the lanky, shaven-headed GI were chipping each new commandment in stone. She took me aside.

"Listen, Chris, I love him. But please don't tell my mother you saw us here in Seoul. Promise? She would never understand."

Utopia closed for curfew, and we went to sit on the curb outside, the staff sliding drinks to us from under its shuttered grille. Having abided by the letter of the law, at 4:00 a.m. the neighborhood clubs presented a middle finger to authority, and we all hurried to enter the Moonlight Bar across the street, as it opened for 'breakfast'.

"I'm sorry, Kwong, I didn't plan this encounter. I'm as surprised as you, probably more so."

"Don't worry. We can never escape our past actions," she said with feeling, "or the disappointment of our dreams."

HONG KONG
September 21, 1991

THE KOREA SHOTS turned out better than I'd expected. I'd tossed and turned all night before picking them up from Color Six photo lab, fearing the worst: that they had been damaged by airport X-rays, or flawed from the start by my own errors of exposure and focus. But this fate was not mine, not this time. I lived to shoot another day. And, looking back on it, the casual intimacy I'd shared with Kwong appeared now less like random chaos, more like another link in the chain of experience. It could not be pure coincidence that I was reading Graham Greene at that moment:

> *"This was victory: somehow to have existed; happiness was an incidental enjoyment: the unexpected glass or the unexpected girl.'*

I always captioned my slides using a green pen. More than one photo editor mentioned looking at them first, since they stood out among all the other photographers' slides captioned in conventional black ink. I could complete 240 slides in the course of the 75-minute ferry ride from Lantau Island to Central.

It was halfway through this self-imposed quota that I spotted Inge approaching, across the deck. I sealed my selection of South Korea shots for *Asiaweek* in their transparent plastic sheets.

"Chris, my mother is sitting upstairs, but I have to tell somebody! Timmy asked me to marry him, and I said 'yes'." The Dutch model's voice danced with an excitement strangely at odds with the concerned expression lining her face. She leaned over, confidentially:

"He is the first person I have ever slept with." Possibly she felt religiously compelled to follow through, make it formal, but she was having second doubts, I could tell:

"Now I'm back here, Seoul seems such a long way away, like it didn't really happen. Do you know what I mean?" I nodded. "And my career is really starting to take off, too, I've got everything going my way ... what would *you* do?" I was hardly the person to go to for advice on matters of the heart, but she looked so desperate.

"Normally, Inge, I write down a list of all the points for and against a course of action. Before I reach the end of the list, I already know my decision. My head and heart are unreliable guides ... I always go with my gut."

Inge sat beside me, calmer now. Occasionally she reached up with long, elegant fingers to tame flyaway strands of her blond hair.

"Wendy had a terrible hangover the day after you left, you know," she said, "I think she felt really bad about you seeing her with Hendrick."

"I can't sit in judgment," I replied, "being with Kwong at the time."

"Was ... is that serious?"

"No. Nothing ever really happened. Mostly we just talked. You know I sometimes think what I'm searching most desperately for is understanding. By comparison sex is, well, a diversion. A pleasurable one, but still distracting."

Inge studied intently the moving Kennedy Town waterfront. A Chinese couple were sitting opposite us, chatting noisily and smiling whenever I glanced in their direction. I smiled back.

"They're criticizing us, you know, making lewd comments," Inge informed me, as we stood up to alight. Reaching her fully magnificent 5 foot 10 inches, her golden mane catching in the morning light, the avenging halo of a furious blond Valkyrie, the missionary's daughter unleashed an unexpected outpouring of righteous indignation in rapid-fire Cantonese that left the startled pair with their mouths gaping like fish, and muttering apologies. "I told them they must be careful because quite a few Westerners can speak Chinese these days."

That's why I resisted learning some languages; generally, it's preferable to think the best about people, and of what they were saying about me.

October 1, 1991

THE VAST RED, white and blue flag of the Republic of China billowed heavily on a breeze carried inland from the bay. It dominated the little hill I had to pass on my way to the ferry. Raising it was an annual ritual, a gesture of defiance from the last handful of stubborn soldiers belonging to Chiang Kai-shek's Nationalist army who, losing the Chinese Civil War, had retreated to—and grown old on—Hong Kong's Lantau Island. Today was the National Day of their sworn communist enemy, on the Mainland.

The civil war between Hendrick and myself had stumbled into stalemate. It had never been that serious, anyway. Photographers never hold grudges for long. We're the only family we've got. Besides, a new enemy had forced us to close ranks: our landlord. He had doubled the rent without warning, so we moved in to a new flat further up the valley. It was a longer walk to the ferry each day, but neither of us planned to spend much time in residence. Apartments were merely photo-equipment storage units.

October 3, 1991

TODAY, A VERITABLE who's who of Hong Kong high society turned out at wreath-bedecked North Point funeral parlor in honor of Sir Y.K. Pao, the shipping magnate. Deborah asked me to cover the event for *Asiaweek*. Caught up in the press crush, I chatted with new-arrived reporter from *The Standard*, Greg Torode.

"Who's that?" he asked, as Stanley Ho, the eminent Macau casino king stepped out of his Rolls Royce. Sir Y.K.'s pallbearers included the unlikely alliance of movie magnate Sir Run Run Shaw, HK's richest mandarin Li Ka-shing, Director of the Xinhua News Agency — and Beijing's de-facto representative in the territory — Zhou Nan, and Y.K.'s golfing buddy, Dennis Thatcher. I'd been expecting him.

"There's Dennis!" I exclaimed, possibly at a volume unbefitting the somber mood. Dennis turned his head in passing and frowned. Made for a nice shot, though. Hong Kong's Governor, the elegant, aristocratic David Wilson assumed his seat on the front row and soon we, the unruly Press, were ushered out.

"Here are your films." I handed over three rolls to Karen, formerly of Lucky Guesthouse, now working as picture librarian at *Asiaweek*.

"And here's your backpack. Have fun!" she said, handing over in return the bag I'd dumped in her office before the funeral. I now had to rush to make the jetfoil to Macau on time. From the Portuguese colony I had a berth booked that same night, on the *MV Macmosa*, sailing to Taiwan's southern port of Kaohsiung.

TAIPEI, TAIWAN
October 9, 1991

THE PUBLICITY DEPARTMENT at Taipei's Regent Hotel were relieved when I called. They'd been expecting me a week already (it being normally accepted practice to fly directly from Hong Kong to Taipei), but I'd been having fun traveling up the island the slow way. I was placed in a Junior Suite at the sumptuous downtown hotel. Derek, my Fairy Godfather editor at *Pacific Traveller* magazine, had managed to wangle this freebie. In exchange, all I had to do was take some shots around the hotel for the Regent's PR department. Posh hotels are just luxurious prisons, cut off from the real world. I aimed to enjoy my comfortable cell for the next couple of nights, and soaked for long in the bath. Then I caught up on all my correspondence using their headed stationary. It was a bit of a waste, though, to be in possession of such a massive room, with its double bed and super-soft mattress, and not have anyone to cavort with in it.

Taipei was in the grip of a tense political standoff. Pictures in local Chinese papers showed students protesting. I suspected it was all to do with the next day, Taiwan's National Day, though Susie, the Regent's PR lady, mentioned something off-hand about 'Wild Lilies' and I didn't pursue it, the set of her mouth told me she didn't agree with their cause.

I called up Martin. Jasmine had passed me his contacts. They were in the throes of an intensely cerebral long-distance relationship, sustained mainly by telephone. He was a member of an elite crew of Westerners working in the Taipei finance industry, trading stocks and shares, and we met downtown at 7:00 p.m. Already the streets were becoming difficult to navigate. Barbed wire trestles had been slung across all the main strategic junctions and smallest of alleyways. Policemen denied access to the inner sanctum around the impressive, red brick Presidential Office, and students were staging a sit-in at the nearby National Taiwan University hospital. My press card allowed me close enough to photograph the central tower of the Japanese colonial-era Presidential Office, bedecked with a massive portrait of the Founding Father of the Republic of China, Dr Sun Yat-sen. Dr Sun had died in 1924, only a few years after the communists came on the scene and, decades hence, forced the Nationalist KMT over to Taiwan. Thus, he achieved the impressive, almost unique, feat of being venerated, simultaneously, on both sides of the Taiwan Strait. His painted patrician gaze stared knowingly down on Martin and me with, what I thought was, an encouraging twinkle in his eye.

We were blocked by police, who ushered us politely but firmly back behind the barricades. We hung around with a group of photographers outside a Family Mart convenience store, among them the Marlboro Man lookalike Robin Moyer, who was shooting for *Time*.

"They won't let us get close to the hospital," complained Robin, bored, "though there may be some action if they try to clear the students out. They've threatened protests to disrupt the National Day parade." The area surrounding the protesters was in lockdown. Only residents living within the cordon were allowed to pass. Martin and I began to probe for a way in. Martin had lived in Mainland China and been aligned with some powerful patrons in the People's Liberation Army. His perfect command of Mandarin disarmed the rookie soldiers we encountered here.

"China," he clarified, "is run by the army—the PLA—and the Communist Party. Both factions need and fear each other." His former affiliation was not of much use in Taiwan, however. "We'll just have to wing it," he conceded.

Humanity is Man's greatest strength, Mankind's weakest link is always human. On this occasion, the Achilles heel was a young police recruit—quite possibly himself sympathetic to the student cause—who nodded us through the first cordon of barbed wire. He only made sure, "Promise me you will not take any photographs."

To save his face, I placed my cameras back in my Domke bag until we'd rounded the next corner. The next alley we tried dead-ended in coils of razor wire. The one after that, however, was not fully barricaded, being left ajar for soldiers in need of the public toilet just down the passageway. Martin and I stepped out here; *behind* police lines, *behind* the ranks of massing troops, and in *full view* of the various TV cameras beaming in from outside. I started shooting wildly at anything that moved. Our luck didn't last long; an enraged army commander ordered us back through the wire, a flash going off as an officially sanctioned CNA photographer recorded our transgress.

Being six-foot-three inches tall, Martin towered above almost everyone in this country. Originally from Ireland, he spoke with a soft northern English accent and informed me of the points where the military would be massing for their big parade in the morning. I made my way back to the Regent Hotel through a city under siege—ugly yellow water cannon trucks now positioned on most every corner—and set two alarms, both for 5:00 a.m.

October 10, 1991

I AWOKE IN anticipation of my alarms, at 4:59 a.m. My footsteps echoed as I was walking down the twisting lane leading from Martin's hilltop community, past the guard asleep in his sentry box, following the line of still-burning streetlamps and on towards the stirring city. Today was the 80th anniversary of the birth of the Republic of China. Flags had been placed across road bridges and outside government buildings; they sagged in the cloying humidity. The ground started to shake long before I got to see or hear the approaching tanks. They amassed in an army base, waiting to breakout from dawn's purple-tinged haze. The military presence at each intersection had doubled from the night before, and I knew I'd not make it past the barricades today. Last night had been a fluke. Besides, observing the show from the perspective of the public was more informative. I could detect in their mechanical displays of patriotic fervor—the platoons of school kids drilled in synchronized acrobatics—a hesitant undertow of resentment against this military heavy-handedness. *Yes, thank you very much for our public holiday, but it really would be nicer to be able to enjoy it shopping or visiting museums and not having to stand here waving our flags and waiting for the politicians and generals to make their speeches.* Taiwan was only just emerging from one of the longest impositions of martial law by a regime anywhere in the world, from 1949 (shortly after their arrival and takeover of the island in 1945), until 1987. Chiang Kai-shek's Nationalist Party, or Kuomintang (KMT), had ruled with an iron fist. The Taiwanese were used to regimentation and, to a large degree, had been cut off from the outside world for this time. The process of repealing these strict laws had begun four years ago.

I jogged to keep pace with a column of missile launchers and open-backed trucks of navy frogmen. Steadying my telephoto lens on a lamppost, I managed some nice long shots of tanks spewing black exhaust smoke and grinding around corners, tearing up the road surface. Similar convoys were converging from all points of the compass, chiefly along Renai Road, and deploying near the Presidential Office. Here, they massed before the military parade, soldiers going over their vehicles one last time with feather dusters. *Where are the disruptions the students promised today?*

Shoving my heavy camera bag before me, I pulled myself on top of the concrete entrance to an underpass. This vantage point had a wide vista above the heads of the gathered public. An out-of-place tinkling sound and flash of silver distracted me: it was the winder arm of my Nikon FA, flying into space. I had just lost the ability to advance the film in my main camera. I improvised by ripping off a length of masking tape, wrapping this around my trigger finger and a NT$1 coin, taping the latter to the former. The exposed edge of the coin fitted neatly into the winder slot on the base of my camera, allowing me to manually advance the film, one frame at a time. Better than nothing. Possibly, to the general observer, this all looked quite cool and MacGyverish, but I'd really just prefer my equipment did its bloody job instead of falling apart all the time.

"You are famous photographer?" a voice drifted upwards.

"What?"

"I see your picture. You are professional photojournalist!"

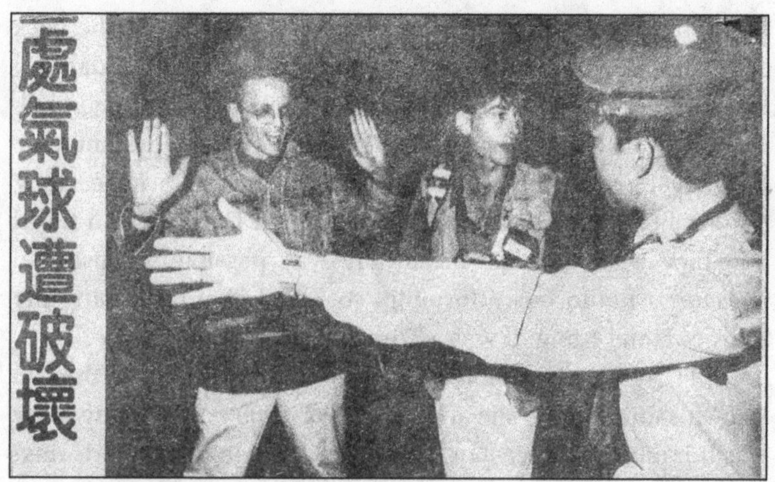

Photo in the Liberty Times *of Martin (left) and I being ordered out of a restricted area near the Presidential Office on the night of October 9, 1991.*

"You must have me mistaken for someone else," I shouted down through the passing rumble of heavily armored personnel carriers. But the young Taiwanese persisted. He waved the newspaper he was carrying at me.

"You, look," and he thrust the latest issue of *Liberty Times* into my hands. There, undeniably, was a photograph of Martin and me being expelled from behind the police cordon the night before.

"Yes, that's me," I admitted, impressed. "Listen, do you have transport? A scooter?" The student nodded, eager to assist the Free Press. "Let's get out of here. Can you take me to the university hospital? Wild Lilies, you know?" He knew. More than this, he updated me on their latest game plan.

"The students were kicked out of the hospital last night. They now are at the NTU campus."

So that's where we headed.

One of the elemental thrills offered by Taiwan was to weave

through traffic at high speed, helmetless, perched on the back of a smoke-spewing Vespa. Today being a public holiday, we reached the protesters at National Taiwan University in no time.

From a call box, I contacted *Asiaweek's* Taipei representative. Miss Huang mercifully broke into English, just as I was reaching the extent of my Mandarin. She confirmed Deborah had faxed that they were to assist me in any way possible. I sensed an *Eyewitness* photo essay forming, so asked about shipping my films to Hong Kong. It was a Thursday, tight for deadline.

"DHL will make a pick-up from our office at between three to four this afternoon," she advised. It was 1.00 p.m. already. Why was this job always feast or famine, manic rush or the doldrums?

"OK," I heard myself promising, "I'll be there."

Most of the protesting students were snoozing in their sleeping bags when we arrived, having just braved a second night in a row on the tiles. Despite the unmarked police cars and plainclothes security personnel—identifiable by their military-style haircuts, polished shoes and unsmiling faces—a festive mood reigned. Someone handed out yellow armbands and headbands, similar to the pro-democracy paraphernalia in Hong Kong. And a young, attractive girl thrust a bunch of lilies in the crook of my arm along with some anti-Article 100 literature. This referred to Article 100 of the Criminal Code, which made it illegal to advocate Taiwan independence—something the KMT government, which still considered itself the legitimate government of *all* China—viewed as sedition. One student told me they were arguing for the law to be amended.

"We have to force the old regime to change. Taiwan is an independent country." This was fairly contentious stuff, despite the relaxing of rules and regulations under new KMT President, Lee Teng-hui, but then these kids were, for the most part, the offspring of the rich and powerful elite themselves. They were rebelling against their parents as much as any passionately held belief in the existential nature of Taiwan's standing in the world. Still, given the number of very real tanks churning up the streets today—and remembering how similar events snowballed out of control in Beijing just two years ago—anything could still happen.

There was a furor in the median of nearby Roosevelt Road, as two protesters sprinted away from a national flag they'd just hung upside-down there. It was a display of deep disrespect, not to mention an arrestable offence. The pair of police cadets standing close by faced a conundrum: whether to chase the fleeing offenders, or to pull down the flag? They chose the latter option, it being too hot, now, to go running around being booed and jeered at.

At 2:30 p.m. loudspeakers coughed into life, and an elderly, white-haired gentleman climbed slowly up to the podium. Professor Lee Chen-yuan taught at the prestigious Academia Sinica, and had founded the 100 Action Union group that was rallying against Article 100. He was one of several academic heavyweights lending his name and moral support to the students' cause. The students listened, some with tears in their eyes, to his stuttering, heartfelt oration, and applauded long and loud at the end. And then a face, even I was familiar with, strode up and presented Lee with two bunches of lilies: Shih Ming-de, the moustache-wearing political activist and lothario—heartthrob of every woman, and hero to every man in attendance. He, and many other leaders, had been jailed for his involvement in the December 10, 1979, Kaohsiung Incident, a KMT crackdown on some of Taiwan's most important political leaders, intellectuals and writers.

Traffic started moving again, with a vengeance. What I needed was to get to Chungshan Road, halfway across town, in a

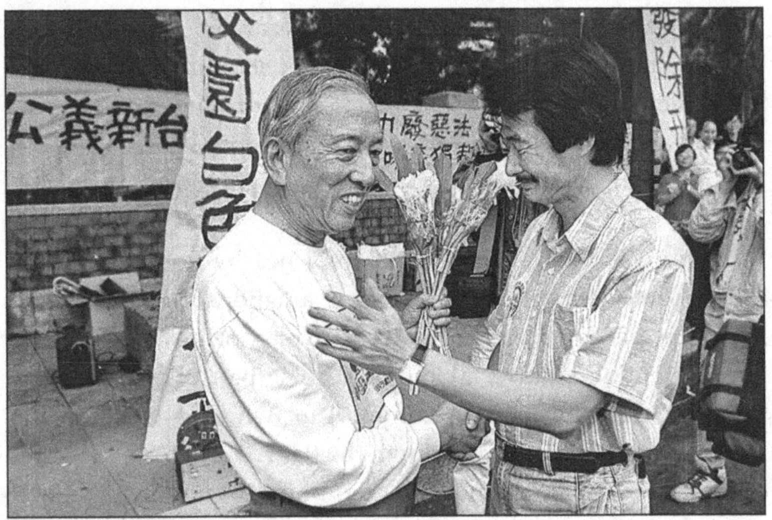

Professor LEE Chen-yuan (left) and political activist SHIH Ming-de at main entrance of National Taiwan University during the Wild Lily Protests. October 10, 1991. Photo: Chris Stowers/PANOS

maximum of fifteen minutes. Taxi drivers ignored me, very likely not wishing to deal with a foreigner and his incomprehensible directions. There was nothing else for it: I waded into the flowing stream of buses, blue vans and two-wheelers, and commandeered a scooter when the lights turned red. The young rider had a camera slung across his chest and didn't seem too perturbed at my jumping on his pillion. Maybe he subscribed to the *Liberty Times*, too? I thrust the local address of *Asiaweek's* office under his nose, and off we smoked.

It was 3:15 p.m. DHL hadn't arrived. I called Martin from the *Asiaweek* office, while I had free use of their phone.

"I'd like to buy some blue chips, some red chips ... and a bag of salt and vinegar chips."

"Very funny," the stockbroker replied. "Listen, can you get to the Hyatt? I'll come down and pick you up on the bike," he said, adding, "I take it you spotted our moment of glory in the local press?"

Martin lived up in the hills in a vast, unfurnished flat. He never seemed to eat. I admired his Spartan existence. He had his act together, as I could only dream of doing (I suspected having your act together was related to having more money than you knew what to do with). But, although his wallet overflowed with wads of blue NT$1,000 notes, his ride was a bashed-up 125cc Yamaha trials bike.

"What do you actually do?" I asked.

"It's easy, I just answer the phone: the guy says *I want to buy so many shares in such and such company* and I phone someone who's got some of these shares and buy them off him." This was false modesty, of course: he was doing all this in Chinese, and had had to work bloody hard to make all those contacts in the first place.

"Oh, it's not so difficult. There are very few foreigners here, so we sort of stick out like sore thumbs. It can be an advantage as much as a pain in the butt. Couple of years ago at New Year, for instance, I was out drinking, bonuses had been paid, the cognac was flowing. I must have stumbled out of the bar around dawn, flagged down a taxi and passed out on the backseat. Next thing I remember, the sun's hitting my face and I'm being shaken awake by the driver, here, outside my flat. "Did I tell you my address?" I quizzed the driver. "No, but I picked you up when you were drunk this time *last* year, and remembered where you lived'."

Martin tossed over a can of Taiwan Beer. "Bought the motorbike after that. Figured having to ride home would keep me from ever getting so drunk again."

We raised our glasses to this and all other doomed resolutions.

<div align="center">~~~</div>

DHL were closed for the public holiday on Thursday. My films only went out to Hong Kong yesterday, a Friday. Looks like I missed the issue. Today, being my final one in Taiwan, I lazed around Martin's flat wondering what all the bother had been about, anyway. Shooting news was a lot like drunken sex: in its grip you burnt, nothing else mattered. But the morning after, you awoke with a bad taste in your mouth, wondering if the whole experience had been worth it. On the spot, it was easy to become overly excited by the deafening roar of war machinery, too involved with the teary-eyed protest, and forget that, to the remote reader, these senses and emotions were not so explicitly felt. *Nothing becomes old as fast as news.*

HONG KONG

November 8, 1991

DEBORAH WAS APOLOGETIC. We were discussing my Taiwan National Day material. "Sorry, but I couldn't interest the editors in week-old news of a military parade during which nothing violent occurred. Long term, there's value in the protest shots, of course, as an historical record." Which was great, but historical records wouldn't help pay that month's rent.

And then she smiled and handed me a copy of the latest edition of *Asiaweek*. My heartbeat quickened as I opened it to the central *Eyewitness* section and recognized my photo essay from the Korean martial arts dojo on Jeju Island I'd visited in September. Sensing I was on a roll, I checked out the current issue of *Asiaweek's* Chinese-language sister publication, *Yazhou Zhoukan*. I had the *Eyewitness* in that, too! This one was even more of a surprise, being a spread of my Orang Asli material. Finally, all the thankless foot-slogging around the Cameron Highlands for Mr Fong last year had paid off. Certainly, I could do with the money; it would help cover my costly, speculative Taiwan trip, films and repairs to my camera.

I loved *Asiaweek*. I finally felt I belonged to something. Mind you, what I was fitting into was a bunch of social misfits and individualists living separately in isolated parts of Asia—like some dysfunctional family—only reluctantly brought together for weddings and funerals by the urgency of a weekly deadline. Still, it was a start, and with it the growing self-confidence brought by more regular publication. I chose my subject matter—or it chose me—and was shooting now with keener awareness of what was marketable. Crucially, I had access to an expanding network of people who could help realize my endeavors where it mattered: in print.

From the evidence in my hands, I needed to stick to slow-burn social features, and not go wasting energy chasing the phantom of Spot News.

∿

A dark and lofty column hung permanently above Hei Ling Chau, posing a smoky question mark about what exactly was going on at the small, rocky island we passed each day on the Lantau ferry.

"The HK government are burning impounded Vietnamese boats there," Hendrick informed me. The number of boat people in detention in Hong Kong had risen this month to almost 65,000—an eight-fold increase since my first arrival in HK, four years ago. Hardly surprising—given all the reports of Thai fishermen preying on these refugees, raping the women, and of the Malay authorities pushing boats back out to sea—that they had started sailing north in greater numbers, and beaching themselves on the more lenient shores of British Hong Kong.

But our official bleeding-heart welcome was now being stretched, and opinion on the Cantonese street—always less generous of spirit—from people, many only a generation removed from being refugees here themselves, had become resentful of funding all these uninvited Vietnamese arrivals with their hard-earned taxes. Or, as an American working for the Save the Children charity explained to me,

"The general stance of the authorities is the situation is not Hong Kong's fault. The refugees are an unexpected and unwanted burden and the government has carried out an extensive and expensive operation caring for them in a timely and humane manner."

We spoke as I visited one of the euphemistically titled 'transit centers' — Bowring Closed Camp — a vacated former British Army barracks housing several thousand refugees out in Tuen Mun.

"Between the lines, of course, you know they just wish the bloody problem would go away," she said.

To that end, it had been announced in the previous month that Hanoi was agreeing to take back all refugees who had fled poverty and persecution under their communist regime, even though many of those refugees had said on record they favored death over repatriation.

"So, see you in the evening, then? I'll get the tickets." I shouted to Hendrick as we parted at the SCMP Bookshop. I jumped on the Star Ferry across to Kowloon to purchase advance tickets for tonight's showing of Oliver Stone's latest movie, *The Doors*.

On impulse, I called up *Asiaweek*, and chatted with acting photo editor Albert Buenaflor. Albert was a wiry and well-meaning oddball, always saying I should get a haircut.

"You look like an Indian," he complained.

"I think Indians look cool," I retaliated.

"Listen, you're in Kowloon? Good. Camera with?" He needed pictures from Kai Tak Airport, this afternoon. "I'll fax GIS and put your name on the list," he said, referring to the Hong Kong Government's Information Service. "They're putting the first refugees on flights back to Hanoi."

I arrived at HK's characterful airport at 3:00 p.m. It was not difficult to spot the Press scrum. Dozens of photographers supported stepladders and massive telephoto lenses, and girls in pencil skirts and hairspray held huge microphones and rehearsed their lines from scripts pinned to clipboards. All milling around the VIP Lounge in the departure area. An ITN TV crew was there, too, passing through on their way to Cambodia. I spotted Luisa: it wasn't difficult; her untamed tresses were so extravagantly coiffed and dyed, it was as though she'd strong-armed Jackson Pollock into doing her hair for the occasion. She was celebrating:

"Hi Chris. It's my very last day working for Commercial Radio, so I had to have my hair touched up. I'm joining the SCMP tomorrow!"

A GIS representative ushered us all into a guardhouse, marking our names off his list as we pushed past, his colleague handing out ID tags on lanyards. Next, our bags were searched. The *Standard's* Mark Ralston was there, dressed smartly as always in crisp blue, long-sleeved shirt and brown chinos. Never a drop of sweat; how did he manage it? We nodded to each other across the commotion. All the other photographers, I noticed, were carrying very big lenses. My longest focal length was the 180mm. Excellent for street photography, but totally inadequate for this kind of paparazzi press job.

The refugees, many of whom had reportedly been resisting the move, were being bused in from camps around the colony. Soon, they would be here, delivered to the doorstep of a huge hangar complex at the end of the runway, where they would be processed and to stay for a final night, prior to repatriation. Before then, we media were given an advance tour of the vast cargo warehouse, emptied now of aircraft, in which rows of cots had been set up as temporary overnight accommodation for

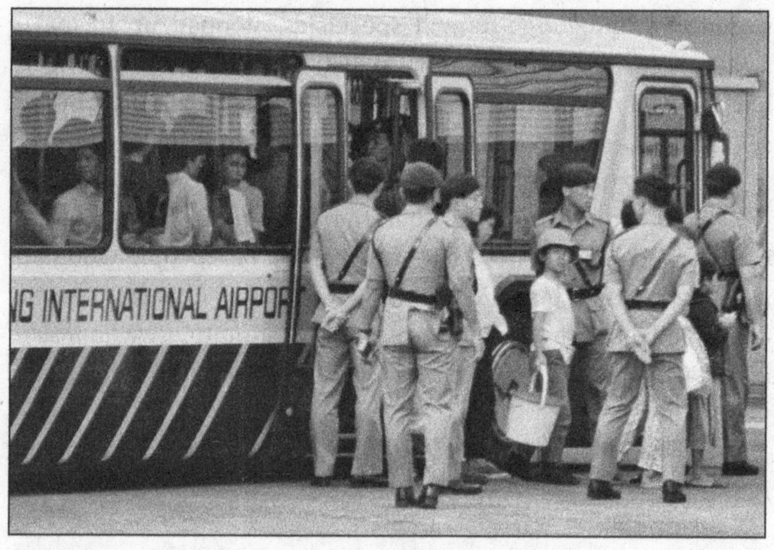

hundreds of souls. And then, just as promptly, we were herded back out to stand behind a rope some 100 yards distant from the hangar.

Three airport buses slowly emerged from the haze. They paused momentarily before hydraulic doors hissed open, letting out a bewildered array of women, children, and men, some carrying rice sacks full of belongings, others clinging to toys. They filed, resignedly, between tight rows of policemen into the hangar.

My only chance for a shot came when a gap in the police line briefly opened, and a young boy wearing a floppy hat and carrying a paint bucket—like he was off for a day at the beach—turned to look at us, as intrigued by the sight of the assembled cameras as we were of him. Some reporters shouted, trying to attract the refugee's attention, hoping to stir a reaction, a wave, maybe, but I guess we were too far away to be heard. The government refugee coordinator, Clinton Leeks, a man of proud chin and large-framed spectacles, stepped up to make a statement. There was a general jostle now as we all changed lenses and brought out our flash units. The sun was starting to set behind Leeks, creating an issue with backlighting.

Asked by one reporter — possibly with rhetorical intent — how well he'd thought today's operation had gone, Leeks replied that they'd had to 'direct' *one or two* of the boatpeople who had protested earlier, but said, in 'no way was this forceful.' *Yes*, he continued, choosing a lighter-weight question to answer, *they'll have lots of nice things provided tonight, like a dinner and videos to watch.*

"What films?" shouted one journalist, others chipping in helpfully:

"*Platoon?*"

"*Born on the Fourth of July?*"

"*Apocalypse Now?*"

<hr>

"Sumatran Mandheling, Acehnese, or a fruity little number from the acidic soils of Mount Bromo?" Hendrick tempted from the kitchen. His taste in coffee was strictly Dutch, colonial. Either he was purposefully testing my resolve, or he didn't think I'd meant it last night when I told him I was going to cold turkey quit the stuff. I drank too much of it, too strong, and was worried about the persistent ache stirring in my gut. Quite possibly this was not associated with caffeine at all, but rather a warning my appendix was on the way out. I'd lain awake all night creating doom scenarios. In the most terrifying of these, I found myself in the middle of Borneo having to perform an emergency appendectomy with nothing but my Swiss Army knife, and a branch to bite on.

Caffeine deprivation, however, left me grumpier and less

coordinated than usual. In the rush for the ferry this morning, for example, a fresh cowpat blocked the middle of the path. Only its head, twitching as my foot came down near it, alerted me to having just dodged a coiled and venomous snake!

Feeling irritable already, I now had to team up with a new reporter—Maggie from *Asian Business*—for an interview session with Aussie businessman, John Faulkner. An Australian, herself, Maggie introduced me as her 'snapper' … one of these days, I was going to turn the tables, announcing, "This is my scribbler." See how *she* likes it. Maggie was sniffling and coughing her questions through a heavy flu, and took up nearly all of our forty-five minute time-slot with no concern for the fading light outside or how increasingly rushed my shots would have to be. We were in Faulkner's impressive office on the forty-ninth floor of the Hopewell Center. The setting was spectacular: a circular skyscraper, its offices radiating outwards, like the segments of a sliced grapefruit.

Faulkner was the Hong Kong head of Leighton, a huge regional construction company. The *Asian Business* article was, ostensibly, about one of their smaller projects—a sewerage treatment plant on Stonecutters Island—but the subtext, of course, was that the materials from the hill they were leveling, would be used as landfill to connect Stonecutters to the Kowloon mainland. This, in turn, would create a vital stepping stone for the much-anticipated and criticized road and rail infrastructure to Hong Kong's planned new airport on Lantau Island.

Maggie got all local with Faulkner, gossiping about the Sydney Harbor Tunnel:

"I mean, that's a *monstrous* mistake, you'll have to admit," she coughed.

The Leighton man paused only briefly:

"We're doing that project," he said, the epitome of droll.

"Look, it's a good *idea*, just the positioning of it that's maybe not so wise?" Maggie backtracked, trying to hide her embarrassment sneezing into a tissue.

Faulkner was a fair dinkum bloke, though. He could see I was up against it with the failing light, so, having posed him for a few standard shots by his desk, he suggested I accompany him to Stonecutters Island on an inspection tour the following day. 'Snapper', indeed. I would show them.

November 28, 1991

"CHRIS, PHONE!" HENDRICK tossed the cordless unit into my room, where it missed the bed and went clattering across the parquet floor tiles.

"Chris?" It was Deborah, the *Asiaweek* photo editor. "Listen. I have the assignment of a lifetime for you."

Briefly I wondered how she'd been able to arrange for me to helicopter in and cover the Fall of Saigon. But I never did think straight in the morning without coffee.

"Really?" I asked, noncommittally.

"Yes, there's a press meeting in the Mandarin Hotel this afternoon ..." Pages rustled at her end of the phone line as she sorted through a fax release, "... *the well-known lingerie company, and sixteen international models to display these items ...*" It was instructional to learn I was considered *Asiaweek's* underwear man. From the common area came the waft of waffles and scent of forbidden Java. This had all the makings of a memorable day. Hendrick had the radio cranked up, full volume; I recognized

Maria's South African accent, and what sounded like a revolution going on behind her. She was reporting from Kowloon Walled City. Hendrick slid a copy of today's *Hong Kong Standard* across the table, before disappearing to tend to his griddle. In the paper, an article explained:

> *Government today will forcibly evict 39 families from the Walled City despite granting a last-minute reprieve yesterday to another 33 families ... Residents last night moved out valuable items, such as refrigerators, to avoid damage in today's expected confrontation.*

"Hendrick," I called. A nose poked out from the small kitchen nook, followed by the sweet, syrupy smoke of slightly singed pancake mix. "I have an early birthday present for you. The assignment of a lifetime." When push came to shove, I was much more of a riots and social injustice sort of shooter. Pretty, near-naked women just caused my hands to shake and confuddled my exposures. It was best to leave *them* to the professional.

The Walled City was *the* story of the moment. Due to its location — directly beneath the flight path on the perimeter of Kai Tak Airport — the ramshackle conglomeration of tower blocks had been restricted to a moderate height of fourteen floors. This was the only restriction that had been enforced in this otherwise lawless enclave. Originally a Qing Dynasty fort, the settlement grew, and indeed thrived, inside British Hong Kong, largely independent of British rule. Until recently, according to a 1987 HK Government survey, upwards of 33,000 people lived in the 6.4 acres, giving it a square kilometer population density more than 100 times that of New York City. Not only was Kowloon Walled City one of the most densely populated places on earth, it was also a bolt hole for triad gangs, and the prostitution, gambling and drug empires that enriched them. It was a rat-infested, *Blade Runner*-style, high-rise slum that had expanded many-fold by Chinese refugees escaping from communist rule both during and after the civil war.

I'd visited to shoot there on a number of occasions, but had never been able to find my way through its maze of dripping, dark alleyways — strung with electric cables and lit by bare bulbs — to its heart. Here, it was rumored, stood an ancient temple, part of the *Yamen* administrative complex, a former residence of official Qing Dynasty magistrates. I desperately wanted to photograph this antiquity before the scheduled demolition got underway.

The police had cordoned off half the complex, posting men to guard all main points of access. In between and around them, residents and protesters had erected protest banners. One burly young man smashed a clay pot at the feet of some officers and then charged at their line before being tackled to the ground and swamped by a mob of local photographers. He would probably make the front pages tomorrow.

The police — and my competition — thus occupied, I snuck round to the park-side of the Walled City, and in through the window of a vacated, ground-floor barber's shop. Once inside, I pushed through the salon's unlocked front door, stumbling into a dank and moldy corridor, more of a tunnel, and blindly felt my way to an interior stairwell. Electricity to the entire complex had been cut, and some corners of the stairwell were completely devoid of light. I used my camera flash to burn irregular staccato images of the way forward on my retina. The day was overcast, but the sudden bright light as I crashed through a metal door onto the rooftop stunned me. I waded out into a sea of bent and rusting TV antennas, bamboo ladders and denuded clotheslines. The crackle of a walkie-talkie alerted me to the presence of the enemy. I crouched behind a water tank, heart thumping wildly, as a patrol of three policemen passed close by.

The rooftop constituted an informal fifteenth floor, open to the elements; an additional layer of illegal dwelling atop an already condemned and illegitimate complex. An eerie vacuum filled the lean-to shacks of wood and tin. The former tenants couldn't have been given much time to clear out: their pots and pans remained hanging on nails, drawers still contained old passport photographs, and crumbled pornographic magazines littered the floor. I took a piss in an ash-filled pot (surely, the former owner wouldn't have forgotten to take along his ancestors?) and absent-mindedly walked out, right behind a duo of police officers. I took a few shots. The noise of the shutter gave me away. Confronted by authority I played the old press card trick, but it didn't wash here, today.

"OK, OK, I go down to street." I pointed over the edge of the tower block at the pinprick heads of the media mob, gathered below. The uniforms were unconvinced of my sincerity, and one of them took it upon himself to escort me safely to the ground floor.

Back in the press throng, a writer raced up, announcing breathlessly, *"They're dragging people out around the corner!"* This information spread like fire in a gasworks, inciting a hell-bent-for-leather rush along the main road. In Hong Kong press photography circles, the only rules were to get in first and get up close. Shooting from the front row with a wide-angle lens was the way to go. There seemed to be no gentlemanly pact, as in some other parts of the world, ensuring everyone stood back and got a fair shot at the action. I machine-gunned a few frames, mostly featuring the backs of my fellow photographers. *Sod this for a game of soldiers.*

I headed off to hunt on my own again. About twenty minutes later, I emerged back on the rooftop through a two-foot-wide

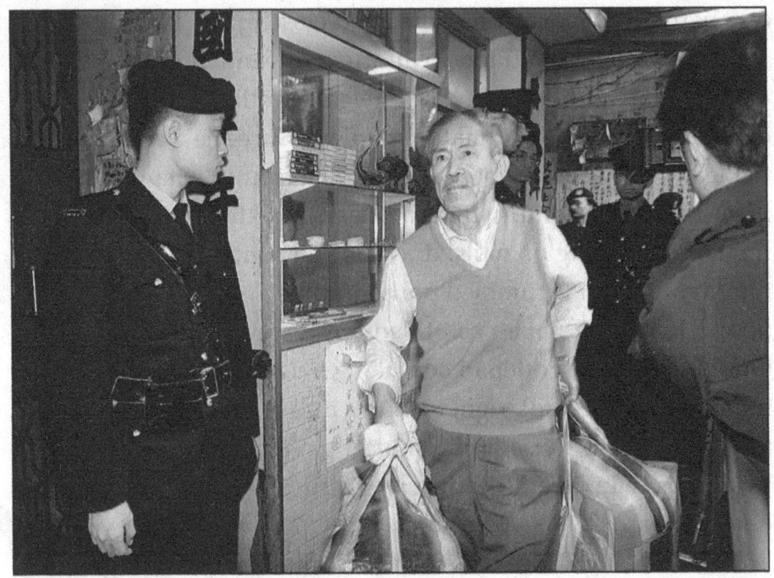

Elderly resident being evicted from the ground floor of Kowloon Walled City on November 28, 1991.

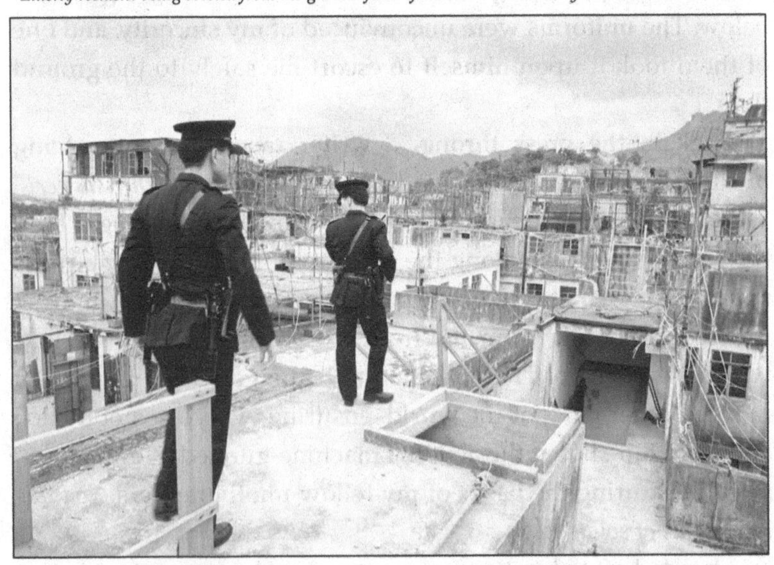

Officers of the Royal Hong Kong Police Force patrol the rooftop of Kowloon Walled City making sure all residents have vacated their homes. November 28, 1991.

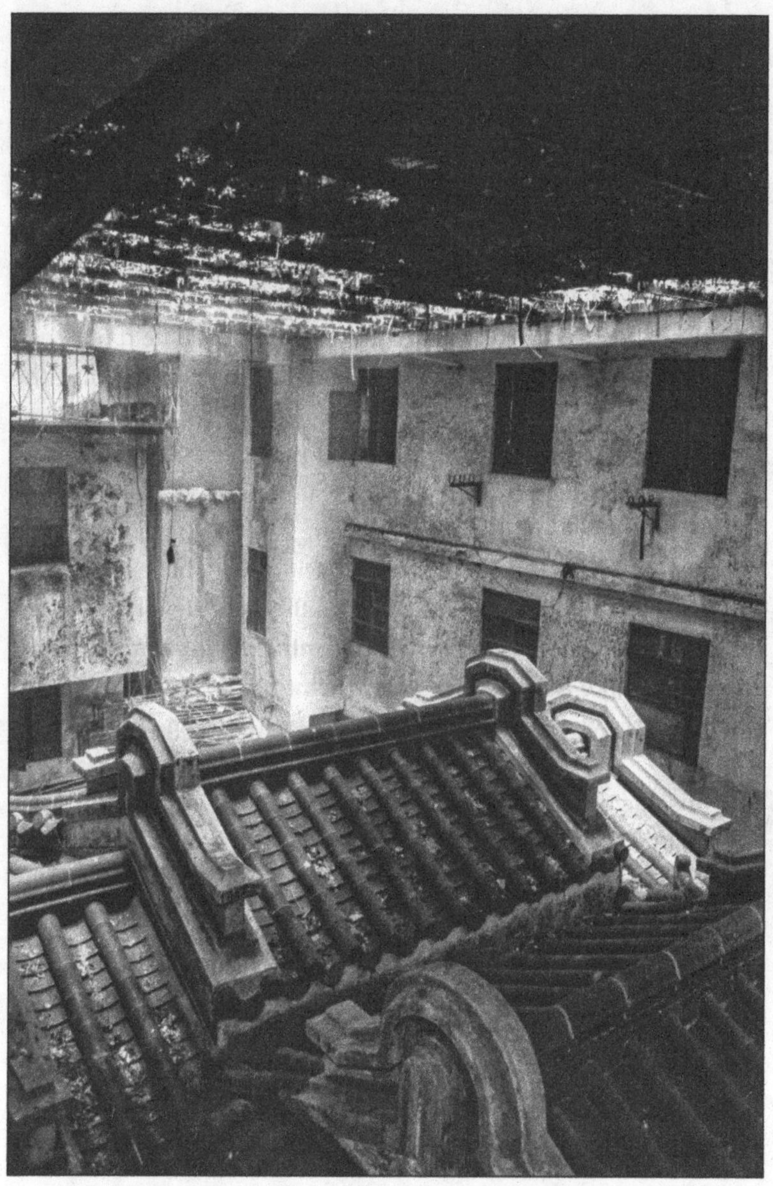

Original temple at the heart of Kowloon Walled City. November 28, 1991.
Photos: Chris Stowers/PANOS

iron trapdoor. It squealed open on unoiled hinges. Below, twenty yards away, five environmental protection agents dressed in white dust suits—fearful of asbestos contamination—stood around, studying a clipboard.

I rattled off a few shots before again being betrayed by my clicking shutter. I waved to them as casually as possible, wheeling around to escape before they raised the alarm. And that was when I walked straight into a policeman who was taking a pee over the railings. He was as surprised as me to find he'd not been alone in his duties. I made a dash for my foxhole, bolting the cover behind me.

It is odd how often storms of blind panic leave you stranded on the shores of Serendipity. Now was one of those moments. I had no idea where I was—direction, floor, or block; even the concept of gravity was starting to get a bit wobbly—though I figured I must be somewhere towards the street level and in the center of the entire, crumbling labyrinth, as right in front me, developing like a black and white print in the chemical tray— emerging slowly, layer upon layer—was the long-searched-for *Yamen*.

Constructed originally alone, in open fields, the historic temple-like structure now found itself dwarfed and surrounded on all sides by crooked, grimy apartment blocks. The musty shrine shimmered dully at the base of this deep and mournful urban pit, covered over by a rusting, metallic grille. Dripping shafts of exhausted sunlight filtered through the stinking stratum of refuse that had built up upon this grated platform, illuminating buried roof tiles that weakly flashed their presence, as if hopeful of rescue. I felt like Indiana bloody Jones discovering a lost Mayan tomb.

I was out doing my regular round of editors in Quarry Bay a week later when I bumped into Maria. She was entering the SCMP office as I was leaving.

"Hullo! What brings you over to these parts? Looking for a new job?" I joked.

"Yes, actually. Listen, Chris, you lived in Indonesia, right?"

She suggested we grab a coffee together. I was back on the brew now, appendix be damned, and happily agreed. Besides, I sensed she was about to start mining for information of a more personal nature. Journalists were programmed that way.

"Yes," she exclaimed at louder volume than necessary, as though phoning a story in over a bad line, "I'd love to be posted to Jakarta for the *Post*; everything's so flat here, now that all the Tiananmen shit has fallen off the map. It may be glorious to get rich," she posited, using the phrase that was on everyone's lips at the time—and most commonly, if erroneously, attributed to China's paramount leader, Deng Xiaoping (though there was no proof Deng ever actually uttered those words. The expression most likely was apocryphal, and taken from the title of Orville Schell's 1984 book, *To Get Rich is Glorious: China in the 80's.*)— "But it sure leads to some dull stories."

"I'm with you on that," I said, patiently sipping my cappuccino. Then Maria got down to brass tacks.

"Listen, it's sweet you'd think of helping Luisa out with a passport by getting married and all. What a lark." I waited for the 'but' … there was always a 'but' after an action had been qualified as being 'sweet'. "But Owen *really* loves Luisa. Maybe they should be given a chance to work it out?"

Owen was Luisa's fellow reporter at the paper. A hopeless romantic myself, I was happy to relinquish my marital claim, as frail as it ever had been. Besides, lately I seemed to have been being blown out of, rather than in to, relationships. Fortunately,

I was not in any hurry to settle down. *When I get married it will be for real, too.*

———— ∽ ————

The annual *Asiaweek* Christmas party was being held at the Hilton Hotel, and I didn't have a thing to wear. Albert had only issued me the invitation because he'd spotted me roaming around the office earlier looking, he said, like a *half-starved fox, skulking for scraps of food.* He said I should come and stuff myself on *Asiaweek's* luxury spread instead.

"You see? You should have gotten a haircut."

"Never mind the hair, Albert, you're just jealous," I said, rubbing his bald pate for good luck. "What clothes do you have lying around?" There was no way I could make it out to Lantau and back before the event started. "And by the way," I made clear, "that wasn't a skulk. I am not a skulker, and am not prone to skulking, off, or otherwise."

Hendrick complimented my new attire an hour later when we met in the hotel lobby. "Nice zoot suit, brother." It was some Americanism he must've picked up off a gangster movie — one of the cast of which I now resembled.

"It was all Albert could find," I excused the tight black dinner jacket with white lapels. The silk scarf was Karen's addition to my fancy dress garb. I wished it hadn't been such an arresting shade of yellow. Hendrick himself had gone for the Oriental Lounge Lizard look. Clad in a black silk kungfu tunic, with his long hair pulled back in a ponytail, he resembled the granular lovechild of Steven Seagal and a stick insect.

"Come on, let's get a drink."

On the surface this should have been a simple mission. But our immediate access to alcohol was aggravated by having to run the gauntlet of impressively suited and bejeweled publishers and editors, lined up in greeting at the entrance. It seemed unlikely they'd have donned their best tuxedos to welcome the likes of Hendrick and me, the hired help, so we dived past them, into the welcoming sea of excess. Here, waiters bobbed like tethered buoys, offering endless glasses of booze from silver trays. Trestle tables groaned like trawler decks, barely managing to contain their catch of smoked salmon sandwiches, slices of sashimi, prawn cocktails and fish roe canapés. Beyond this, the main ballroom heaved with a thousand souls. Central to all the decadence sparkled a fountain of liquid chocolate, itself guarded by huge sentinel ice sculptures. Food stalls serving exotic fare from all the Asian countries the magazine's reporters were based in were dotted around the perimeter. I was just complaining to Hendrick, "Maybe they could improve their photo rates, instead of splurging like this," when I spotted Max, and in tow, Jasmine.

"Miss Jones! Maximilian. What are you two doing here?"

"Christopher!" Jasmine swiveled to face me, her bulky jewelry clinking like ice cubes in a whisky glass. "You don't think these magnificent sculptures carve themselves, do you? Max has been madly chiseling for three days. They are based on my designs, well, all but one of them. Honestly, a whole room full of photographers and not one of you has thought to bring along a camera to record my work!"

Just then Deborah sauntered up, her hair down and eyes doing a horizontal scan from the ice statues, ignoring Jasmine and me, before settling possessively on the diminutive figure of Max. The artist, best known for his painted series of spectacularly magnified vaginas, was dressed this evening with rebellious flair, as though he'd just mugged Rupert the Bear and decided to put on all his clothes.

"Max, is it? I've just been admiring your work," Deborah grasped the master ice chipper authoritatively by one of his leather elbow-pads, and guided him towards a dripping example of his more X-rated *oeuvre:* "I particularly like this one. Tell me, is it some sort of butterfly...?"

We photographers stood together in the same corner, corralled by primal herd instinct. Karen, the *Asiaweek* picture researcher, made a late but show-stopping entry supporting a little black dress and, on her arm, Fred Scott, the BBC soundman. Fred had been in Iraq, following the chaos, part of a documentary crew. He'd started taking pictures in his spare moments blessed, as he had been, with that key ingredient—that which I had tried to attain by stowing away on the Gulf-bound *Prosperity*—access. *It doesn't matter how good your camera is; if you're not in the room, you don't get the shot.*

Carl was here, as was Greg Girard, taking rare time off from his photographic book project at Kowloon Walled City, where he'd been racing against the wrecker's ball.

"Chris, have a cheroot," Carl was in ebullient mood. His run of good luck had continued since Bangladesh. He'd made more money in the last two months than in the entire preceding year. Taking his role as mentor seriously, he continued: "Good job on the *Eyewitness* articles, by the way. Stick at it and remember, focus on the story. There shouldn't be any wasted elements in your frame."

The reception was scheduled to end at 9:00 p.m. but it was now 10:30 p.m., and both champagne and conversation were flowing unabated. This came as no surprise: since co-founded by maverick Kiwi journalist Michael O'Neill, in 1975, *Asiaweek* had never seen off a month in profit. Instead, the magazine built its reputation championing worthy local and regional causes, and nurturing a misfit band of writers and photographers at the start of their careers, many of whom may never have been published elsewhere. Not a recipe for financial success. But they sure knew how to throw a party.

Hendrick and I circled the jam-packed ballroom, never letting a tray of drinks pass unsampled, and in competition with each other to see who could pick up the most business cards. Eventually, we were forced to leave—the last ferry to Lantau waited for no one. We departed, firing off a fusillade of elastic bands across the hall at Fred, who joyfully retaliated.

December 11, 1991

HMS Tamar wasn't a ship, but a building. The "upturned gin bottle"—as its distinctive shape was known—was headquarters of the Royal Navy in Hong Kong. It sat on the waterfront, the Fleet Arcade running beside it. Fleet Arcade had long been the place to stock up on American magazines and get a cheap haircut. Today the mighty United States Seventh Fleet was visiting. *Ready Power for Peace* its motto.

A yawn-worthy press conference ended with the assembled hacks ambushing the US Navy spokesman, a mild-mannered Vice Admiral: *'What is the US position on losing Subic Bay? Do you fear the growing strength of the Japanese Navy'?* And they hounded him on the most pressing issue of the moment: *'Are your vessels carrying nuclear weapons?'*

"It is official policy to neither confirm nor deny the existence of nuclear arms aboard these vessels," came the standard reply, to groans all round.

"We're on," grunted fellow shooter Ralston, as the journos packed away their notepads, and we photographers were let loose aboard the mighty USS *Blue Ridge* command ship. The electronic gadgetry packed below-decks was reminiscent of *The Hunt for Red October*, minus periscopes. The tall ship shadowed some of the neighboring skyscrapers. Its bridge afforded a wonderful opportunity, this sunny morning, to take stock shots of the Hong Kong skyline from a unique perspective. I was very careful to avoid putting my camera bag down on any prominent red buttons.

〜〜〜

When you consider the mechanics and manpower required to physically deliver a letter to any number of locations around the world—and the variety of things that could derail the entire process—it's a wonder, not only that the service costs the price of a mere stamp, but that anyone would chance their penned thoughts to such risk in the first place. Today, for example, a letter my best friend Mark had popped into a slot in a wall in a small town in Germany, had found its way to my box—itself one of thousands of identical boxes—inside the General Post Office of Hong Kong. It really was quite miraculous.

... I'm back from the frozen Falklands. The penguins were friendly, though the locals were a bit dim. In Krautland now, on the alert for messages being beamed across the Iron Curtain. Can't say much. They've got me learning 30 new words in Russian every day. Do keep your eye on the news, though. Who knows? Your job and mine may not be so dissimilar, after all. I envisage a scenario where we get to meet up on some Eastern European battlefield, and I'll have to drag your sorry arse to safety. Like in that Rolf Harris song about the two little boys.

I've got a very serviceable Kawasaki 750 now. Let me know if you're coming home again, and we'll get some touring in this summer ...

Funny, I'd not given it much thought in ages: going 'home'. 'Someday', I'd always assumed, but *what's the rush?* A lingering sentiment, a curiosity, always remained, though. Usually, it surfaced when I was drunk, defenses weakened; and what was nostalgia if not a sober form of inebriation? *'Be careful'*, my inner voice cautioned, *'avoid commitment': there's nothing worse than being nailed down by a schedule.'*

Christmastime in Hong Kong was traditionally cool, gray, bleak — very British, really — and decidedly familiar. With 'Handover' — that invisible giant Panda in the room — only six years away, what better excuse was there to live it up while opportunity existed?

As a possible harbinger of change to come, we basked in an unseasonably warm temperature of 25°C. But, with a turkey roasting in Luisa's oven, and Owen preparing the Brussels sprouts and gravy, all the signals were for a welcome continuation of tradition and normality.

They'd wasted no time in moving in together. Luisa and Owen. I supposed it was for love, economy, or both of the above. I couldn't imagine giving up my freedom for anything less. Luisa's gift to each man present was a pair of red socks. We played *Twister*, and I remember becoming rather contorted with Maria and Ira Chaplain. Ira was the towering Black Star photographer who was so laid-back, any more relaxing would tip him out the window. And then, all of a sudden, it was daylight — iris-burningly bright. Dehydrated, I located my consciousness where I'd left it, in a bar in Wanchai. *How the hell did I end up here?* And I was being berated by a drunken Scotsman who worked for British Airways and hated the English. What a wanker. The mid-morning ferry back to Lantau was full of similarly ashen-faced and constitutionally delicate reprobates as myself. Hauling my corpse up the three flights of stairs to the flat, I found the note Hendrick had taped to my door:

*Chris, your mother called last night to wish you a Happy
Christmas.*

This was slightly unnerving, since I'd neither made nor
received a telephone call home in five years. Long distance calls
were a pointless extravagance; all you did was shout clichéd
phrases down a crackly line, discuss the weather and worry the
whole time about how much it was costing. Why would she start
phoning now? Had someone in the family died?

The Soviet Union expired over Christmas. It felt like a lifetime
ago I'd been in Pakistan, teaching English to the children of
Mujahedeen commanders at the Dr Omar Khyam Public School
in Peshawar. Back then, in the spring of 1987, it had seemed
impossible that the Russians could ever be defeated by a ragged
and often barefoot bunch of Afghan freedom fighters. But their
dogged persistence (aided by timely supply of Stinger missiles
courtesy of the CIA) had helped turn the tide in that conflict.
In doing so, they'd cracked the façade of Soviet invincibility,
leading inevitably to the collapse of the whole house of cards.

December 31, 1991

A MYSTERIOUS TUBE plastered with Korean postage stamps had
arrived at the post office. Inside was a rolled-up rice paper scroll
depicting sprouting bamboo stems and a passage of beautiful,
ink brush calligraphy. It bore the personal red chop of its creator,
Master Ko Kwang-ho, and a small note thanking me for the
publicity the *Asiaweek* Eyewitness had given his small dojo.

There was also a letter in Wendy's familiar hand. Out of habit, I sniffed the scent left faintly, where she'd licked the envelope. Inside, she revealed she had "fallen in love with a Tomboy".

I popped a New Year's card to Derek in along with my latest selection of slides of Hong Kong; he seemed more agitated than usual — maybe he was trying to quit coffee, too?

"Have you seen the news?" he jabbed his editor's red wax pencil at the offending article in today's *Post*. Some countries outlawed gun ownership or homosexuality, or fined you for jaywalking or littering. Singapore did all the above, and had now gone one better, banning chewing gum, too. Then he brightened up, eager to show me his layout for a back issue of *Pacific Traveller*, celebrating the opening up of Vietnam, fifteen years after the Fall of Saigon. Derek had been there in '75. And for this anniversary issue he'd used his own black and white photos to illustrate the piece. He'd only been twenty-five years old when he went to Vietnam. I'd be that age in a few weeks. It seemed every generation was destined its own war. I couldn't help wondering if I'd missed mine.

Hong Kong
January 1, 1992

HOME — PERHAPS IT was inevitable, after five years ignoring the place, that my thoughts turned in its direction? No resolutions this year, just resolve: to explore as much of Asia as possible before returning to England. So, I purchased a one-way ticket to Singapore, intent on taking it from there — my cameras loaded, wallet less so.

SINGAPORE
January 4, 1992.

THE FIRST DAY spent in Singapore always comes as a relief; the second, a guiltily joyful wallow in the city's material abundance and efficient plumbing. By the third day, the sensitive soul is clawing its graffiti-free walls and contemplating the emptiness of modern life. *What am I doing back here — again?* I feared I was losing focus — that righteous sense of mission all photographers need as armor, and without which are nothing but wandering voyeurs.

It would be easier if I had a skill to fall back on, but I hadn't been blessed with an innate understanding of computers, like my best friend Mark. And I hadn't inherited the practical intelligence of my father, with his ability to fix anything, grow anything, and enjoy getting his hands dirty. Nothing I've learned could be taught at university. *Hang on, though — doesn't that mean anyone can do what I do? If that's the case, how much longer can I rely on 'Plan A' — luck, basically?* My talent, if it lay anywhere, was being able to size people up at a glance, empathize convincingly, and muddle along in any social situation; I felt at home just about anywhere. I guess that was what made photography so attractive, and natural. The same qualities had earlier helped me to teach. Possibly I had the makings of a tour guide. Or a spy.

There was no 'Plan B'.

I re-established contact with Shusse publishing's art director Wai-fong today. She let me use the electric typewriter at a spare desk in her office to type up my Kowloon Walled City story. I'm like a traveling salesman, hawking words and pictures at each port of call. She offered advance payment in the form of *Laksa*— our lunchtime tradition—at the Carlton Hotel. Latest gossip: Nigel recently quit Cheney Communications and was now her boss, and chief editor. Later, I met up with Roger Mitton, *Asiaweek's* Singapore correspondent. He mentioned a pilgrimage called *Thaipusam*, about to kick off in Kuala Lumpur, which would attract over a million Hindu penitents to the Batu Caves.

Jakarta, Indonesia

February 24, 1992

KEITH LOVEARD, ASIAWEEK'S Indonesia correspondent, lurked behind a huge bushy beard. An Australian, twenty years my senior; he was a compulsive smoker and owner of a rich, baritone voice. His face, he joked, was "made for radio". In the evening, he drove us to a nightclub in his old Toyota Land Cruiser. Along for the ride were Julie, his feral girlfriend—closer to my age than his—and her friend Lulu, whom they were trying to set me up with. The omens did not bode well. I spoke only village *Bahasa*, and Lulu no English. More than this, she was shy. Never match one shy person with another.

I needed an outgoing woman, someone to drag me out of myself; one who must also like staying at home as much as I did (or at least contemplating the thought of that eventuality). I wanted a modern girl with traditional values.

What I desire is a contradiction, and that will be very hard to find.

Next pages: A Hindu devotee to the diety Lord Muruga has his tongue pierced whilst in a trance-like state, during the incredible annual Thaipusam *festival held at Batu Caves, near Kuala Lumpur, Malaysia. January 1992. Pictures from this story ran as an* Eyewitness *spread in Asiaweek magazine. Photo: Chris Stowers/PANOS.*

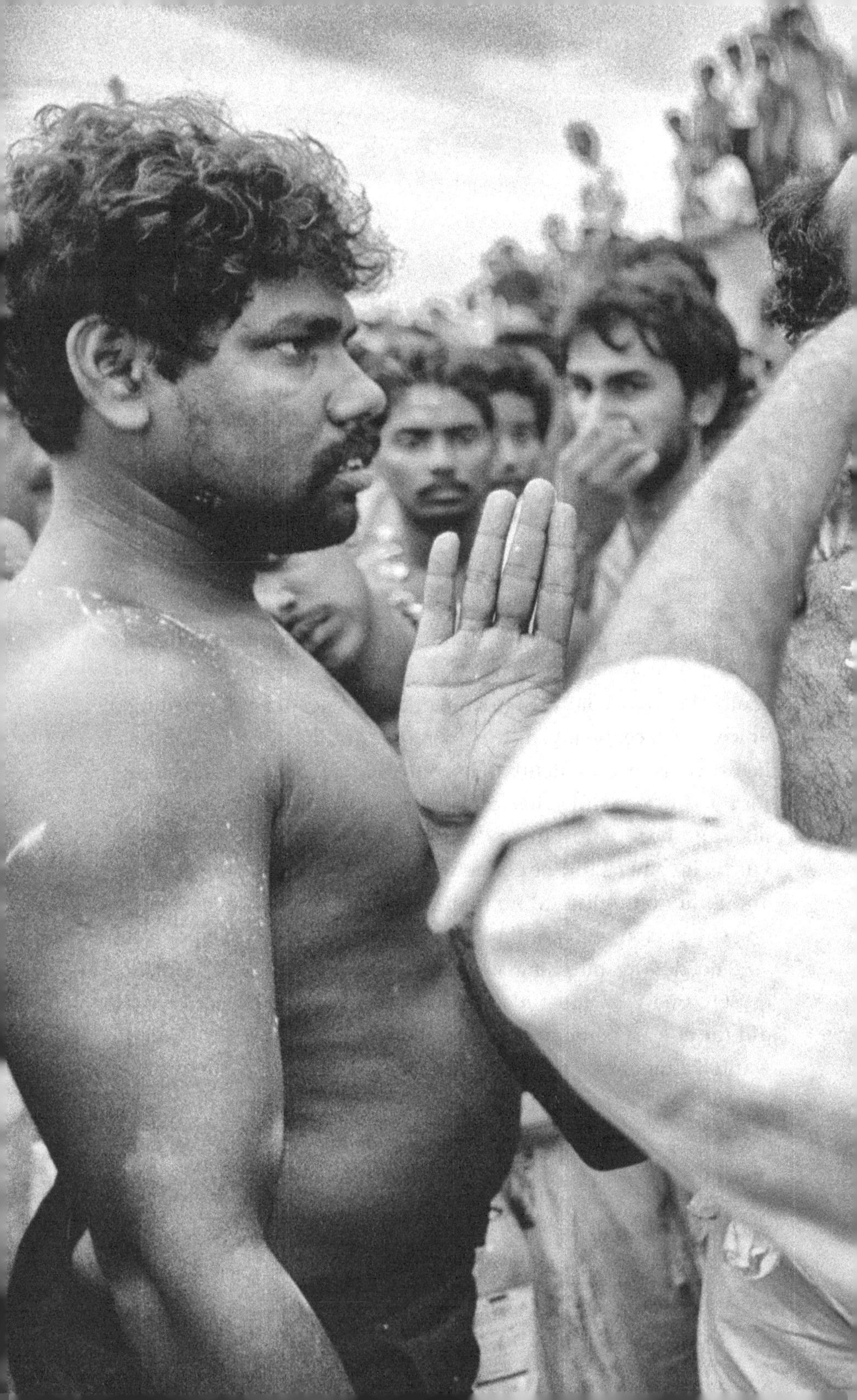

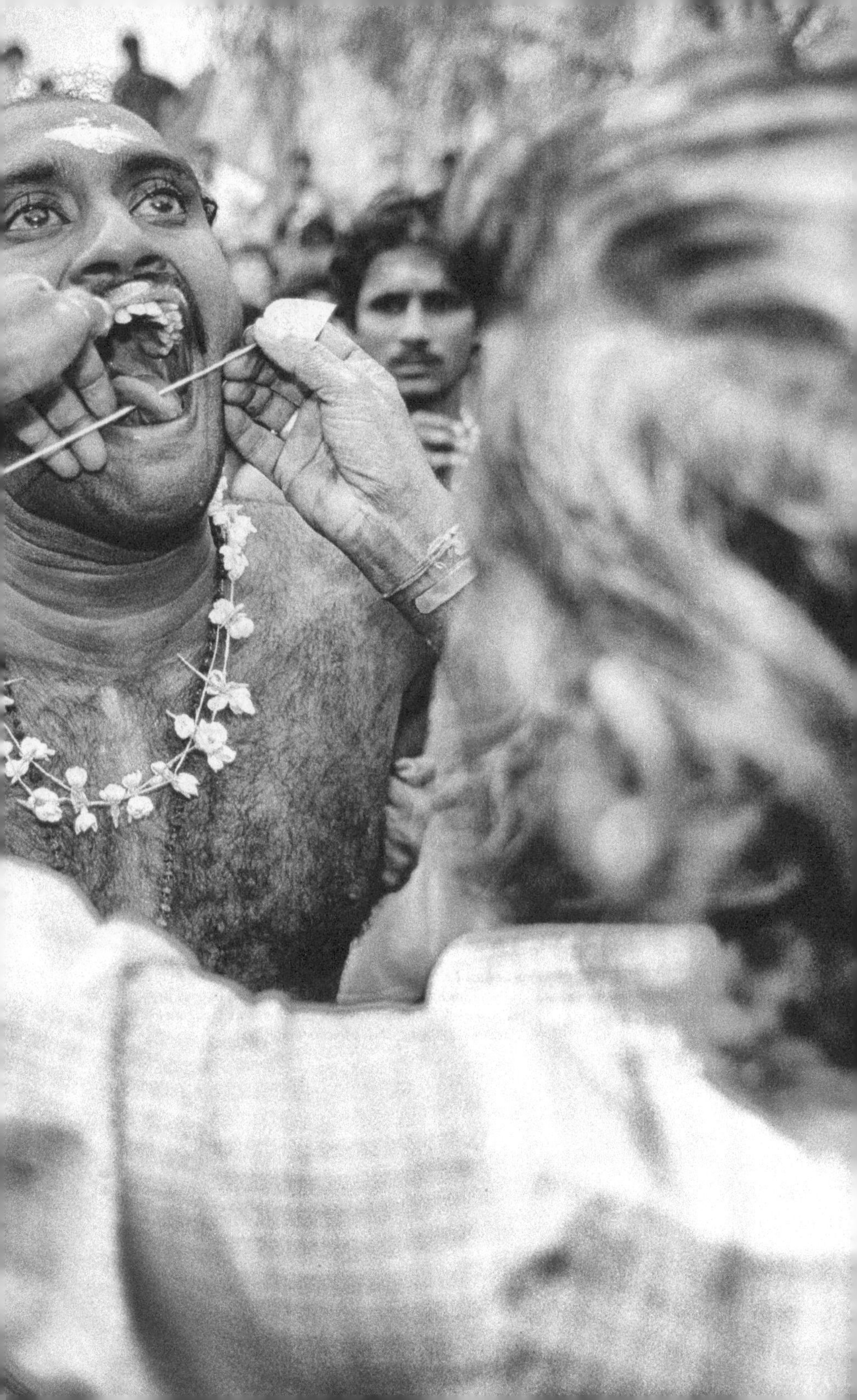

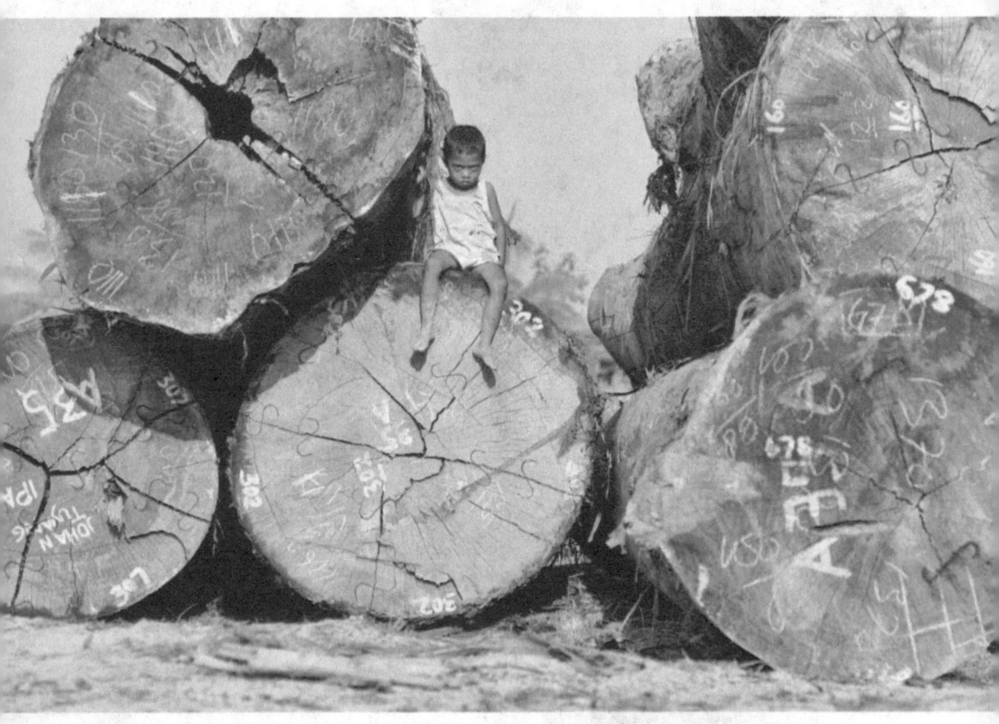

Giant logs at a transmigrasi camp in East Kalimantan, waiting to be floated downstream to the voracious sawmills of Samarinda. As simple as the image was, it became one of my best-selling stock photos – including, later on, as my 2nd Asiaweek cover shot - as 'The Environment' became a hot topic in the 1990's. March 1992. Photo: Chris Stowers/PANOS.

Keith suggested I join him on a trip he was planning up the Mahakam River, deep into the interior of Borneo, in search of transmigrant settlements for a story he was working on. The policy of *transmigrasi*, started by President Sukarno, was being continued and ramped up by his successor, Suharto. Essentially, it was a land redistribution policy, entire communities—and some political opponents—being forcibly uprooted from overcrowded Java and dumped in remote parts of the archipelago. Critics claimed it led to increased deforestation and cultural 'Javanization' of the country. There were reports of starvation, too.

Next pages: A mother and her children – members of a recently settled transmigrant community (forcibly removed from their native Yogyakarta, in Java) – putting on a brave face outside their new home in a transmigrasi *camp near the Dayak village of Long Nah, East Kalimantan. March 1992. Photo: Chris Stowers/PANOS.*

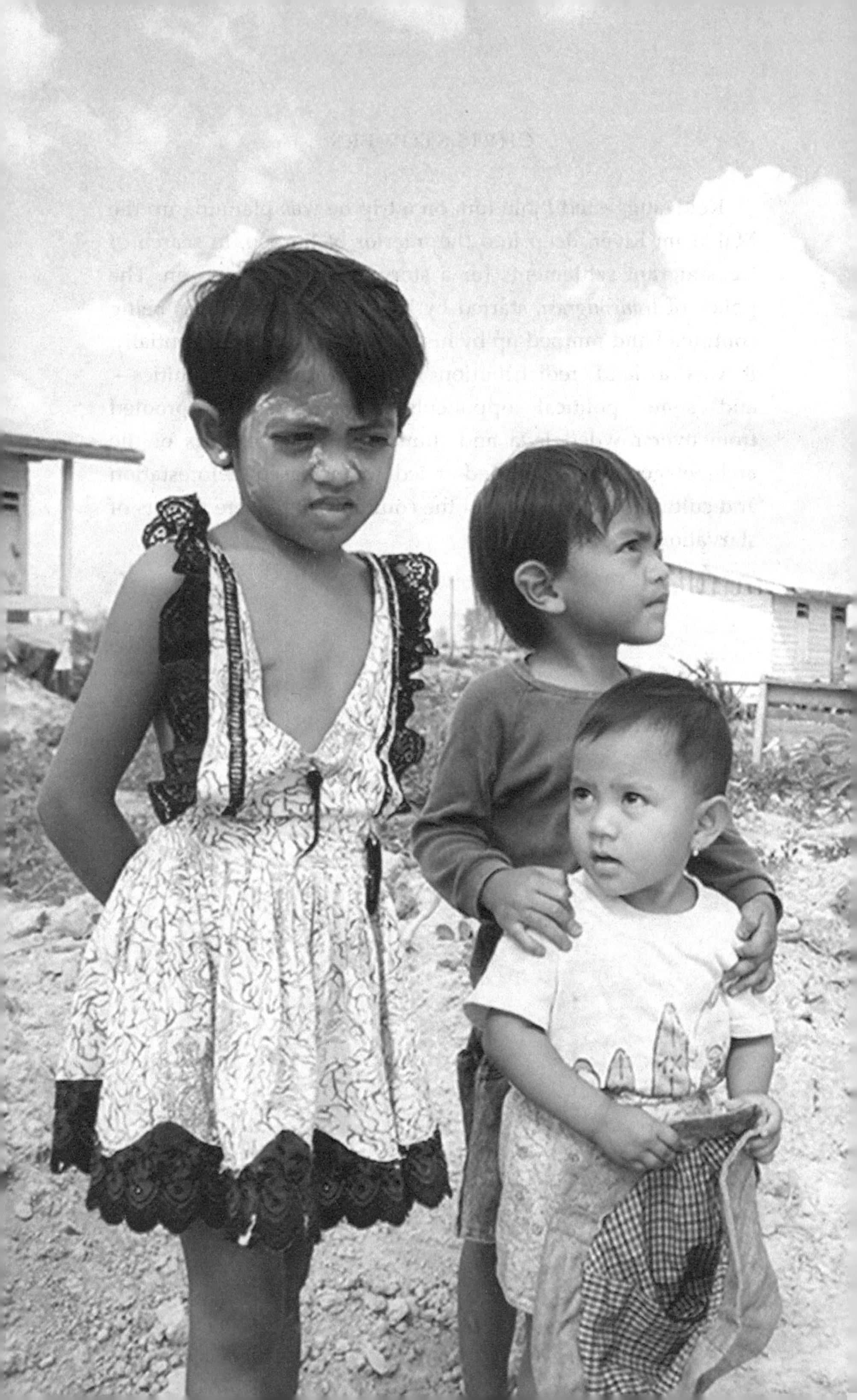

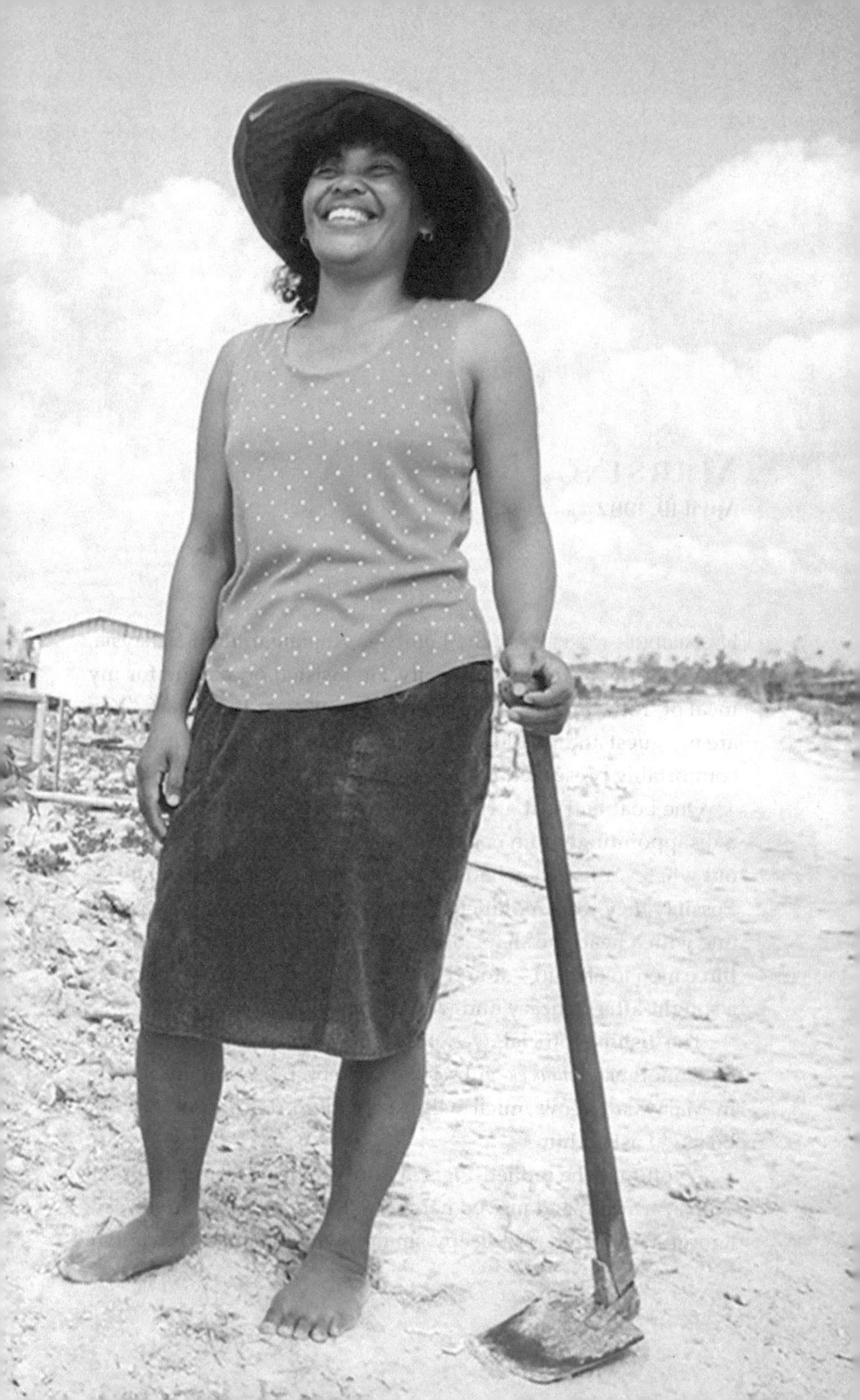

MERSING, MALAYSIA
April 19, 1992

NAZARUDHIN WORKED FOR the Lembaga Kemajuan Ikan Malaysia, the government fishing authority. He insisted on paying for my meal of 'roti canai' at *Zam Zam* restaurant, near the wharf. "You are my guest and would do the same for me in your country," he comfortably presumed.

One boat had just arrived back from a four-day voyage with a disappointingly thin catch, yet its crew were happily handing out whatever fish they had for free to friends and acquaintances. Possibly they were mollified by the two seven-foot-long sharks — one with a head the shape of an arrow tip that took a winch and three men to offload — stored in their forward hold. The fins were a sought-after delicacy and would fetch a high price.

The fishing official was only a few years older than me, and another *Asiaweek* subscriber. I kept bumping into them in Malaysia. "How much will it cost to go out on one of your boats?" I asked him.

"Nothing," he replied, "it is my duty to help. I'll ask around."

Nazarudhin had moved here from Kuala Lumpur three years ago, and now preferred sleepy, small-town Mersing to the capital.

He thought it important to preserve the traditional Malay way of life, where everybody knew everyone else, or at least someone who did.

"Malaysia is not such a big place; move to a new town or state and your past will follow you, by word of mouth. The whole system is based on trust. I wasn't born in this region, so naturally, people were curious about me when I first arrived. They made an effort to find out about my background. They'll always find a relative or friend who knows someone in your home village, and then trust is established."

"I'd find that restrictive, like being spied on," I told him.

"Here spirit of community counts for more than the self. Just submit to it and everything is taken care of. I will never go hungry or be without a roof over my head; I am freed of such responsibilities and concerns. When I first arrived, for example, I didn't worry about finding a home. One of my new co-workers approached me, asking if I had sorted out my housing? 'Not yet', I told him.

'Come with me, I know four or five places, I'll show you', he said. And I had a house by the end of the day. There are no estate agents in Mersing."

"Where I come from, people think it impolite to ask questions; personal privacy is valued extremely highly," I interjected, thinking *but everyone is nosey, they all gossip.*

"But how can I be expected to concentrate on my work if I am worried about finding a house, or a wife? It is to everyone's benefit to divide work from home and pleasure so they can give themselves completely to each need. My wife doesn't expect me to discuss my work with her and she doesn't argue if I have to work late. But I must devote myself to my family as soon as I get home. Here, there is no shame even in asking for money. Never ask to *borrow* from someone. 'I'll give you the money if you need it,' they'll tell you, 'but don't borrow it from me.'"

"If you don't repay them, of course, just don't expect anyone else in the neighborhood to ever help you out again. Likewise, I work at the port, people are always giving me fish; it would be an insult not to accept, or to offer to pay; on the other hand, I can't sell the excess, I have to find others to pass the gift on to."

"What goes around comes around." I mused, having recently encountered just that from plantation manager Jerry in Sabah.

"Precisely. Though it's not perfect. There are drug users here. I threw one of them into the harbor once. But commit a crime and you will be given a chance to redeem yourself. You will be scrutinized very closely, of course. Should you fail again, *then* you'll be written off. A small town is a very lonely place in which to be a pariah."

Over several cups of sweet tea, I found myself falling under the spell Nazarudhin was weaving. The intricate social fabric of Mersing, I became convinced, was a precious and valuable heritage more of the world could benefit from duplicating. After all, it was not so dissimilar from the world I had so eagerly left, five years ago—my small village where everyone knew everyone else, too. Maybe I was just tired of being ever the polite guest: a privileged alien, always on his best behavior, never hanging around anywhere long enough to get involved in settlement.

I returned to the port office later in the afternoon. "I've found you a boat," said Nazarudhin. Fishing vessel #1872, with its crew of eighteen men. "They sail tomorrow at 11:00 a.m.," he continued, adding, "No conditions, I trust you."

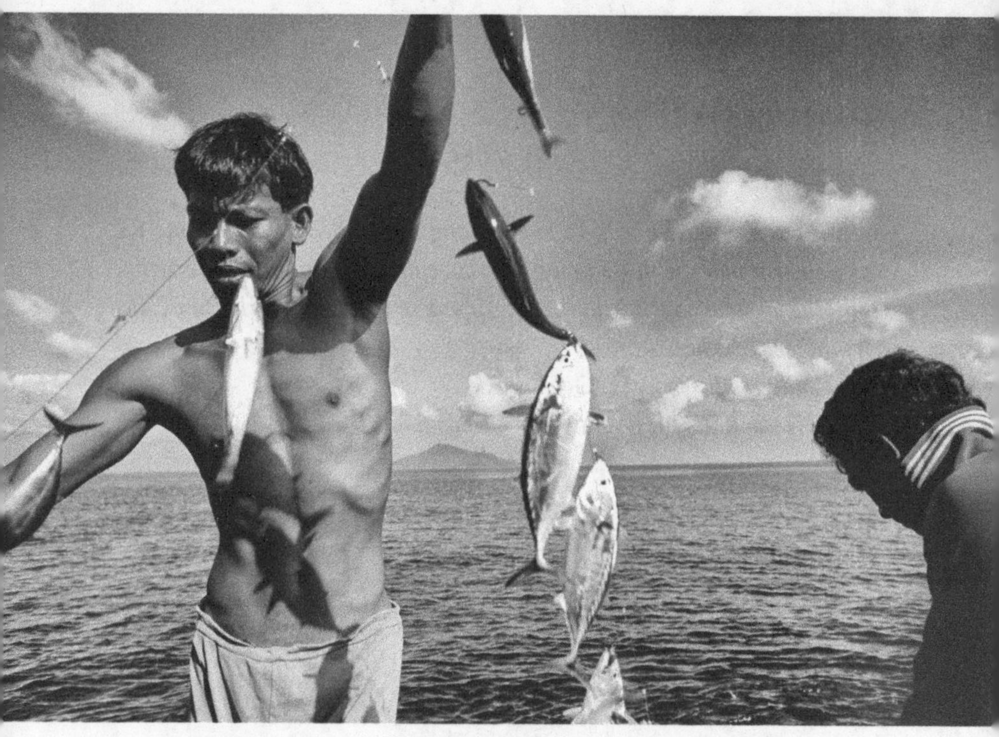

*A crew member of fishing vessel #1872, out of Mersing, catches our breakfast off of Tioman Island.
April 1992. Pictures from this story ran as an Eyewitness spread in Asiaweek magazine.
Photo: Chris Stowers/PANOS.*

Deliver by hand:

Rex Hotel, Stowers, Room 5 – 03.05.92

Chris,

I'm being posted back to Hong Kong soon. Please contact our KL office when you are in Kelantan. We have an up-coming issue focusing on Hudud laws and the increasingly severe policies of Kelantan Chief Minister Nik Aziz.

Could be the cover ... Good luck!

Peter Comparelli (Asiaweek – Malaysia).

Kota Bharu, Kelantan, Malaysia

May 8, 1992

Islam is the official religion of Malaysia, practiced throughout most of its states in moderate form. The only time I'd come up against regulatory intolerance was posting a letter to my friend Uval in Tel Aviv from the General Post Office in Kuala Lumpur. The clerk picked up my offending missive disdainfully, with the tips of his fingers, and laid it flat on his counter while rummaging in a lower drawer. Finally, he located the rubber stamp he was looking for, took his sweet time inking it, and proceeded to brand my envelope with the government-approved position: "Since no country as Israel exists, this letter cannot be posted." It was a sentiment the Menteri Besar (chief minister) of Kelantan State, Nik Aziz, would have fully endorsed. He was reportedly turning the northeastern state — one that borders Thailand — into his own private caliphate. Kelantan was already the most conservative state in Malaysia. Now, in addition to the signs outside offices and government buildings advising women to cover up in approved Islamic fashion, men and women were routinely being divided into separate queues in shops and supermarkets. *Asiaweek* was doing a piece on the place, and Peter Comparelli had helped set up the interview at the government complex in Kota Darulnaim through Nik Aziz's vaguely sinister PR manager, Hushan.

"What do you think of the Hudud laws?" Hushan asked, vetting me before letting me in to photograph his boss. It was a rhetorical question. "They are quite fair." He went on, "For example, if a car owner is stupid enough to leave his keys in the ignition, we would be more lenient when sentencing the thief tempted into stealing that vehicle." Laying his elegant, bony left hand across a copy of the Koran, he continued, "The maximum penalty is there as deterrent, it would seldom be used. Besides, we don't just chop off the hand willy-nilly," he prodded expertly at his prone wrist joint with the long fingers of his right hand, like a surgeon preparing to operate. "We know the best place, so it's not so painful."

I was ushered into Nik's office. The room had no windows, eliminating any disturbing influence from the real world outside. It was like a nuclear bunker or the interior chamber of some vast pyramid. The great man himself, almost lost in a huge, polished hardwood chair, was gracious if not particularly welcoming. As befitting the spiritual leader of PAS (The Pan Malaysian Islamic Party), he resembled a Biblical prophet, his gray goatee bobbing beneath a loosely wound white cotton turban. And he sounded quite calm and rational as he propounded the most radical ideas concerning crime and punishment.

After the shoot, Hushan, perhaps sensing a convert, offered me his personal Koran as a gift. I had to decline, though; the volume was too bulky to fit in my bag.

Next stop was the ruling UMNO party headquarters, where I started to track down the organization's charismatic Finance

Minister Anwar Ibrahim. It seemed he was staging a rally up the coast at Tumpat. I cadged a lift with a high-ranking UMNO official in his chauffeur-driven Range Rover. "Oh yes," he said, "Anwar, he's quite a card!"

This same official later introduced me, fleetingly, to Anwar as "The Man from *Asiaweek*."

The Finance Minister used his address to slam the very same Hudud Laws I'd just been hearing such glowing reports about down the road, and then—to great applause from the rustic crowd who had gathered expecting entertainment—lambasted the Sultan of Kelantan's avoidance of import duty on his Lamborghini.

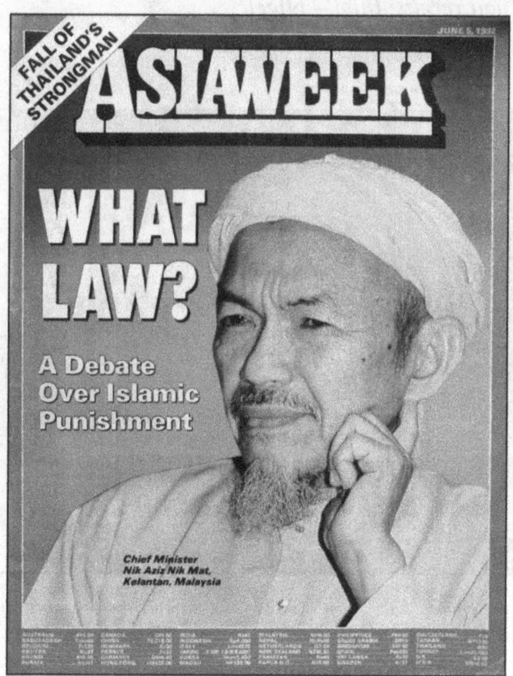

Then Chief Minister of Malaysia's Kelantan state, Nik Aziz.
My first cover on Asiaweek magazine. June 1992.
Photo: Chris Stowers/PANOS.

Anwar oozed populist charisma and the crowd lapped it up. The editors at *Asiaweek* tipped him to become a future Prime Minister of Malaysia ... (and, of course, thirty years later — in November 2022 — they were eventually proved correct).

URGENT FAX — 15MAY92

From: Shusse Publishing, Singapore

To: Chris Stowers c/o Asiaweek (KL)

Chris mate,

Don't come back to Singapore! I have a wicked assignment for you in Malaysia. Motorbikes involved. I believe you have a valid license? Details to follow. Please fax me your acceptance and eternal gratitude the moment you receive this! — Nigel

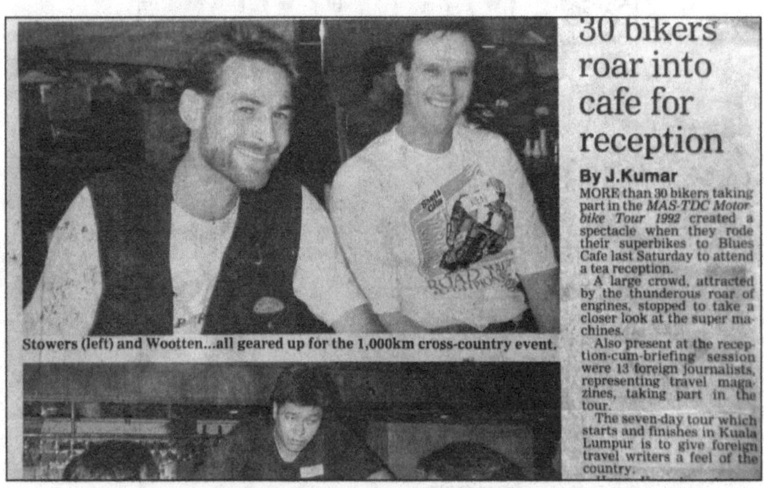

Stowers (left) and Wootten...all geared up for the 1,000km cross-country event.

30 bikers roar into cafe for reception

By J.Kumar

MORE than 30 bikers taking part in the *MAS-TDC Motorbike Tour 1992* created a spectacle when they rode their superbikes to Blues Cafe last Saturday to attend a tea reception.

A large crowd, attracted by the thunderous roar of engines, stopped to take a closer look at the super machines.

Also present at the reception-cum-briefing session were 13 foreign journalists, representing travel magazines, taking part in the tour.

The seven-day tour which starts and finishes in Kuala Lumpur is to give foreign travel writers a feel of the country.

Grinning like the cat that got the cream. Local press coverage of our all-expenses paid motorcycle junket around Malaysia, courtesy of the Malaysian Tourism Board.

To: *Lance Corporal Mark Morgan, BFPO, W. Germany*
From: *Coral Beach Resort, Kuantan, Malaysia.*
4th June, 1992

Hi Matey,

Sleep-eat-ride-eat-sleep. Repeat. This has been the decadent mantra of my life for the last week. A few death-defying scrapes: narrowly avoiding impact with a water buffalo at 110mph on the approach to Kuala Lipis least among them. Yes, the Malaysian Tourism Board has entrusted thirty of us petrol-head hacks to a manic circuit of the peninsula and its beauty spots. Wish you were here!

So far, I've ridden the range of bikes, from a Honda Goldwing to a retro Kawasaki 750, a freight train of a Suzuki 1100 and the most insane 1500cc V-twin Vulcan chopper. I don't even have my international driving license with me, but the police are escorting rather than trying to stop me, for once. Guess I'll have to come up with some words and pictures in exchange for all their generosity. Makes me think we should try for a big bike tour of Europe next summer. What d'you think?

Unrelated subject: what the hell is going on in Yugoslavia? Is that anything your department monitors? All this conspicuous consumption, as Asians play Yuppie catch-up, is boring and futile. By comparison, the disintegration of Eastern Europe seems ancient and epic and I can't help but feel I'm missing out on a big story.

Your Bro, Chris

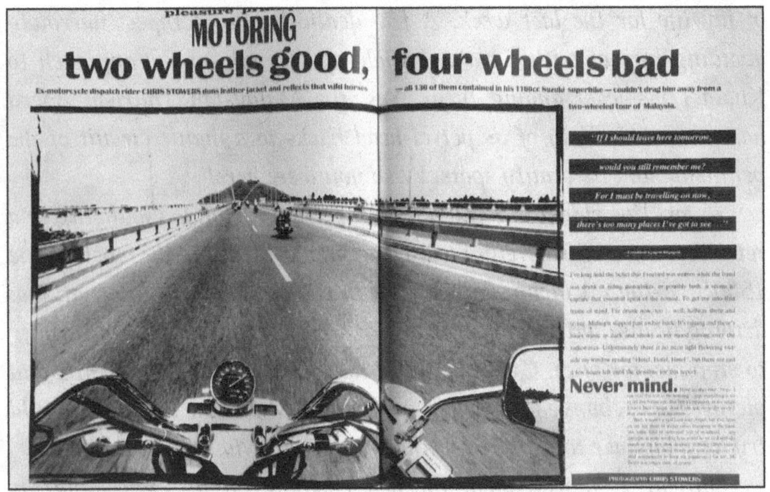

Opening spread of resulting article about the motorcycling freebie, as it appeared in Singapore's MAN Magazine, June 1992.

Hong Kong
July 9, 1992

Back in hongkong, and a new Governor, Chris Patten — the Territory's twenty-eighth and last — had arrived to much fanfare. The old order was ending. I should be on my way. First, though, I needed to lighten my load. *Never carry more than you can run with*, that had been The Mouse's wise advice, long ago in Peshawar. It would take a donkey with panniers to carry all my slides these days. Hendrick faced the same dilemma. So, we spent all day sorting out strips of negatives and slides, prizing open plastic mounts until our fingernails bled — keeping the good stuff, throwing the rest in a bin liner. Hard. Dispassionate. We crammed our discarded slides into the dissected oil drum we used for barbeques, on the rooftop. Hendrick sprayed the lighter fluid and I flicked in the flaming match.

You wouldn't believe the way celluloid goes up!

I was enveloped by a funeral pyre of imperfect memories, consumed by a dark plume of noxious smoke; the ghosts of every place I'd traveled danced in a tempestuous black vortex. Mesmerized, I stared as faces appeared, contorted, converged and were sucked high into the bruised evening sky, like inverted sooty stars. I sensed I would be following them soon, too; *the fragments of our lives can only possibly fall again to earth at the one place we've striven so hard to ignore and avoid all this time – HOME.*

PART 3

The Long Way Home: July–September 1992

"My vision of hell is having to stay in one place –
my idea of a holiday is going home."
Paul Theroux

6. Home.

To paraphrase the old American Express tagline: 'Home. Don't leave home without one.'

Home is a mother's love, infinitely patient, always waiting to forgive and let you back in. The stronger that love, the more emboldened you are, the further you stray. My home lies within a house in a small village, across the fields, up a hill, down the crunching driveway and along a shadowy hall leading to the room in which I was born. We all start out between the confines of four walls. And then we begin to explore. We sail away.

I left on my twentieth birthday, commanded by curiosity and, let's face it, lack of any greater ambition. I haven't yielded to the urge to return yet ... and yet? And yet the tide rises relentlessly. Up and up, it percolates the timeless strata of our native soil, bringing us all, inevitably, back home ...

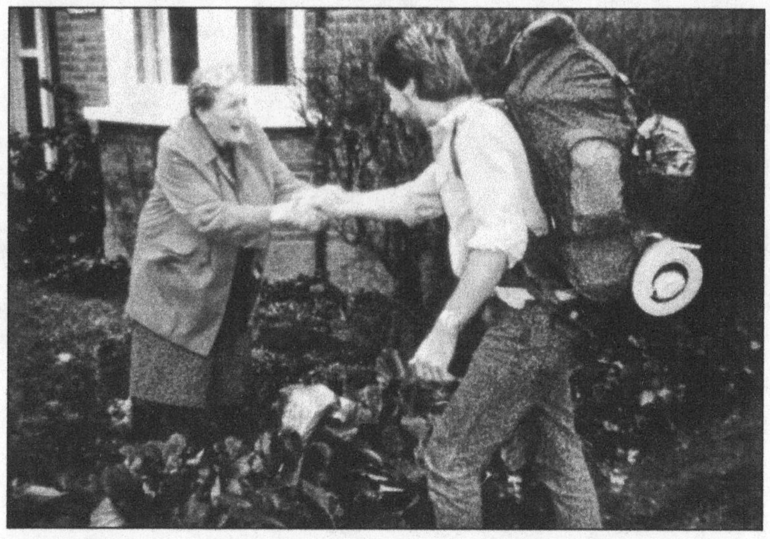

My grandmother, in her mid-80s, seeing me off on my travels from the garden of her house — next doors to ours — on January 23, 1987. It would be almost 6 years before I returned.

HONG KONG
July 10, 1992

I WAS CATCHING up with my diary on the ferry ride into Hong Kong. Everything I owned was squeezed in the backpack beside me. Adjusting my hat against a sudden gust, I let my thoughts wander. Green fields and country pubs had begun to seem exotic after my long time away. I hadn't considered the move any deeper than that. Something would turn up. Something always did. And Fate would make sure that that 'something' was more interesting than anything my imagination could conjure by itself. Mainly, though, I was just curious to see if home had changed in the last five-and-a-half years. I knew *I* had. Hong Kong was my reserve parachute, a place to retreat to if it all went pear-shaped.

Hendrick approached, his wiry, thick-veined arm offering forth a Styrofoam cup of syrupy coffee.

"Been meaning to ask," said my flat mate, "what is it you write in that book of yours? Is there really so much you need to remember?"

"I don't write a diary to remember things but so I can forget them," I informed the lanky Dutch photographer, realizing how pompous it sounded, at the same time knowing he knew me well enough to understand.

"So, you're going ahead with this, then? Have you considered what you have to go back to?"

"I don't really know. Two thousand days is a lot of freedom; it won't be easy." I'd lived like a fugitive for five-and-a-half years, on the run from responsibility.

"Well, it's not as though it takes more than twenty-four hours to reach anywhere from even the remotest part of the world these days." Hendrick concurred, "You can always fly back if it doesn't work out."

"I'm done with flying. I'm going all back by train." I needed the time to think, to let my thoughts escape from the prison cell of daily activity and to run riot.

"You'll last a month, two at tops! You'll be back. Besides, have you given any thought to how things have changed since you've been gone? England hasn't been sitting still, anxiously awaiting your return. You'll be as much a refugee back there as a nomad here. Where you come from, that state of mind you inhabit *circa* 1987, that's gone, man. It was only ever in your head, even at the time!"

He had a point. Though I believed a crucial distinction existed between the global nomad and the refugee. Refugees were rather prone to settling—they were, after all, reluctant nomads. They desired to establish a new version of the home they'd been forced from, and were quick to demand and establish rights in any country that gave them shelter. Global nomads, on the other hand—coming for the most part from better-off countries and more stable backgrounds—chose instability. We didn't have a leg to stand on. It was not considered 'normal' behavior to seek a less secure existence in an under-developed part of the world for lower monetary reward. That degree of disengagement bred distrust.

Refugees had UN treaties. There was no legislation, no international protocol to deal with global nomads (though I believe our numbers to be growing). Just look at any immigration form or voting register, hell, even an application for a credit card: what's your address? In which country do you reside? Who is your employer? What's your salary? 'Variable' was the only honest answer I could give to all of the above. Refugees longed for civic status; global nomads resisted any such categorization. This was what I was thinking.

What I said was "I'll send you a postcard."

The ferry began its turn to dock. I took the overhead walkway linking the Outlying Island ferry piers to the GPO. There was nothing in my post office box. No last-minute distractions. No possible excuse to stem the tide of destiny. I was going home and would have to set off quickly, before I changed my mind. Or had it changed for me.

I met Jasmine at the rail terminal in Kowloon. She had an assignment in Guangzhou and had asked me along to photograph it.

"You've not forgotten to wear your hat, I see." She approved. "It shows your degree of resolve. You'd never attempt serious travel without it."

It is frightening how much of an open book I am to some people.

Beijing
July 14, 1992

Two thousand days! What a magical amount of time to have spent away from England! I mentally recited the figure during the forty-hour train journey from Guangzhou to Beijing. My trans-continental rail journey would continue from the Chinese capital to Mongolia and then through Russia. The iron rails laid across countless miles of hostile territory, in interests of economy, defense and industrial progress, would see me to my ultimate destination. It was comforting to be resuming the basics of forward motion, too.

Following a couple of days working together in Guangzhou, Jasmine had returned to Hong Kong. A painter and illustrator, fluent in Italian, she was moonlighting in leather these days. The Italians were moving their factories to southeastern China, tempted by all the cheap labor and the lack of environmental regulations.

"One must move with the times, Christopher," she said, excusing her unromantic embrace of commerce, "and the Italians are an inherently artistic race. It's not as though I've given up art altogether, I'm just searching for inspiration through unconventional means. Besides, they pay very well for my factory reports, and I don't see you complaining."

She was right, of course. Accompanying her interviews had allowed me to bypass all the security guards. I'd gathered many useful images of indentured laborers and polluted sweatshops with which to trade, once I arrived back in London.

"Oh, and you may do worse than look up an outfit called The Panos Institute. They're a charity that need pictures. Nobody's heard of them, but they are into worthy causes. Just like you." And she'd scribbled down their address in Angel Islington, North London.

The coal fumes in the Chinese capital were so thick I wished I smoked: at least my lungs would've benefited from the filter. I rented a Flying Pigeon bicycle for less than one yuan a day. The ancient two-wheeler's center stand bobbed up and down on its weak spring, ploughing the receding tarmac in intermittent furrows. I had both cameras slung across my chest like bandoliers, the 24mm lens affixed to one and 85mm to the other, ready for action. Their presence, slapping against my body on each push of the pedals, was reassuring, and confirmed me in my craft lest I should capitulate to stage fright. Rudimentary stabs at free market commerce bled across Beijing's spacious sidewalks: watermelons stacked like giant green bowling balls beneath plastic drapes, and boxes of Longevity and Hatamen cigarettes displayed in colorful pyramids.

I joined a sluggish peloton of identical bicycles at one particularly wide and daunting road junction, overshadowed by a huge sign outside China's first-ever McDonald's restaurant. It displayed the optimistic boast: 'Billions served'. I decided to check the place out, joining a throng of excited Chinese epicures about to experience their initial capitalist gherkin and Imperialist cheese slice (though most were drawn in by the model of the clown Ronald, before whom a queue had already formed for photographs). I caught up on correspondence using a placemat for stationary, and contentedly watched the pouting girls cycle by in their knee-high nylon stockings and short summer dresses.

Visas are a traveler's campaign medals, our proudest mementos in a tireless war against bureaucracy. I needed to organize three of them, all from communist embassies, before even thinking of leaving China. The representatives of Mongolia, Russia and Romania lay scattered across the vast capital. I aimed my first assault at the Russian visa office.

"So, you vant to go to Russia?" sighed the dragon at counter number three. "But vair will you enter? Ven will you arrive, and vair depart? This I need to know." It seemed I should have started at the end, with the Romanians first.

"This you have to do," she leaned forward confidentially. Maybe she was not all scales and fiery nostrils, after all. "Go first to Ulaan Bator." The Mongolian capital.

"Yes," I edged closer.

"Next, get your Russian visa from the embassy there."

"Yes," I breathlessly awaited her Third Commandment.

"Trust me." Strangely enough, I did.

It took me an hour to cycle across what, on the map, appeared to be a tiny segment of Beijing. I parked my rented bike near the Friendship Store, walked a while, and joined the tail end of a snaking line of visa seekers leading towards the Romanian compound. Apart from one rather confused-looking Indian, every else in the line was Chinese, the Eastern Bloc countries — led by Hungary — having recently relaxed visa regulations with communist allies like China to encourage trade. A detachment of PLA troops marched past silently, their feet clad in black cotton

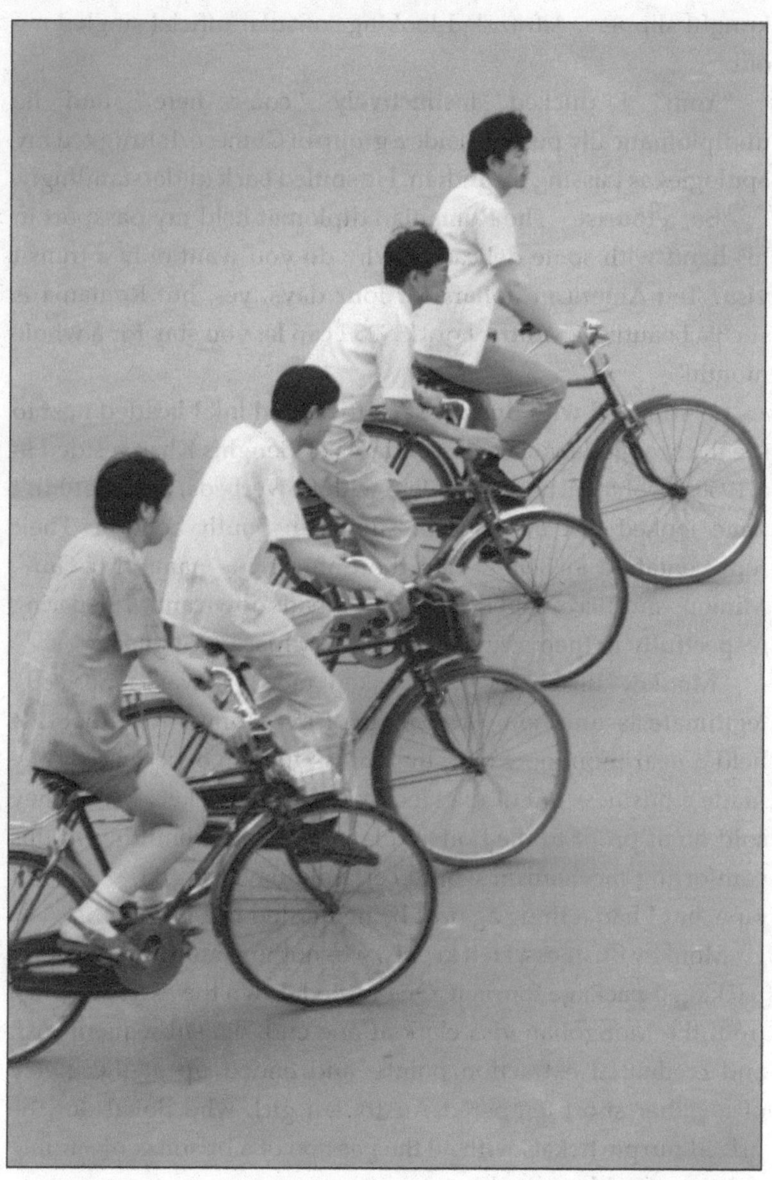

Cyclists crossing Tiananmen Square, Beijing. July 1992. Photo: Chris Stowers/PANOS.

kungfu slippers. A frazzled-looking consular official singled me out:

"You!" I ducked, instinctively, "come here," and he undiplomatically pushed aside a group of Chinese. I shrugged my apologies as passing the Indian. He smiled back understandingly.

"So, a tourist!" The Romanian diplomat held my passport in his hand with some delicacy. "Why do you want only a transit visa? Ten American dollars for four days, yes, but Romania is such a beautiful country. For US$25 I can let you stay for a whole month!"

Legitimized with Bucharest's official red ink I headed next to see the Mongolians. The descendants of Genghis Khan resided in a 1950s pebbledash villa, replete with flowerbeds, that wouldn't have looked out of place in suburban South London. Their representative in Beijing had the unforgiving name 'Mr Gun'. Minions shuffled about his presence, heads down and whispering respectfully in their secretive schlicky-schlacky tongue.

"Monkey Business?" Gun asked me. His was a perfectly legitimate assumption. After all, the travel company of that title held a near-monopoly over the Trans-Siberian experience. They made a business out of the block-purchase of tickets which they sold on at profit to the Lonely Planet crowd. Submitting to this comforting mechanism would certainly have simplified the red tape, but I had a thing against being herded in a group.

Monkey Business, I felt keenly, was nothing more than cleverly packaged package tourism. One rattled down the assembly line, from the Mongolian visa clerk at one end, via subsequent cash and credential extraction points, and ended up at the mercy of a rather short-tempered Australian girl, who doled out the prized purple tickets with all the passion of a prison cook ladling dollops of cold mashed potato.

"No," I said, a little too defiantly.

Gun looked up from his desk, paused to scrutinize the rare non-conformist standing before him, and slowly stretched out his hand for my passport.

"Good, good. Come back Friday, I give you two-week visa." Monkey Girl scowled from her corner.

MONGOLIA
July 20, 1992

ACROSS MOST OF Asia, every third doorway opens to reveal a restaurant. Often, they don't bother with the door. This was not the case in Ulaan Bator.

Here, if you were lucky to hunt down food at all, you faced a long queue before ever reaching its source. There was something devotional and essentially Buddhist about the way these resigned shoppers shuffled forward in columns. I had once, in Tibet, toured the Potala Palace; it was like being squeezed through the fetid innards of a whale lit by oil lamps. I had no desire to repeat the experience for the sake of procuring a bloody sheep's tongue. The only type of meat still in plentiful supply was horse. Those boney nags lucky enough to have escaped the butchers' knife were ridden, clattering through the capital's streets on unmaintained shoes, where they greatly outnumbered the bashed-up *Volgas* and *Trabis*—Soviet cars that became useless chunks of scrap once the fuel in their tanks was used up, or tires perished. I was alerted by band saw screeches to the approach of more than one car being driven along on sparking metallic rims.

Reverberations of the breakup of the Soviet Union were taking their own sweet time to wash up on the far, grassy shores of Mongolia, its most distant satellite. Any Russians still based here were in frenzied retreat, taking with them everything not bolted down, and then coming back to unbolt and take that, too. Stores were empty and it was rumored only two weeks' worth of oil was left to run the city's sole power plant. After that—lights out. The Mongolians, to their credit, seemed to be taking impending disaster in their stride, as though they relished the coming war of attrition with their old Soviet masters. They had mostly, by this stage, exchanged the city center and concrete suburbs in favor of their cozy, tented encampments in the hills surrounding the capital. Here they awaited the end game.

Over the years, I'd lost the habit of scavenging for food, having been softened by its natural abundance in more tropical lands to the south. Life was no picnic in UB (as everyone abbreviated the Mongolian capital city). Mid-summer temperatures hovered around 13°C and a dusty wind blew in off the ever-present steppe. Soulless concrete tenement blocks—Soviet structure and uniformity brought to tame the wilder extremities of empire—lay vacated, projecting the desolate appeal of urban warfare training camps. In an unlit state-owned department store, overshadowed by a monumental T34 tank, disconsolate pairs of injection-molded plastic shoes, yellowing sets of chemistry goggles and plastic raincoats gathered dust behind cracked display windows. Passing Mongolians were not tempted inside, since they were toasty enough wrapped in their traditional fur parkas and their feet planted inside knee-high, felt-lined leather boots.

The Mongolian national currency went by the delightful name 'tugrik'. The highest denomination available was the 20 tugrik note. I exchanged US$20 on the black-market. I was thumbing through the hundreds of notes received in exchange, when a voice speaking English of the American variety interrupted me.

"Come on, I'll buy you a meal." The mild accent was attached to the squat, smiling personage of Ron Gluckman (I'd seen his byline), "I'm with *Asiaweek*." The reporter assumed kinship due to the cameras hanging off my shoulders. *Do I look so hungry that strangers are now resorting to charity?*

"Chris. I shoot for *Asiaweek*. What're the chances?"

"Here? Pretty good actually. The only place to eat is the restaurant of the Ulaan Bator Hotel." Ron pointed out the grand, gray façade of this landmark, across the empty square. Any neo-classical delusions its architect may have entertained on the drawing board had been, plainly, sacrificed on the brutal anvil of Stalinist constructivism, and to the forced economy of cement.

"I'm doing a story about the Mongolian Navy," Ron continued. Mongolia is a landlocked, desert-rimmed country: Ron was either the most optimistic fool I'd ever met, or an absolute genius.

"I've tracked them down: a father and his son running two leaky cabin cruisers on Lake Hobsogol, up on the Russian border."

We entered the hotel's cool foyer through double doors that kept winter out the nine-months of the year it was raging. Ron hadn't been exaggerating. The entire, ramshackle expat community, ranging from itinerant Polish power plant advisers to the visa secretary of the Russian Embassy, visiting geologists and professors studying the ethnomusicology of Mongolian throat warbling: all were gathered here during the institution's strict feeding hours.

"There's a two-tier system in operation. No one really knows the value of money; it was always skewed due to the subsidies of the Russians," Ron advised. Now they'd left, he went on, some interesting inconsistencies cried out to be taken advantage of. For example, you had to pay for hotels using US dollars, in cash. But food and local transport could all be paid using tugriks, and these were linked to the official Tugrik-Dollar rate, which was currently valued twenty times lower than that offered on the black market. For the fortunate owner of hard currency, communist economic mismanagement was a bonanza.

"I'll pay for us all," Ron magnanimously beat everyone else at our table to the draw, "I need to get rid of these tugriks, somehow." Ordering from the extensive, two-page menu which offered such delicacies as 'barbeque lamp' and 'fillet stake' was simple: only the schnitzel was available. The bill for our meal, including ersatz coffee and a dessert of tinned North Korean pears with ice cream, came to 200 tugriks—a little over fifty cents—for seven people. I began to view UB as being my kind of town.

The Altai Hotel was positioned on the urban threshold, where the city surrendered abruptly to rolling grassland; out beyond the Russian cemetery with its rusted Orthodox crosses, and the neglected shell of the half-finished Holiday Inn. This, the most futuristic-looking structure in town (reportedly financed by a Yugoslav business consortium), had missed its completion date for the celebration of seventy years of Mongolian communism, 1921–1991, and occupied a deserted worksite, beneath frozen cranes: the most recent memorial in a long line of unfulfilled aspirations.

On Peace Avenue a long queue led to a food kitchen. My attempts to photograph here were frustrated by small rocks and pebbles launched at me, wordlessly and with pinpoint accuracy, by people standing in line, irritated I was recording this shameful evidence of their current national economic plight.

A little farther down the road, a riotous crowd gathered

outside what I took to be an employment office. No stones this time. Instead, a policeman grabbed my arm and marched me inside. Showing unusual knowledge of the workings of a camera, he rolled back the film, pointed the lens at the window, and proceeded to count off each frame as he double exposed it in the bright daylight. He made sure to wind each frame on slowly to maximize the extent of my demoralization.

Feeling rather pissed off by the general negative reaction toward my profession, I decided to wander along the railway tracks until I either bumped into a station or broke out into the countryside. The station arrived first. At the counter, under a sign reading 'MOCKBA', I was told it would cost US$92 to travel halfway round the world to Moscow. This news cheered me up a little. Although, thanks to the inefficiency of Soviet bureaucracy, the ticket could only be purchased through an official government travel agent, back at the Ulaan Bator Hotel.

Having wasted my entire morning being pelted with stones, getting sworn at, arrested and misdirected, retiring to the UB Hotel for a restorative lunchtime schnitzel was gaining in appeal. I was caught in a thunderstorm crossing the square and arrived drenched and shivering. The meal was a bit of a wash-out, too. Despite the presence of the Mongolian Symphonic Orchestra, gathered to serenade us in their penguin suits and shapeless white dresses, there was a shortage of actual food today; just biscuits and ice cream, and a generous concession of *arkhi*, the local vodka. The label on the bottle featured the inevitable Genghis Khan — the only universally recognized Mongolian.

Ron introduced me to Vladimir, the suave Head of Visa Section at the Russian Embassy, and I told him I'd be around in the morning. Taking care of business, I booked a seat on next week's Moscow train and put through a call to the British Embassy. Their building was just down the road, but the line was too crackly to make out much of the conversation.

Afterwards, I rejoined Ron and his varied gang of hangers-on in a nameless bar, housed inside a 'ger' (the Mongolian version of the Tibetan yurt) near the Russian Embassy. This place had a stock of genuine Czech Urquell pilsner. Alcohol, for the moment, seemed to have avoided the severest of rationing.

The invitation arrived yesterday, when I was out. Upon the thick, creamy stationery lay embossed The Royal Coat of Arms — imperious and golden:

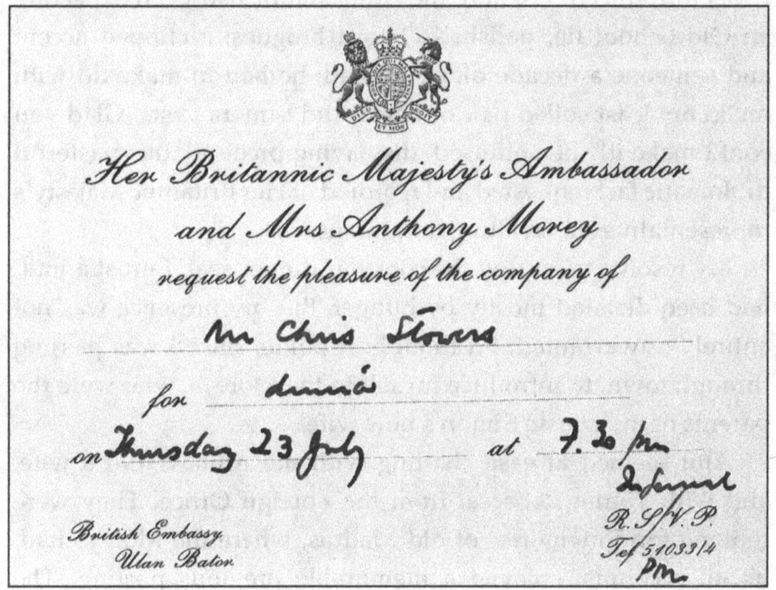

'Dress Informal'. Thank god. There had been no room to fit a tuxedo in my backpack.

There was no fence to keep inquisitive or ill-meaning Mongolians from straying into the British Embassy, merely a grassy knoll and a dirt track, well-trodden, that lay between it and the Indian Embassy next door. A dark man in a light suit came towards me out of the obscuring dusk. This was Anil, Second Secretary at the Indian mission.

"I was just over there, nobody's answering. Let's try again, shall we?" This time Anil headed for the side entrance, via a sunken vegetable plot. I caught sight of a substantial body, clothed in tweed, emerging from the greenhouse.

"Ah, caught red-handed!" Ambassador Morey greeted Anil as an adopted son. "Just been inspecting my prize onions ... and stashing the reserve bottle of whisky," he added, conspiratorially. I was introduced. Possibly the Ambassador had been expecting an Old School tie, polished Oxford brogues, a clipped accent and someone a decade older. Instead, he had to make do with me in my least soiled pair of Levi's and camera vest. "Glad you could make it!" he enthused, displaying precisely the masterful diplomatic tact requested and required of Her Britannic Majesty's representatives in far-flung dominions.

My resolve to occupy the consular dinner seat, I must admit, had been dictated mostly by hunger. But my presence was not entirely unwarranted: I'd thought it polite, since I was passing through town, to introduce myself to the Moreys, who were the parents of my cousin Simon's new wife.

Anil seemed at ease chatting with the Ambassador's wife, and with young Rebecca, from the Foreign Office. They were reliving fond memories of old Madras, where the Moreys had, by all accounts, enjoyed a memorable previous posting. The remaining male guests were all named Peter. Peter from Reuters had been based in Mongolia a year and was leaving soon. He was looking forward to the limitless food options of his new post, Beijing. And there were two retired British Army majors. I asked the youngest of these — who looked barely forty — what he was doing here.

"QM. Queen's Messenger."

"Young Peter gets to guard the mail," chipped in Ambassador Morey.

"That and go hang gliding. Have you been able to arrange something for me this trip, Tony?" Assured that a foray to the steppes had, indeed, been organized, the younger QM went on, "Yes, glorified postman, really. Entire compartment stuffed full with diplomatic pouches in London, then I sit on it, dishing out documents all the way to Hong Kong." It sounded the perfect job, I told him, for an ex-motorcycle courier such as myself.

"Only catch is, old boy," piped up the elder Peter, also a QM (the world was suddenly full of them; possibly he was heading in the opposite direction), "have to've served. In the army, I mean." He hesitated, looked me up and down, took a sip of dry sherry and passed judgment, "You haven't, have you? No. Thought not."

We were led through to the dining room, its twenty-foot-high ceiling ornately plastered with cornices and lit by a sparkling central chandelier. I concentrated on the extensive feast being wheeled in on silver trays and serving trolleys pushed by dutiful Mongolian servants. Soup and croutons were followed by a variety of meats, none of which appeared to be of horse.

"Is this turkey?" inquired Anil hopefully, washing his down with a glass of chilled Riesling; and I'd wondered idly where on earth you'd locate a turkey in Ulaan Bator? Images of disheveled QMs struggling to contain gobbling sacks of live foul aboard the Orient Express sprang to mind. A superb Pineapple Romanoff was seen off with cheese, biscuits and coffee. Chocolates and port bringing up the rear. Cigars optional.

I recounted for general consumption my interview that morning with Zolzukhan, the chain-smoking, self-proclaimed boss of the fledgling Mongolian Stock Exchange. His trading floor was located next to the Dollar Store in the main square, and housed in a grand, peach-colored building I'd initially taken for the Opera House, until I'd stepped close enough to decipher its brass plate. The Asian Development Bank had recently handed the Mongolians several million dollars to experiment in the free market economy. I'd photographed Zolzukhan, cigarette in hand, seated against a backdrop of brand-new computer terminals, all sheathed in their original plastic dust covers and obviously unused.

"Bit premature, wouldn't you say?" the elder QM opined. "Country has to walk before it can run, what? I mean to say, none of their chaps knows how to use the technology. They've always had the Russians do that sort of thing for them, and now they expect the West to take over that role."

Peter of Reuters, who had interviewed the Stock Exchange chief, himself, pointed out: "Zolzukhan often refers to 'his' stock market as being a car he helped to build but anyone could drive."

"Yes," countered the elder QM, "but what he didn't tell you was he takes the bally steering wheel with him anytime he parks it!"

Rebecca swooped, perhaps sensing not only that my guard was down but, following the consumption of a third brandy, I'd lowered the drawbridge, run a white flag up the pole, and hung a sign on the castle door reading, "Come on in, it's open." She quizzed me intently about what I planned to photograph on this trip, and handed me her card. "Come and see me when you're back in London. The Office would be awfully interested in having a look at your photos." *Is this how agents are recruited*?

"So glad you could make it," Ambassador Morey shook my hand warmly, swinging the heavy door shut behind me. It was 1.00 a.m., and the garden gateway was caught like a distant ship in the sweep of a lighthouse beam. Ron had warned me not to set foot on the streets of Ulaan Bator after dark. Wolves roamed freely, emboldened by man's shrinking footprint, and gangs of thieves preyed on those stupid or drunk enough to ignore the protection of sunlight. The laughter and partying continued, silhouetted behind the embassy's glowing curtain drapes. I stooped to pick up some rocks, and ventured forth into the silent city. Footsteps sped up behind me. I turned, but there was nothing there, just my heart beating in the diminished airspace of my chest.

The Moscow train must have arrived. At least thirty Russians were milling around outside the Altai when I arrived back from lunch at the UB Hotel. Dressed in uniform dark blue adidas tracksuits, the traders made discreet currency deals and tried to sell their goods to the Mongolians from out of huge woven plastic sacks. Forget Zolzukhan's disconnected computer terminals: here was your *real* free market economy.

Batbilik, the dwarf, was a familiar character, who could always be found hanging around the main square, attempting to sell trinkets to tourists; I'd spotted him in the afternoon as he emerged from a Chuck Norris film screened at the Lenin Club.

"How is it hanging?" he began his pitch using homemade American slang. I'd never seen him dressed without his floppy fishing hat, and a camera vest very much like my own. The conversation always started the same way.

"Concealed in each of my many pockets are numerous bounties and treasures. You would like to see them?" And before I'd had time to tell him 'no', he was pulling out postcards and stamps, dinosaur eggs bearing a suspicious resemblance to stones, faded Russian maps from the 1970s featuring a newly cemented UB Hotel, an exquisite 1911 Hong Kong silver dollar, and tin badges featuring the likeness of Soviet-Mongolian hero Sukhbaatar. I admired his indefatigable spirit of enterprise, and changed some excess tugriks back into US dollars, allowing him to benefit slightly on the rate.

Most everyone was glued to their TV that night, watching the previous day's opening of the Olympic Games in Barcelona. The last time I'd picked up distant news of an Olympics was four years back, tuning into a Singaporean broadcast on Xavier's shortwave radio on the deck of the *Kurnia Ilahi* as we drifted in the Java Sea. I felt similarly marooned here in Ulaan Bator, this time in a vast ocean of grass, rather than of water.

The restaurant in the UB Hotel was less crowded than usual. Only the horse fillet and coffee were available today. Vladimir sat at the table next to mine, making a show of cutting all the gristle from his steak, his face a mask of astonished disbelief at how little edible meat was left at the conclusion of this operation. He was, I could tell, trying to avoid eye contact. My train was scheduled to depart the next day. I would have wasted the fare—a huge chunk of all the money I had left in the world—if he failed to issue my visa in time. But if all these years in Asia had taught me anything about dealing with officialdom, it was to not worry or kick up an unnecessary fuss. Of all the things beyond our ability to control, those of a bureaucratic nature were the most elusive: either you learned to sway with the senseless meanderings of civil servants, like a bamboo in the wind, or you would be snapped by them in two.

There was no guard outside the Russian Embassy the next morning, so I walked straight in. Vladimir was cheerfully handing out passports to a bunch of equally delighted Pakistanis.

"Ahh, Comrade Chris. Tell me, how is your feeling after the

meat last night?"

"Thought it a bit … gamey …" I ventured. Why all the pleasant banter?

"Bear with me, I can't seem to, ah, locate your passport. I had it here somewhere …"

Distractedly, he emptied all the draws in his desk, and then began working through a filing cabinet, mumbling to himself in English for my benefit, "transit visas, 'S' … that's strange, should be here …"

I was sitting in the Patience Department, on the verge of losing my bamboo-like flexibility, when the Visa Secretary made his triumphant discovery:

"Aha! Here it is, filed under 'R'," (my middle initial) "my apologies. Ten-day transit. It is the maximum I am authorized to permit." Just in time, too. The train was scheduled to depart that evening and it would take six of those days just to reach Moscow. Getting out the other end of Russia before this paperwork expired was going to be tight. But I'd take anything I could get at the moment. Problems always seemed to resolve themselves once you started moving.

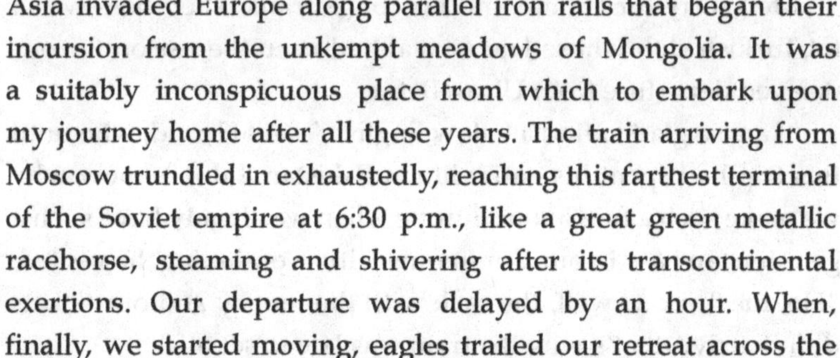

Asia invaded Europe along parallel iron rails that began their incursion from the unkempt meadows of Mongolia. It was a suitably inconspicuous place from which to embark upon my journey home after all these years. The train arriving from Moscow trundled in exhaustedly, reaching this farthest terminal of the Soviet empire at 6:30 p.m., like a great green metallic racehorse, steaming and shivering after its transcontinental exertions. Our departure was delayed by an hour. When, finally, we started moving, eagles trailed our retreat across the rolling wilderness, hopeful of our tossed scraps. As we clattered along, I grabbed some shaky shots of the Mongolian Army out on maneuvers, mindful of the distant geopolitical interests expressed by a certain brunette representative of Whitehall.

We slowed to a standstill sometime around midnight. Chinks of lamplight escaped through the train's chintzy curtains and kindled the nearby steppe into brief blaze. The station was a desolate spot. I saw no place name but guessed it was Darjan. All these places looked the same, at night especially. A wolf, unbothered by its captive audience, continued to gnaw through the carcass of a sheep at one end of the platform. Russians, their breaths reeking of vodka, boarded at the other end carrying cardboard suitcases and straining plastic bags. Glass jars of pickles swung on lengths of string looped around their necks.

"I'd like to say Russian men need these beds," growled a bear of a man, one of these new arrivals, who directed his ire at the shrinking Pakistanis. The Asians couldn't fit in their own cabin since that was already stuffed to the ceiling with the more than forty straining sacks of fake adidas tracksuits they were helping transport.

"He means," I interpreted for the benefit of Hamid with whom I'd been reminiscing about Anarkali Bazaar, in his hometown of Lahore, "that you're occupying his cabin."

I felt sorry for Hamid and his compatriots. Their boss was a fat Turkish slob whose late arrival had been the reason for our delayed departure from Ulaan Bator.

"I am so glad to find a fellow English," said Hamid, who until this trip had spent his entire life in Pakistan. I don't know why we make such a fuss about Europe when we already have such a genuine fan base in our Commonwealth. Continuing, he vented, "He, the Turk ... well, the sack with the money and our tickets didn't arrive, that's why the train was late to set off."

When, back in 1807 Sir Humphry Davy, experimenting with

his primitive, two thousand cell battery, managed to send a spark of light across the span of four inches between two charcoal sticks, thus creating the first arc lamp, I very much doubt he foresaw his invention being exported to the Mongolian steppe, or that one of its monstrously magnified descendants would be thrusting me under inquisitional glare, now, at two o'clock in the morning. But that was the wretched time chosen, specifically, I imagine, to maximize discomfiture and mental anguish of the weary Russia-bound traveler. An eagle soaring above our stalled train would have observed in the outspread sulfur-yellow wings cast by this row of floodlights, and the fainter illumination of the body of the train—lying perpendicular to this—a representation of itself, daubed perhaps by one of the early-Impressionists.

Back on board, and the Mongolian customs guards made a beeline for the Pakistanis, lining them up in the corridor and insisting they offload half of their sacks. They made a show of checking for smuggled goods beneath all the piles of sportswear, and then accepted a tracksuit apiece for their efforts.

No man's land followed our release; an invisible swell of grass that took a further two hours to traverse at trundling speed. At the far extremity of this forbidden territory slouched Russian border guards, stony-faced and dragging AK-47s. Again, the Pakistanis were targeted. The Mongolian traders smirked as the contents of their competitors' compartment were once more transferred from train to platform and back. The Russians extracted their fee of six tracksuits from out of the load. The Turk reappeared at this point, long enough to cadge a cigarette off of me. He didn't even nod in thanks. By such gestures do we learn the measure of a man.

SIBERIA
July 29, 1992

FOR SEVERAL DAYS we rumbled, surveying savannahs of sage and forests of larch and birch. A permanent feature of the narrow, swaying corridor beyond my cabin was the empty vodka bottle, propping open the upper window to let stale air and smoke escape. Obviously, this gap also let the train's own diesel fumes in. These olfactory stimulants blended perfectly with those of passing blackberry, honey and pinesap, together forming a pungent aroma that stirred memories of my brief romantic interlude with Claudia in Tibet, and could easily have been marketed as a new air freshener: 'Siberian Summer'.

"Drink, Chriskin. Tea!" insisted ten-year-old Maxim (universally called *Maximka*), dispelling my daydream. How could I have been so wrong about the Russians? Until now I'd been conditioned to view an entire people unfairly and secondhand, through the skewed and muddied lens offered by my Afghan students and Mujahedeen friends back in Peshawar, where my travels began. The bombs detonated by their agents, and fear of their helicopter gunships, had left me smeared with a thick veneer of prejudice.

My present travel companions, to the contrary, were the salt of the earth; they couldn't be farther removed from the cold-hearted, stereotypical Soviet invader described so ghoulishly in the propaganda posters of the refugee camps in Pakistan's North West Frontier Province. Not only did the Englishman share with his Russian counterpart a healthy degree of fatalism and appreciation of a good game of chess, but he, like us, loved to drink tea and was a passionate dunker of biscuit. The Russians were the most misunderstood of all Europeans, and we would possibly have more in common with them than with the Americans, if the chips were down. Where we differed, perhaps, became understandable once you began to travel across their vast and under-developed landscape. Russia enjoyed the luxury of so few people and so much space. It was a glorious interval of a country, during which one was forced to slow down and contemplate life. It was a quality that 'The West', rushing madly to escape its past, was in danger of losing: a quality that rail travel allowed time to appreciate, and gave the Russians, with their rich heritage of national literature, the vocabulary to explore.

Maxim's father, Alexander, had the bearing of a schoolmaster, though he was an engineer by trade. Right now, he was part of an exodus of skilled workers flooding back to Mother Russia. He'd been in Ulaan Bator for the last six years to oversee the setting up of a car production plant there. That project had derailed, along with the rest of the Soviet economy. All the most valuable machinery and assembly line components had been scavenged, repacked and sent back west. He and his sons, being humans, were more expendable, and had been left to make their own way home.

Alex assembled Maxim, and his eleven-year-old brother Vova, each morning and afternoon, assuming responsibility for their extracurricular education. They delved for treasure between the pages of hundreds of volumes that strained the straps of their suitcases. When not reading, they perfected their chess moves.

"Russia is a very fine country," Maxim exclaimed proudly in English, looking out the window. "Ahh ... Polyana!" he sighed, a 10-year-old already versed in Tolstoy. Alpine scenery flowed by like reflections rippling in a wide river. Log cottages, their gables and window shutters painted soothing pastels of green and blue, formed hamlets along tenuous, rutted tracks. Pitchforks held back flowing tresses of golden hay piled high upon horse-drawn carts. Allotment fences buckled amid an explosion of sunflowers and beehives. Then the curtain fell—zinc and shadow, white and black—as thick forests of silver birch trees reasserted control.

At night, just beyond Irkutsk, we skirted Lake Baikal, menace lurking in its placid depths. The earth became scorched, drained of dark blood. Three giant incense sticks tapered to the heavens disgorged a foul fog. They were silhouetted by the combustible glow of flare stacks, like so many fire-breathing dragons. The stench of industry clawed at throat and lung, peppery and sweet like a rotting corpse.

The following day my chess education continued. There was little else to do except read, write, play cards and take potshots at the passing peasantry with my camera. I lost first to Vova and then his younger brother, Maximka. I dared not challenge their father. A frisson of excited chatter ran the length of the corridor as we pulled into Krasnoyarsk. Mongolians leaned out of their compartments, feeding t-shirts bought for a dollar in Beijing to the outstretched arms of frenzied traders on the platform below. The traders paid twice that price, and then rushed off to sell them for three dollars each at local markets. I felt vulnerable alighting the train, my mobile home for several days now, to purchase a paper cone of boiled new potatoes from a rosy-cheeked

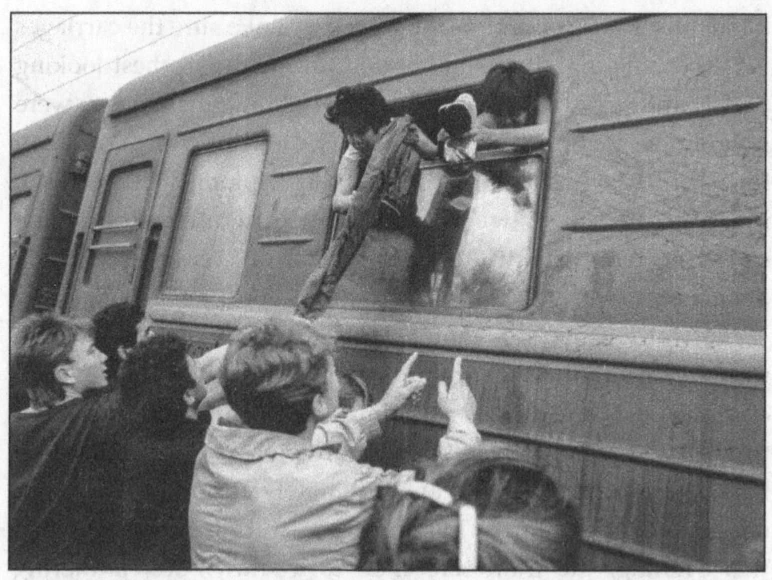

The Great Railway Bazaar. Mongolian traders sell hard-to-come-by consumer and fashion goods from the window of their carriage to Russians on the platform in Krasnoyarsk, Siberia. July 1992.

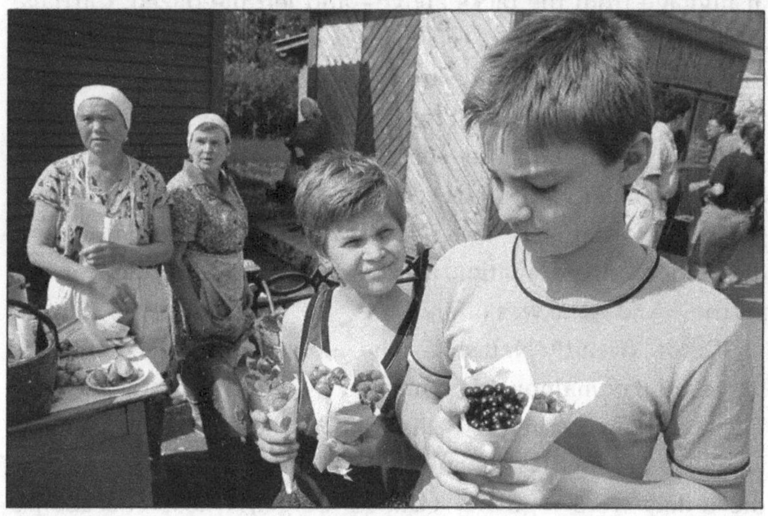

Chess 'maestro' Maxim (center), and his elder brother Vova (right), having just bought berries from a Babushka during a brief stop somewhere in Siberia. July 1992.
Photos: Chris Stowers/PANOS

Babushka. My eyes kept darting back to make sure the carriages were not moving off as she selected for me the freshest-looking packet and sprinkled it with chives. My Mongolian loaves were holding out just fine. I had purchased three kilograms of bread for all of seven-and-a-half tugriks at the 'Diplomat's Store', back in UB. I ladled on strawberry jam to help disguise their growing staleness. Wary of future famine, I kept my tin of Pyongyang pears in reserve.

Forward again for another straight day. The comforting, routine jolts and sways of the carriage, the regular morse code clacking of wheels over rail joints, the sleepy rhythm of rail travel fused organically with the neurological networks of those being transported. One became intimately attuned to any faint change in the routine. Thus, it was disturbing indeed, when this evening, the train screeched to a drawn-out, juddering halt. Silence fell, audibly — along with any poorly stowed item of luggage from the racks above — and left me dazed. Carriage attendant Natasha unlocked the rear door to peer out. I seized this opportunity to stand out on the step-plate and breathe in the cool, menthol mist as it rose, laden with dew and scented by peat and pollen. This was what the middle of nowhere smelled of. Soviet citizens long ago became accustomed to accepting their government-stamped fates. None of my traveling companions demanded an explanation for this sudden interruption of our journey. And none was offered.

Plump, friendly Natasha — who, along with Sergei, her gaunt to the point of malnourished husband — controlled carriage No.3. The couple lived on board the train, making sure the samovar was kept boiling, bed linen folded and accounted for, and that the toilets were regularly cleaned. Sergei, whose cheekbones protruded like the ledges of a cliff, would give anyone a fright down a dark alleyway, let alone in the swaying corridor of a night train. Belying his appearance, he turned out to be a patient and perceptive sort. He presented me with a 'Moscow-Vladivostok' railway badge, and I gave him a postcard with a nice view of Hong Kong that he immediately stuck up in the window of their compartment. Natasha insisted on making me a mug of strong tea, and I chatted to Sergei in English as the train rumbled back to life. He replied in Russian. Language is as much tone and expression as it is words and grammar; we understood each other perfectly, immersed in the communion of patient respect.

Unless the world — as some continue to contend — is flat, then every mile traveled away from home, inevitably and eventually, would bring me a mile closer back to it. I felt very much on the homeward run now, though I was dreading the end of the ride. Now I had direction, sense of purpose was next on the list. Attempting to gauge public opinion, I mentioned to Alexander that, after Moscow, I was heading to Yugoslavia. His reaction was to grab hold of an imaginary machine gun and start shooting it at me.

Hamid wandered into our compartment carrying a chess set he'd found, looking for someone to play against. He had a glazed look about him and failed to conceal the half-finished bottle of *arkhi* in his pocket. Since he wasn't in top form, our game ended in a draw.

"I'll come back tomorrow, with more ... concentration. Then I play proper game," he meant against a more challenging opponent, like Alex or, quite possibly, Maximka.

"But we are arriving in Moscow tonight," announced Vova, as the Pakistani zigzagged away. Already? I had lost all track of time. This cabin was as much home as I needed; the strangers in it, sufficient family. Cocooned from the real world and its stationary problems, I'd been sleeping better than for months. How could it be all ending so soon?

I spent the remainder of the morning in carriage No.6. Running this car were two male attendants, both named Yevgeny (I differentiated them by age, Junior and Senior). It seemed like an odd arrangement, but nobody questioned it.

"Why you not visit yesterday?" Yevgeny Senior reprimanded me, his close-cropped moustache twitching as he poured coffee into three mugs, spiking them with some of his home-brewed vodka. I handed over a pack of precious Marlboros by way of apology, and the podgy thirty-nine-year-old transferred half of the sticks to an empty glass jar for his younger namesake. Duty done, he then lit one for himself. He sat for a moment, lost in reverent puffing.

"Ah, Amerikanski tobacco!" And through a smoky cloud he changed topic. "Hey, you miss Soviet *soldat*, ten of them last night, all drinking much, much the vodka. Make the best photo for your Amerika magazine." To Yevgeny, the West *was* Amerika. Dispensing with the coffee, we started tipping back neat vodka.

"To Gorbachev!" I toasted, "Glasnost." One of my verbal darts hit the board, the other missed the target wildly:

"*Nyet, nyet. Nyet* Gorbachev. Yeltsin!" Yevgeny corrected me as to who the real mover and shaker of the New World Order currently struggling to its feet in Moscow was. Yevgeny Junior arrived, swigged his vodka from the jam jar as though it were water, and proceeded to complain to his co-worker about the Mongolians. *Up and down the corridors, always the doors they leave open.* The willowy, clean-shaven attendant had, due to a swollen knee joint, an oddly swaggering gait. He thanked me for the Marlboros, made sure to save them for later, and opened a pack of local smokes — a brand spelled 'PEUC' (they smelled even worse).

Yevgeny Senior had taught himself English from a 1961

textbook, and the occasional 'Amerikanski' passenger such as myself. Before this, he used to drive a taxi in Leningrad. He seemed to be doing well for himself. Not only did he own a two-room apartment and a Dacha in the countryside, but whenever he was not working on the train he rode around on a motorcycle and sidecar, and he was saving up for a secondhand car. Each month he teamed up with Yevgeny Junior, and they would spend the next twenty days on the rails. In return for this sacrifice, he received 5,000 rubles and — in a sign of changing times — US$80 in hard currency.

"Poor people, if not have Amerikanski dollar, food, everything very expensive — my ruble worth ..." Yevgeny searched for a suitable comparison, ending up tearing off a single sheet of toilet paper, "... this is what is worth now!"

All afternoon we sliced through an infinite yellow carpet of oilseed rape, closing in on the elusive capital. I was roped in to filter Hamid's Sub-Continental English into standard British format. The results I related to Alanya, a delectable nineteen-year-old I'd spied walking her Alsatian at various stations along the way. Beautiful girls and dangerous dogs being equally unapproachable, I relished this excuse to get to know her better. She translated my English back into Russian for the benefit of the two Yevgenys. The concerned attendants felt responsible for sorting out onward travel arrangements for the Pakistanis, who needed to catch a connecting train to Kiev. From that city they still had to find a way to transport their forty sacks of fake adidas sportswear to a border town named something like 'Ivana Forovskaya'. By one of those extreme coincidences, the proliferation of which no longer astounded me, this very same 'Ivana Forovskaya' was the hometown of Alanya and her parents.

"Tell lady, she find lorry for tracksuits, we drive her no charge," enthused Hamid.

Every journey must end for a new one to begin; it was just the intervals between travel I found uncomfortable. At midnight, the multiple carriages of the Trans-Siberian Express finally caught up with the engine they had been chasing all the way from Asia to Moscow's Jaroslavsky Station. Maxim and Vova asked for my home address and a passport photograph each.

"It is because you go to Sarajevo," explained Alexander, "they think you will be shot."

"Da!" chorused the two boys, worry etched in their faces. Charming. We waved goodbye across a choppy sea of departing soldiers, scurrying passengers, greeting and weeping relatives; and the luggage belonging to all of the above. I gifted an old baseball hat to Natasha, and my paisley proofreading tie from Hong Kong to Sergei.

"You are not leaving?" It was Yevgeny Senior.

"I guess I have to ..." I left the door ajar for opportunity to sneak through. The train was my sanctuary; Moscow, by contrast, a dark, unknown and deeply threatening, foreign landscape.

"No, you must not. We have spare cabin. Like hotel. This Moscow, it is not safe at night."

Finally, I was able to synchronize my watch to the famous 'Moscow Time' everyone had been complaining about, all the way from Siberia. Yevgeny Junior, his sad, deep-set eyes perhaps mourning the premature loss of his hair, set before us a meal supplied by his mother, comprising salad, salmon, German sausage and sponge cake. The vodka was of his own distilling.

Tonight, in the toilet compartment of a nondescript train carriage, parked in the expansive sidings of a railway terminus on the northeast outskirts of the capital of the 'Evil Empire', I luxuriated in my first shower since leaving Beijing.

MOSCOW
August 2, 1992

IN DAYLIGHT, MOSCOW felt more approachable. I bid farewell to both the Yevgenys who were distracted now, anyway, having to sort out their carriage for the return trip to Mongolia. Having spent just 86 rubles during the past five days of rail travel, to now fork out 2,000 of them (around US$13 at the black-market rate) for a single night of accommodation, went against the grain. But the hotel was the cheapest I could find. Even its address tried to defy me, the closest identifying landmark being Petrovsko-Razumovskaya underground station, the longest tongue twister on the Metro map.

Big cities are always impersonal, and Russia's capital — like the territory it nominally represented — was vast: Moscow was one tough dame. She'd been through her fair share of abusive lovers over the years. But you'd never find this tragic heroine weeping or feeling sorry for herself. No! At the end of each doomed affair, she would slap on a new layer of makeup, ignite a fresh cigarette, and get back out on the streets again. I felt the best approach to my relationship with this soft-hearted yet fearsome Amazon would be to take a deep breath and jump in with the daily commute.

My love affair with public transportation was instantly reciprocated as getting about was practically free. A one-ruble Metro token allowed you to ride any distance and in any direction. Descending two hundred feet into the bowels of the earth was like stepping into the tungsten-lit movie set of a Flash Gordon flick; angular revolutionary heroes peered down from high pedestals, and elaborate chandeliers awaited their removal for the next scene. Prominent by their absence were those twin banes of capitalist existence: graffiti and advertizing.

In the little hut at the base of the escalator sat a large woman, her face as gray as her uniform. The booth grew inexorably in size as the ancient conveyor belt brought me closer to the platform. Beside me was Tatiana. She had been helping me navigate the many bureaucratic obstacles around town, and had even secured, through some trick of native guile and passionate plea, a much sought-after seven-day visa extension. She was explaining that, despite how bad life was just a few years back: "Some people refuse still to believe the securities of the old system are gone now."

The woman in the booth issued an order through her loudhailer that reverberated up the steep, moving mineshaft. Tatiana paid it no attention. The tinny message was repeated, this time with more irritation. Coolly, relishing the moment, Tatiana purred in her smoky voice:

"Do you know what she is shouting about?"

"I have no idea. Some delay in service, maybe?"

"It's you."

"Me? What've I done wrong?" It was so dimly lit down here, surely all commuters were indistinguishable?

"She's ordering you to take your camera bag off the handrail. You are only allowed to grip the handrail with your hands." And she laughed at the ridiculousness of the situation. Her country—an entire orthodoxy—was crashing down, but here in the murky depths of the Metro, the big lady with the loudspeaker still reigned supreme.

We headed to the Pushkin Monument to meet Evgeny Kondakov. Tatiana and he had been friends since their university days. Evgeny was a *Moscow News* photographer, and I had been carrying a packet of slide sheets for him all the way from Hong Kong, a gift from Hendrick, who'd met him on a trip six months earlier. Emerging from Pushkinskaya Metro station, I faced a dilemma: two compelling scenes were playing themselves out and I couldn't immediately decide which I should start to shoot.

"Go on," laughed Tatiana, habituated to the uncontrollable urges that seize photographers, "I'll wait for you at the feet of Pushkin."

To the left, a huge crowd was squeezed behind metal barriers, eagerly anticipating a Big Mac. McDonald's may well have established this, their first restaurant in the Soviet Union, over a year ago, but the masses were still eager to sample a taste of The West. To my right, a demonstration held by mothers and widows was taking place. The bereaved cradled portraits of lost sons and husbands, all of whom were pictured posing proudly in their service uniforms. It would seem the State had failed to show an equal degree of respect to its martyrs. I opted for the demonstration.

I was shooting a close-up, focusing on the wrinkled hands of an old lady clasping a strip of medals, when a voice beside me explained: "They have gone missing, with no explanation from the authorities, and in peacetime. Meaning none of the relatives can receive the military pension."

"Evgeny?" My assumption was an educated one; the photographer carried an incredible Nikon F4 camera, so costly it must have been supplied by an employer.

"Chris? I knew it must be you. Yes, it's a tragic situation not limited to these few protesters. More than one hundred thousand soldiers and sailors have gone missing since Perestroika."

Just then, a large lady pushed through the police line; in her hand she waved a placard. Suddenly, a bunch of men ran in to grab her, screaming into walkie-talkies, and a squad car appeared, tires squealing, from around the corner. Three of the uniformed men bundled the aggrieved Babushka into the rear of the comically small Lada, as commotion erupted all around them. The car weaved off in a splutter of exhaust smoke and blaze of sirens.

"McDonald's?" Evgeny suggested.

We picked up Tatiana on the way.

"Just look at them," she nodded disparagingly at the people queuing very slowly for their fast food. Evgeny gallantly helped her down from her perch upon the statue of Russia's greatest poet. "For so many years we've had no choice; we all had to wear the same clothes, buy the same radio sets, read the same newspapers. Now we have a choice, and what does everyone wear? Tracksuits!" I had a flashback to Hamid and his crew of harassed sportswear smugglers, and wondered if they'd made it to the border yet.

"Yes, and the streets are full of drunks," I added.

"That's nothing new, though, Chris," Evgeny was quick to correct me. "After all, it is sung:
'There cannot be too much vodka,
There can only be not enough vodka.'"

"It's the black marketeers, all these beggars and mafia from the Caucusus, that are the worst," Tatiana opined with feeling. "As you see, the police are happy to arrest poor Russian mothers, but they turn a blind eye to the crimes of uncivilized louts. It's a ticking time bomb."

Evgeny made his apologies and rushed for the airport: he was flying to Kazakhstan to shoot nuclear test sites out on the steppe. Tatiana and I enjoyed a relaxed stroll together along Arbat Street, where drunken, off-duty Spetsnaz troops dressed in berets and blue and white striped t-shirts reveled, serenaded by a busker on accordion. Tatiana slipped her arm through mine and steered me away from their volatile, vodka-fueled merriment when I began to raise my camera.

We enjoyed a long chat beneath the elegant vaults of The White Swan café. Afterwards, Tatiana flagged down a taxi. The decrepit *Moskovitch* had seen better days; its engine stalling several times on our way to Kievskaya Station. The flat-capped driver flogged his vehicle like a stubborn mule after getting it running again. He started talking to Tatiana. I saw her face redden and then she exploded, berating the driver for whatever it was he had just suggested. He, in response, jammed on the brakes and abruptly ejected us, short of the railway terminus.

"He wanted me to tell you to pay US$25 for this ride, and then said he would split the difference with me!"

In order to improve my chances of success at the railway ticket counter, Tatiana started to coach me, patiently:

"Repeat after me, and seriously this time … *'Ya zjhe vu Tal-in-in, ya no g'voro-po Ruski, po-zhalust'* … none of those Estonians can speak Russian properly, they'll take you for a guest worker. Try again, 'I'm from Tallinn, sorry, I don't speak Russian' … OK, a little faster this time."

I was queuing for a ticket to Kishinev, the capital of the Moldovan Republic, a former Soviet satellite state. This shared a border with Romania, was presently caught up in a bitter civil war, and lay directly across my route to Yugoslavia. Throughout Russia, foreigners were still compelled to purchase tickets through the State-run Intourist agency. Their official rate for the thirty-six-hour journey would set me back US$70. By comparison, locals traveled the same distance for US$3. Tatiana faded into the shadows, leaving me less conspicuous. The queue shuffled forward. A chap to my left asked a question in Russian, and I practiced my sentence on him. He resorted to tapping the back of his bare wrist, and I told him the time was *che-ti-ryeh*, four o'clock. I inched closer to the counter and readied my sheet of paper, the one on which Tatiana had written down my destination and train number in Cyrillic. Mentally, I rehearsed my lines. The person in front of me moved aside. I stepped forward and opened my mouth ... "*Ya* ..." at the same time a perfumed arm reached through the crowd and yanked me away. It was attached to Tatiana, who was jabbering something convincing in Russian. She winked at me.

"I have your ticket," she whispered. She had found a black-market dealer just outside the station entrance and bought it from him.

This evening it stayed light until 10:00 p.m. On the way back to the hotel I bought a heavy loaf and three huge tomatoes from an old woman with a headscarf, her wares displayed on an upturned cardboard box at its entrance. *Naked Gun* — following me around the world — was being shown on the television in the lobby. Dubbed in Russian, all the parts had been voiced over by the same, mono-toned male actor. The room phone rang at least twice before midnight; bored hotel prostitutes trying their luck.

The following morning, I set out to meet Tatiana, and together we visited VDNKh Park. She showed me the Friendship of Nations fountain: fifteen golden figurines representing the various republics of the USSR, all looking outwards, their backs turned to each other. Later, we passed Red Square and the Moscow Hotel, with its twin wings built in different styles.

"The architect submitted his blueprint to Stalin, offering the choice of two different facades. Stalin, they say, hardly glanced at the plan before okaying its construction. And so, the hotel was built with unmatching wings, since nobody was brave enough to point out to the Great Man his mistake," Tatiana informed me. She was a bubbly, confident soul, able to move any bureaucratic mountain and pry open any official door. Her 'crime', that of her generation, was to have been born too soon. She was doubly disadvantaged. Having grown up a free-thinker in repressive, suspicious, yet intelligent Soviet society, she now entered the second half of her life as an innocent, thrown to the wolves of capitalism and chaos. Money and hustling, not fine words and ideals, now ruled the roost.

Tatiana lived with her seventy-nine-year-old grandmother in the ground-floor flat of a tenement block indistinguishable from all those around it. Her bedroom was her only truly private space. A huge poster of Marilyn Monroe hung above her bed. I slipped a US$10 note behind a postcard propped against the mirror on her dressing table that Hendrick had posted her. It featured the Hong Kong skyline.

"Yesterday I accepted your money for my work, but now we are friends," her pride had argued when I tried paying her earlier in the day. As in every country, in Russia there were good people and bad people; the difference between good Russians and bad Russians, however, was significantly greater.

The atmosphere that evening was thick and muggy. In Tatiana's apartment kitchen, we feasted on thick, brown bread laden with the sweetest of tomatoes and delectable homemade jams. We sipped coffee from dainty bone china teacups and

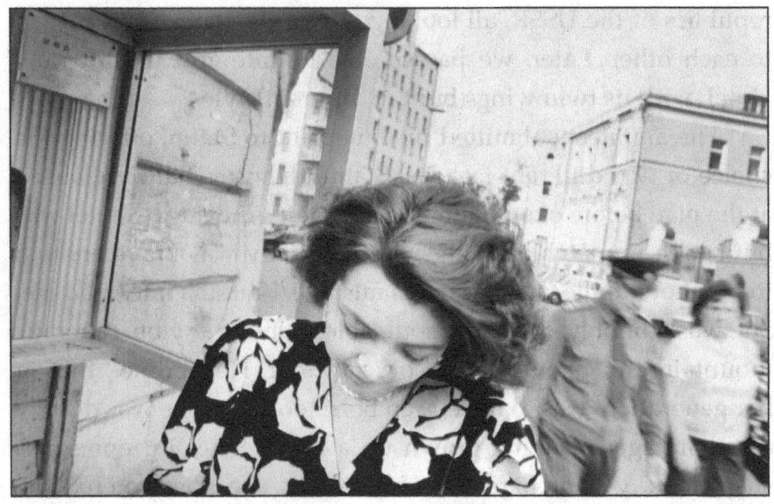

Tatiana. Moscow, August 5, 1992.

washed down the remainder of our food with 96 percent vol. medicinal vodka. Her bright red dress clung to her abundant figure like wallpaper as Tatiana accompanied me through the descending twilight to Kievskaya Station. The train for Moldova was scheduled to leave at 11:30 p.m. Half-drunk, I felt like a sailor with his girl on shore leave. We strolled arm-in-arm along the platforms, searching for my train, dwarfed below a cliff face of dark green carriages.

"If only I were ten years younger, Chris ..."

Yes, dear Tatiana, and if only my visa were not expiring ...

At midnight, Tatiana ran to catch the last Metro service home. We hugged and kissed goodbye and I was happy and sad all at the same time — as, I sensed, was she, too. The Kishinev train didn't pull in until 1:30 a.m. Its conductor told me this often happened with the service from Moldova, due to it being shot at.

〜〜〜

The magician's cloak of nighttime swirled away to reveal a compartment bathed in golden reflections cast by the sun as it rose across endless wheat fields. I awoke languidly, rocked by the familiar, somnolent sway of the train. We were already rolling through Russia's bread bowl, the Ukraine. The only other occupant of the cabin was an army officer in full dress uniform, on his way to Kiev.

Mid-afternoon, and a long stopover at Kiev Station. I had the cabin to myself now. The sky was a peerless deep blue, and Radio Kiev played tunes over the stations' tannoy system: a solid half-hour of *Air Supply* and *Earth, Wind & Fire*. Couples were out with their children, ice creams dripping in the heat, and my mind was transported back to Pakistan in 1987. Then, at the start of my travels, high in the remote Hunza Valley, the young daughter of two German hippies, her face creased in concern, had asked her proud parents whether the milk in her *chai* came from "before or after Chernobyl?" We had passed through *that* ill-fated station a few hours back.

That night I discovered a small plastic bag of ground coffee that Tatiana must have stashed in my camera bag when I wasn't looking. The samovar steamed, and so did the train, into a second night, and through Bessarabia. I brewed up a mug, went heavy on the sugar, and settled in for the unsettling.

MOLDOVA
August 7, 1992

PATRICK LEIGH-FERMOR, memorably, traveled this region in the mid-1930s. Shacked up with his lover, the Romanian noblewoman Balasha Cantacuzene, the couple pursued the arts — she painting and he writing — until their idyll was interrupted rudely by World War II. He described enjoying a "knight's-eye view from a horse" of Bessarabia; it was pretty spectacular from the raised vantage point of a railway carriage, too. The traces of Asia, which had clung to Soviet rails across the expanse of Russia, wore thin this close to the West. For the first time in over five years, I was back in Europe. The landscape was part that of France — flat acres of corn and sunflowers — and part England's grassy meadows and cabbage plots. Above all, there was a reconnection with language (passing railway stations declared their allegiance in the Roman alphabet, above the Cyrillic). The very light itself was keener, more contrasty, released from the lethargic haze of the Orient.

Geographically, the distance from Odessa to the capital of Moldova, Kishinev, was short, but many obstacles lay in my way. The disputed territory of Transnistria being a case in point. The hours of slow rumbling in the carriage started to drag. I tried keeping my eyes open during the long, sweltering night; a darkness of shunting and halts, convincing me that at any moment the cabin door would be smashed open by armed guards demanding documents, or that the windows would waterfall in a hail of bullets. Moldovan independence had only been recognized a few months earlier, on March 2, and I felt rather inadequately documented carrying a — by now, possibly obsolete — transit visa for the territories of the *former* Soviet Union in my passport. 'The Moldavian Soviet Socialist Republic' was a part of that family of nations, of course, but had just bloodily detached itself from any association with Moscow. In doing so, it left stranded the tiny rebel region of Transnistria, sandwiched between Moldova and Ukraine. That enclave now was stubbornly intent upon abusing its dwindling authority by harassing all passing traffic, a duty it jumped to with doggedly sentimental devotion to Soviet-era bureaucracy.

Dawn arrived as a benediction, the rays of a young sun blessing the glistening west bank of the Dniester River and the border of Moldova proper. Fortunately, practical reality hadn't yet caught up with realpolitik, and for all intents and purposes Moldova remained, diplomatically, a member of the extended and squabbling Russian Commonwealth. My transit visa was begrudgingly accepted and stamped.

Reaching Kishinev, I checked in to the Cosmos Hotel. The massive structure dominated a major intersection up from the railway station, and was impossible to miss. I was shown to a vast and vacuous room — replete with bathroom and balcony — on the eleventh floor. The staff encouraged payment for the night using a combination of three US$1 notes and fifty Russian rubles. At this point there was no alternative Moldovan unit of exchange (only on November 29, 1993, was the Moldovan leu introduced as legal tender).

As surely as a first determined step transforms into a journey, so possession of a single contact will lead, eventually, to establishment of a valued network of friends. In the case of Kishinev, I was very fortunate to have the name of Nicolae Pojoga, one of Hendrick's contacts from his journey six months earlier, jotted in my notebook. Nicolae answered the phone like a hunted man and kept initial conversation short, habituated by a lifetime of caution. It took me a few hours to track down the elusive Pojogan at the end of a dark corridor, in a back room of the national Press Building, up near the new Parliament. The tall, heavy door of *Moldova Press* creaked open, and a pair of brown eyes twinkled from the gloomy interior. Nicolae — their owner for the last forty years — attempted to direct attention away from these unguarded windows to his soul by thrusting forward a full beard capable of concealing any amount of conspiracy.

The Kishinev native exuded the quiet nature of an academic. It was of small surprise to learn he was a physicist by training, until the civil war had come along and forced him to investigate reactions in the less quantifiable, and often more volatile, world outside the laboratory. His iconic photograph of the victorious Moldovan flag being raised atop Parliament at the end of the recent war of independence, had established his reputation as The Nation's Photographer. Though he was too modest to ever admit it.

Nicolae wrote me a letter of introduction to the Ministry of External Affairs and connected me with a lady friend of his there, Alla. Alla told me, "You really should have a Moldovan transit visa ..." while having to admit the Russian one was still acceptable. She rushed off to sort out my Moldovan press credentials, leaving me to drink tea with an impeccably dressed and manicured government minister.

"Perhaps you could give me some advice?" this suave gentleman sought my advice on setting new government policy. "How much do you think we should charge for a tourist visa? Is US$25 too much?" (I recommended a more backpacker-friendly US$10.)

Alla soon returned bearing a newly laminated Moldovan press pass and my passport, the latter neatly stamped with a ten-day Moldova transit visa, "just in case you fall in love with Moldova."

I met up again with Nicolae at the Press Building, eager to celebrate my new temporary legal status. 'Procrastination' is my middle name. I think it is for all us nomads; we relish any excuse to linger, to avoid a little longer the responsibility of arrival. And we become excessively fond of any place that recognizes and affords us such freedom. I was, indeed, already beginning to fall in love with tiny Moldova.

That evening, Nicolae introduced me to Sergey, a battle-toughened photographer, his muscles knitted from steel cable, and to Tudor, soft of belly and large of moustache, the local representative of Reuters. Tudor's house was located just off Kishinev's main artery, the former Lenin Street, rechristened a few weeks back as Stefan cel Mare—Stefan the Great—after the ubiquitous 15th Century National Hero, vanquisher of the Ottoman hordes at the Battle of Vaslui. Pushing through a vivid green wooden gate, we entered a courtyard shaded by grapevines and pregnant with summer fruit.

"Moldovan cognac is held in high regard as far away as Siberia," I was able to report from recent personal encounter.

"Then we had best keep Tudor's cherry brandy and his wine a State secret," suggested Nicolae, our host basking in praise. Tudor reportedly produced 3,000 liters of wine a year, most of it destined for home consumption. He was famed for it.

"Yes, it is imperative we drink the evidence," Sergey put an end to all discussion.

At the end of the evening, Nicolae gallantly, and necessarily, escorted me back to the Cosmos Hotel. The lobby was a throng of people and cigarette smoke through which I wove with deliberation, my grape-fueled feet, like those of a deep-sea diver, carefully weighing each step. No one paid me the slightest attention. All eyes were glued to the cheesy Mexican telenovela playing on the communal TV. *Bogaty Toszhe Plachut* — "The Rich Also Cry" — was an instant hit across all ex-Soviet States from first broadcast, in the summer of 1992. Cities frequently became paralyzed during the hour of the soap's broadcast, and the day following its final episode was set aside as one of national mourning. Even the prostitutes seemed less pushy than usual, preferring to relax and watch the televised antics of bed-hopping Latino yuppies rather than to engage in their own less glamorous version of the ritual. I did, however, get one call on my room phone:

"Hello, who is this?" I answered, the chatter of TV dialogue and female giggling in the background.

"I am nice Russian girl, you want, no?" She sounded bored already. I let her get back to her show.

Bendery was what the cold, impersonal science of geopolitics boiled down to. Perched on the western bank of the river Dniester, the little town occupied one side of a disputed border on the edge of a breakaway region within the contested republic of a self-destructing empire. This solemn settlement had witnessed some of the most vicious fighting during the civil war, and its inhabitants and buildings continued to smolder. I joined Nicolae's photographer colleague Sergey, who was eager to see if his birth house in the town remained intact. Tudor offered to drive us the forty miles from the capital in his old *Moskvitch*.

Now, some people carry icons of their name-Saints, or a piece of lucky shrapnel as a talisman. Tudor's good luck charm was the word 'PRESS' which he had taped in huge capital letters across the bonnet of his little car, on both its doors, and obscuring half the windscreen. We were halted at multiple checkpoints along the road from Kishinev, nervous machinegun barrels tracing our progress from bunkers constructed of sandbags and empty ammunition crates. The approach to the bridge across the Dniester—beyond which lay Transnistria—was peppered with the distinctive fan-shaped hollows left by exploding hand grenades. A Russian tank barred our way. Peacekeeping troops lazed beneath the Russian flag that hung limply in the midday heat above their command post, its white, red and blue stripes flowing out like squeezed toothpaste.

Tudor lit one of his foul Kosmos cigarettes, and violently reversed the tiny car. We shot down a side street pitted by bomb craters, lined with singed houses, their cracked walls knitted together by burned grapevines, like tendrils of black blood. The closer we came to the center of town so evidence of violence intensified: windowpanes smashed, brick walls blasted into rubble, and fences and gates perforated by bullet holes. A truck, fitted with makeshift armor plates and a mounted machine gun, lay fire-blackened halfway through the sidewall of the political headquarters it had been used to ram.

Sergey peered out between the letters 'SS' on the windscreen. No doubt, he was trying to reconcile his childhood memories of Bendery with the bombed-out building site we were currently navigating. We parked the car a little way from a communal pump. The stringy photographer started interrogating the people lining there to collect water in a pathetic collection of buckets

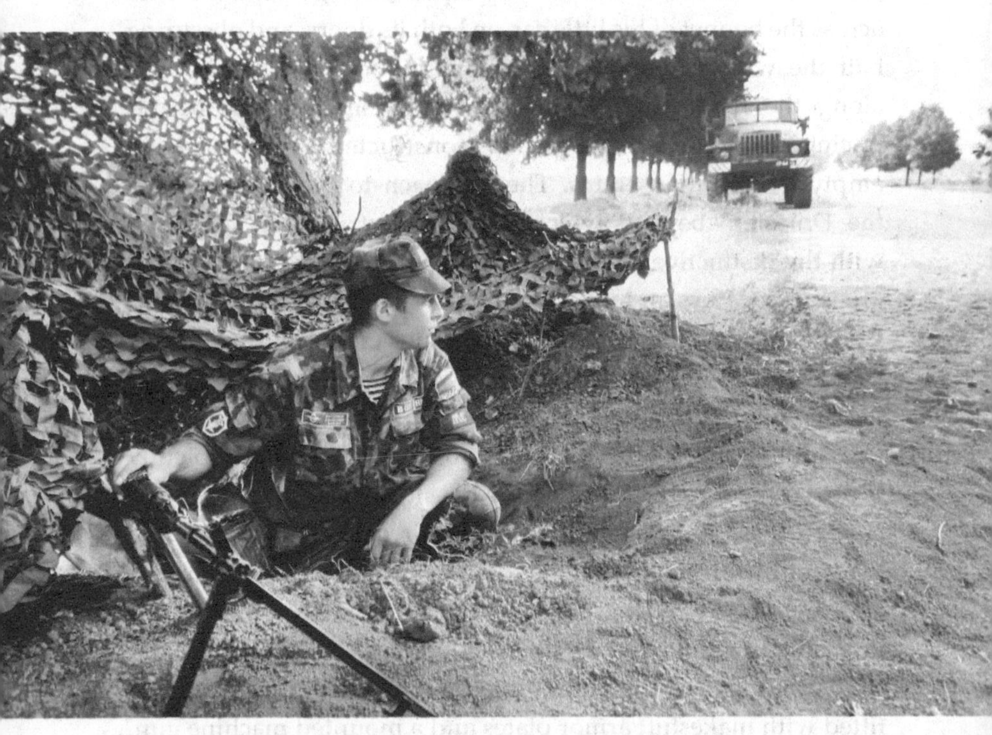

A CIS peacekeeper mans a gun position along the approach road to Bendery, Moldova.
August 8, 1992. Photo: Chris Stowers/PANOS.

and bowls, vases emptied of flowers, and bottles once used for wine. He returned and muttered some directions to Tudor, who stubbed out a half-smoked Kosmos and revved the motor.

It was getting hot, quickly. The noonday sun forced the streets into shimmering submission. Baked air rampaged like a Mongol horde borne from the furnace of Central Asia. It assaulted the ramparts of the Dniester here in a final defiance of cement dust, desert sand, and hoof-crushed sage. I was parched but all the shops were shuttered and I could find nothing to drink.

"Here," indicated Sergey as we drove up a narrow lane and parked in front of a tumbledown cottage. Mortar bombs had caved in the building's roof and gutted the interior, but the external walls remained untouched. "This is where I was born," he growled. We were invited inside by the current owners who were shoveling out the wreckage. Taking a rest from their efforts, they plied us with potent homemade wine that made my head spin. I drank it too deeply and fast, wishing it were water.

A child, commissioned earlier by Sergey as our eyes and ears, pedaled up breathlessly on his bicycle. He pointed back down the road and Sergey began to gather his eclectic array of exotic equipment—a Russian Horizont panoramic camera, the heavy 6x7cm large format Kiev with fisheye lens, and his workhorse, a Nikon F SLR that looked as though it had seen daily action since the Tet Offensive. He muttered, "Russian troops, down by the cinema."

We jettisoned the car and joined the platoon; multiple uniformed arms reached out to pull us aboard their open-backed truck. The young conscripts were minesweepers, brought in to clear any explosive devices that remained strewn around town. They were heading to a factory behind the railway station suspected of being mined. Their senior officer used an electronic metal detector, the rest of his squad having been issued poles

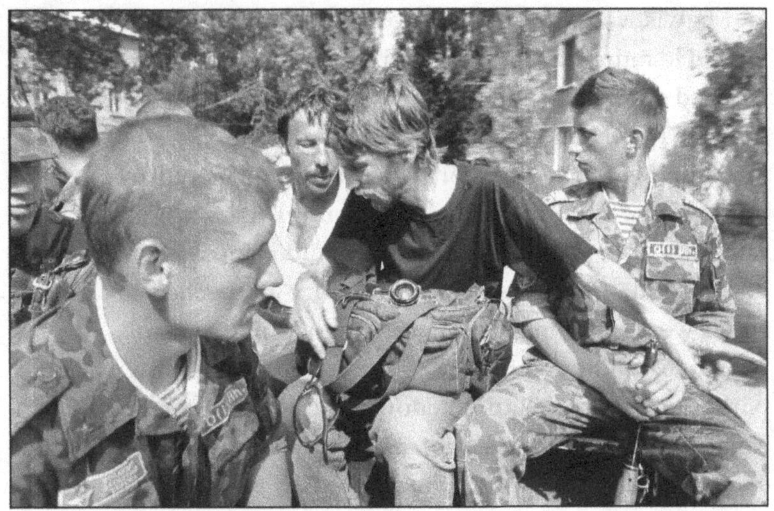

Tudor Iovu of Reuters (center, in white shirt), and the Moldova Press photographer Sergey Voronin (with camera bag), sit aboard a truck along with CIS peacekeepers who are going in search of landmines near Bendery railway station, on August 8, 1992. Photo: Chris Stowers/PANOS.

with metal tips to probe in the ground at an angle. I noted that each soldier had his blood type sewn on his jacket, in case of emergency transfusions. This was a sound idea, and I have, ever since, marked my own blood type clearly on all my camera vests.

I stood well back, utilized my telephoto lens, and thought of Moscow: how many more mothers, wives, sisters and fiancées would have joined the ranks of protesters in Pushkin Square by the conclusion of this particular 'peacetime deployment'?

We arrived back in Kishinev at 8:00 p.m., the sun still a little off the horizon. Nicolae joined us after his work, eager to hear our tales from the border, and we once again gathered in Tudor's courtyard. Ever the host, Tudor cooked up a stupendous stew, adding to his groaning table local French-style baguettes and 'Manchuria'—a golden fish roe—sausages and yogurt, sour cream, sheep's cheese that squeaked when chewed, and cooled grape juice. Summer nights in Moldova were made for celebration, under the stars and in the company of good friends, with copious amounts of wine. Money could not buy such happiness. Though possibly it would leave you nursing a slightly higher-quality headache.

The next few days passed pleasantly, hanging out with Nicolae and Sergey at the *Moldova Press* office. I wandered Kishinev's potholed streets shooting queues of weary shoppers as they shuffled around state-run stores. Only three essentials of the Moldovan diet appeared free from rationing: bread, cheese and honey (fortunately my three favorite food groups).

Back at the hotel, I was hooked on 'Super Channel', some sort of EU-sponsored version of PBS. It came through in sporadic bursts on my TV of an evening, and was the only channel broadcast in anything but Russian or Romanian. One memorable program was a French documentary about a species of African frog that hibernated beneath the drought-crusted surface of a lake for ten months of the year, only to miraculously emerge and engage in an orgy of consumption and copulation for the two months of the rainy season. Rather like Siberians in summertime. The main news item was more somber, and delivered in German. It featured the gaunt inmates at Trnopolje camp, near Prijedor in Bosnia-Herzegovina, where the Serbs were holding around 3,500 Bosnian-Croat and Bosnian Muslim prisoners of war. I may have just missed the conflict here in Moldova. But where I was headed to, Yugoslavia, was bursting into flames.

I met up with Nicolae on the steps of the Press Building early next morning. He immediately dashed off, leaving me guarding a wooden swivel chair he'd scavenged for his office, and his five-year-old daughter, Alyana. It was pointless to guess how long he'd be gone, or to where, as he habitually mumbled his sentences and would halt altogether whenever hijacked by thoughts more interesting and profound, which was frequently. Abandoned, the two of us sat obediently on the chair, facing the wide pavement, playing a game of nodding at passing pedestrians. Nicolae remembered where he'd left us an hour later, returning tied up in a cable he'd scrounged for his fax machine, and carrying a plastic bag in which were concealed the separated components of a heavy-duty 6x6cm camera. *That* mechanism appeared to have more in common with a tractor gearbox than any instrument of precision optics. He complained,

"The only thing Russia knows how to make good is the Kalashnikov."

Possibly the last Soviet parade ever to be held in the region was rumored to be taking place later that day in the Transnistrian capital, Tiraspol. This was a big deal, Nicolae convinced me. Sergey joined us. He looked more haggard than usual after working all night in the dark room at *Moldova Press*. We commandeered the newspaper's staff car—an ex-army jeep— and prepared to enter 'enemy' territory. For me, this required a visit to Alla in the Ministry of External Affairs to be issued a note to take to the Interior Minister asking for his permission to cross into rebel territory. For Sergey, it meant popping back home to pick up his swimming trunks. He was planning to carry on to Odessa after the parade to join his wife and kids at a resort on the Black Sea.

The road to Bendery was becoming familiar. On this visit, Sergey had come prepared to persuade. Utilizing a combination of natural guile, and the distribution of cigarettes and some of the black and white photos he'd been up all-night printing— they featured the soldiers from our last visit—we made it past the embedded Russian tank, right to the door of the local Government Press Office. Here Nicolae, by pure chance, 'discovered' a few bottles of Tudor's finest cherry brandy at the bottom of his camera bag. Negotiations continued inside for most of the afternoon.

While awaiting the outcome of this dual charm offensive, I wandered the vicinity, alone, feeling a touch vulnerable without my chaperones. In a war zone, the street photographer becomes an easy target for the mad, drunk and dispossessed. A camera, to them, is less visual recording device than it is a beacon of hope. Your physical presence—no matter how dangerous things may seem—offers the first hint of return to normality. Refugees, the tormented, the victimized latch on to you with a burning compulsion to unload their story. It doesn't matter if you are unfamiliar with the language, they don't care. A sympathetic ear is sufficient, and I sat there that afternoon nodding my head and agreeing '*da*' a lot or, when I sensed it the more appropriate response, '*nyet*'. At such times, the photographer is as much social worker as shooter.

By 5:00 p.m., I felt the day had been wasted. I regretted not staying back in Kishinev and being productive organizing my onward trip to Romania. But suddenly, Sergey rushed out, taking the steps of the press office three at a time. Waving some official-looking papers at me he shouted, "Come on, Chris, let's go!"

When I'd passed through Tiraspol a week back it had been nighttime. I was half asleep, and alighting the train had not been an option. Now, in daylight, I appreciated the horizontal red and green stripes with hammer and sickle—flag of the former Moldavian SSR—as it rippled atop the Stalinist spire of City Hall; the bust of Lenin at its entrance, and the touching devotion to Moscow in place names such as Karl Marx Street and Gagarin Boulevard.

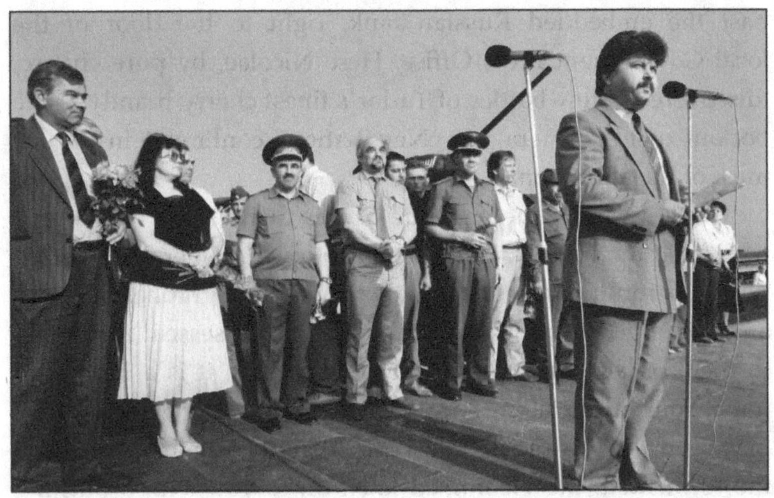

The President of Transnistria (back row, center) and his generals, in the territory's capital, Tiraspol, on August 14, 1992. Photo: Chris Stowers/PANOS.

The President of Transnistria—a plump man with a Lenin beard, dressed in a gray short-sleeved shirt—was speaking from a platform in front of City Hall, surrounded by his generals. The war-wounded and veterans, school children carrying flowers, and civilian on-lookers gathered around. The occasion was somber, memories still fresh of fighting and loss; their futures anything but secured.

Next up to the dais came the Transnistrian Army Chief, who was heaped with praise for his running of the campaign, even though it had led to stalemate, the disbanding of his forces, and their duties being taken over by peacekeepers from the recently founded Commonwealth of Independent States (although Moldova was among the former Soviet Republics who had signed the Alma-Ata Protocol on December 21, 1991, it only formally ratified the agreement on April 8, 1994. Russia-loving Transnistria, on the other hand, had no qualms about welcoming CIS troops on its soil). The Army Chief spoke through gritted teeth, fists clenched and arms stuck rigidly to his sides. Soon, many people had tears pouring down their cheeks, moist tracks glinting in the soft evening sunlight. Sergey was disappointed, though. There had been no procession of tanks. We shook hands, and he headed off to the Russian Riviera. The rest of us, appreciating the rare opportunity, dashed up Lenin Street to the Kvint Distillery to stock up on Transnistria's famed cognac. Along with sunflower seeds, it was (and still is) the rebel region's main export earner.

My transit visa close to expiry, I knew I had to drag myself away from Moldova and re-establish forward motion. Nicolae came bearing bad news: there were no tickets available for that day's train to Bucharest. He went off to enlist Tudor, admitting the Reuter's man had connections superior to his own at the Railway Bureau. Frankly, I was beginning to hope I could stay in Moldova a lot longer; I couldn't remember the last time I'd felt so involved in a place. And then there was Natashe. Long-haired, brunette Natashe — part-time assistant at *Moldova Press*, and recent graduate of the Foreign Languages Institute. Tall, wearing the skimpiest of hot pants, and only eighteen, she was a few years younger than me, and how I wished I'd met her on my first day in Kishinev, rather than this, my last. Her voice was husky and her hands shook when she stylishly angled her cigarette. I wanted to grab hold of her wrists and calm them. Possibly, Nicolae had arranged this convenient time alone so Natashe could present me her case for getting out of Moldova. If so, she was disillusioned by all the glittering West had to offer. As disillusioned, in her own way, as was I about the simple joys offered by life in Kishinev. We desire most that with which we are least familiar.

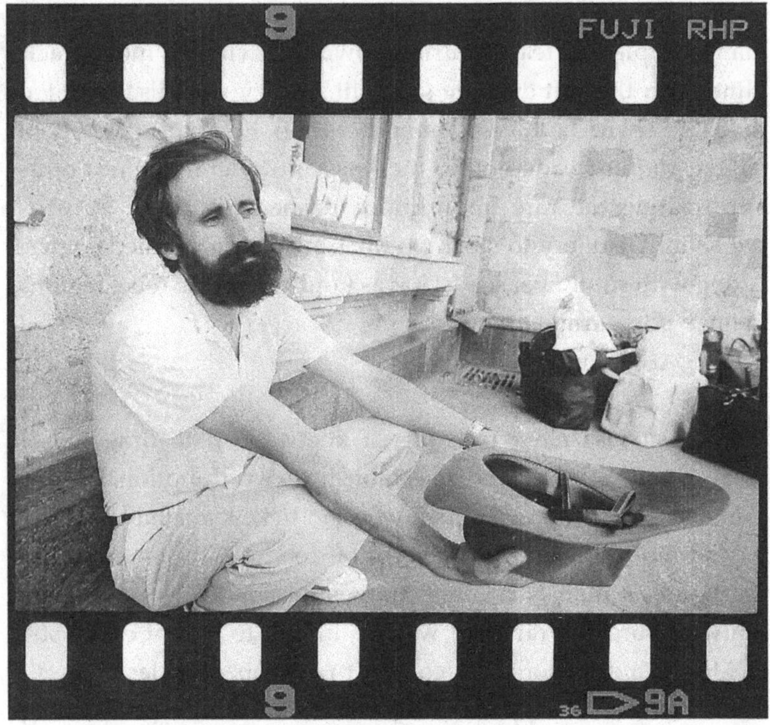

Nicolae clowning around with my hat at Kishinev station as we wait for the train to depart.
August 15, 1992.

It was by now midday. Tudor had been unable to pull any strings, transport-wise. So, Nicolae, Natashe (wearing my hat and looking like Indiana Jones's sexy kid sister), and I jumped in the jeep and headed down to the Gara. The railway station's impressive arched façade overlooked a plaza scattered with people squatting among piles of thumb-worn books, used clothing, watches, screws, radio components, old tin badges featuring Lenin—in short, all the elements of their washed-up lives—and hoping to make a sale. I purchased some faded Soviet-era postcards featuring triumphant fountains, orderly parks and glistening apartment blocks.

A train pulled in and Nicolae dashed along its row of dark green carriages, trying to find a sympathetic attendant. He signaled us from afar, and we jogged along the platform.

"This lady," he said, introducing a buxom and good-natured female cabin attendant named 'Ilyana', "thinks she can find a place for you in her carriage. Also, she will make sure you have no trouble at the border." I handed Ilyana a US$5 note. A seat magically materialized, stripping me of any excuse to remain. Hardly was I released from Nicolae's bear hug before the train jolted forward, its reluctant wheels groaning. Natashe threw my hat through the open window at the last minute, and along with it, a kiss, the intent of which I had a long journey ahead to decipher. Ticketless, I exited the mighty Soviet Union.

Earlier I'd felt certain Kishinev was the start of Europe. I was wrong. Direct Russian influence ended, instead, at Ungheni, an hour farther west of the Moldovan capital. Here, for four long hours, we were held prisoner as the carriage was hoisted six feet off the ground, its bogies being changed to fit the narrower gauge Romanian track.

"Drink?" offered one of my cabin mates, Ion. He pushed across a two-liter bottle of *Joke*, its label otherwise identical to that of a more famous American brand of soda pop. He and his companion Vlad were smugglers from Romania. Their plunder of electric cables, radio transistors, stereo speakers, switches and other assorted widgets was concealed behind the ceiling panels, and inside the cabin's light fixture. Joining us at the border were two Moldovan girls, with the darker complexion and free-spirited nature of gypsies, Ala and Alona. They didn't appear to be smuggling anything, except possibly, if the reports were to be believed, their bodies. Everything is relative, direction especially so. When you travel through Europe toward the east, each country becomes progressively poorer. For Moldovans heading west, however, Romania was the Promised Land.

At midnight we crossed the River Prut, coming to a stop in Iasi. Ion distracted the young Romanian customs official tasked with searching our cabin as Vlad cracked open a bottle of vodka and a two-liter container of paint-stripping red wine. The guard left our cabin swaying slightly, a bottle of *Kvint* shoved in his pocket for good measure. Ion winked at me in complicity, and then started chatting up Ala, the more pneumatic of the two girls.

We were traveling beneath a full moon and Transylvania passed by in negative, a selenium-blue world of trees, haystacks and lengthy shadows. Flitting meadows blinded like snow. A warm foot began to explore my groin. Through the slit of my eyes, I confirmed it was attached to the leg Ala had extended from her bunk, opposite. I feigned sleep. This accidental positioning of limb to organ had to be the byproduct of her earlier alcoholic overindulgence.

I briefly considered extrication; but that would have risked alerting her to the fact I was more conscious than I was pretending. I decided, instead, to lie still and see how things developed. Quickly, as it would happen: damn my over-active imagination. An inquisitive hand joined the foot. *You don't get this on British Rail.*

Call me prudish if you will, but I was aware of a potential audience of at least three other passengers simulating sleep in the higher-up bunks. I made an exaggerated yawn and sat up. Ala gestured I should join her in her bunk. I was saved from decision by some complex shunting in Tandarei where, beyond the stockyard, the faintest glimmer of life had begun to seep into the eastern sky.

ROMANIA
August 16, 1992

MANKIND HAS BECOME numbed and complacent traversing physical distance. It is still disconcerting, though, to travel through time. As I stepped off the Kishinev train in Romania's capital, Bucharest, I was transported to Paris: the year 1930. Riotous early morning sunlight uprooted the cobblestones and set the dewy tram lines on fire. I wandered starry-eyed past architecture that was a mix of French Colonial and brutal Constructivist; the odd flourish of Art Nouveau here, a soupçon of Stalinist structuralism there. There were very few billboards or signs of any sort, though political posters took up some wall space, reminding people of their novel and democratic responsibility to vote in elections the following month. The aroma of freshly baked pastries wafted temptingly from the open windows of numerous bakeries. I stayed at the Opera Hotel, a down-and-out Art Deco joint with tall window shutters, high ceilings and worn-out carpets.

A photographer has to hit the ground running in any new town. Bucharest being the biggest and most confusing I'd been in since Moscow, I called the British Embassy to talk to a friendly voice. I was patched-through to the press attaché, Laurie Bristow (who would rise, over subsequent decades to become, in 2016, British Ambassador to Moscow). Turns out he used to be posted in Taipei, and knew *Asiaweek*. He said he'd make some enquiries with Belgrade "and see if our Embassy is still there ..."

———— ∞ ————

Status Report:

Finances ... US$270 (cash) / 6,500 lei (US$17)
Films ... 57 rolls exposed / 53 rolls unexposed

———— ∞ ————

Nicolae had left me an introduction to Reuters' photographer in Bucharest, Radu Sigheti. I climbed a steep flight of stairs to the news agency's office, startling the receptionist.

"How did you get in?" she asked. Elegant, dressed in couture, she accepted my explanation that the door had been open. "That lock, it never works. I hate electronic things! So, you want Radu, you say? He's in the darkroom, please wait." And she'd offered me strong coffee and an unfiltered cigarette for my patience. After five minutes, Radu emerged, eyes squinting as they re-adjusted to daylight. Romania had been—and was still—a hotspot for news, and Radu hectically and heroically reporting every aspect of it since communist-era dictator Nicolae Ceausescu and his wife Elena had been executed on Christmas Day, 1989.

"Let's get something to eat," he suggested. I liked the cut of his jib, and followed him out of the building. His Ford Fiesta XR2 straddled the pavement, where he'd dumped it in earlier rakish assault of the curb. He reversed blindly into a screeching, swerving and honking flow of oncoming traffic, executed a tire-burning 180° turn, and headed off towards the People's Palace.

"We call it 'Ceausescu's Folly'," Radu said, pointing to the massive white edifice that was quickly consuming the windscreen. We zoomed down the wide, empty boulevard, "There's a nuclear fallout shelter and twenty kilometers of tunnels under the building. Ceausescu was petrified of atomic war, but it was a simple bullet that killed him in the end."

Radu skidded the car to a halt, allowing me to jump out and get some shots. A sentry was posted at each corner; I offered the closest of these my unsmoked Reuters cigarette. He seemed grateful, only too happy to break the tedium of his day job by posing for my lens. Before I could make it back to the car, though, two policemen had swooped in, demanding documents. Radu laughed at my indignation. "Romania is a very open place, you will see. But some," he nodded in the direction of the policemen who were jotting down his license plate, "are still suspicious. It's as if they are not completely convinced this is not some kind of dream, and tomorrow we will wake up with Ceausescu back in power."

Democracy had unleashed a diverse range of opinions, if the prolific graffiti was anything to go by. 'Jesus was a skater', read one. 'Fuck You', basically, another. There was also a plaintive cry for the return to Monarchy, 'Viva le roi Mihai!', Romania's King Michael von Hohenzollern-Sigmaringen, at the time, still being exiled in Switzerland. Radu and I drank coffee strengthened with schnapps at a shaded street café beside a cinema. *American Ninja 4* was being shown.

"Life was bloody bullshit under Ceausescu," Radu's English came studded with colorful profanities he'd picked up working with his British and Australian editors. "My job in those days was to air-brush his face on huge portraits, can you believe it? *Before* the communists, that was Romania's Golden Era. Look at our people in movies and documentaries from that time; they

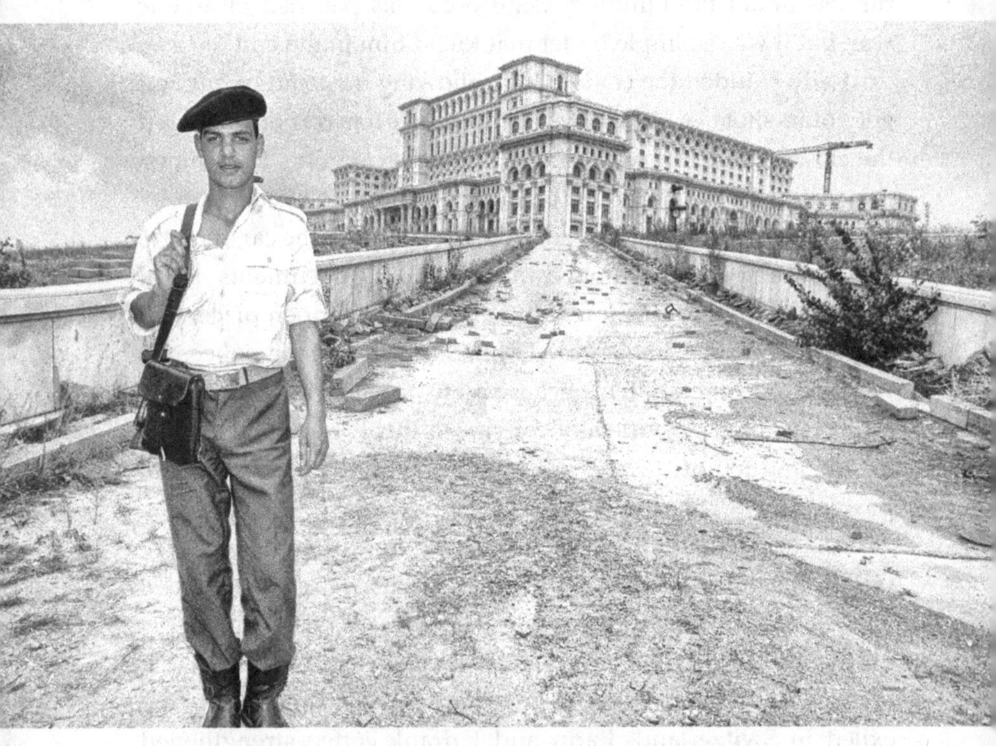

A guard at entrance ramp to the white marble 'Ceausescu's Folly' – now the Romanian Parliament building – a tribute to the megalomania of Romania's Soviet-era dictator, Nicolae Ceausescu. August 17, 1992. Photo: Chris Stowers/PANOS.

are taller, better educated, proud. Ceausescu killed off many of the intellectuals and we suffered years of bad food, and then with all the mixing of the races … you see how things have come down," he said, referring to the communist's determination to 'Romanianize' the nation. Romania had long hosted significant Hungarian, Gypsy, German and Jewish minorities, and Ceausescu attempted to assimilate them; merging the children of minorities into schools with majority Romanian ones, forcibly relocating minorities to predominantly Romanian areas, and outlawing minority languages in order to create a greater 'Dacian' identity. Apparently, the results of this great experiment had been patchy.

The delectable desserts offered in Bucharest were, following my recent dietary privations, just too tempting. I ordered a second '*Africaine*' — a sweet dark chocolate filling held in place by a pair of fluffy white meringues (55 lei, about eight cents) — and oriented myself with Yugoslavia using Radu's *Road Atlas of The Balkans*.

"By the way, do have a bullet-proof vest?" Radu asked, dropping me off at the peeled-paint entrance of the Opera Hotel. Suddenly, people were so concerned about my safety.

I had to move on from Bucharest. The Opera was a fabulous hotel, but at US$10 a night, it was draining my hard currency fast. I couldn't merely transit through Romania, though: what a waste of a visa that would have been. Radu suggested the alpine town of Brasov. A train was leaving at 2:00 p.m. Transformation from industrial river-plain to mountain paradise was swift and definitive. A wheezing old gent greeted me on Brasov's platform and offered me a room in his house for US$5 a night. I let this asthmatic stranger guide me on the trolley bus to his home, just off the medieval town center, the Kronstadt. He and his wife occupied an apartment in a building centered around an Escheresque courtyard of tilting floors and non-vertical walls. The place was inundated with potted plants and indoor vegetables. Grapevines and ivy bound the exterior of this ancient structure, offering a degree of organic integrity that denied its crumbling brickwork. He presented me with a six-inch-long key to the communal toilet, and tediously mimed instructions as to the correct operation of the water heater.

At 9:30 p.m. I called it a day. The Kronstadt was bathed in a prawn-hued and lingering sunset, and I was enjoying watching the girls strut by sipping at weak local beer on the terrace of Café Bimbo. Served in bulging one-liter plastic cups, the brew was cheaper and safer to drink than the bottled water.

I have never been a fan of horror films. Real life seems to offer more than enough genuine opportunities to be scared shitless. But, being so close, I felt compelled to make a trip to Bran Castle. The place was a bit of a disappointment: more of a mansion, with turrets. No Dracula memorabilia. They were missing a trick. The surrounding countryside, however, presented a perfectly Elysian idyll. Haystacks glistened as though still drying on Monet's canvas, and farmers wearing narrow-brimmed Bavarian-style hats worked their way down steep pastures swinging long-handled scythes. The women were dressed in black with headscarves, their occasional unguarded smiles revealing a treasury of gold. I bought a pound of cherries from one of them. I hadn't made it far down the hillside before a Dacia taxi skidded to a halt beside me. The driver poked his head out the window and introduced himself as 'John', asking if I would like a 'free ride', since he was heading back to Brasov, too. His generosity was explained by the fact that taxis in Romania, at this time, were still all State owned, the driver receiving a fixed salary of about US$30 a month, no matter the number of fares driven. There is no such thing as a free ride, of course, and John—recently married—used the half-hour journey to unleash a torrent of gripes and observations about the institution upon me, his captive audience.

He paused for a moment, distracted by a piece of passing scenery. "You like that girl? I can get her for you, if you want. There's nothing else to do here, anyway, only eat and drink and fuck and wait for a visa out of the country."

John dropped me off on the outskirts of the old city, and I left him with half a pack of Marlboros; it seemed he'd been hit by a wave of sudden remorse, "My wife doesn't know I look at other girls ..."

If it hadn't been for John's desire of confession, I'd never have ended up standing where he'd dropped me off, staring at the entrance of the Brasov Hospital of Obstetrics and Gynecology. A wooded hill rose behind this imposing edifice, promising a suitable vantage point from which to shoot Old Brasov's church towers and rooftops. I set off up a narrow lane to the left of the main clinic, but didn't get far before being distracted. A window, its shutters open, compelled me to tiptoe a look inside. A metallic bed with leg stirrups and straps stood alone in the center of a bare room, bringing to mind some contrivance of medieval torture. Possibly its function was quite innocent, for helping give birth, say, though my mind tilted toward the sinister. With a blinding flash of certainty, I knew I would not be able to leave Romania until discovering what was going on behind those pale hospital walls.

Fortunately, the next person I bumped into was Dan. A lively and inquisitive twenty-year-old economics student, he was making some extra cash as tour guide at Brasov Town Hall. He walked me around a display of photos of detainees from the pre-Ceausescu 'Stalinist' era, and artifacts prisoners had crafted in jail. Among these was a small crucifix whittled out of bone, and poetry tied on string in morse code, one knot for 'dot' and two for 'dash'.

"Most of our visitors are Italians. They drive here for cheap sex," he informed me matter-of-factly. Despite never having left Romania, Dan already spoke English, French, Italian and German with near native fluency and was working on his Japanese. He was evasive when questioned about the ringlets of hair stowed behind each of his ears, marking him out as Jewish.

"It's my own style. I release them whenever I spot a girl with a ring through her nose. She will have a spark to her!" *I should introduce him to Jasmine ...*

Most of all in the world, Dan wanted to become a photojournalist. He handled my press card with reverence, and asked me to post him a fake one the next time I was in Bangkok.

"Write in it that I am Swiss, nobody questions the Swiss."

I opened up to Dan, telling him of my revelation at the hospital window.

"What're the chances of getting in there to shoot, Dan?"

"Let's try. Anything is possible with a press card and a little *Bafta!*" Seeing the baffled look on my face he explained, "*Bafta!*" (the exclamation mark, apparently, was vital), "it's Romanian for 'good luck', but more than this, it implies a hint of the perfume of adventure. It is very effective." And with this we set off through the Kronstadt, Dan giving wide berth to an innocuous gray brick structure we passed on the way.

"It was the headquarters of the secret police. Ceausescu has been dead for two years but we still avoid walking near it." Lightening the mood, he continued with a joke:

"Ceausescu orders a new series of stamps bearing his portrait. One day he visits a vendor and asks him how sales are going.

"'Not so well,' the vendor replies, 'people complain they don't stick very firmly.' So, the dictator, fuming, tears off a stamp, spits on the glue and sticks it to an envelope.

"'It seems to be holding perfectly well.' he declares.

"'Yes,' the vendor informs him, 'but most of my customers are spitting on the other side!'"

We rounded a corner and started up a gentle slope to the hospital entrance.

"This is a very important journalist. He has come all the way from Hong Kong to report on the state of our healthcare system," Dan assaulted the gatehouse guard. Sometimes two people are less conspicuous than one. After all, no self-respecting foreign correspondent would travel without an interpreter, a role Dan was handsomely equipped to ham up.

"Where is your car?" demanded the guard, anxious to regain authority.

"We're parked around the corner. Please go and fetch your top doctor!" And the man in uniform scuttled off, suitably impressed. Ten minutes later we were ushered into an administrative building, there to meet Dr Iacob Codrin, a 6-foot-6 giant of a man, in his late twenties, with embryonic traces of salt and pepper hair. His looks were drawn, and I worried I was dragging him out from some life-saving operation. He accepted a cigarette easily enough, though.

I may have just missed photographing the war in Moldova by a few weeks, but suffering, emotion and human interest don't always have to come with guns attached. I was beginning to get an idea of just how Dr Codrin made his living, and this was a story I wanted. It would, if nothing else, go some way toward justifying my lengthy and — to the ill-informed skeptic — aimless wanderings around half the world from Hong Kong. Serious social issues, rather than ephemeral spot news, were sort of becoming my theme. It worried me briefly that I may have been turning into some sort of misery junkie; in danger of becoming one of those cynical journalists I'd always been so critical of.

As incongruous as it seemed, I was excited, shaking with anticipation at the challenge of gaining access to a medical operation, and nervous about how I'd react to, and handle the responsibility of, recording the truth; eyewitness to a very private moment few people would ever contemplate, let alone endure. At that moment, though, I had to put on a performance. I needed to unleash my ego sufficiently to persuade and gain access to the surgical theater; yet, once inside, I'd have to instantly repress that boisterous urge and become a mere passive observer. I knew I was up to the mental gymnastics, but gaining access at all hung, right now, on how I read, reacted to and got along with the hospital overlord, Dr Codrin.

Dan made the required formal introductions. Then he withdrew to snap pictures with his Instamatic camera of premature infants in oxygen chambers, and trays filled with ominous-looking surgical instruments. We were then fitted with surgical gowns, and Dr Codrin took us on a swift tour of the wards.

"Currently, around a million abortions are carried out each year in Romania," he explained, confirming my worst fears—and greatest hopes—about what was going on in the room with the open shutters. "Around six million of the women in this country are of childbearing age, so you can calculate for yourself, one in six are having an abortion each year. We carry out between fifty to eighty such operations here every day," he glanced at his watch, letting me know how short his time was. "Is there anything else you'd like to know?"

I decided there was a time to be oblique and diplomatic, but that time was not now. "Actually, yes. There is one thing. Would it be possible for me to photograph during one of these abortions you mentioned?" It was a big ask. I tried to keep any nervous excitement from my voice, making it in casual tones, a perfectly neutral, procedural request. Codrin inhaled, glanced up and down the ward, frowned momentarily at Dan who was holding up a test tube, examining the amniotic fluid contained within. He seemed at this instant to make up his mind. Sighing, he said, "It's best you return tomorrow morning, it's a bit late today. We'll have plenty of abortions for you and your *interpreter* then." Dan looked up sharply, and I couldn't tell if he was offended by the tone or overjoyed by the title. Codrin offered a rubber-gloved hand to shake; I could barely restrain myself from clicking my heels and bowing in response.

"I know, Dan, I know!" I pre-empted my good-luck guide when we were safely out of sight of the hospital. I broke into a celebratory jig: what were the chances? "It's your bloody beautiful *Bafta!*"

I lay awake that night, pondering those very chances: where else in the world and at what fateful moment of history could an unannounced photographer walk straight into an abortion clinic and start shooting? The window was small. Romania had only recently been released from the grip of totalitarian dictatorship. It was a nation so anxious to prove its newly won democratic credentials that it temporarily exceeded the openness of the very democratic countries it aspired to imitate. Privacy issues and threats of litigation would block such access in the US or Western Europe. And in Asia? There, cultural sensitivities would lead to a war of polite attrition, *'yes'* meaning *'no'*, *'perhaps'* implying *'not a chance'*, and *'come back tomorrow'* being code for *'I'll not be on duty then.'*

———— ∾ ————

Early the next morning I waited for Dan at Café Bimbo, sipping strong coffee and cleaning the dust off of my lenses and filters. I gave my bronze Buddha a rub for good luck, too, before loading my Nikon FM2 with Tri-X black and white film, and the other body, a Nikon FE, with 400 ASA color chrome. Both of the films I pushed one stop, to a more light-sensitive 800 ASA. The higher speed should, I reasoned, eliminate the need for artificial lighting and keep my impending mission as natural and non-invasive as possible. Photographing an abortion would never be dignified, but at least I could try to make it discreet.

"Bafta!" Dan ambushed me from behind, and we set off over the cobblestones, as if to battle. Dr Codrin was waiting for us at the hospital entrance. He escorted us into the abortion clinic along a cream-colored corridor lit by bare bulbs and furnished with a single bench. Upon this sat a dozen women ranging in age from around eighteen to fifty. They disguised any nervousness or embarrassment by knitting, or avoiding eye contact all together.

"Abortion was outlawed by Ceausescu. Families were forced to have four or five children, though there were always poorly trained midwives willing to perform illegal acts in the villages. Pretty bad all round, and then the 'revolution' happened and they're all coming to our hospital to terminate their pregnancies. This is nothing to a year ago, by the way." It was not expensive; the clinic charged 900 lei—around US$2—for the operation. I dutifully jotted down his words.

"Of course, if a woman does not realize after three months she is pregnant, there is nothing we can do for her, and certainly we wouldn't consider performing an abortion after that period," he stressed, absolving himself and the hospital of any potential claims of malpractice. Indeed, proud of the quality of service his unit provided, and not wanting to let me down or look bad in the eyes of the world he added, brightly, "Let's hope we find a beautiful woman for your pictures, eh?" And with that, he pushed open a swinging door and led me through to the operating theater.

Women had been entering this room while we were talking, one every five minutes or so, for pre-op check-ups. Or so I'd thought. It turned out they were in there for the real thing: the operation was that quick. Once inside, Dr Codrin impressed upon his staff the necessity of my presence. A lady doctor with short hair, efficient manner and ironic set to her mouth was seated at one end of the table, her head framed by leg stirrups. A motherly nurse was on hand to assist. This nurse was helping a middle-aged woman off the bed. I took a light-meter reading and compensated mentally for backlighting from the tall, frosted-glass windows. The room was diffused with enough light to allow a lens aperture of F11. But the luxury, that of depth of field, would bring my shutter speed down to the borderline territory of 1/30th of a second. I prayed my hands would stop their trembling.

The nurse cleared the table of blood and goo from the previous operation. She dropped the sopping red tissues into a huge bin of discarded swabs and fetuses in front of the lady doctor. Then, as casually as if setting a new place for dinner, she laid down a clean paper napkin, covering the remaining wet stain. The next patient was summonsed, a girl in her mid-twenties. Her face was pallid and she was visibly shaking. The nurse smiled at her, soothed and guided her into position on the table, lifting up her legs and splaying them in the clamps.

I'd pared my options down to the 24 and 85mm lenses. I was, by now, so used to their perspectives that I viewed every street scene, each passing action, within their compositional frames. I knew every knob, button and dial on my cameras, too. I could focus by instinct, change films while being tear-gassed, and strip them down in the dark. The two hefty Nikons were my sole excuse for being in that room, and through them I received

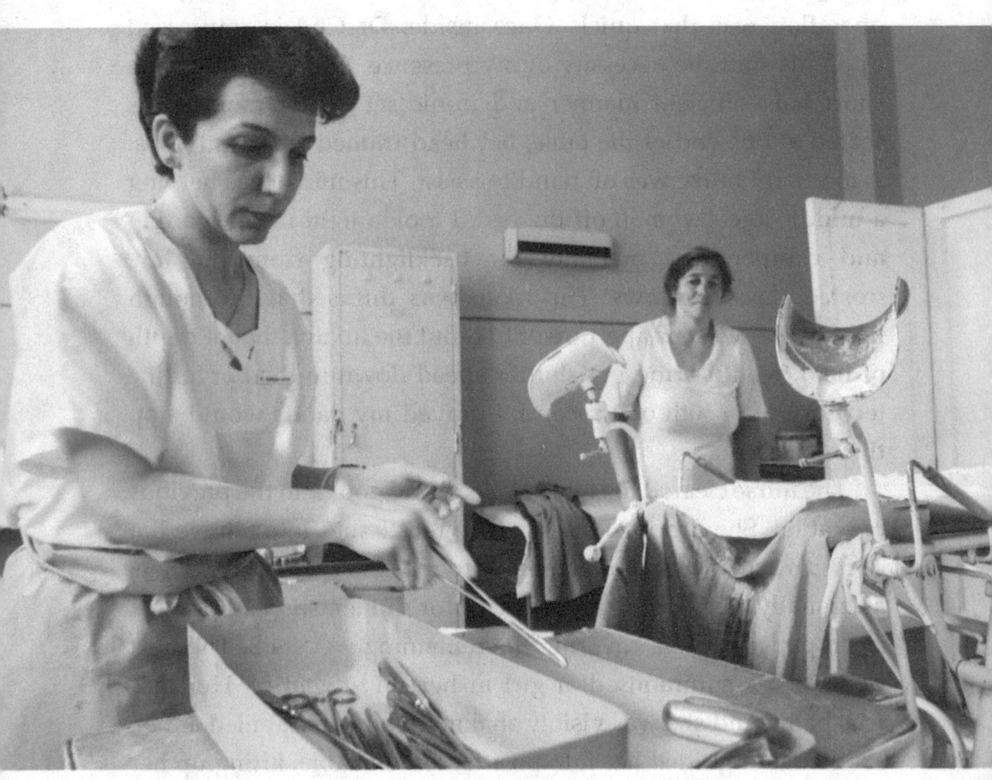

Lady doctor at the Brasov Hospital of Obstetrics and Gynecology, Romania, preparing her instruments before performing an abortion on the middle-aged woman (right) who is warily entering the clinic.

assurance—that I was not a fraud or a voyeur, but a professional with a job to do. Just like the lady doctor, who began to slide a stainless-steel implement that resembled an extended shoehorn, deep inside the suddenly surprised girl on the bed.

I focused on the girls' teardrop earrings. They disturbed me. They didn't belong here. Who gets dressed up for an abortion? *Was she intending to go out clubbing as soon as the procedure was over*? Through my lens I probed her face, her eyes; the traditional hunting ground for emotion. But the human element, the soul of the shot, was missing there. Then I spotted it, not in the girl's pale, determined expression, but further down, where the motherly assistant nurse gently held her hand.

I acknowledged Dan, at the edge of the room; his mouth was moving but it was as though he were shouting from behind a soundproofed window. Blood was pulsing violently in my head. My throat was constricted, and I struggled to control my intake of air and tame my racing heartbeat.

PomPom, Pom-pom, pom—pom, pom——pom.

That's better. I felt the heft of my camera body, its familiar surface texture, the reassuring weight in my hand and position of buttons under my fingers. I got my breathing under control. "Pom" beat my heart, and then, during the pulmonary pause, CLICK—pom … I wound on … clicked again. Exhaled.

Next pages: A motherly nurse holds the hand of the girl with the oddly out-of-place earrings. August 21, 1992. This series of photographs was later featured in Marie Claire magazine, and elsewhere. Photos: Chris Stowers/PANOS.

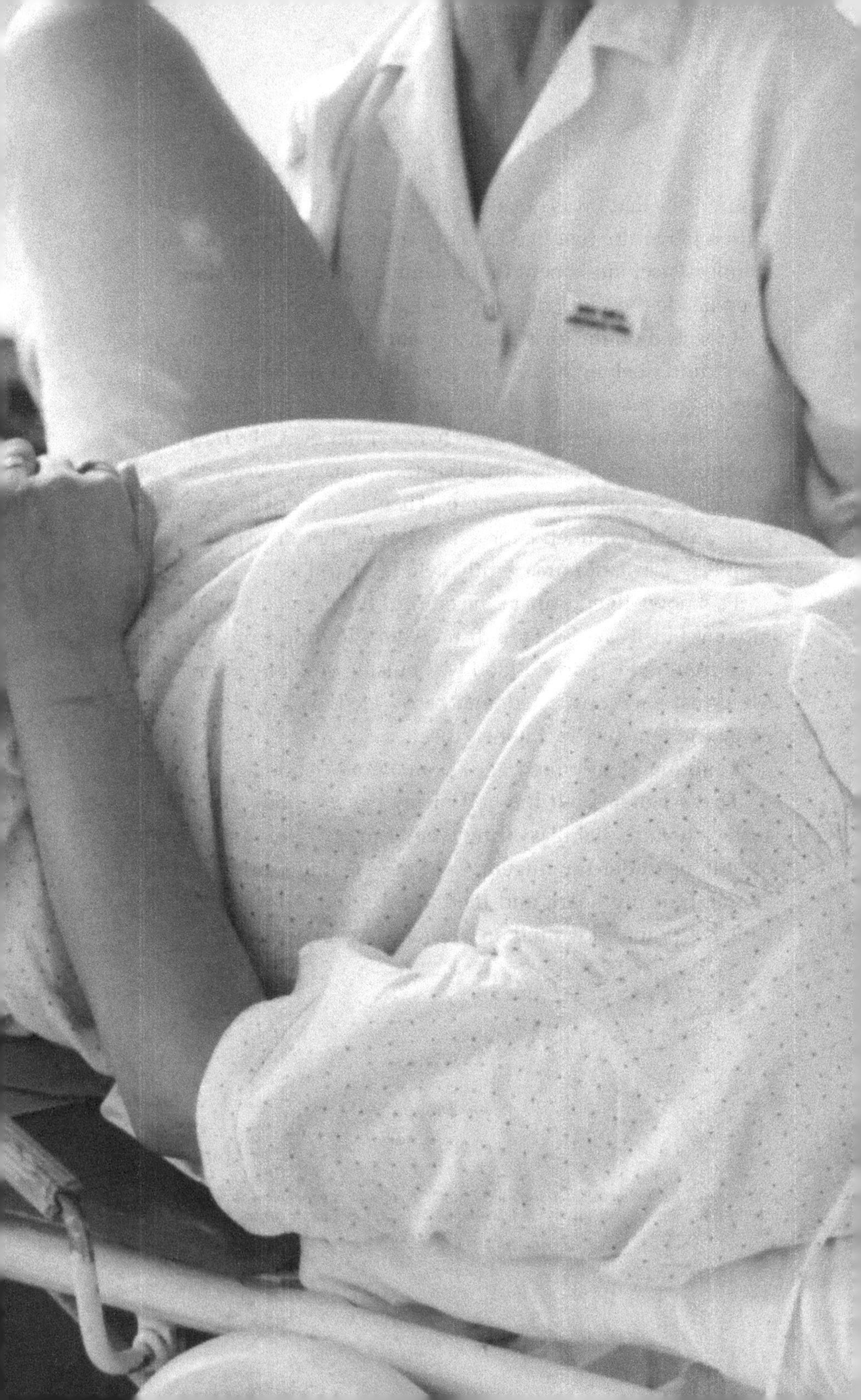

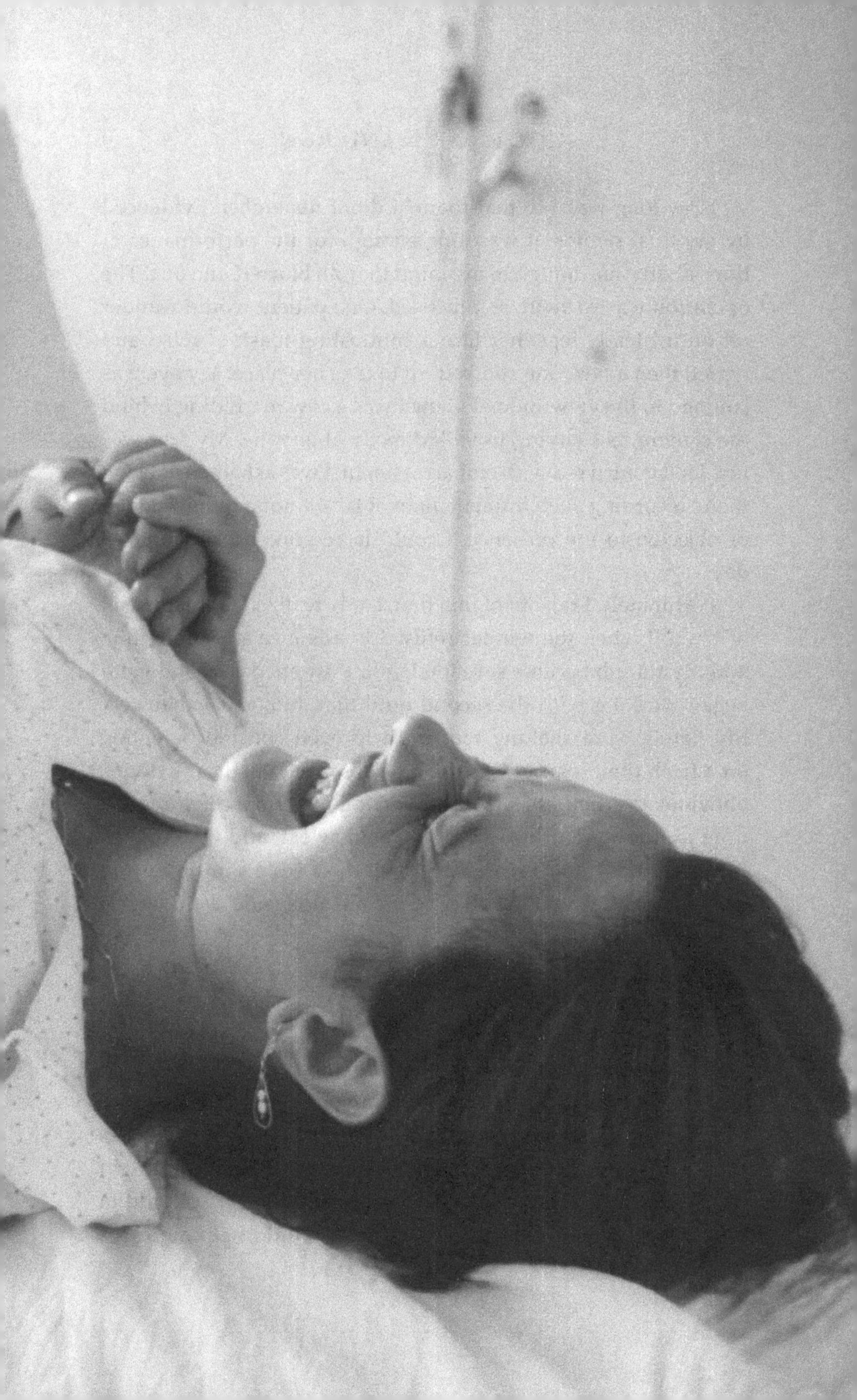

How long was I in that room? I don't remember. Evidenced by my final photos, it was long enough for the performance of three abortions, though in my mind they all blurred into one. The operation was so swift, so practiced. One patient would wander off on unsteady legs, her face a contrasting mask of relief and regret; then a new one climbed up to take her place. My eye was jammed to the viewfinder. I knew I was a coward, hiding behind the camera, not having to look directly at anyone. My face was hot. I felt it burn red with embarrassment. I was ashamed at being there, recording such intimate moments. Yet nobody questioned or objected to my presence: I could have gone on shooting all day.

Fortunately, I ran out of film first. I only realized I'd hit the end of the roll when the winder refused to advance any more film, and my thumb became sore forcing it. I dropped that body and began working with the second until that, too, was exhausted. My hands were shaking too much to even consider spooling on a fresh film. Instead, I made a dash for the tall, heavy doors, oblivious to whether Dan was following me or not. Fighting the urge to throw up, I broke out in a cold sweat, and the nervous ladies waiting their turn on the operation table shuffled up in silent sympathy, making a space for me alongside them on the bench.

———— ∞ ————

Due to the morning's drama, I'd missed the 12:20 p.m. train to Timisoara. Dan deciphered the railway timetable.

"You can take the night train to Hungary and get off at Arad. There's a train from there to Timisoara at 5:00 a.m." This was all suitably whimsical, and would save paying for the night in a hotel. Besides, I could do with a few hours of solitude in the railway cafeteria before departure. It would help me focus on writing a story I'd been mulling for a few weeks now: *From Tiananmen to Timisoara.*

The great travel writers are all strong on historical detail, philosophical observation and local color, but often frustratingly vague when it comes to practical experience. Or perhaps I'd not yet come across the specific paragraph detailing where Bruce Chatwin got caught short in a diner, or Eric Newby interrupted the call to prayer to answer a more pressing call of Nature?

I think they're missing a vital cultural constituent. Take the public toilets at Brasov station. A vital insight into contemporary Romanian society would be lost by their avoidance. To start with, a 5 lei coin was required just to get in. These practically worthless discs were in short supply, forcing the purchase of one for 10 lei from a rough-shaven alcoholic with a penchant for smoking my Marlboros and kissing my hand in gratitude.

Once inside the Men's room, the adventure had only just begun. The floor was flooded with urine. Trusting no one to guard my luggage outside, I sloshed into the cramped cubicle fully laden, assaulted at eye-level by various hand-drawn genitalia and carved telephone numbers. Squatting Asian-style on the rim of the shit-smeared bowl, I rested my backpack on my knees, and angled its top against the door to act as a lock, thus replacing the absent original. I balanced the camera bag on top of my head, holding it in place with one arm. Of course, there was no toilet paper, a discovery I made rather too far into the process to be of any practical use. I had a newspaper, but it was secured inside my main pack …

At 8.00 p.m. Dan came to see me off at the train station. He handed me the most recent copy of *Newsweek.*

"Here, for your mental digestion." It featured a story about 'concentration camps' in Bosnia. I knew enough about how the news worked not to trust the report blindly, but it was the most up-to-date information available about my self-imposed destination. "Don't forget," Dan pointed out, "today is one of incalculable *Bafta!*" He was itching to tell me about a letter he'd just received from a Belgian girl he'd been corresponding with. "She's planning to visit next month and together we'll besiege the Belgian Embassy for my visa ..." I was very happy for him, and for the combined dose of good fortune unleashed by his powerful Romanian rune. Dan was practically bursting to deliver his next piece of good news, "... and Chris, guess what? She has a ring through her nose!"

Eleven p.m. I was forced to write my diary entry standing in the unstable corridor of a slow-moving train. A group of soldiers lay slumped at my feet, spilt pools of their cherry brandy soaking into the spare carpet, and cigarette smoke billowing out through the opened windows of the carriage, the incense of some particularly brutal religion. Earlier, I'd fought and elbowed through them, as the train moved out.

"Here, you sit next to me. I save you seat." I'd leaned into the cabin, better to follow the commanding female voice. Its owner was pulling a brush through long, flowing hair. A few rebellious strands escaped into and around the deep, green pools of her eyes. A wave of nostalgia kicked me in the gut. It came out of nowhere: *Claudia.* It's all different; a different continent, a different long journey, a different hot night. A different pair of green eyes.

I'd better go and see what she wants.

7. *Sic Transit Gloria Mundi.*

Thus the world in all its glory passes us by, out beyond the cracked and dusty windows of a thousand bumping buses and rumbling railway carriages, releasing our thoughts to float freely in the varied landscape of imagination. I used to be concerned that my choice of a life of near-continuous travel exposed some irredeemable character flaw and was indicative of an essentially idle nature. Am I running because I don't know how to do anything else? But then I gave up worrying and settled back to enjoy the scenery.

Seems to me the difference between the daydreamer and the philosopher comes down to which side of the glass you're sitting on; and the divide between nomad and photographer is no different: in both cases it is merely a matter of positioning and perspective.

On one point we can surely agree: Man's desire for Paradise is just a longing to return to the place he started out from, and like faith, it grows stronger the longer it is denied. 'Arcadia', 'Eden', 'El Dorado', 'Nirvana', 'Shangri-La', 'Utopia' (and perhaps 'Home' should be added to our endless list of illusions) ... that we have so many terms for the condition of perfection surely points to a lack of that quality in ourselves. We ought to be careful what we ask for, anyway. Heaven, I am sure, is great, but what the Hell are you going to do when you get there? Personally, I'd last three days, tops, in any Promised Land. I'd rather continue to wade through the chaotic swamp of reality, clinging to the dream of Elysian Fields, than actually arrive at them and risk disappointment.

Home is terminal, anyway, like Waterloo Station, or Southampton Docks. It's where we start out from and end up at, and it colonizes the sentimental part of our mind that dwells on mortality. In transit — the space between terminals — we live. Do we truthfully seek Home's embrace when, eventually, we condescend to return? Or merely smug confirmation that we've moved on, while it remains mired in the past? If so, why should it take us back in?

Those of us who travel most broadly, who observe and record the wildest habits and excesses of the human tribe, cling most stubbornly to what we know and where we came from. It's a form of self-defense, and it always comes as a shock to discover that Home doesn't value our loyalty as highly.

I don't suppose my grandmother had put much thought into how things would turn out when she set sail for Cape Town. She simply followed her gut instinct, and never doubted anything would go wrong. Had she been able to predict marrying and raising three children in the tough conditions of Bulawayo, of only being able to return to the grassy meadows of her beloved Kent after twelve long years, then she may have hesitated. But Destiny doesn't indulge the undecided.

Perhaps it was Destiny now, tugging at my sleeve, rather than Eva tempting me into her cabin with outstretched hand? I've often looked back on this moment with the luxury of hindsight and recognized it as one of the more blatantly signposted and obvious forks in the road encountered. Can anyone alter their Fate, or willfully sway it, even for a moment? Is the nomad programmed solely to wander, the photographer only to observe — shielded from the messy responsibility of involvement, mesmerized by the passing blur of illusory borders?

Why does life flash by so quickly?

Sic Transit Gloria Mundi ...

I'd spotted Eva at Brasov station. She'd boarded without a ticket, too. We had laughed at our audacity, then she'd called out something in Romanian, I'd been unable to reply, and we'd lost each other in the uniformed tide. Just another of those achingly wasted opportunities with which the traveling life is littered. But now I found myself sitting next to her, the cabin lights dimmed, a half-moon casting blue shadows across a ghostly sea of wheat. And I experienced the opposite of that earlier melancholy — euphoria.

"I like your *barba*," Eva stretched out a smooth arm to caress my beard with two fingers. I felt relief at this statement. When it came to facial hair, women tended to fall into distinct camps of love or hate. Sitting side-by-side, her soft tresses tumbled over my shoulder. Next, I accepted the gentle impress of her cheek upon my upper arm, as she trustingly surrendered to sleep. I was hypnotized by the potent fumes of chance encounter, the motion of the train, its regular clack-clacking pulse. I lay my head down softly in the springy nest of her piled-up hair.

"*Bafta!* Dan," I whispered, scared to disturb the dream.

The cabin lights were switched rudely on at 2:00 a.m. Disheveled passengers sprang up, straightening their clothes, brushing at crumbs of food, and checking their hair was in order. A ticket inspector entered, noisily demanding payment. Those with official tickets were in the minority. As soon as he left, we were plunged back into merciful darkness and the soothing realm of sleep. The compartment expanded and contracted hypnotically with the lights of each passing town. Eva, curled up now on the crowded bench, laid her head on my lap. She turned to look upward as I succumbed to gravity and the attraction of her soft lips.

The cobblestone platform of Arad railway station was damp when we arrived at five o'clock in the morning. A solitary streetlamp reflected in its multiple shattered mosaics. Eva and I stood entwined, illuminated under its sulfurous cone. I willed it to beam us up—to preserve for eternity this exquisite moment. But then the train's whistle blew and shattered such foolish aspiration. We kissed with increased urgency, each nerve sizzling electric desire; her body was warm, willing, homely; her scent, combined with that of the train, an unforgettable musk of lavender and diesel. The carriages began to crawl and I jogged along the platform keeping pace with Eva, our fingers clasped … but there is only ever contact, and then its loss. A fraction of a millimeter might as well be a light year.

I retrieved my backpack from the puddle I'd dropped it in and hitched it, uncaringly, onto one shoulder. I hadn't had to get off that train. I could have gone through to Budapest with Eva. I'm a damned idiot, letting opportunity slip away so cheaply. And for what: some misguided attempt to test my nerves in a warzone? A feeling of inadequacy continuously nagged me: *you're not a real photographer unless you've been in battle*. It's like 'home' would have won if I returned to it not having faced down my fears. There'd always remain that element of doubt. It seemed I was destined to place a higher value on the tragedy of others than in my own happiness and security. To be so easily distracted and lured into situations sensible people run away from was evidence, surely, of a certain addiction to thrills? Yet I'd always viewed myself as the most balanced and rational person in the world. Photography and travel had taught me to juggle and reconcile extreme situations, people and emotions. But somewhere along the way I must have let the ball slip: I'd become unhinged, seriously deluded. I lifted my free hand and breathed Eva's fading scent. It smelled of sanity.

A simple wooden cross stood in Timisoara Square, placed in remembrance of the students and citizens killed in the demonstrations of December 1989 that ultimately triggered the downfall of Ceausescu's despotic regime. Fleetingly, this unremarkable provincial town had gained a moment in history. I wished it a future of peaceful obscurity.

SERBIA
August 24, 1992

"THE LESS YOU understand a language, the more sensible you are to the melody or harshness of its sounds," Thomas de Quincy once observed. Over the past few weeks, I'd become accustomed to the lyrical emotion, as well as etymological familiarity, of Romanian. But this was a Yugoslav train, and my papers were being demanded again in muscular, unsentimental tones. The cabins seated six people, like those in Russia, not eight, and the signs were all in cyrillic script. Following a brief Latin reprieve, I'd re-entered the Slavic world.

At the border, Romanian customs officials made a show of seizing every second carton of the cigarettes people were carrying to sell in Belgrade. They left unmolested the numerous sacks of toilet roll occupying much of the cabin floor. Sanctions must have been hitting Serbia hard. I thought it a wise precaution to hide the copy of *Newsweek* Dan had gifted me, along with its anti-Serb article, in anticipation of even tighter border controls on the other side. But the Serb immigration officer barely glanced at my passport.

Watches were reset. I was now an hour closer to England

than I'd been in almost six years. We crossed the Danube at 11:00 a.m., passing through industrial suburbs. The black-market moneychangers at *Beograd-Dunav* terminal accepted only Deutschmarks. Following the imposition of sanctions, the US and, by extension, its currency, were now viewed with distaste. Fortunately, I found a few Teutonic notes crumpled at the back of my wallet. I counted out all I had left in the world: US$200 and an assortment of change. That's the approximate day-rate any self-respecting journalist would pay his fixer. Hotels, it soon became worryingly apparent, cost US$50 a night, or more. I wasted eight hours—time that would have been better spent shooting or organizing my journalistic credentials—slogging my backpack up and down Belgrade's steep avenues in search of affordable accommodation. It took an hour just to locate a shop where I could buy a 20 dinara token for use in a public phone. *I bet this never happens to John Simpson.*

Once installed in a phone booth, I utilized my best MacGyver skills and an unraveled paperclip to force my jammed token through the slot.

"British Embassy," a distinctly flat, foreign accent answered. I was put through to the Press Attaché, who, by contrast, sounded as though he'd just come off the playing fields of Eton. But this refined product of a rare and costly private education; this fortunate son, recipient of life instruction from the learned dons of England's most elite school, the hallowed halls of which have been training ground for diplomats and prime ministers for hundreds of years, was not, I sensed, particularly interested in my inquiries about the availability of cheap hotel accommodation in his neighborhood. I'd have had more luck asking the receptionist. The attaché did, however, leave me the names of the BBC and *Telegraph* hacks, both currently in town and, after audible discussion with his colleagues, suggested,

"Try the Turist Hotel, old chap. It's pretty basic, I must warn you." Pretty basic it may have been to a government official. But the Turist was still 45 bucks a night. My search continued.

Reuters, as was becoming habit, came to the rescue. Peter, Radu's opposite number in Belgrade, told me UNPROFOR (the acronym for the UN mission in Bosnia) organized a food convoy, and that this left for Sarajevo each Tuesday, setting off from their base in Pancevo, a small town twenty miles out of the capital. Today was a Monday. "You may have better luck finding a hotel out there, too," he added.

I took a bus back across the Danube. It dropped me off in sleepy, deserted Pancevo. The town's medieval spires needled an endless indigo sky, and I traipsed along cobbled streets beside a small river, where sailing boats lay moored beside weeping willow trees. There, the girl operating a kiosk—its windows displaying the most unbelievably hardcore porn magazines— offered to change some of my US dollars at double the bank rate. Sladana was around twenty, luminously gorgeous and spoke excellent English. Her parents were career diplomats. Due to the brewing chaos in Bosnia, her family had been recalled from Argentina, where they'd been posted for the past four years. She shuttered the little shop, took my hand (a trustingly innocent gesture that stunned me into meek submission) and we strolled back into central Pancevo. The Sloboda Hotel was run by a friend of hers. A free room was located—no running water before 10:00 p.m. It cost an agreeable six dollars a night.

The idea I formed that night was to be gone for a week. I'd start by heading into Sarajevo with the UN convoy. But ideas are deliriously simple things. Firstly, there was my burden of seventy-plus rolls of exposed film to deal with. I tossed up my alternatives. *Ought I take them with me, or leave them secured in the Sloboda Hotel's safe?* Instinctively, I favored freedom of movement … but Sarajevo? What if I couldn't make it back again to retrieve them? In the end I decided to leave not only my films but backpack, too, with the manager. I would be compelled to return to Pancevo, but at least my images—from Beijing to Bucharest—would stand a greater chance of survival. This plan had the distinct advantage of allowing me to travel light; not even a change of clothes would be required. It would be easy, I assumed, to just hop in the back of a UN truck for the ride.

The following morning, before the sun had risen, I walked to the UNPROFOR supply depot, my footsteps squelching water from cracks between loose cobblestones. A few shadowy characters already loitered at the entrance to the depot—hopping up and down to kick-start circulation, blowing into cupped hands, stubbing out cigarettes—members of the Press. A young French national service conscript in UN garb, displaying his peace credentials via a defiant CND pendant, guarded the gate. He assured me I'd not missed the convoy.

The sun broke cover in the cornfields and the ground shuddered as thirty white trucks started their engines. The lead vehicle emerged from behind the iron gates. It was a jeep. In this rode a trim military figure, his blue beret positioned at a defiant angle. He bore a face I recognized from TV. The Press clustered around him. As their onslaught was dying off, I asked if I could borrow a UN flak jacket and join the convoy. '*Non*', he replied to each request. The convoy pulled out slowly, I searched for places to stowaway, but the trucks were too securely fastened.

"They don't usually 'ave ze ambulance. Maybe zey are expecting trouble today, *non*?" the pacifist conscript noted. This only added to my frustration at not being allowed along for the ride.

Just then, a dirt-streaked VW Passat hatchback roared up. The driver, a tall Japanese man clad in designer suit, jumped out:

"Have they gone yet?"

"They went that way," I pointed.

"Hop in!" he said. I happily obliged. The only problem being to find a space to hop in to. The big estate car was loaded down with Betacams, batteries, hefty tripods, boxes of video film, cables and lighting equipment, a tent, food supplies and water in huge plastic containers. I squeezed in the back, on top of a dozen jerry cans of petrol, my head angled against the ceiling, already intoxicated by the fumes.

"I'm Haji," he introduced himself, "and this is Cinzia," his Serbian translator. They both lit up cigarettes, unaware or perhaps unconcerned we were traveling within a mobile Molotov cocktail. Haji gunned the motor and sent us skidding out toward Belgrade, there to join the highway heading west. We soon caught up with the UN convoy.

"Pass me that camera, will you?" Haji asked.

Winding down his window and steering with his knees, Haji began to film the trucks as we overtook them. We zoomed ahead by a mile or so, and I helped set up his tripod. Haji attached his camera just in time to 'ambush' the convoy as it passed below us.

Having bought the car in Hungary, Haji had driven non-stop to Belgrade on a hunch that entering Sarajevo from the Serb side would prove more interesting than, like most of the media, going in through Croatia. Cinzia acted cool. Like most interpreters, she valued words highly and didn't go in for small talk. She spoke Japanese, though, and was progressing through Haji's Marlboros at a steady clip. She wrote out two cardboard signs for the windscreen, one reading 'PRESS', the other its Serbian equivalent 'PRENZA'. The letters 'TV' were already taped over the hood and on the doors. Rounding a corner, we almost rear-

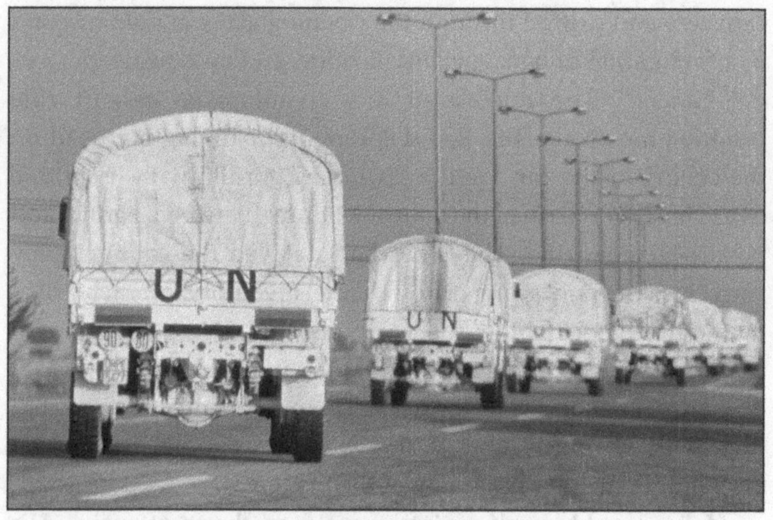

Shot through the windscreen of Haji's car, this is the UNPROFOR convoy we tailed to the Serb border with Bosnia-Herzegovina, at Zvornik. August 25, 1992. Photo: Chris Stowers/PANOS.

ended the tail UN truck. The convoy had halted for the troops to dress in bulletproof vests before crossing the river into Bosnia-Herzegovina. Haji and I hit the ground running, and shooting:

"*Bonjour, ça va?*" The UN troops were mainly French, young and personable. Among them was a small contingent of Belgians and Egyptians, too. Haji pulled out the latest in Kevlar waistcoats, black, with a high anti-shrapnel collar. He'd purchased it last week in that army-surplus haven, Brussels. I began to feel distinctly underdressed.

The lack of a flak jacket was a worry, but I had a more pressing concern: for how much longer would my *Asiaweek* press card continue to protect me, so far removed from its Hong Kong powerbase? I hadn't been in Belgrade long enough to sort out any more relevant local credentials. Fortunately, we were slipstreaming the UN convoy, getting waved past most roadblocks. I wedged my documents between a couple of video

393

canisters and drifted through the ripening acres of golden grain in a fumigation of benzene and nicotine, and on into sleep.

"Papers!" The muzzle of a semi-automatic assault rifle prodded me awake. Startled, I sprang up, banging my head on the ceiling of the car. We'd arrived at Zvornik, with its bridge over the River Drina, the natural border between Serbia and Bosnia-Herzegovina. The Serbs had delayed the convoy. They were insisting on going through the inventory of each truck methodically, searching for weapons the UN were rumored to be running to the Bosnian Muslims in Sarajevo, along with humanitarian supplies. No incriminating guns were found, but there was obviously no love lost between the UN troops and Serb militia that held this side of the bridge.

Haji wound himself up into a one-man charm offensive. His Asian appearance afforded him a certain elasticity of interaction with the guards, who found him an amusing but harmless oddity. I recognized the trait: it was how I, the novel Westerner, was often treated in Asia. He broke out some Polish vodka and handed around cigarettes, joking and backslapping with a particularly grizzly looking bunch of gunmen. I envied him his non-aligned status.

"Why do you support the Muslims?" A gunman had approached me from behind. 'You' can be a dangerous little word: never more so than when muttered by an unshaven brute holding a Kalashnikov in one hand, and a jug of peach-tinted, sedimentary hooch the other. I sensed he was linking me — by guilt of association — to the parliamentary decisions of my far-away government. The teetering soldier continued with feeling, "In ten years' time it will be *you* in the West having to fight these Muslims. And yet here you are supporting them!"

Haji intervened, possibly sensing I was on the verge of doing something stupid, like answering. He dragged me back to the car. The guards were apologetic but firm: they had their orders, and what kind of soldiers would they be if they didn't follow them? They left us with half a bottle of moonshine to console ourselves as they stripped the car of its fragile and inflammable load. Haji kept his cool, and smiled more and more broadly. That was how I could tell he was really pissed off; but the Serbs were not attuned to so fine a degree of Far Eastern pique.

I kicked irritably at the dust, considering other ways of getting into Bosnia. The river was swollen at this point, about 300 meters wide. I could discount the heroic stupidity of swimming such an obstacle. Then I spotted an old rowboat at the foot of the bridge. The vessel tugged absently at its rope — oars crossed inside like the arms of a slain Crusader knight. It would have to be nighttime before I could 'borrow' that ... but then the UN trucks coughed into life; diesel fumes belched from exhaust pipes and offered an end to stagnation. Cinzia waved to me from Haji's reloaded car, and I ran to join them.

Haji and Cinzia had arranged their paperwork through SRNA, the official Serb News Agency. This was sufficient to get us through the checkpoint on the Serb side of the bridge. The tarmac of the bridge itself had been scarred, like the streets of Bendery, by exploded grenades. The first Bosnian rooftops rose into view as we crested the central span ... and, then, another checkpoint. My heart sank.

Both Haji and Cinzia valiantly pled my case, but the gorilla with the Kalashnikov was having none of it. I did not have express permission from SRNA to step onto Bosnian soil. A pathetic sheet of paper, the silly little inky stamp, an illegibly scrawled signature: bureaucracy crushed the life out of adventure, every single time.

"Thanks Haji, get out of here. You don't want to lose that convoy," I bid them bon voyage. The three of us hugged and swore we'd meet up in Sarajevo a few days hence. Cinzia jotted down the address of SRNA in Belgrade, and I recrossed the Drina on foot, just another pedestrian. A civilian on crutches squeezed past. "Sloboda," he greeted me. 'Freedom'. And my anger drained away.

Back on the Serbian side, I bought a liter bottle of Fanta from a kiosk and downed it in one go. I started walking out of town. No one was around to stop me. The place seemed deserted. The suburbs of Zvornik only stretched a hundred yards before countryside took over. I followed the course of the River Drina south. It contoured with deceptive tranquility the splayed purple toes of forested hills. Spring water burbled in ancient stone fonts at the base of each escarpment. I filled my empty soda bottle at one of these. The water tasted creamy and had a slight natural fizz reminiscent of Perrier.

Soon I came to a well-defended dam, its obstruction responsible for the swelling tide upstream. Suspicious glares trailed me along gun barrels and I walked rigidly past. The sound of scattered light arms fire reached across from the other side of the river, but it was the heavier retort of cannon fire, coming from further along the twisting gorge, that telegraphed an anticipatory tremble to my knees. Around the bluff, a red, blue and white Serbian flag sagged above a walled luxury villa. Both had seen better days. Mounted on the rear terrace of the building was an anti-aircraft gun, aimed at the opposite bank and manned by a burly crew wearing Russian Special Forces t-shirts, with bandanas tied around their heads. I avoided the wrought iron gateway to the compound, and plodded on down the road.

"Oi!" a shout came from behind. I acted deaf. "OI!" Three strikes and you're out, in this game. I turned slowly, readying myself for persecution. The militiaman grabbed hold of my arm and marched me back to the villa. Half a dozen skinheads were lounging around, sharpening their commando knives, playing cards and swigging moonshine. Occasionally one of them would disappear to strafe the Bosnian riverbank with a few thousand rounds of 20mm tracer. The least thuggish-looking of my captors was a young chap of studious demeanor sprouting a head of ginger hair. My passport was handed to him. He interrogated me, first in Serbo-Croat, then in French. I remained convincingly blank. Lastly, he resorted to my mother tongue.

"So, you're English, are you? Not a spy … from over there …" using his toothpick he gestured across the river in the direction of Bosnia, "'cos you don't look very English."

I assumed he was referring to my beard, and the state of the jeans I'd not had a chance to wash in six weeks. There were holes in them where my camera bag rubbed. But nothing had to last more than a few weeks now. I'd been away for six years: this was the final stretch, and issues of personal hygiene and dress took second place to the specter of imminent arrival. I grasped at Ginger's familiar accent, asking him,

"You've been to Manchester, right?"

"Yeah," a spark of humanity brightened his face, "four years, at uni." He nodded to the guard strangling my upper arm, who released his grip slightly. "Right shyte'ole — full of foreigners. Good music, mind. Listen, Pal, I could have you shot just for being here. No one would ever find you."

He had a point. The staff at the Sloboda Hotel back in Pancevo would divide my belongings between them; Peter at Reuters would assume I'd made it through to Sarajevo. And my parents … well, they were still under the impression I was on holiday in Ulaan Bator, that being the story I'd fed them to keep my return home a surprise.

Never before had I considered my nationality a liability.

Being born British was like drawing first prize in the lottery of life. But that was before the advent of satellite TV channels beaming incriminating footage back the very same night into the countries they were filmed. Bloody CNN. Ginger had a bee in his bonnet, and a pistol on the table. I felt it unwise to question his politics too vigorously. Everyone was a critic nowadays.

"You TV reporters, why do you make the Musselmen into saints?" Ginger was perplexed more than angry, and only too quick to lump me in with the TV media, "The Bosnians and Croats supported Hitler! Only us Serbs fought against the Nazis and helped save Jews. Have you forgotten that?" He flared, bringing up 'The World War II Argument'. Indeed, some prominent Israeli media personalities were presently taking the stance that Israel—and by extension 'The West'—had a clear and irrevocable historical obligation to side with the Serbs in this conflict.

A pot of strong coffee was plonked on the table, accompanied by a flagon of plum brandy. This Ginger uncorked.

"Drink up, yer wuss," he urged, and I passed around my ritual Marlboros with shaking hand. I assumed Ginger's particular peeve was with ITN. Their coverage, of the so-called 'Death Camp'—that which I'd seen on *Super Channel*, back in Kishinev—was being viewed by the Serbs as a distortion of the truth, detrimental to their cause. I emphasized my neutrality in all of this:

"I'm just a photographer. We don't take sides."

"Don't give me that pansy bullshit! Neutral? Only the rich can afford not to take sides. When the shyte hits the fan, who you gonna trust, your multi-kulti friends? Everyone takes sides, Pal. Tribe with tribe, religion against religion. Look around you. It may start out with fucking pan pipes and cute adverts for Coca-Cola, but it always ends in barbed wire and bullets!" With that, he'd slammed his fist on the table. "Wake up! You English have been ruling the world so long you've forgotten what it's like when you have to fight for your own home. You preach tolerance, but you've just gotten soft."

A police car drove up. It was a Serbian police car, the man driving it dressed in the uniform of a Serbian policeman. The police officer was a friend of Ginger's. He had a long beard and was, by religion, a Muslim. I really could not get my head around this place.

"He'll see you back to the bus station, all right? Just don't let me see you here again."

And I thought: *No chance of that. Pal.*

The bus arrived back in Belgrade at 7:30 p.m., the setting sun silhouetting the city's dominant hill, a church cross glinting gold at its pinnacle. Back in Pancevo, I sat at the battered table in my bare room. Some of the hotel staff had been in there during the day; they'd left behind an almost full bottle of red wine. Its contents were local, rough and—by the time I finish writing two letters, one to my parents and the other to my best friend, Mark—empty. I snuffed out the candle and called it a day.

I took a lonely bus into Belgrade from Pancevo the next morning. I needed some passport photos for all the IDs and paperwork getting into Bosnia would require. But the 100 dinara black and white photo booth ran out of paper after I'd pushed my coins in the slot. Then the 200 dinara color photo booth took so long to work, that I was looking down at the slot—trying to figure out where best to direct a good kick—when the flash went off. The resultant, surprised shot, made me look like young Josef Stalin at the height of his Tblisi bank-robbing fame.

The technical delay caused me to arrive late at the SRNA office. Fifteen minutes *too* late, to be precise.

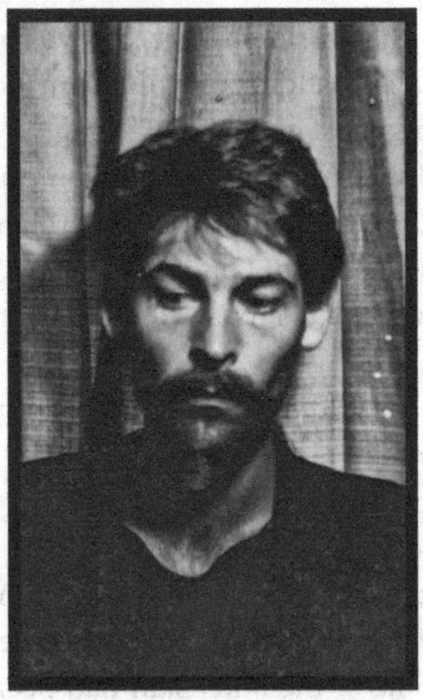

ID picture, taken in photo-booth in Belgrade,
the moment I looked down to see where to
deliver the faulty machine a good kick.
August 27, 1992.

"The order came in fifteen minutes ago; the old passes for Bosnia are no longer valid," the secretary was apologetic but unbending. This was in reaction to the two-day International Conference on Former Yugoslavia (ICFY) currently going on in London. Bosnian-Serb President, Dr Radovan Karadzic, was in attendance. The most contentious issue for the Bosnian-Serbs was being forced to notify the UN, within ninety-six hours, of the positions of all their heavy weaponry. The stage was being set for a frenzy of activity — by all sides — to grab territory and conceal weaponry before this deadline expired. The clock would start its countdown tomorrow, August 28. In retaliation, Karadzic's government was demanding greater scrutiny over whom they allowed into their territory, and their intent. I was directed to the new SRNA office, nearby, on Mose Pijade Street. This was run by Radovan Karadzic's daughter, Sonia. Security was high. An armed guard at the entrance searched my bag and wafted a hand-held metal detector about my body. Several goons, clad entirely in black, lounged around, portraying menace. To a man, they were wearing mirror sunglasses. I didn't spot Sonia. Perhaps she was out back trying on leather trench coats? They took down my details and told me that even if I made it into Bosnia-Herzegovina, I'd only be allowed as far as Pale—the former ski resort and acting seat of the Bosnian-Serb government—Sarajevo being outside of Serb control.

Since I would have to wait until seven that evening to pick up my credentials, I had an entire day to kick about in costly Belgrade. I soaked up some of it attending a protest of Serb civilians venting their anger against the Western media. As a member of the offending tribe, I was relieved they allowed me to take photos at all. Graffiti on a wall close to Hotel Moscow set the scene. 'Human Beings are the Problem!'

"The West is being bullshitted," one old gent informed me urgently, "It is not you, but your government and President Bush who are blind to the schemes of the Muslims."

Afterwards, I headed to the Press Center, the welcome discovery of which, along with its limitless supply of free coffee, I'd made a day earlier. The gossip was all about ITN pulling their crew out of Sarajevo, and of the BBC's Martin Bell, who had been wounded Tuesday, the same day I was detained by Ginger and his crew at Zvornik Bridge. Bell's most likely replacement was the doleful radio reporter, Allan Little, standing beside me now at the hot water urn, topping up his Gold Blend. He reminded me more in appearance of my Hush Puppy-wearing liberal arts teachers than any cigar-chomping, hell-raising gonzo war journalist. Allan joined the queue of concerned individuals asking if I had a flak jacket, and looked genuinely sympathetic when I told him of the UN's lack of generosity in that department.

"Last person who went in without one was killed," a posh accent chimed in—Alec Russell, of *The Telegraph*—he couldn't be much older than me, but exuded the effortless confidence afforded by an expense account. "Anyway, can't stop, have to find a car to hire."

As much as I enjoyed the gallows humor and valuable information gleaned by mingling with other members of the wandering, vagabond press circus—who, alone, were able to share in my doubts, worries and dubious victories—at the end of the day, *they* got to sleep in plush hotels and order room service. I, on the other hand, had nothing to look forward to but the darkened corridors of the Sloboda, and a pile of underwear to wash that had been ignored since Moscow. I know we all have to start somewhere ... but it was beginning to feel like I'd been 'starting' for the last five years.

At UN Headquarters in Novi-Beograd I picked up a funky blue and white UNPROFOR press card. A shopkeeper spying me wearing this, later insisted I take a bottle of water for free. It didn't wash with the policeman on the main bridge over the Danube, though.

"No photo!" he shouted. The world over, it's the same. What is so damned important about bridges? My argument, that I was merely standing *on* the bridge, shooting *from* it, was too delicate to survive in his binary world: bridge, good; camera, bad. The only problems we have are those we insist on inventing.

The press-liaison officer at SRNA was called Olga. I arrived to pick up my credentials, as ordered, at 7:00 p.m., just as she was heading home. She countered the door guard's stony-faced demeanor with genuine warmth and friendliness. We started chatting as she stamped my letter of transit. The Sarajevo native was missing the cosmopolitan gaiety of her hometown terribly.

Her husband had been 'lost' in the fighting, and she herself barely managed to escape the twelve miles to Pale along with a single bag of possessions a few months back.

"I was skiing in the hills in January, and a refugee fleeing across them by May! This job SRNA gives me is charity, until I can support myself. But I'll never be able to go home," she confided, "how can I, when I see how much they hate us Serbs? Yet we continue to allow the Muslims and Croats to flee to safety in Belgrade. Thousands of them have come to escape the fighting in Bosnia, but we can't go back there." And she mentioned a word I was familiar with from the Afghan students I used to teach, and the Mujahedeen groups based in the bazaars of old Peshawar: 'jihad'. Her ex-neighbors had become Holy Warriors.

BOSNIA–HERZEGOVINA
August 28, 1992

BY ALL ACCOUNTS, the road to Pale was a disputed and dangerous one, and I arrived at Belgrade bus terminal expecting to find our vehicle blood-streaked and riddled with bullet holes, its chain-smoking driver having to be coaxed into running the gauntlet. Instead, the coach was a luxury tourist one with soft leather seats, and the driver clean-shaven with a smart uniform, slip-on shoes and slicked-back hair. The single hole in the windscreen could easily have been made by a falling rock.

My fellow passengers were all locals. I thought how bloody stupid I'd look if I were the only one puffed up like the Michelin Man in a bulletproof vest. It would have had the unintended disadvantage of making me more, not less, of a target. The bus retraced last Tuesday's route to Zvornik. I held my breath as we crossed the bridge. On the far side, guards came on board and checked everyone's paperwork. I was singled out and escorted off the vehicle. My new SRNA pass, however, was found to be in perfect order, but they needed to copy it using a Xerox machine at the petrol station. I rejoined the coach, my fellow passengers displaying patient understanding, delay being a condition they've become conditioned to. A fresh batch of passengers boarded, bidding adieu to tearful relatives. From here on, Olga of SRNA had assured me, the territory was Serb-held, all the way to Pale. Though the situation, she'd warned, was "changeable".

A symbol began to appear painted prominently in the windows and on the doors of perhaps half the houses and businesses we passed: a white cross, with the Cyrillic letter 'C' in each corner, pointed outwards, like horseshoes. Many of the soldiers back in Zvornik had the same talisman carved into their gunstocks, too.

"'*Samo Sloga Srbina Spasava*'," the man in a crumpled jacket beside me translated, "'Only Unity Saves the Serbs'," and he cackled to himself in some privately meaningful way. A soldier with a machinegun rode upfront with the driver. He was in charge of two crates of beer, distributing bottles liberally at each checkpoint we passed. The coach cruised silently up through forests of dark emerald conifer. At Han Pijesak, the highest point on this road, there was a famous spring. Everyone jumped out to refill their bottles with spa water, and then we continued, past shuttered holiday homes and pastures void of cattle. Haystacks wilted like ice cream cones on a hot day at the beach. It started to drizzle, the first rain I'd seen fall since Ulaan Bator. Through the window, I searched in vain for sight of the ski lifts and toboggan runs that'd been built here for the 1984 Winter Olympics.

We arrived in Pale as mid-afternoon shadows started to coat the cold, east-facing slopes. A cameraman from the local TV station, Mandic, drove me at great speed to the SRNA Press Center, which occupied the ground floor of the Bellevue Hotel, a mile out of town. He swigged a quick coffee, plugged his batteries in to charge for a while, and then zoomed back to his office. The only electricity in Pale came from private diesel generators. Their high-pitched rumblings lent an eerie, primal vibration to the approaching dusk.

Sanja worked at the SRNA Press Center. She was twenty-three and, as seemed to be the mold for all young girls in Serbia, serious supermodel material. This point had not been unappreciated by a 'famous' Italian journalist who, just the day before, had offered to take her to Rome and give her anything she wanted. She'd turned him down, she said, preferring to stay in Bosnia and fight until the war finished. She was briefing a Japanese woman reporter, Yasuko Nakayama, who was based in Greece (the Orthodox Greeks, along with their co-religionists, the Russians, being supportive of the Bosnia-Serb cause). Sanja gestured me to join them.

"Ahh, Haji and Cinzia, yes," Sanja shed some light on the whereabouts of my friends, "they went through to Sarajevo a few days ago. You may be able to join some of our people going there tomorrow ..." I have always been wary of press junkets, being rushed from site to site, introduced to hand-picked victims, unable to independently confirm events. One needed time, patience and calm to coax stories out of people. On the other hand, I didn't have the funding to argue, and reasoned that some access would be better than none at all.

Meantime, Sanja explained the workings of the Press Center, its free coffee and breakfasts. All the professional journalists were staying with the politicians, up at the flashy Olympic Hotel: bees swarming around the honey pot. Sanja said she'd see what she could rustle up to suit my more 'moderate' budget, and I consoled myself I'd be having the more authentic experience; the type money shields you from.

Yasuko and I were treated to a hot meat stew, potatoes and bread, softening us up for the digestion of some blatant propaganda in which SRNA speculated the Bosnian-Muslim President, Alija Izetbegović, had AIDS. This was based, their logic ran, on his lengthy spell in Soviet prison camps ('where homosexuality is rife'), that he'd visited an AIDS clinic on his recent trip to Belgium, and that he was often seen in close proximity to his attractive young male secretary, Haris. Yasuko did that inscrutable Japanese trick of appearing genuinely interested and eager to hear more.

This gained us a free dessert.

It is evidence of an optimistic streak in Man's nature how often we place trust in those we know least well. Sanja left me in the protective custody of a shady, unshaven local black-market fixer named Najor. I followed Najor to the unstaffed Panorama Hotel—a former ski resort—where he found me a room at the just-affordable price of US$10 a night. I assumed this included his unspoken commission.

Blacked out and silent, the hotel was a fifteen-minute walk through the woods from the Bellevue. Lending me a Kalashnikov bayonet in case of Muslim raiding parties, he added, unhelpfully, "The enemy isn't far away." I made my way down the candlelit corridor, past ghoulish figures huddled beneath blankets. These were Serb refugees in transit from Sarajevo to Belgrade. Fir trees reached out their arms to brush the windowpanes, and the heroic international war photographer dove beneath his duvet, into the protective cover of sleep.

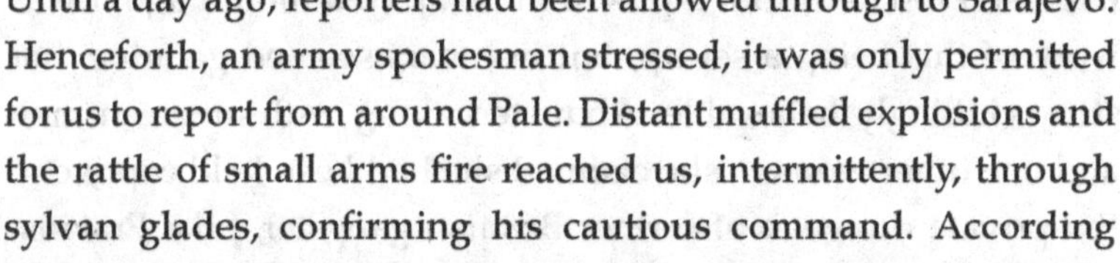

Until a day ago, reporters had been allowed through to Sarajevo. Henceforth, an army spokesman stressed, it was only permitted for us to report from around Pale. Distant muffled explosions and the rattle of small arms fire reached us, intermittently, through sylvan glades, confirming his cautious command. According to Sanja, the London Conference had triggered a new ground offensive, and Bosnian-Muslim forces were closing in on Pale, from the northwest.

"They are trying to grab as much new territory before the four-day window closes, and to provoke us into retaliating with our big guns. If we do, The West will impose even more sanctions on Serbia." She said, adding with impatience, "I do not have your local press card ready yet."

Yasuko was stared at like an alien as she entered the canteen. The only Asian they knew in Serbia was Bruce Lee. I think she found it a relief to talk to me. After six years away from Europe, I found myself a stranger here now, too. She told me she worked for a socialist newspaper in Athens.

"Have some coffee. My treat," I offered, generously, and we sat down for a chat.

"You know, in Japan we drink a lot of coffee. But nobody really likes it. It's just something we do to be like the rest of the world. Maybe I always found that façade to be stupid, or maybe I was always strange, because I actually like coffee." She went on to explain how restricted she felt by the rigid conformity and expectations of Japanese society. Like me, she had left home at the age of twenty. She had lived in Athens ever since. I sensed she was having some difficulty squaring her leftist-pacifist credentials with the more extreme attitudes and actions of the Bosnian-Serb leadership she was embedded with.

Sanja dragged us down to the TV station. Here, we were seated facing a taciturn fifty-two-year-old Serb woman who had been rescued from a prison in Sarajevo a month ago. I was wary of this being a set-up, but her tears seemed genuine, her story chillingly believable. Abducted along with nineteen men and one other woman, she claimed she had been held captive in the private dungeon of former Bosnian gangster, Juka Prazina. He now commanded a private militia of around three thousand followers—known as 'Juka's Wolves'—and had an official position in the Bosnian-Muslim army, we were told. (His body was discovered—with two gunshots to the head—in a canal in Aachen near the German border, on New Year's Eve 1993). Apparently, each neighborhood in Sarajevo now contained private prisons of this sort, often concealed beneath supermarkets or petrol stations.

For twenty days the prisoners had been subjected to beatings. One fellow detainee had died in her lap. She claimed to have been raped by her ex-neighbors. No reason was ever offered for their detention, other than that they were Serbs. Finally, when she had been beaten so badly there was no further use for her, she had been dumped on the streets, and later rescued by a UN patrol.

By this stage, Yasuko was holding the poor lady's hand. How could her persecutors—people she had formerly passed every day in the market, waved to and borrowed cups of sugar from—have become so brutalized, so quickly? It must all stem from fear. Man isn't intrinsically evil; he is intrinsically scared. At base, we kill in order not to be killed. Natural enough. But rape? Torture? We haven't progressed far from the cave. At best we've covered over some rocks with flowery wallpaper. Given the right conditions, all hell can and will break loose. What was happening in Bosnia was proof of that.

Aided and abetted by ITNs 'Death Camp' coverage, the Serbs had been vilified as the black hats in this particular conflict. Alarmist headlines, such as 'Belsen '92' in the UK's *Daily Mirror*, with its direct inference of Nazi extermination camps, didn't help. The people at SRNA silently seethed at what they considered to be persecution. Partly it was their own fault, letting the press walk in and around so freely in the first place. They had been naïve. They should have reckoned on the shock factor inherent in modern-day newsgathering. With editors and producers breathing down their necks, media teams were increasingly harassed into finding ever-more dramatic, harrowing footage. It was inevitable the skinniest-looking camp inmate was focused upon. I'd have done the same. It's a flaw inherent in a system that can only represent a snapshot of a single moment on a single day. It is selective. And despite the best intentions of the vast majority of those involved—who, I know, strive to represent the truth as closely as possible—any image or collection of words can be taken out of context, serving to fuel the very hatreds and prejudices they were attempting to expose.

Yasuko and I headed off to a makeshift hospital operating in the former Koran Hotel, out near a sawmill on the outskirts of town. Here, exhausted doctors worked around the clock, tending to a new influx of patients, injured two nights previously, when their convoy of cars had been attacked evacuating Gorazde. I shot black and white film in the hotel's former restaurant, partitioned now into crowded wards. Most of the wounded had been hit by exploding grenades and mortars. Shrapnel was being extracted from legs and stomachs. We interviewed the head doctor in his sandbagged office. He pulled heavily on an unfiltered Drina cigarette and sipped at thick, Turkish-style, coffee. He and his colleagues hadn't the energy to resist our inquisition.

Yasuko insisted on visiting the TV station on our way back. She was desperate to gain access to the army camp at Lukavica that overlooked Sarajevo. Local 'Channel-S' cameramen were driving out there all the time. We were passed along to a local Serb, Yadran. He was six months younger than me, and it was uncanny how well he spoke English. He was learning Arabic, too. Tall, willowy and urbane, Yadran stared beyond us with the faraway gaze of the poet or philosopher, or one who had recently misplaced his car keys. He told us that no transport would be available until the next day. I hoped I'd be able to hold out that long. I was down now to my last US$100 hard currency, with a few thousand Serbian dinara in local coin. Shopkeepers handed me brand new bank notes in change. These were issued by the Bosnian-Serb authorities in their new capital, Banja Luka. Yadran told me they were interchangeable with Serbian currency, here. "Just don't try using them in Belgrade. They are worthless there."

I found Najor lounging in the Bellevue lobby surrounded by his grim coterie of cardsharp buddies. I handed him my daily room rent/protection money. In exchange he suggested I might find something 'interesting' going on in Sokolac today. The flight of the Bosnian-Serb population from majority Muslim Gorazde had all the makings of the next big story, and many of these persecuted people were gathering in that small town.

The old bus, from Pale to Sokolac, was a far cry from the luxury coach coming here. It chugged for half an hour into high pastures through a scenic gorge. I'd failed to differentiate Sokolac from any of the other numerous, sleepy pastoral communities I'd passed through when arriving, a few days back. I paid it more attention now.

The bus dropped me off at the petrol station. The courtyard was overrun by dozens of tiny, Fiat-style cars — flattened beneath luggage that teetered on roof racks — and trucks laden with escapees, all coming from Gorazde; old men, women and children, many looking shell-shocked, their vehicles sprayed with bullet holes, their windscreens shattered. I tried to purchase a lone pack of Camel cigarettes to distribute as gifts. The stallholder refused my handful of Banja Lukan notes, insisting on Deutschmarks. This confirmed Yadran's assessment of the shaky foundations of the new Bosnian-Serb economy.

A tough-looking bunch of men squatted on a grassy

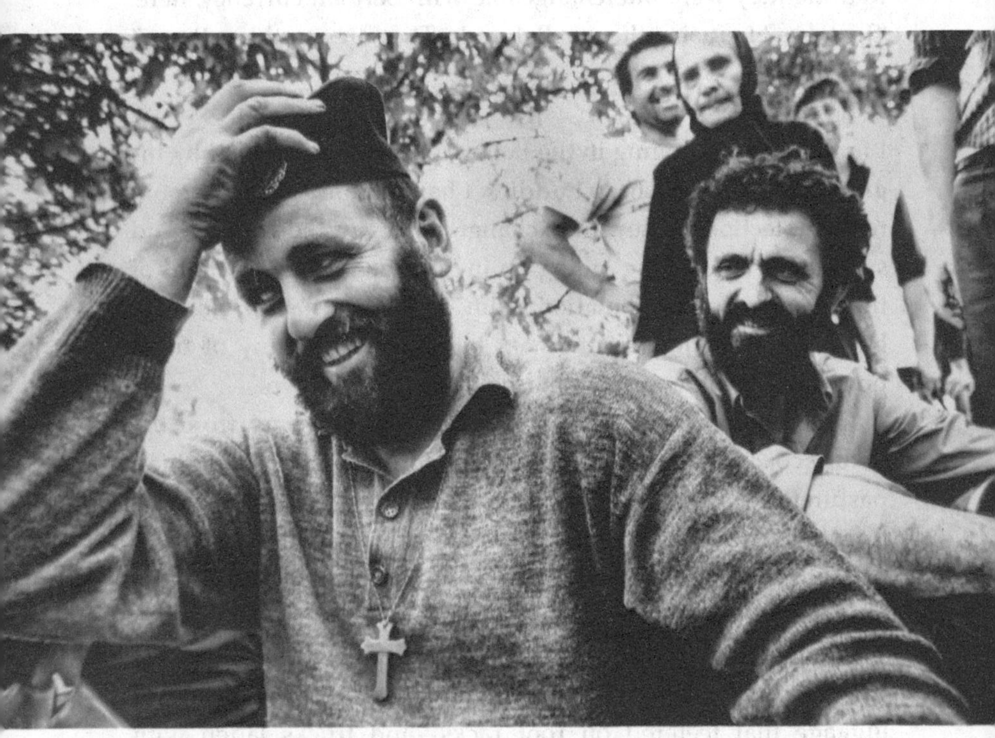

Sharing a light moment with some Chetniks on a stopover in Sokolac, Bosnia-Herzegovina, as they flee from their hometown of Gorazde. August 30, 1992. Photo: Chris Stowers/PANOS.

A family of Serb refugees, from Gorazde, rest in Sokolac during their flight to safety in Belgrade. August 30, 1992. Photo: Chris Stowers/PANOS.

embankment, sharpening their knives and bayonets. They identified themselves as Chetniks, intensely patriotic and heavily bearded Serbs—famed as World War II guerrillas by some, and collaborators with the Axis forces by others—they each wore a crucifix and had the ubiquitous Serb 'CCCC' motto tattooed on their arms and necks. They'd been run out of their hometown and had revenge on their minds.

Thinking the hospital would offer up the best material, I began to trek back in the direction of Pale, snapping away at road signs, landmarks, passing traffic; willing my fortune to change. Along the road I came across a well-dressed middle-aged man, his young wife and their child, who happened to be walking the same direction. What luck! He was a doctor at the local hospital and spoke English. He quizzed me about my work and I asked him permission to shoot inside his clinic.

He led me through the lunatic asylum—an assembly of rooms banished to the perimeter of the hospital, as though craziness were infectious—and we arrived at the main guard post. He told me, "I will have to ask permission, please wait here."

I smiled in solidarity with the soldier on duty, offering him a local Drina cigarette. Oddly, he refused. Probably he was expecting something American. A few minutes later, my friend reappeared, in conversation with a couple of military-looking officials. I waved to him across the courtyard, glad to see his familiar face. He would be able to get things moving now. Instead, I heard,

"That's him! That's the man I saw earlier photographing troop movements on the road to Pale," and he pointed at me.

It only ever takes a moment for everything to go to hell. Understanding the danger you face arrives later, in retrospect. A pair of militiamen approached from behind. One tore the camera bag off my shoulder. The other roughly shackled my hands behind my back. I was pressed firmly into the front passenger seat of their VW Golf. The guard sitting behind me jammed a pistol in my neck.

"Problem," the driver growled, meaning for me.

The cuffs forced me forward until my head almost touched the windscreen, which was pierced at eye-level by twin bullet holes.

So, this was it, the 'thrill' I'd been seeking ever since kissing goodbye to Eva on the nighttime platform in Arad and embarking on this frivolous detour into danger. A danger that suddenly felt worryingly real and very personal. To be honest, it was a path I'd been on a long time, ever since the first wave of bomb blast adrenaline back in Peshawar. Six years of experiences and escapades: and they had all been secretly in cahoots, patiently leading me on to this one day — a specific set of map co-ordinates deep in some unseeing glade of the Dinaric Alps — and an unmarked grave, unremarkable among so many. I was not special after all. I'd had a good run. But I should have guessed I'd never really be allowed to make it home.

Worst of all, I had only myself to blame. What degree of idiot goes strolling through a country under siege casually snapping away at vital parts of infrastructure? What kind of foreign correspondent can't afford to hire a car or interpreter? I cursed myself for not having told anyone at the Bellevue where I was heading.

The AK-47 that belonged to the unshaven driver lay across his lap, its muzzle pointing at my knees. The weapon wobbled and slipped each time he changed gear or slammed on the brakes. My leg joints began to shake, and not entirely from indignant rage.

"I'm not a spy," I croaked, an octave higher than aiming for, my throat scratchy and dry. Even my traitor voice was in on the act. With his right hand, free between gear changes, the driver turned to me, and slowly drew a thumb across his throat.

This wasn't the first time I'd been threatened by an armed man. That was back in 1987, at the very start of my travels, in Pakistan's Swat Valley. But instead of getting used to the experience, the habit had progressively unnerved me. Perhaps, that first time, youthful optimism and ignorance of real-world perils had shielded me from any sense of fear. I'd even managed to persuade the tribesman with the rifle to pose for my camera, chalking the whole experience up to one of cultural misunderstanding. With the passage of time, however, I'd become increasingly concerned whenever someone jabbed a weapon in my direction. Like Russian roulette played with an ever-decreasing number of empty chambers, each round drew me exponentially closer to my last.

So, I was wondering whether to make a grab for the machinegun or try and jump from the car at a slow bend, and run for it. Wouldn't that present my captors just the excuse for target practice they were itching for? Instead, I sat and stewed, working myself up into a right stomping mood. *Why the hell did I ever leave such a comfy set-up in Hong Kong?*

We drove back through Sokolac, past the petrol station, past the police station, and out the other side. Turning up a dirt track, the car skidded to a halt outside a nondescript concrete blockhouse. I was led from the car to a detention cell. I glared at everyone, attempting to convince myself of a bravado I did not feel inside. A person has more control over their life than they care to admit: start thinking yourself a victim and sure enough you'll end up becoming one. A flustered official arrived demanding my papers. I indicated with my chin the top right pocket of my camera jacket, saying,

"I wondered when you'd ask!"

But in order to be successful, sarcasm requires a receptive audience. The officer confiscated my IDs: passport, UN press card and SRNA's Belgrade accreditation.

"Your government allowed me here, I was trying to do my job and report the true situation in Serbia." The official flicked through my paperwork distastefully, showing zero interest in my excuses.

"For my efforts I have been ignored, cajoled, shoved and accused, threatened, shackled, had my neck skewered by a gun and been threatened with slow and needlessly sadistic decapitation. If this is how you treat your friends, I'm not surprised your enemies are winning the support of the media and wider international community."

"Enough!" he snapped. "Your papers are no good. Permission from Pale, you have?"

"Call Sanja, at the Bellevue." *What was her surname?* "She knows me."

"You are spy, I think. You wait."

No alternative option presented itself, so I waited and worried I'd overdone the indignant foreigner act. By 4:00 p.m., though still locked up and under arrest, the handcuffs had at least been removed. I rested awkwardly against the institutionally pale-green walls, my legs stretched across the doorway, fully intent on tripping up the next person who came in. I channeled my indignation into penning a report:

BOSNIA-HERZEGOVINA, 30AUG92, 15:00 GMT
SOKOLAC—A convoy of exhausted Bosnian-Serbs
escaping the besieged town of Gorazde halted here for fuel
today. They arrived in the back of lorries, shot-up 'Zastava'
bubble cars, and aging Ladas that groaned beneath the
weight of all their transportable possessions. The evacuees

were visibly relieved to have reached safe-haven in this Serb-held town, thirty miles northeast of Sarajevo ...

In Sokolac, anger was directed equally toward the Muslims and Bosnian-Serb President, Radovan Karadzic, who had called for all Serbs to evacuate mainly Muslim Gorazde. Thickly bearded Slavko Zirkorvic, identifying himself as a Chetnik, said, "We have no allegiance to Radovan. Yes, we will go to Serbia now. But then we will return along the Drina (River) to Gorazde to take back our homes and slit the throats of the Muslim animals. We have lived in Gorazde for hundreds of years, the same as the Musselmen, why should we leave?"

Darkness settled upon the forests of Sokolac, like a lace shroud landing delicately on the shoulders of a young widow. I regretted not having brought any warm clothing, as it looked like I'd be here overnight. Around six o'clock, though, there was a commotion in the corridor. A key rattled furiously in the lock, and a flustered man wearing a camera vest not unlike my own entered, his body blocking the doorway. He hesitated momentarily, eyes adjusting to the interior level of gloom. It was Mandic, the cameraman and volunteer interpreter. Someone must have contacted SRNA in Pale. He had come racing out of the twilight and dust in his VW Golf (it was always a Golf. Instead of selling arms, the Germans seemed to specialize in equipping the world's rogue republics with nippy, economical hatchbacks). I asked him how he knew I was missing and where to find me.

"It was Najor," —*bless his gleaming, golden teeth*—"yes, he said he had received a call from angry Sokolac police. "'You have rude Englishman in fishing vest staying there'?"

Mandic dropped me off at the Panorama Hotel, almost forgetting to add, "Oh, here's your press pass. And Yadran says to prepare to for Sarajevo tomorrow. I'll pick you up in the morning."

СРПСКА РЕПУБЛИКА
МИНИСТАРСТВО ЗА ИНФОРМАЦИЈЕ PRESS

ДОЗВОЛА Бр. A–015/92
за несметано кретање и рад

HONG KONG
CHRIS STOWERS
ИМЕ И ПРЕЗИМЕ   МЈЕСТО   ДРЖАВА
C 339249E   PALE,SOKOLAC
ПАСОШ   PRESS БР.   СВРХА
ASIAWEEK   HONG KONG
АГЕНЦИЈА   МЈЕСТО   ДРЖАВА
ВАЖИ ОД 29.08. ДО 5.09. 92. ГОД.
М.П.
ГРАНИЧНИ ПРЕЛАЗ

The next day I made sure to bring along all my lucky charms. These included Ata's talisman, hung around my neck, and the 'lucky' Bic biro (gift from Tatiana), placed in my lower-right jacket pocket, along with my Tibetan Buddha. These, I hoped, would protect the contents not only of my wallet, but my ascending colon, too. A portrait of Layla I kept in my top-left pocket, over my heart. Photographers are not overly superstitious or sentimental; we just happen to find ourselves in more frequent need of psychical armory than those employed in the more sedate professions.

Thus prepared, I strolled downhill from my refugee camp chalet to the Bellevue. Early morning sunlight lanced through rising mist. The fir trees dragged green tendrils over my shoulders, soaking my camera jacket with their tears. Mandic, an amateur rally driver before the war, came roaring up in his Golf. As he was intimately familiar with all the back roads, in no time we were sliding in a controlled arc into the car park at the Olympic Hotel. Yasuko was already in the lobby finishing off what looked like her fourth cup of breakfast espresso. She introduced me to a new arrival joining us for the trip, Pazit Ravina, a senior Israeli journalist of serious demeanor and a slight limp, who was reporting for the conservative newspaper *Davar*.

Israel was ignoring the sanctions imposed on Serbia by 'The West'. The two nations instead found themselves bonded by mutual instinct for self-preservation against a common Islamic foe. It was an indication of how complex the formulation of any meaningful political analysis of the Bosnian situation had become that I found myself squeezed at the dining table between a radical left-wing Japanese feminist, and a right-wing Israeli die-hard, both of whom had been invited as guests of the same government. I scrounged a cup of tea and two slices of toast from their leftover spread, happy to be a simple photographer, free to duck out of the conversation and polish my lenses and fiddle with my dials.

For the second day in a row, I found myself hurtling towards a hesitant future in the front-right passenger seat of a Volkswagen Golf, though thankfully, this time, without the handcuffs. Mandic stuck to mountain tracks in an attempt to avoid the main road that ran down into the valley and Sarajevo. This had been labeled by the Western press, predictably, as the "Highway to Hell". We arrived at a gap in the trees and he slowed the car to a crawl. Leaning across me, he pointed out my open window.

"See that hill over there? It is popular with snipers." I mentally willed my body to shrink, and expected little red laser dots to start dancing on our foreheads. Pazit, on the other hand, wanted Mandic to stop the car and get out for a stroll. A little further down the hill, we located an encampment of Serb army regulars. They walked a shallow trench, its excavated earth heaped up to form an embankment on top of the ridge, creating a safe zone away from enemy sniper scopes. Here they sat on ammunition boxes and boiled coffee in billycans.

From these grim troops, Mandic extracted the latest news: "the road to Sarajevo is not open, far too dangerous. Even if you go, you will not be allowed back across the frontline again." Sarajevo continued to defeat me. But I did get to see the forlorn city a few miles away. It sprawled across the shallow valley floor, gray and smoldering, like a half-sunk battleship.

The source of the rumbling artillery that had unnerved us these past few days—now sounding much closer, firing in regular salvos—was Lukavica Army camp, just around the bend. We were permitted a visit. Pazit was happy. She had been searching for proof Syria was supporting the Muslim forces, and was delighted when shown a stash of munitions—captured from an overrun Bosnian-Muslim position—with Arabic lettering printed all over it. My own research dug up several incriminating packs of US Army ration Tootsie Rolls—I destroyed as much of the evidence as my stomach could take, and filled my pockets with the rest—though it remained unclear whether these were US Army rations that had been issued to the Serb military, or rations the Serbs had captured from the Bosnians or Croats.

Yasuko, meanwhile, had gone unusually shy. Like a love-struck schoolgirl, she was hanging on every word and gesture of the camp commandant. He was the ruggedly handsome sort, whose creased eyes and jutting chin were forever doomed to attract and arouse the passions of peace-loving and exiled Far Eastern femme fatales, those with a weakness for strong caffeine and men with huge Howitzers.

We were invited to interview Ismail, one of dozens of Muslim troops being held prisoner at the camp. Despite the litany of people forever telling us, 'it's never this hot here at the end of

August,' Ismail was shivering, a bundle of nerves. Hands balled in his lap, each time the big guns went off—rattling the duct-taped windows of the commander's office—he jumped. His bootlaces and belt had been removed as a precaution against self-harm. Pazit reckoned she could crank out an article on Ismail for *The Mail on Sunday* (she was impressively well-connected), and I got my camera out, deciding to use the 85mm lens, stepping back to give the prisoner a bit of space.

In a low and unsteady voice, Ismail explained he had been a miner, before the war, that he'd been forced to take up arms. Given a gun and minimal training, he was sent to the front. He'd only been on the ground for three days before his unit was overrun. Pazit showed me a handwritten note that had been

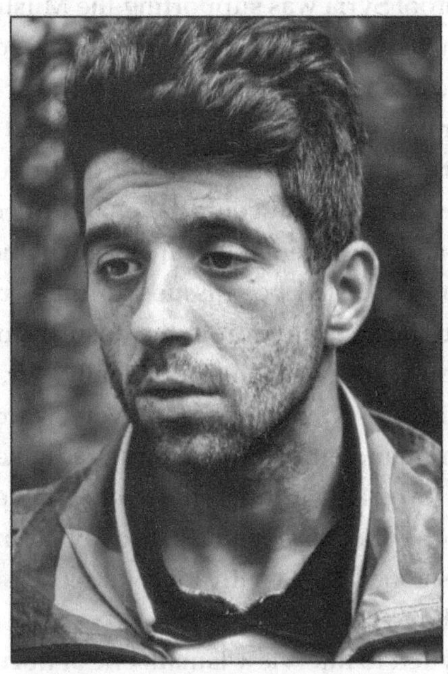

Bosnian Muslim prisoner, Ismail, photographed in
captivity at Lukavica Army Camp on August 31, 1992.
Photo: Chris Stowers/PANOS.

found in Ismail's possession.

"It's from an imam," she enlightened me, "a religious exemption that includes sections of the Koran said to offer a soldier fast-track martyrdom, if they're killed in battle."

Ismail admitted to Pazit he was scared of what would become of him at the hands of the Serbs. On hearing this admission, the Serb officer who accompanied us as translator, laughed. It was a disturbing laugh, one that occupied a narrow corridor of sanity between two opposing doors. Call them 'Door A' and 'Door B'. Door A opened to reveal Serb brutality towards prisoners was nothing but absurd myth, the invention of biased Muslim propagandists; open Door B, however, and you were teetering at the top of an impossibly steep staircase, one that descended to a black basement torture chamber.

Right now, the spotlight of our media attention kept both portals fastened. I wanted to assure Ismail he'd be OK; that he'd soon be released through Door A. But what did I know? I had no right to go around raising anyone's hopes.

A few hours later we were back in Pale. Mandic dropped us off at the Olympic. Pazit had an appointment to keep there with a mysterious, elderly Israeli called 'Raffi'. Raffi admitted to being an 'ex-spy', who, now retired and with nothing much to do, thought he'd come to Pale and see if he could be of some use. He wanted to set up a press center, like that of SRNA's, right here in the Olympic Hotel (where most journalists stayed, anyway) and needed Mandic's computer technician brains to get things up and running.

The only 'ex'-spy was a dead one, I mused. *He must still work for Mossad.*

After dinner, I let Pazit know of my intention to travel into Sarajevo with the UN convoy on their way through Pale the next day. She displayed concern. Considering the nature of her job and the company she kept, I realized it was quite likely she had access to information far more detailed and up-to-date than my own. "Don't go," she said. It was neither threat nor entreaty, but guarded advice. This only made me doubly anxious to join the trucks.

Next, she attempted to entice me to stay. Opening her bag, she brought out a spare, all-expenses paid ticket to some place called 'San Stefano', to cover a chess match. I declined her generous offer. I have never liked being told what to do, even when it was for my own damned, ignorant good. And as for chess, my ego hadn't yet recovered from the bruising it took from ten-year-old Maestro Maximka, on the Trans-Siberian Express. Not long afterwards, but already far away from Bosnia, I would spot a report in a newspaper that made me regret making that rash and moody decision. The accreditation Pazit had so kindly offered was for the legendary Grandmaster clash between former World Champions Bobby Fischer and Boris Spassky. The match was held on Sveti Stefan — an exclusive island off the coast of Montenegro that was, at that time, part of the former Federal Republic of Yugoslavia. The tournament would continue, famously, in Belgrade, with Fischer eventually winning the encounter 10–5. Due to UN sanctions, however, Fischer's involvement led to conflict with the US government, the IRS, and a warrant being issued for his arrest. It would have made a good story.

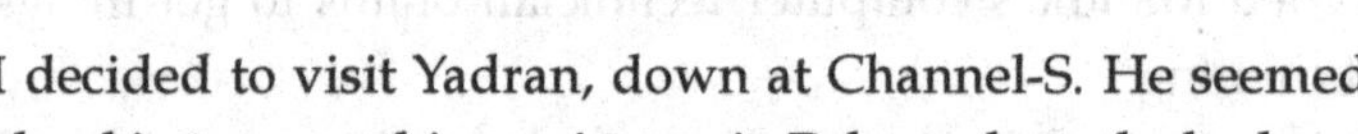

I decided to visit Yadran, down at Channel-S. He seemed to be clued in to everything going on in Pale, and maybe had some dirt on this Raffi character, too. I found him, as usual, seated behind a bank of TV monitors.

"Ah, Chris, come, come, look at this." He was shifting in his seat, agitated, and inhaled one cigarette after another. He streamed a news broadcast Sky TV had sent out earlier over the Channel-S satellite transmitter. It showed footage of an old woman, clad in black, crying in a cemetery. Yadran was outraged: the woman wore the traditional mourning garb of the Orthodox faith. She was clearly a Serb. "But the reporter called the people in the cemetery Muslims!"

I offered him some chocolate biscuits, an effort to curry favor and show we're not all alike and uncaring, the wicked Western Media. But then an ITN crew barged in and I could see it was going to be an uphill battle. Fresh back from filming the Gorazde convoy, they were looking to commandeer Channel-S's satellite link in order to broadcast their 'scoop' on that night's *News at Ten* back in the UK. Time was of the essence.

"Who are these, the Three Stooges?" asked Yadran, his face drained of color. I turned to examine the new arrivals. Yadran's eyes were angled down, glaring at the legs of the invading trio, uniformly clad in Bermuda shorts and sandals. Their lead negotiator wasn't even wearing socks. His sense of sartorial propriety mortally offended, Yadran refused to delay his own scheduled news bulletin for that of this slack foreign crew.

"We'll pay," shouted the leader, a cockney, as short of hair and limb as he was of dress sense and good manners. "Cash."

Yadran was forced into negotiations between his Channel-S boss and the ITN crew.

"'Chubby', is that the word to use?" He was referring to the head ITN 'Stooge'.

"Yes, he's 'Chubby' all right," I marveled at the range of Yadran's self-taught vocabulary.

"Oh, sorry, Mate," Chubby overheard me speaking, "didn't know you was English. Is 'e your interpreter, then?" He talked right over Yadran, who sat there, impassively, fuming.

"No, he's my friend."

"Right," I was dismissed, and Chubby turned back to Yadran. "So, Mate. How about it? We only need half a bloody hour."

After some pretty vigorous dealing, the Channel-S boss caved in to international demand, and their hard currency. At least Yadran had been able to gouge a decent rate. I admired his restraint. Yadran hovered over the shoulder of an ITN cameraman who was now hastily editing his footage on Yadran's personal desk. "So, where are these people from?" he asked.

"Gorazde, Mate."

"I see. And, so, who are they?"

"Serbs, Mate, bloody 'ell."

"Good," pronounced Yadran, "just checking."

Even though the job was turning him into a chain-smoking neurotic, Yadran managed to put his head down day after day. He towed the line and coped with all hassles encountered along the way. He had, thus, been forged into early maturity by a series of unavoidable, character-building events. Events that I, on the other hand, could always escape. That was the joy, and the unbearable lightness — to steal Kundera's phrase — of being a freelancer. I could always skip town when the pressure became too great, a story too repetitive, or the situation too dangerous. With no skin in the game, I could remain the eternal child.

September 1, 1992.

AUTUMN ARRIVED OVERNIGHT. The guns had fallen silent. Pulling back the curtain, I faced gray dawn skies and damp, denuded trees that made me think of England. The enthusiasm to get to

Sarajevo, burning so hot in me a day ago, had correspondingly cooled. For the first time since leaving Hong Kong, my ultimate destination, like the tree branches, was laid bare. My entire, foot-dragging, circuitous route back across half the planet had been nothing but one long attempt to delay inevitable return.

It would have been a different matter entirely were I being paid for the inconvenience. Were that the case I would invest in a flak jacket, rent a car, travel with a fixer, and play in the big league. Like Jim Lindelof and Lee Shapiro had, back in Peshawar. But then they remain splattered across some random ridge of the Hindu Kush, courtesy of a Soviet helicopter gunship (my former Khyber Hotel associates had been killed in Afghanistan on October 11– some reports claimed October 9–1987. News of their deaths taking nearly two weeks to reach US officials in Pakistan). Or The Mouse, his arm crippled by a Russian tank shell. *Who are these people*? I'd once wondered, in awe. Today, given half a chance, I would join their ranks. Against these wilder urges, though, my inner accountant cautioned restraint. Get out! Live, so you can shoot another day.

I needed caffeine to help uncoil my brain, so I headed to the press center. It was abuzz. Lukavica had been attacked in the night and was now caught in the Bosnian-Muslim offensive around Ilidza, a Serb-held suburb near Sarajevo airport. Najor, sensing the end of his get-rich-quick scams, was calling in his complex web of debts. If Bosnian-Muslim troops made it to Pale, it'd be every man for himself. I persuaded him to sell me the bayonet, something he begrudgingly did for US$15. I was not convinced I could plunge it into the heart of an enemy, but you discover many new and surprising talents in the heat of a moment. Besides, it incorporated a nifty wire-cutter function that could be quite handy around the house.

"The road to Zvornik is under threat," Yadran informed me,

referring to the N19 lifeline to Belgrade. The buses had stopped running. Effectively we were stranded. "This is the action you've been looking for," he piled on the pathos, "We may have to fight our way out, after all." Then he relented, "Look, it will be safer if we all stick together. The Panorama is too exposed. Why don't you stay in town? Some of my colleagues and I are looking after the house of a priest who went back to Belgrade. Join us, you do not need to pay."

And he let me sit in a corner of the studio to type out my Gorazde report on the office typewriter. The process was lengthy on a keyboard so fond of Zs, Ss and Cs with inverted hats above them. Much white-out was involved.

It was rare I felt the urge to smoke. Today, though, I reasoned an exception could be made. I walked to the little Orthodox chapel near the TV station, slid my back down its rough wood-paneled exterior, and puffed earnestly on a cheroot. I vowed to return in time of peace, and pass another such lazy afternoon on this same spot. This plan, of course, remained contingent on making it out of here at all. The lack of artillery fire from Lukavica took on extra significance: now all was quiet on that particular section of the western front. Pale was likely to be the next target of the renewed Bosnian-Muslim offensive.

It was not until late afternoon, after Channel-S had finished broadcasting its news, that I was allowed access to their fax machine. I quickly jotted Luisa's name on top of the sheet, bylined my story from Pale, and dialed in the numbers for the *South China Morning Post* newspaper. It was a long shot. It would be very early in the morning in Hong Kong. But my conscience demanded the time I had spent here not be a total waste. I tried getting the message through several times. The machine repeatedly spat out a receipt: 'NG'.

"Negative," explained Yadran. The fax hadn't gone through.

He jogged off to confer with some of his colleagues clustered around a large map, the entire group smothered in cigarette fumes. He returned a moment later, the bearer of bad news. "The Muslims have captured the road to Zvornik. They have destroyed our transmitter on the hill at Majevica. All lines are down. Please, excuse me …" he was called outside: ITN needed his help, urgently. Their van had broken down.

Amid all the chaos, Allan Little and Alec Russell turned up. It was after dark, and their faces displayed evident relief at arrival. Allan told me he hadn't been able to get into Sarajevo during the last five days, either, so I didn't feel such a failure. His translator, Dragan, a sensitive soul disguised beneath a skinhead haircut, told me he was being paid US$500 a day in danger money. He added, "I would not go back to Sarajevo for even US$5,000 a day!" This somewhat vindicated my cowardly intention to bug out in the morning.

Meanwhile, squatting in the stairwell, Alec was shouting down a fragile line to London. He was becoming increasingly frustrated reading in his story to some dozy night desk subeditor who was obviously unaware of the gravity of the situation.

"No, no, no, 'Ilidza', I, L, I, Dz, A … you have to accent the 'z' of the Dz with an inverted circumflex diacritic … an inverted … you know, like in French … hello? Yes, like the French … the one that looks like a hat, only turned upside down … right … begin transcript: 'Ilidza, which Bosnian President Izetbegović (sigh) I, Z, E, T, B, E …'"

"There's a curfew after 9:00 p.m.," warned Allan. I stole a glance at my watch. It was past ten already. I followed Yadran outside. We wove blindly through a graveyard to the priest's residence beside the church. Once inside, our voices were absorbed in the religious texts lining its walls. I prepared our evening meal of tinned food, and this we ate by sacramental candlelight, beneath the glinting silver and gold of abandoned crucifixes. I'd like to think that God became frustrated with the pious and their mundane litany of daily peeves. Surely, he would appreciate the odd message from an old acquaintance, one with whom, perhaps, he'd thought he'd lost contact?

"Dear God," —I muttered, having first checked Yadran was in the bathroom and out of earshot—"it's not that I've not been thinking about you. I've just been busy. That's a pathetic excuse but, as an all-seeing entity, you'll know I'm not lying. Anyway, I don't often ask for favors, so if you could bump this one up the 'to-do' list a bit sharpish, preferably by tomorrow morning, I'd be extremely grateful. Please, Lord, let the N19 be cleared overnight and the road to Zvornik be a safe one. Lots of love, etc."

Before falling asleep, I asked Yadran if he'd ever used a gun.

"No," he replied, sounding mildly offended, "Never touched one. But, were I forced to, I'd rather fight than run away from here to live in Serbia."

As I hovered on the edge of sleep, I wondered if I would do the same were my home ever threatened? I'd like to think I would. But where and what was my home these days? An empty room in a humid Hong Kong flat? My parent's house, a deep freeze of adolescent memories? Rather, my home was here, tonight, and I'd fight for it if I had to. And tomorrow it would be some other place I'd traveled to, and I'd fight for that, too. Because no man should have to go to sleep worried his world will still be there come morning.

Not even a Western nomad.

<hr>

The following day was painfully cold. I put it down to all my years in the Far East: my blood had thinned, I'd become Asianized. But Yadran, brewing coffee on a camping gas stove and lost in a cloud of rising steam, was feeling the sudden chill, too.

"You should try for the bus at seven o'clock," he shivered, "Our troops countered the offensive last night so the road is open, but I don't know for how long ..." This was the most recent intelligence doing the rounds and I wanted to believe it, though I felt like a traitor to even consider deserting my new friend — after all, I was not exactly in any to rush to get back to England — but what justifiable reason did I have to stay?

At Pale bus station it was difficult to tell if more tears were being shed on the friends, relatives and lovers being seen off on the unpredictable drive to Belgrade, than those left to stay behind and face likely encirclement and evacuation, like the residents of Gorazde.

The bus pulled out. I smeared a circle in the condensation using a corner of the lacy window curtain. I waved through the pane to Yadran. He stood lost in thought, hands thrust deep in his jacket pockets, a cigarette dangling from the corner of his mouth, a Balkan James Dean. I don't think he saw me.

On the outskirts of town, we made an unscheduled stop at the end of the lane leading to the Panorama Hotel. Yasuko clambered on board and sat next to me. It was comforting to know I wasn't the only one deserting Pale that day. Soon we were gliding past Sokolac. I noted, with a judder, the police station and little cell block just beyond it. Here, there were signs of recent shelling: the burnt-out cottages and holiday homes I'd passed a few days earlier were smoking anew. I grabbed some shots from the window as Serbian soldiers crouched and ran through a hamlet. It felt weird to be so detached, viewing the action from on high, in plush seats, as though we were in the upper circle of the cinema.

As we descended, autumn rose to greet us. We reached Zvornik at noon. We were close to Serbia now, but there was still the bridge blocking our path to freedom. I seemed to have a 'thing' with this crossing point; it was like a playground bully, waiting to steal my pocket money each time I tried to pass. At the roadblock, Yasuko and I were made to alight while our bags were searched. A fierce-looking Chetnik demanded, "Do you have films?" My stomach began to tie itself in knots as I envisioned losing all my footage right here, on the very point of escape. *Just let us out of this madhouse*! Yasuko, commendably, lost her patience. She screeched at the rugged militiaman, who was twice her height, and many more times that in bulk.

"Of course, we have films!" Shocked into submission, he meekly nodded us through.

A few miles farther, and the bus pulled over at a café. The pig that rotated on a spit at its entrance signaled a return to normality; of food over fear. Juicy slices of salted pork were served between doorsteps of bread, and relieved, excitable chatter erupted from mouths so recently muted in dread.

Leaving the Sava River to flow and join the Danube away on our left, the gray suburbs of Belgrade rose grittily through unromantic mid-afternoon light. Yasuko headed off to file her stories from SRNA's Press Center. I had more urgent business to attend to, and jumped on the next bus to Pancevo. Fortunately, my exposed films were still where I'd left them, secured in the hotel safe, but the town was less welcoming this time around. Gone was the gaiety of summer; an icy wind stripped leaves of copper from the trees, and huddled pedestrians eyed me with suspicion. I felt like Frodo returning from his adventures, only to find his beloved Shire pillaged and polluted. Sladana's kiosk was boarded up. I couldn't find her anywhere. Worryingly, the room rate at the Sloboda Hotel had almost doubled, to 4,000 dinara.

I'd kept some local currency in reserve to fund a celebratory binge with—nothing wild, but I'd been dreaming of a beer and bar of chocolate all week. All that would now vanish to pay for tonight's room. Prices in the capital had risen 40 percent, across the board in the short week I'd been gone, the byproduct of biting sanctions and international isolation. I couldn't afford the bus to Berlin now, but there was a cheap train to Hungary leaving in the morning.

The next day I awoke at the crack of dawn feeling change was in order. Accordingly, I shaved off my beard. For a moment I considered keeping the glamorous, cavalry officer moustache that remained, but then shaved that off, too. I'd put myself through the same facial transformation coming out of the jungle of Borneo a few years back. Then, as now, my body shivered involuntarily, bursting with sap and juices. I felt electric; it was the euphoria that accompanied survival. That, and finally having nothing holding me back from the making a direct dash for home.

BUDAPEST
September 3, 1992

IT WAS TIME to check out of the hotel, and Serbia, too. The authorities were starting to become malicious, as I discovered down by the train station when, for no reason except that I was an obvious foreigner, a policeman insisted on rifling through my backpack. He was about to uncover the Kalashnikov bayonet when I remembered my UN Press Card. This counter declaration to his own authority punctured his self-confidence, and he gave up his search when his colleague in the car began to hoot the horn with impatience.

With no fanfare, the train bound for neighboring Hungary slid out of Belgrade station. And with no sunlight to enliven it, the passing landscape was condemned to unremarkable status all the way to the border at Subotica. The Land of the Magyars wasn't much of an improvement. Here burnt brown battlefields of corn soaked up the cement dust spewed by dreary factories. Or was it my mood? Had I fallen out of love with travel? Even the exotic place names failed to ignite my normally hyperactive sense of wanderlust.

We pulled into Budapest's Keleti Railway Station in the late

afternoon. An eager little gentleman in a hand-knitted cardigan —
and of moustache so lustrous I wished I'd kept mine a day longer
so we could have compared whiskers — introduced himself as
'Mr Rats' (I imagine it being spelt with a 'z' and an extra 's' or
two. Life in Hungary would come to a crashing halt deprived of
these essential consonants).

He offered me room and board in his apartment for US$10.

What was the local currency even called? I doubted I'd
be in the country long enough to spend any of it. Across the
communist bloc, the parallel US dollar economy happily co-
existed with national ones. Its people, long forced by financial
necessity and innate distrust of the authorities, had become
savvy to the minutest shift in exchange rates. Everyone knew the
best place to make a trade. By comparison, where I grew up —
where I was heading to — it was part of the vacation experience
to be ignorantly short-changed on your 'holiday money'.

The Ratses lived in a grim tower block — in a suburb full of
them — called Barta. That was the impression I gained of the
place at first sight, externally. The scene improved dramatically
as soon as the front door had shut behind me and I'd ventured,
by way of thickly carpeted hallway, into the main salon. Here was
a realm of obvious domestic bliss and affability, not to mention
a close-to-military degree of tidiness. Mrs Rats, the prime mover
behind this domestic dexterity, ran a tight ship, and was quick to
serve her weary lodger his nightly goulash.

Maybe I shouldn't be in such a rush. Today was a Friday; by Monday
I could, if things went smoothly, find myself back in England!
I'd been so pre-occupied, it had sort of crept up on me. Having
survived 2,052 days away, it was of vital importance I squeezed
these last few moments of freedom for all they were worth.

By 10:00 p.m., I was squeezed on the sofa in the living room with the entire Rats family, and their flatulent beagle, 'Bobbie'. The central heating was cranked right up. I was sweating, and they were all laughing uncontrollably at an indescribably crap local TV game show.

I'd rather be in Sarajevo.

BERLIN
September 5, 1992

BUDAPEST RUMBLED TO life at 4:15 a.m. with the first stirring of the trolley buses. These transported yawning workers to the city center from the dripping bus shelters of any number of suburbs identical to Barta, in all but name. The economy coach from here to Berlin used up my remaining dollars. A rookie traveler at this point might well have panicked; luckily, I had some experience in being broke. A solution would present itself. And if not, I could always stand at a corner and juggle, badly. It wouldn't be the first time my hat had been used as a collection bowl.

Mitteleuropa passed my window, a procession of toy towns and manicured farmland. From Hungary through Czechoslovakia to Germany in half a day: each productive acre was allotted its task, its people living in abundant boredom. As the bus progressed from east to west, so official scrutiny given my passport descended from flippant flick of the photo page down to a mere glance at its cover. By the German border, my stately, black hardback British booklet was waved through on color alone. What lack of concern! Don't they know there's a war going on just down the road?

This fortunate population, bound within the protective perimeters of Western Europe, must imagine themselves immune to the troubles besetting the world outside. Was memory that quick and determined to forget? To delete all recollection of the rubble left by Allied bombing raids, the bitterness and privation of Cold War ideology and of occupation?

No, those memories hadn't been forgotten: they'd been buried. Europe was enjoying its present state of self-indulgent denial precisely *because* those memories were so raw and painful, and its citizens so unwilling to countenance a repeat of such chaos on their very doorstep:

It can't happen to us, not now that we have shopping malls and ATM machines and children to put through college; we're too civilized for war.

Blessed with a temperate climate and moderate political and religious convictions, people here had been lulled by decades of peace and prosperity. They refused to recognize the obvious: that in times of economic and social breakdown, diversity evaporates, leaving only division; and tolerance was trounced by tribe. So, don't become too smug and comfortable all of you out there, passing by in your new cars, with your luxury holidays and fitted kitchens. Times of privilege and plenty cannot reign forever — all empires implode. The battling states of former Yugoslavia, a few short miles away, should have been ringing alarm bells. Instead, it seemed everyone here had plugged their ears, pulled down their eyeshades, and popped a Valium.

The bus dropped me off close to Berlin's Zoo station, at 9:00 p.m. Encased in my unwashed camera vest and dirt-stiffened, ripped jeans, I fitted right in with the New Age hippie types dwelling in the city, now The Wall was down. The S-Bahn rumbled overhead, and from its elevated platform I gained a view across a distant 'graveyard' of old cars and airplanes that had been chopped up and welded into weird structures. Around these, performing some sort of atavistic ritual, people danced in jerky movements, lit eerily by huge orange bonfires, like Druids worshipping a metallic Stonehenge.

It was too late to go looking for a hotel, so I found a bench partially sheltered from the chill east wind, and resolved to wait out the night. At midnight, though, two policemen patrolling with huge dogs encouraged me to move on. I felt like standing my ground, like I had when peed on by that expat, back in Hong Kong. *I'm not a bum, I'm a photographer*, I'd protested then. But this time I really did look like a bum. Berlin was a city of the night and, sure enough, a nearby 24-hour McDonald's catered to the nocturnal crowd. I scraped together some coins and ordered a cheeseburger. It came ready congealed. And I nursed my coffee until it froze.

From the McDonald's I moved across the square, passing on the way some really quite explicit sex shops and a group of glue-sniffing punks, and took up new residence inside the 24-hour Burger King. The girl at the counter was compelled to sport a promotional cowboy hat at four o'clock in the morning. *Well, you asked for capitalism …*

"My hat is nicer than your hat," I said, to break the ice. And her smile made me feel human again. I recognized in it something of the spirit of Claudia. *Ah, Claudia, so far away in Bonn: if only you lived here!* In my frantic search for lost pfennigs to pay for the coffee, I unearthed an envelope. It must have been lying there forgotten about, for months, crushed beneath my flash unit. I gently extracted from it one of Claudia's 100 deutschmark traveler's checks—payment for my photos she'd used in her long-ago article about Hong Kong—coming through now, in my hour of need. I suddenly stood a much greater chance of affording to get to the Hook of Holland in the morning. My faith in having faith was restored.

⚬⚬⚬

Come sunrise, despite the sleepless night, I felt no tiredness. It must have been adrenaline. My senses were on high alert; the homing-signal was cutting through the ether, loud and clear. My immediate challenge was to secure sufficient funds to continue my onward journey. It was important, therefore, that I didn't appear too desperate as the man at the money exchange kiosk opened up at the start of the day. I prayed he'd accept my wrinkled deutschmark traveler's check, and I handed him all my remaining cash, too, even an old 20 Hong Kong dollar note. He magically transformed this odd-ball pile of random currencies into a uniform stack of Dutch guilders. This was the final foreign currency standing between me and my own pounds sterling. On the train I discussed the war in Bosnia, US politics, and the state of the monarchy with a Dutch businessman who worked in Berlin for British Petroleum. At Amersfoort he insisted on me trying a *kroket* — the ubiquitous breaded, sausage-like snack available hot from vending machines across the nation — and I learned from him of the deep respect the Dutch still held for their Royal Family, and of the societal order established by compulsory national army service. In my heart I am forever English ... but my head couldn't help wishing I were a little more Dutch.

It took all day to reach Rotterdam. There I changed trains for Hoek van Holland, racing against both the clock and the fading light. I refused to contemplate spending another night on the tiles. Cameras flapping on their straps, I dashed along the platform like a duck attempting take off, hoping still to be able to make the 8:40 p.m. connection to 'Haven', the ferry terminal.

Since setting off from Hong Kong almost two months previously, I'd had plenty of time to imagine what the end of the line would be like. Daydreaming about it had helped sustain me through the Mongolian steppe and silver birch forests of Siberia, the cornfields of Ukraine and minefields of Moldova, the detour to tragic Bosnia, and recent blitzkrieg dash from Berlin to Holland. In the end it came down to this: a desolate, windy freight yard — next stop, the Channel. A hundred miles of choppy gray water were all that separated me from home. The irony would be too much to bear had I ended up, instead, in Dunkirk.

I'd just assumed a ferry would be waiting for me. And one was: the towering Stena Lines vessel, *MV Britannica*. I've always been a sucker for romantic-sounding ships, and *Britannica* had obviously been dispatched by Fate to transport me home. She was scheduled to depart for Harwich at 9:00 p.m., but had been delayed. Smoke was billowing from her funnels. Passengers were pouring through immigration. The fare was 109 guilders. Inwardly I rejoiced, as I was flush with 156.50 worth of the Dutch currency.

"But this is a night voyage," the ticket agent told me, "at night you have to have a cabin. That will be fifty-four guilders more, so … the total is 163 guilders, please." Now, I am filled with praise for the Dutch and their enlightened, practical souls. But when it comes to the subject of money, they are always deadly serious.

The port was going to close at 10:00 p.m., after *Britannica* sailed. I briefly entertained the idea of stowing away, but shuddered recalling my last attempt at the Hong Kong container terminal. Instead, I began the search for some corner to sleep in, one that would offer some degree of protection from the biting wind and discovery by port security personnel. Dark clouds rolled in, snuffing out the sunset and bringing with them rain. The only dry spot was a hundred meters farther up, where an extended rooftop covered the platform.

Of greater urgency was to find food. The little café attached to the station was closing up, its last patrons downing their *Amstels* and heading to board the ship. *Why, for once, can't I be normal, like them? Why does it always have to be such an epic struggle?*

The clock on the wall didn't help matters, its minute hand clicking relentlessly south towards nine-thirty. I chewed a cold *kroket*, and waited for divine inspiration. It failed to arrive. Outside, *Britannica* blasted her horn, lengthily and decisively. Security shutters began to screech and rattle in steely protest as they were lowered. The lights above the immigration booths were switched off. It looked like I'd finally run out of options.

I'd missed the boat.

I wandered, disconsolately, in the direction of the now-shuttered immigration gates, and stared through their metal grille. The *Britannica* was still at berth, and I was determined that only when she became a faint dot on the horizon would I relinquish all hope. At the same moment, an invisible windborne hand tugged at the salt-rusted grating, briefly inflating it, like a sail. Maybe it was the spirit of my Indonesian sailboat, *Kurnia Ilahi*, looking out for me now? The noise of tortured metal caused an elderly, rake-thin official to investigate the state of his shutter. I called out to him, not expecting a response:

"I'm so sorry, but I'm meant to be on *Britannica*." He located me through the grille with not unkindly eyes.

"You have a reservation?" he asked, his English almost extinguished of accent.

"Yes ... well, er ... not exactly. Actually, no," I decided total frankness was called for. I had no tricks left in my box: "I have enough money for the day ferry, but am about ten guilders short for the night sailing."

"I see," he said.

There came a lengthy blast on *Britannica*'s horn. It seemed to galvanize the official into action. Pushing his peaked cap back on his head, he turned around and began barking orders. The lady at the ticket counter remained at her post and a strip light flickered into life above one of the immigration counters. My new friend selected a key from his belt and opened a side door.

"It's 109 guilders for the ticket," the ticket lady repeated, looking down her list, "and for the reservation, do you have forty-three more?" I'd had that amount earlier, but had spent some of it on *krokets* since our last unsatisfactory meeting. I opened my hand and counted out all the coins I had left.

"Do you have twenty-six guilders?" She'd located a cheaper bunk.

"Yes!" I had thirty, and shoved them all across her counter. My savior—who was by now shouting into his walkie-talkie—pointed me towards immigration. The clerk there had earlier removed his uniform and was now dressed in civvies. But that didn't stop him from stamping my passport with theatrical flourish. Then his boss ushered me to the entrance of a long, windowless passageway:

"Hurry, now, they are holding the boat for you."

"Thank you, thank you!" It was not an adequate expression for the relief or gratitude I felt, but at the moment was all I could muster.

"Yes, yes, good luck. And hurry!" he said.

I dashed blindly along the tunnel, unable to suppress the grin spreading across my face. I rounded a sharp right-hand turn and almost collided with two sailors who were lowering the gangplank. I waved my ticket at them and they hustled me on board.

Home! – England
September 7, 1992

CABIN 2042 WAS located down in the bilges, but came replete with a shower, toilet and three beds, and I was its sole occupant. What a turnaround! I felt like shouting out, "I'm coming home after six years!" but it was mostly holidaymakers on board; they wouldn't grasp the extent of my victory. *Britannica* she may have been grandly named, but the atmosphere on board this ship was no more regal than a floating fairground.

I found it impossible to sleep. In a few hours I'd be stepping on native soil for the first time since my twentieth birthday. I was now approaching my twenty-sixth. That huge gap — one I had filled so nonchalantly with the throwaway excuse of photography — revealed itself now as a deep, incomprehensible chasm. How many alternate experiences had I missed out on, and what collective memories would I have been able to share with my peers had I, like they, stayed in England, too? Would I, in future, only ever feel comfortable in the company of fellow nomadic photographers, unable to connect with anyone who was not a thrill-seeking junkie?

I headed to the ship's bar, hoping alcohol would glaze these prowling concerns. Digging deep in one of the pockets of my camera vest I unearthed a crumpled pack of 2-3-4 brand *kreteks*, the unfiltered, high-end brand of Indonesian clove cigarette I'd once photographed being rolled by hand by a vast female army in a factory in Surabaya. The crackle of combusting clove buds; the sweet residue left on my tongue; the paper, sticking to my lips after each luxurious inhalation — my neural synapses were firing on all fronts, transporting me back to the heaving swells of the Java Sea. There, barefoot, I'd run happily about the glistening teak deck of our spice boat, the *Kurnia Ilahi* — yet another home I would never truly escape — one that lurked in the shadows of my subconscious, waiting to be triggered by a familiar scent, tune or tug of the wind.

The ship's horn sounded three long, startling blasts. I must've fallen asleep, after all. I made sure my hat was positioned in a correct and jaunty manner, and secured against treacherous gusts, and then headed up on deck. It was a gray day, and the gray Essex coastline approached across a diminishing expanse of gray sea. The horizon seemed disappointingly short of landmarks. I'd expected white cliffs, and *Land of Hope and Glory* to be blasting over the intercom. Instead, a group of schoolgirls were sitting around, waiting for their teachers to lead them down to their coach on one of the lower vehicle decks. The docking procedure took forever, and one of the girls — her orange hair ablaze — became tired of waiting, crossed her legs and made to sit down on the deck. She was caught, midway, by a sudden tempest that lifted her tartan skirt, flashing a brief glimpse of pale inner thigh. She turned to look at me, acting coy.

"I didn't see that," I muttered, and she laughed.

"Where did you come from then, the jungle?" her malfunctioning wardrobe already forgotten.

"If only you knew."

Jessica and her classmates, despite their present style devotion to the punk popstar Toyah Willcox, were all good Catholic girls from Ipswich. Their class was on its way back from a school field trip to Cologne. I needed a ride, and they felt a Christian urge to offer assistance: we soon hatched a plan. Taking off my hat, I hid myself among Jessica and her friends, who gamboled about — a hockey-skirted scrum worthy of St Trinian's — and smuggled on board their coach.

I squatted on the floor in the back row, my arm on Jessica's knees. She acted ever so prim and proper. I'd hoped the free ride would take me closer to home, but sadly the school bus made a turn north at Colchester, where I needed to get off and travel in the opposite direction. One of Jessica's gang faked a stomach upset.

"Please, Miss, stop the coach. I have to throw up!" Others joined in the clamor. The driver was forced to make an emergency stop at a Little Chef cafe. I hopped out the back door and the invalids staged a miraculous recovery.

During all my travels I'd carried with me £2, in coins, secured in a 35mm film canister. I'd always envisaged using them on this very occasion, for the final fare home. It was all the money I had left. There would be no more discoveries of traveler's checks; all my exotic notes had now been excavated. However, due to inflation, the amount was now insufficient to cover the bus or train ride home from Essex. I would have to hitchhike.

Luckily, I used to crisscross this part of the country when I worked as a motorcycle dispatch rider for Mercury Couriers. I recognized my present location along the A12 as being opposite the spot I'd once run out of petrol on the company's Honda CX500. I wrote the word 'Tunnel' — meaning the Dartford Tunnel, a massive local landmark — in large letters on a piece of cardboard. I reasoned my local knowledge would give me an edge over the New Age types trying to catch lifts with their hopeful references to distant 'Dover'. A former Merchant Navy man pulled up in a Ford Capri and was able to drive me over the River Thames — rather than under it — on The Queen Elizabeth II Bridge.

"That wasn't here when I left!" I exclaimed. *How much else has changed?*

In my dreams, 'home' was untouchable, a mental enclave carefully preserved and curated with museum-like precision. I recalled that fabled time traveler who'd stepped on a butterfly only to return to find his own era ruled over by chimpanzees. But I needn't have worried. As I joined the bus queue in Dartford, I was reassured by the conversation of two old ladies who may as well have been chatting there since the day I left:

"Aw right, Doll? 'Ow you keeping?"

"Oh, not so bad, Mabel, luv. Can't complain. Y'self?"

"Well, it's a struggle these days, innit, what now wiv the knees packing up, and George bein' 'ome all the time an' gettin' in the way. But mustn't grumble."

The No.477 bus came along and cleared out all my old coins. The fare for the three miles to Hextable cost the same as the thirty-six-hour train journey from Moscow to Moldova.

———— ∞ ————

Even now, so close, I couldn't head directly home: I had to pick up my mail from Fred, who lived in the neighboring village to mine. For two months now, his letterbox in Rollo Road had been receiving my redirected mail. Fred, the uncle of a childhood friend with whom I used to park my bicycle each day for school, had been happy to assist in the deception.

"Lucky you didn't turn up ten minutes ago or you'd have bumped into your Auntie Barbara," he greeted me. That would've done it: news of my return would have reached home before I had! Fred brewed up a pot of PG Tips, for old times' sake. I stuffed the jumble of assorted letters and postcards into my backpack, thanked him for his collaboration, and set off on the final leg of a long, long journey. One that, somehow, felt right to be completing on foot.

I hastened past the Methodist church where I'd been baptized, up the hill and across the fields where I used to have to run to keep up with my father's striding pace—my fields, finally, my hill, my village—leading to the house in which I was born. Visibly, nothing much had changed. I turned into the driveway. My sister Jennie spotted me first, from her bedroom window, instantly vanishing, leaving the curtain fluttering. I approached the porch, feet scrunching the old, familiar gravel, my heart in my throat. I had no keys to let myself in—a stranger here, now—so waited on the doorstep as my sister and mother fumbled open the locked door, their excited voices shrilling, "It's Chris, it's Chris!"

I am home.

Later that evening, I hid from my father when he came back from work, creeping up from behind as he was peeling off his dirty work coveralls: "Penny for a homeless traveler?" I asked from out of the silence. It was only the second time I'd seen him shed a tear.

We popped next door to surprise Granny Stowers soon afterwards. I wondered if she was aware of the waves she'd set in motion when she had rashly jumped ship from England to South Africa almost seventy years earlier? And that they continued to reverberate through her grandson, today ...

It took a while before she recognized me—age finally cashing in its chips—but upon hearing my voice her eyes moistened and she urged us through to the living room. As a boy, I would lie on the tribal rug between her piano and the fireplace, studying intently the black and white photos in her old hardback albums that documented her early married life in Rhodesia: a life that was gaining for her importance and clarity, just as surely as the one she was daily living started to fade out of focus. Here, I too had planned my escape. Placed where the carpet had once lain was a decorative antique Japanese screen. On it she'd taped a huge map of the world. Little red, white and blue pins stuck all over it, pretty accurately tracing my travels for the last six years.

Uncle Martin, my Dad's older brother, came in from the kitchen like a doddery old butler, shakily bearing a silver tray replete with steaming teapot and bone china cups clinking in their saucers. The mound of demerara sugar, contained in a small silver bowl, was covered by a weighted fly net, and the milk jug, I knew, had seen daily service since Bulawayo.

"Oh, thank goodness," my grandmother sighed, "I don't know what we'd do without tea!"

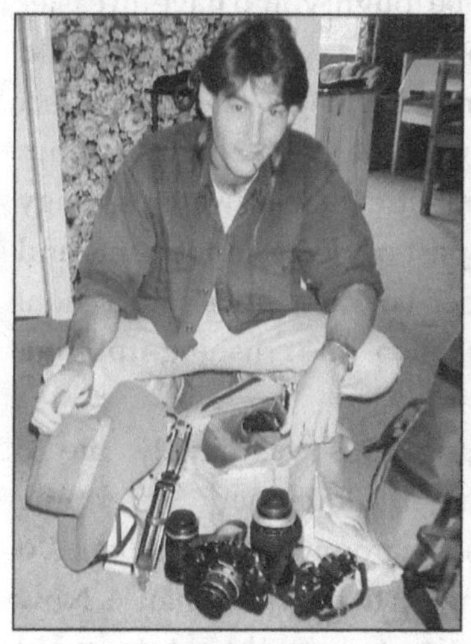

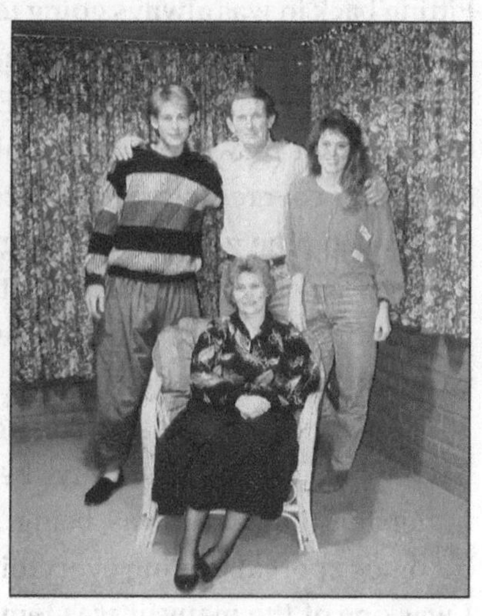

Back home again, after almost six years away…
September 7, 1992.

And with my parents and sister, just before heading off again, to Hong Kong. November 1992.

EPILOGUE

England. September 16, 1992

ENGLAND SUFFOCATED AND enthralled, in equal measure. And, although the protagonists remained the same—namely: a) My country, and b) Me—one of us had been off having a merry old time, making new friends and merging with the wider world. Fitting back in was always going to be tough: you'd have an easier time trying to squeeze the milk back into a cow. I wandered old haunts, as ghosts are wont to do. English villages offer the perfect environment to wallow in nostalgia. The crooked gravestones and moss-covered steeple; the root-strewn pathways, springy with fallen pine needles, winding past neglected allotments and through wooded dells; the weather-boarded pubs, old school playground, and memorial to The Fallen. The crushing-uplifting paradox of all of bloody History.

I found cities just as challenging. This was largely due to having become used to always being 'the foreigner'. Never fully understanding what was being said around or about me, I'd become expert at leaving everything up to luck and chance. Now I was one of the many, it was tempting to keep the act up, avoid responsibility, pretend to be something exotic, like a Latvian. On the other hand, total literacy — what a lark! No longer did I need anyone's help deciphering signposts or timetables; a newspaper reverted to its primary role as source of information, rather than emergency umbrella or fly swat; I could eavesdrop on the conversations of others on the train (ultimately a futile exercise, as they tended mostly to be complaining about being on the train). Unlike the majority, I found it impossible to get worked up when the bus to Dartford was running ten minutes late, having become conditioned to the elastic and random nature of public transport in places as diverse as Peshawar, Sulawesi and Ulaan Bator.

Reverting to type, the first week I was back I bought a secondhand Kawasaki GT550 motorcycle, *the* dispatch-riding bike of the day. After all, if the photography game didn't work out, I would have to go back to messengering. I zoomed up the City Road to White Lion Street, in Islington, for my first appointment with Panos, the charity outfit Jasmine had recommended back in Hong Kong. My old *Mercury Couriers* delivery satchel strained at the seams attempting to contain all the color slides I'd brought along to show them. What was a 'Panos', anyway? Sounded like an aging Greek pimp.

"Anyone order a bike?" the large African woman at reception made the initial, and totally understandable, assumption I was a courier. Off to a good start.

Soon it was established I was a photographer, and not there to pick up a pack of negatives for urgent delivery to a printing company down the Commercial Road. I was led past walls of gray filing cabinets to a cozy back room, and introduced to Adrian Evans, the manager of Panos. Or, to be precise, the head of the photo storage facility currently affiliated to its parent charity, the Panos Institute.

"At present", Adrian explained, attempting to tame a mop of

wild hair that made him look like Hugh Grant backing through a wind tunnel, "the library section is little more than a repository of photos dumped off by the charity's numerous aid workers when they come back from their field trips. Mainly to Africa. We corner the market in black and white photos of people digging toilets in sub-Saharan famine zones." Adrian was stylish, droll, and really quite ambitious. Over lunch at an Indian restaurant in Islington High Street, he sketched his plans to buy out the library and turn it into a full-fledged photo agency. Pointedly, he mentioned he'd be needing to fill the shelves of this new agency with more colorful, commercial material from booming Asia. He said he'd take anything I could give him. *I think it's the beginning of a beautiful friendship.*

⚯

The following day was a red-letter day for letters. Not one, but two substantial envelopes awaited me on the dining room table. The first was from my best friend Mark, posted from a military base on Cyprus:

> *... I arrived here in February and to be honest, I can't stand the place. I have finally tired of the Army and I suppose, in truth, have matured, become philosophical ... it's a big step to leave this secure lifestyle, but I have to have faith in my destiny. I have a funny feeling a whole new world is going to open up for me.*
>
> *Early last year I did think my single days were over, as I met a superb young lady. Anyway, life is a bitch. If it <u>had</u> worked out, you would have to have come home to be Best Man. You do have that obligation, you know! On my last visit, your parents showed me some of your photos in various magazines. I thought your best work was the*

black and white stuff you did in Kowloon Walled City. Maybe we'll meet next in Hong Kong, when I'm freed of the military?

Mark had joined the army the same month I'd set out on my travels. We had ventured over wildly different routes these past six years and, although our paths had never crossed in that time, had always managed to keep in touch. The army still gripped him in its talons but, by the sounds of it, not for much longer. Our long dreamed-of motorcycle tour of Europe would have to be put on hold until *next* summer, though. The second letter was from Stuart. The inveterate Aussie backpacker I'd first met in Peshawar, at the very start of my travels, had recently arrived home in Sydney, following an eventful trip to Yemen that had involved evacuation by sea to Djibouti thanks to some shenanigans involving a civil war. I *knew* he'd not last in his job at the funeral parlor:

… Was surprised to see that you've headed home but I'm sure your family will be very happy. Personally, I wouldn't have left it that long. Six years is a hell of a long time …

That was rich, coming from a man who thought nothing of being away four years at a stretch. All this correspondence helped, though. It confirmed I had another life now, *out there*. A life lived at a distance. I would always favor the fax over the telephone call, and prefer the letter to the fax. The delay between receiving news and having to reply with a decision was liberating. Like shouting messages across a particularly vast canyon—the time between echoes was the time in which we could live.

Two weeks after my first visit, I received a telephone call from Adrian, informing me of my first sale through Panos. The shot had been used quite small—one of people milling around outside the cinema in Ulaan Bator—and had been printed in *The Economist*. The color slide had been reproduced in black and white, and didn't carry my name, of course, but I knew it was mine. After Panos's 50 percent cut I was £30 up on the deal. Enthused by sudden international exposure, I strode to the newsagent opposite my hometown's dominating ASDA supermarket, intent on buying a copy. But the search was in vain.

"The *Whato*nomist?" deadpanned the proprietor, possibly ruing whatever cruel twist of fate had relegated him to sell copies of *News of the World* and lottery scratch cards on the rougher side of S______ High Street (I won't incriminate the place in these pages. It is, for all its flaws, home). "Don't stock it, Mate. People round 'ere don't read big words like that. Better try Bromley."

∽

I continued to meet up with old school friends. But they hardly seemed to realize I'd been gone. This was not their fault, of course. I'd not exactly been concerned with what they'd been getting up to all these years, either. Our formative experiences had been sealed in the classroom and at the disco on a Friday night, untroubled by future intrigues of Asian geopolitics, perilous jungle trips or Balkan killing fields (subjects I now felt somewhat qualified— and yet restrained myself—from commenting on). So, we fell back on predictable topics and neutral territories of discussion; school time antics, deranged teachers and TV soap operas—and attempted to undermine the barriers of awkwardness that had built up between us by drinking more heavily.

Could it be that Norman Tebbitt's cold admonishment to my generation to 'get on your bike' had inadvertently spared me a life of conformity? As a teenager I'd taken the Tory politician's words as a personal challenge. Not only had I mounted my metaphorical penny farthing, I'd ridden it right out of England and never looked back. And had I not escaped then (for the window to make such decisions is very narrow and fleeting)? Well, then I'd probably be married by now to a fat-bottomed girl named 'Sharon', living in a housing estate in Gravesend, driving a Ford Sierra, working in insurance—and never truly understanding the origin of the sudden bouts of rage and emptiness that seized me whenever I opened a map or read of someone else's adventures in some far-off land. *"That's my life,"* I'd cry, *"those are my adventures!"*. And someone else was living them.

Stripped of my camera jacket, I felt naked: no identity, no armor, no more excuses. I started to question, too, the opportunities and alternate futures I had so casually and recklessly tossed aside in the blind pursuit of images. My sole consolation was the gradual realization that every road taken was, ultimately, part of the same road: that what could have been probably never would have lasted; at least I'd lived enough to experience what was. My only hope of explaining all this to those who hadn't traveled as widely, or risked losing the security of a monthly paycheck was, if I were lucky, via the absolution of my photographs.

HEATHROW AIRPORT.
November 15, 1992

I HAD NOT arrived so much as returned to the place I'd set out from, all those years ago. This time, at least, I was better prepared to resume a journey that was only just beginning. My faded Domke bag struggled to contain its growing inventory of camera gear: two Nikon SLR bodies (each with bulky motor winders attached), five prime lenses, a couple of flash units, a roll of masking tape, the mini-tripod and a cable release. The pockets of my camera jacket bulged with light meter, spare AA batteries, film canisters, multiple filters, a lens cleaning kit, press cards (various), and my new passport. In my hand I waved a one-way ticket to Hong Kong.

I'm coming home.

Disclaimer

The best piece of advice I ever received was from my mother who, when I left home, suggested I start keeping a diary, "just in case you find something to write about". The second I have used as the title of this book. The vast majority of events related here really happened and were recorded in dozens of personal diaries, letters and newspaper cuttings, written and saved at the time. I have strived to portray conversations, events and people directly from those diaries, to the best of my memory, and in the spirit of the moment. While all the stories in this book are true, please bear in mind this is a work of narrative non-fiction. Two of the players are composites of several dear friends, some names have been altered to protect the privacy of those involved, and one or two episodes have been embellished to some degree for dramatic effect. To those who gave me permission to use their real names and experiences go my heartfelt thanks and everlasting gratitude. And to the many friends and acquaintances with whom I have lost contact over the course of half a lifetime, or fail to mention individually below, I can only hope that if you come across this imperfect attempt to recreate the magical days of our youth, its pages will bring a smile to your face, and you'll forgive me the rare flight of fancy.

Acknowledgements

Thanks to my parents, and my sister Jennie, who gave me the freedom to travel, thirty-five years ago—the greatest leap of faith of all; to my old friends John Fowler and Cyndia, whose hospitality and generosity I take too much for granted whenever passing through Hong Kong. To my *Windfall* crewmates: Franck Dubois, Pascal Trouve, Fabienne and Frank Le Clec'h. To the incomparable Jana Steiger I extend my gratitude for the countless conference calls halfway around the world and late into the night as you helped me knock this draft into shape. My punctuation and grammar have improved under your watchful eye. It is my fortune we met on that cross-channel ferry, so many years ago!

I have gotten back in touch, directly and indirectly, with many old friends during the course of writing this volume—either seeking their approval and confirmation of events, or in support of what was said and occurred at the time. My especial thanks go to Christine and Stuart Buchanan, Sheila and Peter Grout, Ken and Hazel Smith; and to Hans Kemp, Luisa Tam, Leong Ka-Tai, Becky Cho, Yee Wai-Fong and siblings, and the indefatigable Nicolae Pojoga.

Among the many, many friends and acquaintances—not to

mention ships passed in the night—with whom I've either lost contact over the last three decades, or been unable to get in touch with before the publication of this book (yet who, nonetheless, never stray far from my thoughts, and certainly take up many pages in my diaries) are: The Mouse and The London Bus (who probably would wish to remain anonymous to this day), Ted Martin, Darrell Buchanan, Shanta Curry, the extraordinary Dan Panciu (*Bafta!*) and Eva, Fong Peng Kuan and Ruby, the Said Family, Sarah Hamdan, Fabiola, Rippy Soo, Ata Ur-Rehman, Simon Beck, Kees Metselaar, Owen Hughes, Mariita Eager, Edowan Bersma, Anna Murphy (nee Ross), Sebastian Gulay, Sue So, Connie Cheung, Winnie Chong, Lee Nyhus, Frances Fox, Colin Campbell, Marc Johnson, Ralf Leutz, Mark Allen, Sam Ho, Siao Guang-Ming, Charly Godin, Doryanto and Suderson; Lorne Stockman, Jez O'Hare, Budi Setiawan, Jane Parry, Martin Brennan, Edwin Tuyay, Bill Cranfield, Jill Entwhistle, Karen Ma, Philip Crawley, Steve Shroud, Simon Beck, Liau Chung-ren, Greg Girard, Mark Ralston, Robin Moyer, Richard Jones, Mic & Amy Thompson, Gerhard Joren, Fred Scott, David Sutton, David Smith, Judy Tsou, Judy Tan, Deborah Boyd, Honorata Luna, Leticia Cortan, Helen Fowler, Nigel Simmonds, Rahman Jaffar, Nazarudhin, Dr Milano, Roger Mitton, Chan Looi-Tat, Mr Poon of *Photo Scientific*, Munshi Ahmed, Santha Oorjitham, Ken Wooton, Steve Vines, Ann Smeed; Ron Gluckman, Ambassador and Mrs Morey, Peter Hannam, Peter Dening-Smitherton, Rebecca Hall, Tatiana Fonina, Evgeni Kondakov, Sergey Voronin, Natashe, Radu Sigheti, Dr Iacob Codrin; Ambassador Laurie Bristow, Allan Little, Alec Russell, Dragan, Yadran and Mandic of Channel-S, and Olga and Sanja of SRNA, Haji Hiroshi and Cinzia, Pazit Ravina and Yasuko Nakayama.

Thanks, also, to Adrian Evans, Michael Regnier, and all at Panos, past and present. Kudos to Andy Jelfs for the beautiful formula found on page 19 and who was obviously paying more attention to Mr Smith during our 6th Form Maths classes than I; to Alberto Buzzola, Reed Resnikoff, Al Reyes, David Frazier, Jeff Topping, Uval Daniel, Alan Sargent, Josh Lustig, Scott Weaver, Larry Heron, Don Shapiro, Earl Wieman, Gary Melyan, Paul Ehrlich, Richard McCallum, Max Hirsch and Ralph Jennings for assistance beyond the call of duty, and for providing sobering and, I hope you'll agree, well-heeded readings and reviews. To John Ross for his outstanding and generous editorial guidance; and to Jim Cumming and Paul Hu for keeping the single malt flowing on many an occasion when inspiration began to falter.

In memory of those who appear or are mentioned in the pages of this book yet, sadly, are no longer with us:

Mark P. Morgan, Christiane Hammer, Keith Loveard, Derek Maitland, Jim Lindelof, Lee Shapiro, Albert Buenaflor, Peter Comparelli, Paul Blair, Tudor Iovu, Darren Long, Ira Chaplain, G. Martin Stowers, Barbara Stowers, Fred Lyons, and Bernard Stowers.

About the Author

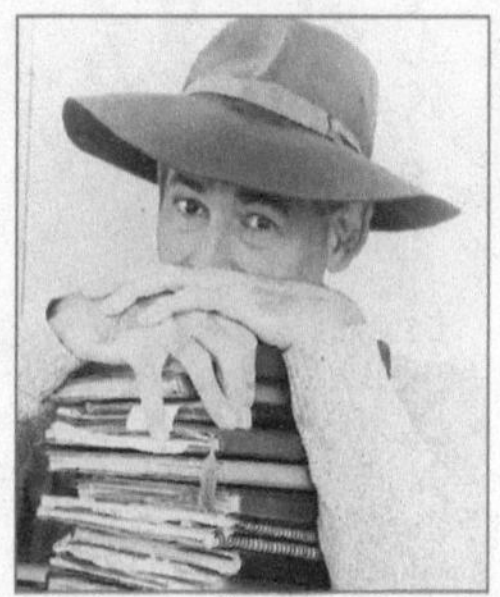

The author is a professional photographer, based in Asia. He is represented by Panos Pictures photo agency in London, and has traveled, lived and worked in more than 70 countries since setting out from his native England, in 1987.

The wise advice given at the start of his travels, to 'shoot first, then ask … and (when that fails) run!', has saved him on many an occasion since …